THE ABSURD HERO IN AMERICAN FICTION

SECOND REVISED EDITION

The Absurd Hero in American Fiction

UPDIKE STYRON BELLOW SALINGER

By David Galloway

 UNIVERSITY OF TEXAS PRESS, AUSTIN

Published with the assistance of a grant from the Ford Foundation under its program for the support of publications in the humanities and social sciences.

International Standard Book Number 0-292-70356-2
(cloth); 0-292-70355-4 (paper)
Library of Congress Catalog Card Number 80-54119
Requests for permission to reproduce material from this
work should be sent to
Permissions
University of Texas Press
Box 7819, Austin, Texas 78712

For Lyle Glazier

CONTENTS

Preface to the First Edition   ix

Preface to the Second Revised Edition   xiii

1. The Myth of the Absurd   5

2. The Absurd Man as Saint   17

3. The Absurd Man as Tragic Hero   81

4. The Absurd Man as Picaro   129

5. The Love Ethic   204

6. Epilogue   228

Notes   231

Bibliography   239

Index   259

PREFACE TO THE FIRST EDITION

In popular badinage, as in serious literary criticism, "absurdity" is the *bon mot* if not always the *mot juste* of this decade. I should therefore point out in the beginning that the concept of the absurd treated in these pages differs considerably from its use with respect to the contemporary theatre—especially the theatre of Beckett and Ionesco. The most obvious differences are in terms of style: the surfaces, at least, of the work of John Updike, William Styron, Saul Bellow, and J. D. Salinger are far more conventionally "realistic" than anything found in avant-garde drama. And as style is above all the writer's method of expressing his point of view, there are also, therefore, fundamental divergences in attitudes. The initial assumptions of absurd literature are, however, compatible: the belief that human experience is fragmented, irritating, *apparently* unredeemable. The ubiquitousness of the absurd arises from the individual artist's vision of the ultimate consequences of this life-denying experience. Albert Camus repeatedly suggested that man could, despite the hostility of an absurd environment, establish a new and viable basis for heroism and thus for human dignity; the "non-hero" who populates so much contemporary drama and fiction is thus not the sole or unavoidable product of such a milieu. In short, absurd literature can be either optimistic or pessimistic; the fundamental and determining issue is whether, in the conflict between man and his "absurd" environment, man or environment will emerge victorious; whether, in terms of the individual, humanistic or nihilistic impulses will dominate; whether, denied conventional social and religious consolation, man is capable of producing adequate spiritual antibodies to resist despair. Thus, when we deal with absurd literature, we are confronted as we are in all styles (but particularly, as an historical precedent, in naturalism) not solely with the immediate image of life which the artist presents, but with the ultimate conclusions to which his work leads us: is absurdity both our birthright and our inevitable doom, or is it merely another vigil through which man must pass in advancing to a new level of human consciousness and new standards of responsibility? Is it senescence or puberty?

Like Camus, the four contemporary novelists discussed in this book share a belief in man's ability to establish a new secular humanism in a world not only postlapsarian, but also post-Freudian and collectivist. If such a man goes beyond the absurd, he does so only by coming directly to grips with his absurd environment; he is thus an absurd hero. The fruits of his labor may also seem absurd in comparison with traditional notions of heroic conflict and reward (or redemption); but they bring a believable promise of rain to the fashionable wasteland, and because they transcend (or promise to transcend) the absurd in terms of the absurd, the challenge which they offer to the choristers of anti-literature possesses vital integrity.

Because the novelists whom I have considered are optimistic chroniclers of the absurd experience, their work is stylistically less extreme than that of Beckett or Ionesco, less preposterously discontinuous and fragmented than a novel like William Gaddis's *The Recognitions* or Lawrence Ferlinghetti's *Her.* For however unconventional the environments and "heroes" of whom they treat, their work is part of a recognizable humanistic tradition; indeed, the only term which seems to me at all satisfactory in describing the redeeming life-stance which they suggest, is "post-existential humanism," a phrase offered by Wylie Sypher in his provocative study *The Loss of the Self.*

A number of reasons encourage me to investigate the optimistic literature of the absurd rather than the pessimistic. First of all, the angry, pessimistic, even nihilistic literature of the postwar decades, in its extremes of attitude and form, has been vigorously self-advertising—however unclearly it may have been understood; the wasteland theory of literature has thus become something of a popular as well as a critical cliché, meaninglessness has often characterized both theme and style (most extremely, perhaps, in William Burroughs), and alienation has become the hallmark of the "serious" novel and the "serious" novelist. This book does not attempt to deny the significance or the richness of the work produced by exponents of the pessimistic concept of absurdity, but merely to suggest that this view is countered by a weight of optimism, and indeed one represented by some of the most skilled writers of our time: writers who grant the absurd premises, but who deny, even decry, the somewhat conventional absurd conclusions. Merely to chronicle the horrors and hazards of a meaningless world may be a significant achievement (and one in which the American gift for gab can be a great asset), and some of these contemporary chronicles—most notably Thomas Pynchon's *V*—have employed exciting and perhaps crucial new narrative techniques; but an obsession with the meaningless can result in art that is puerile, or merely prurient, as contrived and predictable and fashionable as the "mass," selfless world which it purports to reject. Pynchon avoids these pitfalls through his acute comic vision as well as sheer stylistic dexterity, as do a large company of younger humorists—Terry Southern, J. P. Donleavy, Thomas Berger, Bruce Jay Friedman, Donald Barthelme, John Barth, Warren Miller, James Purdy, Ken Kesey, and Richard G. Stern—who promise to usher in a vital new phase in American fiction. And despite the frequent "blackness" of their humor, it serves to maintain a crucial balance, to avoid the pitfalls of preciousness and chic despair.

In our devoted mourning of the giants of the older generation, the flurry of lionizing and then denigrating the Beat Generation, the typically American fascination with cultivating and appropriating such new writers as the black humorists, and in merchandising the hitherto unpublishable like Henry Miller, we have perhaps slighted what may well be the most important development in contemporary American fiction, represented by those writers who have grappled with the meaningless and with great integrity have suggested paths through the modern wasteland, even if they have not always been able to chart those paths with complete precision. Recognizing the discontinuity of much modern experience, they nonetheless have seen man's plight in terms of a continuous humanistic tradition, and not as some uniquely soured modern pottage. They can express despair without succumbing to it, and they can question and deny the validity of traditional consolations without denying the traditions of the human spirit.

I have turned to the work of Albert Camus because his essays—particularly those in *The Myth of Sisyphus*—seem to me most consistently and fruitfully to present the optimistic potential of the absurd experience, and to offer useful terminology for an analysis of that experience in fiction. I have nowhere maintained that he has exercised a direct influence on the four novelists whom I have analyzed, but only that they share impressions of the modern environment and hopes for it which are mutually illuminating. I have consciously avoided any discussion of Camus's own ambiguous relationship to the existentialist movement, which is itself continuously recruiting new founding fathers (or grandfathers—as in Paul Tillich's tracing of the movement to Pascal) and claiming an almost meaninglessly wide circle of progeny. The most fundamental question raised by these novelists is, to be sure, *Existenz*, and the choice between being and nothingness is always with us; nonetheless, my primary interest in Camus has been his vivid evocation of what so often seems the dominant mood of our literary time, and his description of the alternatives which man can choose during the dark night of the besieged soul.

In electing to discuss the work of Updike, Styron, Bellow, and Salinger in light of these theories, I have excluded, of course, other writers who might have been considered with equal fruitfulness. John Hawkes and Edward Lewis Wallant seem to me the most significant contemporary omissions, and I particularly regret that Wallant receives only brief reference in *The Absurd Hero*; but his four brilliant and moving novels surely qualify him for a book in his own right. In the final analysis, I can only resist hiding behind the idea that selection entails omission, for my choice of these particular novelists is also the result of a personal conviction that each has made a major and distinct contribution to our understanding of the contemporary milieu, and that each now presents us with an adequate "critical mass" to warrant such detailed analysis. Nonetheless, it is to be hoped that this book will not contribute to that instant canonization which literary criticism all too often produces in America. Of the four writers presented here, only Saul Bellow has fulfilled what is patronizingly termed a writer's "promise," though all of them have produced works of social and intellectual significance. Updike may still fall prey to his precocious sense of technique (though this seems to me unlikely), and Styron is yet to demonstrate that he can successfully combine in a mature work the compressed metaphysical style of *The Long March* with the more epic and frequently diffuse point of view which characterizes his two long novels. And if Seymour Glass succumbed to the mystical banana fever, J. D. Salinger may never himself recover from Seymour fever; that, in any event, is what most of his recent fiction suggests—in particular, the charmingly inconsequential "Hapworth 16, 1924," published too recently to be discussed in *The Absurd Hero*. But if the final literary merits of these writers must await the verdict of future generations, the value of their diverse examinations of the absurd modern environment is nonetheless of acute significance to this generation, and it is to analyze the significance of their novels, not to canonize the novelists, that *The Absurd Hero* was written.

PREFACE TO THE SECOND REVISED EDITION

Nearly two decades have passed since the initial studies were made for *The Absurd Hero*. Looking back at these pages again has entailed something of that discomforting shock of recognition with which one discovers his own face—startlingly younger, strangely remote—in a forgotten snapshot. But it is not only my own face which has altered; the profiles of John Updike, William Styron, Saul Bellow, and J. D. Salinger have also been remolded. Twenty years ago, they were respected but hardly established novelists, although Bellow had already begun to garner literary prizes, and Salinger had produced *The Catcher in the Rye*, his classic of American innocence. Still, my quartet seemed particularly vigorous, irreverent, ambitious, young, and the message their writings proclaimed struck me then as singularly well suited to the postwar period in which I myself had come to maturity. In part, the challenge of analyzing their work was precisely the fact that it had then received such scant critical appraisal. Today, entire industries of exegesis have grown up round the four, and *The Absurd Hero* can no longer represent for me the uncharted voyage of discovery which it seemed to be in the early 1960's.

My own recent interests have focused on the writing of fiction and on the visual arts. Were I to begin a book today on Updike, Styron, Bellow, and Salinger, it would no doubt be a very different work than the one which follows, employing other critical lenses, other aesthetic criteria. Nevertheless, I continue to believe that there is a recognizable and highly consequential tradition in Western literature whereby the absurd—as defined by Albert Camus—becomes a way of affirming the resources of the human spirit, of exalting sacrifice and suffering, of ennobling the man capable of sustaining the vital opposition between intention and reality. Recent history has not invalidated that message but, on the contrary, extended and enhanced its relevance. Other writers have been more vigorously experimental in pursuing the literary implications of the absurd through the mazes of meta-fiction and post-modernism. Indeed, in comparison to Thomas Pynchon (whose central vision seems to me entirely consonant with Camus's investigations of the absurd), my quartet must appear rather old-fashioned, tuned for four-part barbershop harmonies. All have seemed relatively content with the inherited forms of narrative fiction, although John Updike has shown an increasing tendency to probe literary mannerism and reshape the fictional idiom. The formal conservatism of these writers is, however, an aspect of their search for values, the concomitant of their philosophical conviction that experience can be ordered meaningfully, even in a world which seems chronically disordered.

Formally and thematically, these writers thus illustrate the more affirmative aspects of the absurd, and in that sense ratify established conventions. The arts in America have always had a strong resistance to pessimism and despair; even American naturalism tends to be tinted by reassuring meliorist impulses. Although there are signs that an absurd tradition in something like the "purer" French sense is emerging in the United States, absurd art in its most extreme forms will no doubt continue to be tempered by the essential optimism and the concern for practical solutions that so persistently shape our thinking, serving as a barrier to those darker, more grotesque, more perverse absurdities encountered in Beckett or Genet, or the discontinuities cultivated by Robbe-Grillet. To some degree, perhaps, the writers I discuss can also be seen as representative of America in the 1950's—a generation determined, after the global spasms of depression and war, to build a better world, to reaffirm humanistic patterns despite the steady accumulation of negative evidence. While both Saul Bellow and J. D. Salinger had begun to publish in the 1940's, their first major writings appear in the 1950's, and both Styron and Updike begin their careers in that curious decade shaped by organizational conformity, the struggle for normalcy, the fears of atomic holocaust, and the frostiness of the Cold War. Old enough to have inherited the values of a simpler, prewar America, they were also young enough to respond to new constellations of experience; their writings show a persistent determination to promote humanistic considerations, even if reality seems remorsely intent on denying them. Hence, their own art is a model for the struggles of their heroes, and a very different art from that of the generation that came to maturity in the 1960's.

In the preface to the first edition of *The Absurd Hero* I noted my regret that I had not been able to discuss in detail the four remarkable novels of Edward Lewis Wallant. I have since made good that omission with an entire book devoted to his work. There are other omissions which cannot be made good, even in this second revised edition. Detailed analysis of the writings of Norman Mailer, John Hawkes, and Thomas Pynchon would clearly enrich the dimensions of *The Absurd Hero*, but they would also make it a different book. In the end, I resolved not to tamper with its essential structure, but to content myself with adding "wedges" of new material which up-date the first revised edition and seek to appraise the later development of the authors under consideration.

In the process of re-reading these pages, certain of my own critical prejudices and predilections became clear to me—at least two of which should be specified, as they affect the critical apparatus employed in the following pages. First of all, I grow increasingly convinced that Saul Bellow is overrated as a novelist—partly because he became "it" in the game of literary tag which requires a ruling master-novelist; and that John Updike is generally underrated. My second prejudice is against the excessive length of so many modern American novels, the epic compulsion which needlessly inflates first-rate novels and drops them into our consciousness like great beached whales. Of the excellent longer novels discussed in this study—including John Updike's *Couples*, Saul Bellow's *Henderson the Rain King*, and William Styron's *Sophie's Choice*—there is not one which would not have been improved by being made more compact, more concentrated. And from an aesthetic point of view, the most successful, satisfying works by these authors are almost invariably the shortest—John Updike's *Of the Farm*, Bellow's *Dangling Man* and *Seize the Day*, Styron's *The Long March*, Salinger's brilliant extended short stories, "Franny" and "Zooey." The reader should know these prejudices in order to evaluate my analyses accordingly—or, as Hawthorne enjoined from the Reverend Dimmesdale's experience: "Be true! Be true! Show freely to the world, if not your worst, yet some trait whereby the worst may be inferred!"

Wuppertal,
West Germany

THE ABSURD HERO IN AMERICAN FICTION

I thought of literature then, and I think of it now, of the literature of the world, of the literature of Europe, of the literature of a single country, not as a collection of the writings of individuals, but as "organic wholes," as systems in relation to which, and only in relation to which, individual works of literary art, and the works of individual artists, have their significance. There is accordingly something outside of the artist to which he owes his allegiance, a devotion to which he must surrender and sacrifice himself in order to earn and obtain his unique position. A common inheritance and a common cause unite artists consciously or unconsciously: it must be admitted that the union is mostly unconscious. Between the true artists of any time there is, I believe, an unconscious community.

T. S. Eliot, "The Function of Criticism" (1923)

The Myth of the Absurd

The decay of traditional Christianity as a unifying force in the life of Western man, whether it be mourned, celebrated, or merely acquiesced to, cannot be ignored. Since the death of the Genteel Tradition the theme of the exiled individual in a meaningless universe—a universe in which precepts of religious orthodoxy seem increasingly less relevant—has challenged the imagination of American writers with an almost overwhelming urgency. Despite the persistence of institutional Christianity—as measured by church construction and attendance—modern man seems continually less able to find order and meaning in his life. While he seems increasingly reluctant to take the leap into faith, nihilism rarely produces card-carrying agnostics. Thus, what might be called the "religious quest" continues to exert a powerful influence on the minds of Western thinkers. Albert Camus suggested the reason for this determined questing when he said that "A world that can be explained even with bad reasons is a familiar world."[1] The world ceases to be familiar when even the worst reasons fail to be of any help in explaining or ordering it. All of the old explanations—ethical and scientific—have failed where many modern thinkers are concerned, bringing them face to face with an alien universe in which orthodox "systems" can offer at best only a superficial reassurance.

Camus presented a thorough examination of man's hunger for unity in the face of a disordered universe in *The Myth of Sisyphus*. This persistent appetite for unity appears to be diametrically opposed to the reality which contemporary man encounters, and the disproportion between man's "intention and the reality he will encounter" Camus labels the "absurd." "'It's absurd' means not only 'It's impossible,' but also 'It's contradictory'."[2] In regarding the absurd quest for unity as essentially religious Camus is in accord with the pragmatic anthropological definition of religion as anything which works for a people insofar as it fulfills needs they define as "spiritual." In no sense do Camus's writings attempt to establish a

new religion, but they recognize religion in the broad sense in
striving to suggest an outline of conduct with which modern Western man may face the ethical problems of his age. Critic Charles
Glicksberg spells out Camus's concern with those problems that
have traditionally fallen within the compass of theology: "the absence of God, the relationship of a God who is all-powerful and all-
knowing to the evil and the suffering that exist on earth, the contrast between the routine of life and the crisis of being lost and
alone and doomed that the Existentialist hero experiences, the disruption of familiar, human reality by the knowledge of the inevitability and imminence of death, the search for the authentic life
on this journey to the end of night."[3]
    What Camus eventually describes is a stance which man may
take in a universe in which the old codes of religious authoritarianism no longer suffice to fulfill man's spiritual needs. The stance
of Camus's absurd man is anthropocentric, and its eventual opposition to both suicide and murder is based on the assumption that all
promise of value rests in life itself. In reaffirming the potential
meaningfulness of life, Camus established a new and distinctly
modern basis for heroism, and he suggested both affirmation and
heroism in choosing Sisyphus as the central figure of an essay designed to revaluate "the very warrant for continuing human existence and the possible resources of the human spirit in a universe
that appears no longer to make sense."[4] It is a universe in which
"right and wrong have lost their ancient names, as the ancient
order that named them has crumbled; and the task, as he has seen
it, is not to restore but to create anew."[5]
    Camus's impression of the confrontation of intention and reality
sets the stage for an interpretation of modern man's dilemma as
little dependent on nihilism as it is on supernatural consolation,
and Camus sees the novel as an ideal form for mirroring and confirming this confrontation. Not only does the novel itself represent
a kind of revolt in favor of order, but "the growth of the novel
corresponds, historically, to the beginnings of the modern metaphysical revolt . . ."[6] In his emphasis on art as a form of order
Camus seems clearly opposed to the contemporary French "anti-
novel." By selecting and rearranging elements from reality and
composing them into an imaginative pattern the artist gives them a
meaningfulness and a coherence which they would otherwise not
have possessed. As an imaginative re-creation of experience the
novel can thus, in and of itself, become a revolt against a world
which appears to have no logical pattern.
    If the condition of the absurd is as widespread as Camus argues,

and if the novel does indeed mirror the absurd as well as revolt against it, we might well expect to find contemporary novels of absurdity to which Camus's *Myth of Sisyphus* would serve as a key. Camus himself suggested that the concept of the absurd offered a critical aid in understanding the contemporary novel, and reviewers and critics have frequently noted that a knowledge of *The Myth of Sisyphus* is of great assistance in analyzing Camus's own fiction. While the philosophical essay and the novel are in many respects divergent forms, both are traditionally concerned with the ordering of experience, and Camus saw the novel as a form which harmonized certain of the metaphysical aspects of philosophy with the imaginative structuring of experience which is the traditional province of art. "It is true," as John Cruickshank argues in his study of Camus, "that each activity possesses its own particular climate, but this type of statement merely emphasizes the obvious fact that art is not philosophy and philosophy is not art. Clearly they do not coincide, but there can exist an interpenetration between them and both embody, at the present time, a common disquiet and similar anxieties."[7] It is this suggestive interpenetration between philosophy and art which makes Camus's philosophical writings especially pertinent to a study of contemporary fiction. The demonstration of Camusian elements of absurdity in the contemporary novel does not necessarily prove a borrowing or influence, and certainly does not suggest conscious artistic exercises on philosophical themes. What a demonstration of absurdity does indicate is a sympathetic response to the complex modern environment which Camus demandingly but compassionately explored, both in his fiction and in his philosophical essays. Many American novelists are considering the same disquiet, the same anxieties, and the same apparent lack of meaning and hope which Camus analyzed in *The Myth of Sisyphus*, and they share with Camus a common concern for religious and moral themes, especially in terms of the struggle to find value and fulfillment in a world without God.

The phenomenon of disproportion at the heart of the absurd has been the eternal problem of all great literature, and Camus frequently recognized that the concept of the absurd owed much to thinkers other than himself. Among those whom he cited in *The Myth of Sisyphus* were Husserl, Dostoevski, Nietzsche, and Sartre. What distinguished Camus from the countless other thinkers who considered the conflict of intention and reality was his refusal of all conventional value systems as either explanation for this con-

flict or relief from it, and his desire not to describe a new metaphysics, but rather to suggest the basis on which such a metaphysics might eventually be established. Beginning with a *tabula
rasa*, Camus proceeded to state what he considered the only pressing contemporary problem: suicide. Faced with a universe "suddenly divested of illusions and lights,"[8] man must decide either to
live or to die. If suicide is eventually rejected as a solution to man's
absurd situation he is left with the problem of how he should live.
Camus admits that a recognition of the meaninglessness of the universe may lead man to defenestration, be it physical suicide or the
intellectual suicide of the leap into faith, and his rejection of these
reactions to the universe is largely emotional: he simply denies
their validity as solutions. By eliminating one of the terms of the
conflict between man's intention and the reality he encounters,
suicide avoids the problem instead of solving it. Camus attempts to
show that the only position of integrity is the one in which the
paradox is preserved and in which the individual clings to the resulting tensions and conflicts as the only potential source of meaning. Camus repeatedly emphasizes that the absurd is not a feeling
restricted to the province of the philosopher, but one which is as
significant for the petty government clerk as it is for the conqueror
or the creator. In fact, Camus's own first attempt at absurd fiction,
The Stranger, centered on the colorless and insignificant clerk,
Meursault.

The feeling of the absurd is born when suddenly the chain of
mechanical daily gestures is broken, and in the void which results
man has the opportunity to ask himself, "Why?" Out of this moment consciousness is born. In Camus's words: "It happens that
the stage sets collapse. Rising, streetcar, four hours in the office or
factory, meal, streetcar, four hours of work, meal, sleep, and Monday Tuesday Wednesday Thursday Friday and Saturday according
to the same rhythm—this path is easily followed most of the time.
But one day the 'why' arises and everything begins in that weariness tinged with amazement."[9] A world which seemed to have
order now has only a wearying rhythm. Some are lulled back to
sleep by that rhythm, but those who resist it and remain awake are
the ones who must finally, with heightened consciousness, choose
between suicide and life. There are many manifestations of the
absurd, of which the collapsing stage set is only one. "Likewise the
stranger who at certain seconds comes to meet us in a mirror, the
familiar and yet alarming brother we encounter in our own photograph is also the absurd."[10] But whatever the physical circumstances of his absurd awakening, man becomes detached from his

environment. Like the Joycean epiphany, the absurd moment—which may come in a telephone booth or in a factory or on a battlefield—shows forth to the observer the heart of the world, and in Camus's vision that heart consists of the entire meaningless picture of life, "the cruel mathematics that command our condition." Many American writers—among them the early T. S. Eliot, Ernest Hemingway, William Faulkner, and Wright Morris—have noted similar manifestations of the absurd, but it is not with manifestations so much as with consequences of the absurd vision that Camus is concerned.

The viciously seductive rhythm of contemporary life is the source of Camus's comparison of modern man to Sisyphus, for both are involved in exhausting, monotonous, and apparently unending tasks. Camus's initial vision of the absurd seems nihilistic, but he continually emphasizes that the apparently nihilistic "feeling of the absurd is not, for all that, the notion of the absurd. It lays the foundations for it, and that is all. It is not limited to that notion, except in the brief moment when it passes judgment on the universe. Subsequently it has a chance of going further"; the feeling of the absurd may be based entirely on the objective recognition of "the disproportion between [a man's] intention and the reality he will encounter."[11] Only that individual who takes the absurd as a truth of existence is able to realize the notion of the absurd, and, through heightened consciousness, bind himself so closely to absurdity that it becomes something to live for.

John Cruickshank has noted that while Valéry ironically commented on the well-developed muscles which Sisyphus achieved in the course of performing his absurd task, "Camus wants much more than this. He wants to discover whether some kind of spiritual muscularity can be obtained, and if so, to what positive use it may be put."[12] In the stages of observation leading to a notion of the absurd the world is seen to contain nothing worth living for and, consequently, nothing worth dying for. With the recognition of the absurd as a constant of experience, an observable (not an absolute) truth, man at last has something to live for and something which, under the appropriate arrangement of psychological circumstances, would be worth dying for. "The frustrated search for truth, which made him conscious of the absurd, is at least satisfied on one point in that it attains the truth of the absurd itself. Now this same desire for truth demands, he claims, that one should maintain and defend any truth that one discovers."[13] It is important to emphasize that the notion of the absurd is dependent on two ingredients: intention and reality. To deny either of those terms is to destroy the absurd, which exists only as a consequence of mind reflecting on the world. Thus, the notion of the absurd is one which leads us automatically to a consideration of the individual, and because the individual is essential to the absurd, our real concern is with the absurd man. If, as Camus says, the absurd demands defense as the only truth isolable in the modern environment, we are justified in projecting from the absurd man an absurd hero, one whose concern is with asserting a right to the particular disproportion which he exemplifies. A consideration of the concept of an absurd *hero* is in large part made necessary by the ubiquitousness with which Camus uses the word "absurd"—to refer to the meaningless universe, to the man who suffers in it, to the awareness of suffering, and to the work of art that describes such suffering. Clearly, however, Camus's final interest is not in the man who demonstrates just any kind of disproportion between intention and reality; it does not, for example, end with the individual who, armed only with a sword, singlehandedly attacks a machine-gun nest—although this is an absurd man. Camus's ultimate concern is with the man sufficiently strong to sustain a disproportion on the level of values, a man who persists in his demands for truth in a universe that says truths are impossible.

With the absurd hero, achievement ceases to be a question of victory or defeat but is rather success in sustaining an elemental disproportion. In terms of philosophy the idea that the struggle for truth becomes truth is hardly a new one. Emphasis is shifted from attainment to performance, and in the process of sustaining his performance, of defending his passion for the absurd, the absurd hero achieves fulfillment simply by defending a truth. Absurdity becomes a passion, and the test of the absurd hero is one designed to determine whether he can live with his passions, whether he can accept their law, "which is to burn the heart they simultaneously exalt."[14] Absurdity becomes a defiance of the universe, an extreme tension which will never permit the hero to rest, just as the tormented Sisyphus can never pause in his task. Maintenance of the absurd, moreover, is the only way in which man can rebel against the apparently meaningless universe, since rebellion that does not orient itself to truth is worthless. In the words of Germaine Brée, "The absurd for Camus requires no other universe than our daily world, our earth as we see it, our fellow men, ourselves. Thus integrated into our daily lives, it can be faced at every moment and, by our action, denied. Our revolt against the absurd begins when our consciousness of its existence is followed by the

THE MYTH OF THE ABSURD

refusal to be obsessed and paralyzed by it. It is a state of mind. The emphasis which Malraux puts on death, Camus shifts to life. The emphasis which Sartre puts on the total liberty inherent in man's contingency, Camus puts on lucidity."[15]

Camus is able to draw three circumstances from the absurd: "My revolt, my freedom, and my passion." The absurd man becomes free the moment he recognizes his own absurdity, and thus "The myth of Sisyphus means for Camus that the most appalling truths can lose their power over us once we have absolutely recognized and accepted them."[16] A kind of glory descends on the man who is able to recognize and endure the absurd miseries of the world, and therefore Sisyphus, through such recognition, is not only free; at times he may even be happy. The tragedy of Sisyphus, Camus argues, comes solely from the fact that he is conscious, yet it is his very consciousness which causes the pain of his circumstances to vanish; Oedipus' conclusion that "all is well" is cited as "the recipe for the absurd victory."[17] At the moment of consciousness, tragedy begins, but so, too, does the stuff of happiness: "I leave Sisyphus at the foot of the mountain! One always finds one's burden again. But Sisyphus teaches the higher fidelity that negates the gods and raises rocks. He too concludes that all is well. The universe henceforth without a master seems to him neither sterile nor futile. Each atom of that stone, each mineral flake of that night-filled mountain, in itself forms a world. The struggle itself toward the heights is enough to fill a man's heart. One must imagine Sisyphus happy."[18] Sisyphus becomes the incarnation of the absurd, and the strong appeal which this mythological figure has presented to man's imagination suggests something of the possibilities of the development of an absurd hero of great proportions. For Camus, both Don Juan and Don Quixote are companion figures to Sisyphus. Sisyphus is the hero of the absurd "as much through his passions as through his torment. His scorn of the gods, his hatred of death, and his passion for life won him that unspeakable penalty in which the whole being is exerted toward accomplishing nothing. This is the price that must be paid for the passions of the earth."[19] Obviously Camus's concept of the absurd goes beyond the classic figure of Sisyphus, for Sisyphus was forced back to Hades and his hands placed against the rock by his gods. No absolute or higher power commands the labors of the modern Sisyphus. Thus, Camus must reinterpret the Sisyphus myth to emphasize the fact that Sisyphus' labors are a defiance and negation of gods. "His fate belongs to him. His rock is his thing."[20] "Whatever facet of the problem we consider, the essay leads, nevertheless, to one conclusion: life is infinitely valuable to the individual; only by a clear consciousness of the given data of life can the individual reach happiness; happiness, at heart, can only be tragic. The absurd human being is by definition wedded to life; all evasion of life is a capitulation. Life is our rock."[21]

Camus's arguments on the absurd are impressionistic, and it would be unfair, therefore, to demand of them the logic and consistency of a finalized philosophical system. The author himself continually reminds us that they are neither definitive nor proscriptive. Faced with a world in which man's painful odyssey seems meaningless, Camus determines to find a source of meaning which will deny nihilism while avoiding recourse to traditional absolutes. In his *Lettres à un ami allemand*, Camus outlines this purpose, which was the motivation of his life's work: "I continue to believe that this earth has no superior meaning. But I know that something in it makes sense, and that is man, because he is the only being who insists upon it. The world has at least the truth of man, and our task is to give man his justification against fate itself."[22] Both nihilism and orthodox faith negate the terms of man's conflict and justify fate by accepting it rather than giving man a justification *against* fate. Sartre, who was finally to become one of Camus's most extreme opponents, saw in Camus's very nature the injunction to justify man against fate by living the conflict between intention and reality: "For you bore within yourself all the conflicts of our time and went beyond them because of the ardor with which you lived them."[23] What Sartre saw in Camus was the primary injunction of the absurd: "Live the conflict, for only the conflict can make you free." The decision to live an unending essential conflict does not amount to the renunciation of hope, even though the absurd man does renounce hope in abstract "eternity" and in ever fully comprehending the universe which surrounds him. Life itself—life determined and walled in by absurdities—is now the source of hope.

The underlying, tacitly accepted premise of Camus's study of the absurd is that "man, without the help of the Eternal or of rationalistic thought, can create, all by himself, his own values."[24] The absurd becomes a new and extreme articulation of the necessity of man's appealing to himself as a source of values; its goal is to embrace life rather than to reject it, with the belief that through this embrace man can arrive at the joy of truth. Nevertheless, the absurd theory expounded in *The Myth of Sisyphus* tends more toward a quantitative than a qualitative ethics, as Camus himself suggested: "Belief in the absurd is tantamount to substituting the quantity of experiences for the quality."[25] Although granting the fact that in some cases quantity may constitute quality, Camus is unable—nor does he wish—to avoid the implication that the doctrine of the absurd allows for great latitude in human conduct. In the beginning of *Lettres à un ami allemand* Camus notes that both he and his imaginary German friend had begun from the same premise—that of the necessity of rebelling against the absurdity of the world. Their absurd stances were, in terms of the initial theory of *The Myth of Sisyphus*, equally valid, yet Camus had cast his lot with what he called "justice," while the German had cast his with brute terrorism. Because of his own political involvements, Camus thus found it necessary to redefine the absurd, to make it consider the question of murder as well as that of suicide. *The Myth of Sisyphus* had begun with questioning the latter, while *L'homme revolté* began by questioning the former.

A working definition of the absurd which can be applied to the contemporary American novel should generally avoid the theoretical qualifications Camus made in *The Rebel*. It is precisely because the concept of absurdity appears to have numerous contemporary applications that it suggests itself as a valuable critical thesis, and the unsystematic statements of *The Myth of Sisyphus* allow the individual artist the widest range of interpretation. The first step in the development of the absurd consists in the individual's shocking recognition of the apparent meaninglessness of the universe. The second step consists in the absurd man's living the now apparent conflict between his intention (his inner voice) and the reality which he will encounter; the third step consists in his assumption of heroic dimensions through living the conflict and making it his god. According to Leslie Fiedler, the most honest and promising vision of man which serious literature in our time can present is "not, as so often in the past, a view of man struggling to fulfill some revealed or inherited view of himself and his destiny; but of man learning that it is the struggle itself which is his definition."[26] The development from this struggle of a particular system of belief is not only possible but likely. The ethics of the absurd, however, are implicit rather than explicit. "L'homme absurde is a man without nostalgia. He has accepted his prison walls and the logical conclusion of Camus's argument. He is passionately wedded to life; he is an enemy of death. Therein lies the conscious affirmation of his humanity; he is against the natural order of the universe in which the words life and death are meaningless, against the gods—if there be any."[27] What gives this argument its ethical tone is that man is, through the absurd, affirming his own humanity. Thus far, however, we have at most an ethical direction, not an ethical code: but since man is in a position "to edify, without God, a humanism of high nobility,"[28] he is in a position to restore human dignity and thus to throw his weight on the side of ethical values.

The careful reader of *The Myth of Sisyphus* is well aware that Camus would cast his vote against murder even as he casts it against suicide. It is not the problem of murder which makes *L'homme revolté* inappropriate to the study of absurd fiction, but the fact that its central problem is the determination of the most efficacious channels which political activity should take in order to implement human dignity. What is significant in that work for the purposes of such an analysis is the light it sheds on the position and function of the artist. The novels, plays, and essays which followed *The Myth of Sisyphus* were not simple exercises on a theme, but all of them dealt in varying degrees with the problem of absurdity which that essay enunciates. Their conclusions differ, but the premise of an absurd universe and its absurd opponent remains the same, even when that universe is eventually given meaning by the joy of a Sisyphus-like struggle against it.

Since the words "absurd" and "alienated" have become such popular catchalls for the analysis of contemporary literature, it should perhaps be observed that literary critics no doubt often commit an unfortunate if understandable *lèse-majesté* in regarding the theme of alienation as the unique province of the contemporary artist, disregarding, as they do, the very fabric of tragedy and much that is best and most viable in romantic fiction, but their instincts are surely right, for with increasing frequency and persistence many contemporary writers would seem to suggest that alienation is not the result of the confrontation of a unique human spirit with a particular set of essentially external conditions, but that it is the fate of any and all men who think and feel with any intensity about their relationship to the world which surrounds them. Therefore man does not *become* alienated (the word itself ceases to have connotations of "process"): alienation is his birthright, the modern, psychologically colored equivalent of original sin. Thus, if contemporary alienation is not different in kind from that of previous ages, it is at least different in degree and, because it frequently presupposes the irrelevance of conventional value systems, significantly different in the results which it presupposes.

The four American novelists who are treated in this study—John Updike, William Styron, Saul Bellow, and J. D. Salinger—share a vision of the spiritual sterility and loneliness of the modern environment strikingly similar to the absurd universe which Camus described in *The Myth of Sisyphus*. These authors further share with Camus the belief that man must oppose this universe, even though his demands for order and meaning will make him absurd. Secular humanism is implied in the works of these authors as it is implied in *The Myth of Sisyphus* itself, thus forging an additional link with the early theories of Camus. Like Camus, these authors reject nihilism and orthodoxy, and like Camus too, they end by affirming the humanity of man. The absurd hero is by definition a rebel because he refuses to avoid either of the two components on which absurdity depends: intention, which is his desire for unity, and reality, which is constituted by the meaninglessness of life. The hope which absurd heroes offer to the secular societies of the West is that they may generate values to replace those which are lost as once sacred traditions disappear. Thus, revolt alone becomes revelatory of human values, giving the dimensions to human experience once provided by Christianity; the call to revolt is a call to humanize, to transform the inhumanity of the world. Like Camus, the absurd novelist does not attempt to establish a specific ethical system, but he does point toward a homocentric humanism which may well serve the function of prolegomena to a future ethic.

Just as the premise of the absurd defined in *The Myth of Sisyphus* permits a variety of conclusions—depending on the exact form of the two givens, intention and reality—so it permits, in fictive terms, a variety of forms. Sisyphus, as Camus reminds us, is first a portrait of tragedy and then a portrait of joy. The absurd hero in fiction may remain exclusively in the state of tragedy, or he may transcend that condition by his realization of the sheer joy of struggle; what concerns us here are the varieties of contemporary experience and the degrees of personal fulfillment accommodated by the absurd tension. To some degree, the potential joy following tragedy in the case of the absurd hero is not unlike the *anagnorisis* or discovery which follows the fall of the classical tragic hero: the "all is well" of Oedipus. In this respect, the development of the tragic hero follows Northrop Frye's "Theory of Myths," in which comedy and tragedy are viewed as related aspects of the quest-myth. When he first demonstrates a separation of intention and reality, the absurd man might well be the subject of burlesque, where the essential element of humor would rest in a contrast between the character's apparently exaggerated intention and the environment in which he is placed. At the next level, that of defense of the absurd, the character is involved, according to Camus's definition, in a tragic situation. When the joy that accompanies strug-

gle fills the character, he is experiencing the comic sequel to tragedy. "If we are right [Frye argues] in our suggestion that romance,
tragedy, irony and comedy are all episodes in a total quest-myth,
we can see how it is that comedy can contain a potential tragedy
within itself. In myth, the hero is a god, and hence he does not die,
but dies and rises again. The ritual pattern behind the catharsis of
comedy is the resurrection that follows death, the epiphany or
manifestation of the risen hero . . . Christianity, too, sees tragedy
as an episode in the divine comedy, the larger scheme of redemption and resurrection."[29] At what stage the author picks up the
absurd hero and to what point he carries him along this spectrum is
a question of individual "style," which Camus saw as an order "applied to the disorder of a particular time."[30] In its most exhaustive
development, the absurd hero will be taken through all the stages
from burlesque to comedy, and it is only after the joyous rebirth of
the third and final stage that he may be prepared to derive a value
system from his experience in the absurd. At any stage, however,
the absurd is a symbol of hope. Like the characters in *The Plague*
who give their lives meaning by fighting the epidemic even though
there seems to be no hope of altering its course, the absurd hero
holds out the message that though victory is questionable, defeat is
not final. As a response to the futility which often seems to characterize the contemporary environment, that message is not without
a kind of magnificence.

The Absurd Man as Saint

John Updike's first novel, *The Poorhouse Fair*, was a novel of dismissal in which the author suggested the failure of various traditional systems to fulfill contemporary man's spiritual needs. The novel was an indictment of the life-denying impulses of an age, and while it offered no solution and raised no successful protagonist to this succession of denials, it had to be written to free Updike to create the absurd heroes who appear with increasing authority in the writings that follow. The bulk of Updike's attack in *The Poorhouse Fair* was against the presumably humanistic welfare state whose aim is to give security, coherence, and meaning to human life but which, Updike says, results only in a yet more precarious and obtrusive sterility.

Since the humanist's interests extend beyond the single individual to embrace the human race as a whole, he will eventually look toward the state as the only practicable organ for promoting the well-being and culture of man and for safeguarding the race. Thus, since the welfare state is the ultimate socio-political realization of humanism, almost all utopian literature runs either to criticism of the welfare state or proselytizing for it. *The Poorhouse Fair* is one of the two important books since the Second World War to have been added to this virtually timeless discussion. Its predecessor, B. F. Skinner's *Walden Two*, envisioned a paradise of experimentally conditioned people living together in perfect harmony and happiness. Art and individual expression proliferate at Walden II, and the author devotes considerable emphasis to their importance in the ideal society. Skinner was happily able to overlook the stress or neurosis theory of art—there being, of course, neither stresses nor neuroses at Walden II. The theory that man uses art to order his life is also a meaningless one in this environment, since every detail of life in Skinner's Utopia is synonymous with order. Indeed, there seems no motivation whatsoever for artistic expression—an oversight one would not have expected from an experimental psychologist. Skinner is wholly serious in his suggestion that conditioning is a panacea for the human race, and in advancing it he makes a supreme humanistic gesture to the suffering world. As a scientist he is certain that his plan will work, and as a man he sees no objection to the welfare state in which all needs and wants—the latter conditioned never to exceed the "reasonable" and attainable—are fulfilled.

Updike's examination of the welfare state of the late twentieth century is made through one of its agencies, the poorhouse, and through the humanist who administers to that agency, Mr. Conner. The poorhouse is actually a kind of old-folks home for those people financially unable to provide for themselves in their old age. Updike's criticism of the system comes through the presentation of three variously rebellious inmates, Lucas, Gregg, and Hook.

Conner is, in his own mind, a rebel and an idealist. His zeal for cleansing the world is unflagging. Standing in his office, he hears the gunshot fired by his assistant, Buddy; the fawning subordinate has followed Conner's orders by shooting a diseased cat that threatened to contaminate the grounds:

Buddy's rifle shot had sounded in here like a twig snapping. Conner had no regrets about ordering the animal killed. He wanted things *clean*; the world needed renewal, and this was a time of history when there were no cleansing wars or sweeping purges, when reform was slow, and decayed things were allowed to stand and rot themselves away. It was a vegetable world. Its theory was organic: perhaps old institutions in their dying could make fertile the chemical earth. So the gunshot ringing out, though a discord, pleased the rebel in Conner, the idealist, anxious to make space for the crystalline erections that in his heart he felt certain would arise, once his old people were gone. For the individual cat itself he felt nothing but sorrow. (*PFa*, 64)

There is no question about Conner's inclinations: while he feels sorrow for the individual, he is more than willing to sacrifice him for the good of the "race," for achieving necessary fertilizer. Conner has, unfortunately, been born too late for the kind of life he should have preferred: "he envied the first rationalists their martyrdoms and the first reformers their dragons of reaction and selfishness" (65). The nature of Conner's administrative post would suggest impartial conduct; indeed, he himself felt that impartiality was "a crucial virtue" (15). He frequently falls short in practice: he encourages an informer in the midst of the old people, allowing the man benefits not available to the others, and he has a clear partiality for inmates who were once wealthy or well educated. His aggression toward those whom he feels to be ignorantly prejudiced is extreme. Despite Hook's education, Conner is angered by his defense of the concept of heaven, and the administrator quickly yields to the desire "to pin his antagonist against the rock that underlay his own philosophy" (109). The reviewers of Updike's novels have repeatedly argued that he refrains from committing himself to any of the philosophies which he presents. Updike himself, in a fictionalized monologue on writing, admits that he is "too tired" to attempt to draw philosophy from the scenes which he creates, but he does hope that "once into my blindly spun web of words the thing itself will break; make an entry and an account of itself. Not declare what it will do. This is no mystery; we are old friends. I can observe. Not cast its vote with mine, and make a decree: I have no hope of this. The session has lasted too long. I wish it to yield only on the point of its identity. What is it? Its breadth, its glitter, its greenness and sameness balk me. *What is it?* If I knew, I could say."[1] The mystery of the sea may perhaps eventually be revealed to the writer through contemplation, just as the phenomenon that is modern man may also reveal his secrets and flaws. In *The Poorhouse Fair* Updike is primarily an observer, but he is neither completely dissociated nor completely uncommitted. While he looks with ironic compassion on the entire host of fools and meddlers which he exposes, his final commitment is to the spirit of rebellion. Such commitments are in some respects negative—we are scarcely in doubt of what he disapproves. In standing on the side of rebellion, however, he supports no single character, but rather a germ which resides, with special intensity, in the three old men on whom the story centers.

Updike despises the simple, unthinking handmaid of church or state as manifested through the well-intentioned meddlings of Hook and Conner. Criticism of the welfare state and of Conner as its product is obvious from the opening page of *The Poorhouse Fair*. Two of the old men approach their porch chairs to find them encumbered with metal tabs bearing the names of their "owners." To Gregg this obvious affront to individualism resembles the branding of cattle. Hook's calmer reaction marks him as a well-trained and well-adjusted cog of discipline in that he cautions in favor of tolerating such inane examples of Conner's "tinkering." "'Caution is the bet-ter part of action',' he reasons. "'No doubt it is an aspect of Conner's wish to hold us to our place. An-y motion on our part to threaten his security will make him that much more unyielding'" (11).

Through the novel runs a continuing undertow of criticism in

the form of a letter which Conner has received from one of the
townspeople in nearby Andrews:

Stephen Conner—
Who do you think you are a Big shot? Yr duty is to help not hinder
these old people on there way to there final Reward. I myself have heard
bitter complant from these old people when they come into town where I
live. They call you Pieface you and that moran Buddy. The nature of
there complants I will disclose latter, and will write the U.S. gov.ment
depending. Things have not gone so far these old people have no rights
no pale peenynotchin basterd can take away.

                                                    A "Town's person" (178)

The letter is a double-edged instrument, reflecting as much dis-
credit upon the writer as it does on Conner, but its author has been
chosen with intentional irony to highlight a central theme of the
novel: Conner and his fellows are prolonging life and stifling living.
The final judgment pronounced by the novel, however, is not directed so much against Conner as it is against the sterile world
which has assigned the old people to a poorhouse which reduces
life to its lowest denominator. Resignation characterizes their condition, but their resignation is not an acceptance of the prospect of
death; it is, as the letter to Conner suggests, an acceptance of the
tortuous necessity of continuing to live. Indeed, the old people
revert to memories of the excitement of old wars and political cam-
paigns and "dead" issues because of the necessity of putting some
vitality, however ephemeral, into their lives. Thus, disappointed
that rain has threatened to cancel their annual fair, the poorhouse
inmates recall their former executive, Mendelssohn, and the
warmth and vitality he had carried with him into their dining hall.
In their total recollections Mendelssohn is far from perfect, but it
is clear that the old man possessed a quality of life which won him
their appreciation. Updike is later to describe this intense quality
as "force."

Conner continually abuses the old people's memory of Mendelssohn, and by taking away much of their responsibility for the
fair, considerably lessens its significance. The total boredom and
passivity of these old people's lives remind one of Swift's description of the melancholy and immortal Struldbrugs. While Updike's
comments reflect none of the brutality or bitterness found in
Swift's description, they do contain a strikingly similar impression
of futility.

Of the three "rebels" who emerge in *The Poorhouse Fair* Hook is
the most intelligent: he is much too well disciplined to seek to

reach Conner through violence. Gregg, on the other hand, incites the old people to stone their administrator, and Lucas attempts to defeat monotony with pain, jabbing at his ear with a match until the ear is badly inflamed. Lucas openly defies Conner's authority by buying a bottle of rye and slipping it into the main building to share with his rebellious cronies. It is, significantly, with these three men and their reactions to the dehumanizing humanism of the welfare state that Updike concludes his book:

THE MAN of flesh, the man of passion, the man of thought. Lucas slept. His body, stripped to underclothes and half-covered with a sheet, submitted in oblivion to a harmony of forms. Gregg hopped and chirrupped on the lawn, dazzling himself with the illumination and talking aloud in his self-delight, though tomorrow he would be as cross as ever. Hook sat up with a start. The pillow and his horizontal position had been smothering him, and the phlegm in his throat could not be rasped away. His heart doubled its speed of beating; and gradually slowed. . . . His encounter with Conner had commenced to trouble him. The young man had been grievously stricken. The weakness on his face after his henchman had stolen the cigar was troubling to recall; an intimacy had been there [which] Hook must reward with help. A small word would perhaps set things right. As a teacher, Hook's flaw had been over-conscientiousness; there was nowhere he would not meddle. He stood motionless, half in moonlight, groping after the fitful shadow of the advice he must impart to Conner, as a bond between them and a testament to endure his dying in the world. What was it? (184–185)

To be sure, Updike creates neither a *persona* nor a hero in any of these men. Hook is the most acceptable opponent of the poorhouse system, but Updike's sympathies lie with Hook's realization of his superior's weakness and his simultaneous desire to reach out and help—not with his Christian philosophizing. Hook remains too much a part of the system to be a true rebel. The *significaccio* of Updike's first novel does not rest in a proposed solution, but in the criticism of a system which provides "super" answers to man's physical needs while taking no notice of his spiritual desires and requirements. The lack of attention to the spiritual needs of the poorhouse inmates renders ludicrous the efficient medical treatment to which Lucas is subjected.

As we learn from the townspeople who attend the fair, the poorhouse is but one manifestation of the society which Updike has endeavored to expose. Their talk and their attitudes are shallow: "HEART had gone out of these people; health was the principal thing about the faces of the Americans that came crowding through the broken wall to the poorhouse fair. They were just people, members of the race of white animals that had cast its herds over the land of six continents" (158). They are harmless, but even more dispirited and empty than the old people at whom they gawk. In an attempt to allay the sterility of their lives, the younger Americans seek outlets in extremes of perversion or of respectable platitudinous behavior; and they attempt to regain something of America's once-vital heritage by collecting objects of early Americana and almost anything else which appears to be handmade.

The Poorhouse Fair is a projection into the year 1975, but like most exercises in the pastoral or utopian modes, it is an implied criticism of the contemporary environment. In Rabbit, Run, however, the author made a specific analysis of the spiritual shallowness of his own age. As Whitney Balliett commented after its publication, "Rabbit, Run bristles with enough dissatisfaction to let loose an affecting shout at human fumbling, which the first book never mustered up the indignation to do. There is no pity; nor, peculiarly, is there any humor, but there is a great deal of martinetlike understanding. The Poorhouse Fair was a brilliant but stiff setting-up exercise. Rabbit, Run goes many steps beyond."[2] Harry "Rabbit" Angstrom rebels against the wasteland into which he is born. In consistently opposing the reality which he encounters, Rabbit becomes an absurd hero, and because of the highly spiritual devotion of this gesture against the world, he becomes a saint, although a saint of a very special nature.

Like many absurd heroes, Harry Angstrom is a questing man and, because of the nature of his quest, he is set apart from the world in which he lives. Rabbit is rejected by both his own family and his wife and her family because of his dedication to "'something that wants me to find it'" (RR, 127). The precise object of Harry's quest is never defined in more specific terms, although it is occasionally identified as "force." As a star basketball player, Harry was an idealist who never fouled and usually won. Unlike the idealism of Conner, Harry's is based upon devotion to an inner conviction; Conner's convictions are only the ideals of the state, unquestioningly absorbed. On its most obvious level, Rabbit, Run is a story of the Angst of a young man who strives for the same perfection and skill in life that he had known on the basketball court. But Rabbit does not simply need to be a winner. The methods by which success can be achieved as a middle-class family man and car or kitchen-gadget salesman are not beyond his mastery; they simply do not interest him. Rabbit has broken away from the hypnotic mediocrity of his life long enough to realize its meaninglessness. Stepping apart from this routine, he is able to see himself, and the incredulous vision which greets him is the absurd. Camus argued that "the stranger who at certain seconds comes to meet us in a mirror, the familiar and yet alarming brother we encounter in our own photographs is also the absurd."[3] In a poem entitled "Reflection" Updike expressed a sensitivity almost identical to Camus's sensitivity to the mirror image. What at first glance appears to be an example of *New Yorker* preciousness is actually an extreme statement of the absurd:

When you look	kool uoy nehW
into a mirror	rorrim a otni
it is not	ton si ti
yourself you see	ees uoy flesruoy
but a kind	dnik a tub
of apish error	rorre hsipa fo
posed in fearful	lufraef ni desop
symmetry.	.yrtemmys[4]

Having glimpsed himself in the mirror, Rabbit flees from the apish error of his life, embarking on a quest for his real self.

The theme of the successful basketball star turned middle-class family man is one which Updike has explored in more than one fashion. In a story originally published in the *New Yorker*, Updike described "Ace" Anderson, a former basketball star disillusioned with small-town life and his job as a car salesman. In this story Ace is rejuvenated by the thought of producing a son whose grip and dexterity will match his own. Overcome with this idea, he seizes his angered wife in his arms and soothes her with dancing; as the music swells he imagines that "other kids were around them, in a ring, clapping" (*SD*, 26).

Updike's stories repeatedly urge the idea that few if any causes are worth man's sacrifice, that the world provides little room for heroism. Rafe, another of Updike's unfulfilled young moderns, is described in "Toward Evening" riding the bus up Broadway. Outside the windows numbers on the buildings begin to assume historical significance: "The clearly marked numbers on the east side of the street ran: 1832, 1836, 1846, 1850 (Wordsworth dies), 1880 (great Nihilistic trial in St. Petersburg), 1900 (Rafe's father born in Trenton), 1902 (Braque leaves Le Havre to study painting in Paris), 1914 (Joyce begins *Ulysses*; war begins in Europe), 1926 (Rafe's

parents marry in Ithaca), 1936 (Rafe is four years old). Where the
present should have stood, a block was torn down, and the num-
bering began again with 2000, a boring progressive edifice" (SD,
63–64). The present is a blank, the sky illuminated by a Spry sign,
and the future holds forth only "a boring progressive edifice" like
the poorhouse. The modern world as Updike sees it is a world of
the superlative and the superfluous, but not a world of fulfillment:

> I drive my car to supermarket,
> The way I take is superhigh,
> A superlot is where I park it,
> And Super Suds are what I buy.
>
> Supersalesmen sell me tonic—
> Super-Tone-O, for relief.
> The planes I ride are supersonic.
> In trains I like the Super Chief.
>
> Supercilious men and women
> Call me superficial—me.
> Who so superbly learned to swim in
> Supercolossality.
>
> Superphosphate-fed foods feed me;
> Superservice keeps me new.
> Who would dare to supersede me,
> Super-super-superwho? (CH, 6)

In a world of such hyperbolic and self-defeating superlatives scant
room exists for the hero except in the athletic events which seem
increasingly to occupy contemporary America's minds. Another of
Updike's former basketball stars, "Flick," finds nothing worthwhile
on which he can lay his "fine and nervous" hands once he has retired from the basketball courts.

Updike's young basketball players—especially Harry Angstrom—recall Ring Lardner's innocence stories about the baseball
diamond, and those stories offer a clue to Harry's quest. What attracted Lardner to the game of baseball was that there one could
find rules, that there right conduct was rewarded and wrong-doing
punished, and the prize awarded to the person who dedicated
himself to the game. Real heroism and integrity could be expressed through baseball, and the baseball diamond became a surrogate spiritual environment whose values transcended the individual player. The famous World Series "fix" virtually broke
Lardner's heart. Harry Angstrom is, of course, a perfectionist and

an idealist, but he is not simply a former basketball hero determined to be in all things star and winner. Harry's former coach, Tothero, emphasizes that what he has inspired in his boys is "'the will to achieve'." He adds, "'I've always liked that better than the will to win, for there can be achievement even in defeat. Make them feel the, yes, I think the word is good, the *sacredness* of achievement, in the form of giving our best'" (RR, 61). It is part of Updike's essential irony that this message comes from a pathetic neurotic. One is nevertheless reminded of Camus's suggestion of the great joy which Sisyphus realizes in his apparent defeat.

Harry's quest is for that environment in which he can give his best. He cannot do it in the television-and-booze-tinted world of his wife Janice, nor in any of the other "worlds" which he samples in Brewer, Pennsylvania. Harry's intention is to find that world in which he can again experience the sacredness of achievement. Janice unwittingly touches the core of her husband's experience when she asks after hearing that he has given up cigarettes, "'What are you doing, becoming a saint?'" (9). Whenever he is disillusioned by the world in which he finds himself Rabbit begins to run. The gesture is impulsive, but it is fundamental to his spiritual nature. As he runs Rabbit becomes a social outcast, rejecting his family and the responsibilities which life seems to place on him. These rejections are part of his saintliness. Rabbit has sampled conventional ethics and found them wanting. He longs for total absorption in the present moment, for an opportunity to express his compassion for the human race. This expression of compassion—the desire to embrace the very soul of man—is a concomitant of sainthood. Rabbit hopes that he can give in this fashion to Ruth Leonard, a prostitute with whom he lives after leaving his wife, and that he can give his best in this new experience: "He turns her roughly, and, in a reflex of his own, falls into a deep wish to give comfort. . . . As they deepen together he feels impatience that through all their twists they remain separate flesh; he cannot dare enough, now that she is so much his friend in this search . . . She feels transparent; he sees her heart" (78, 83, 84). While Ruth cannot completely fulfill Harry's desire to give, she is nonetheless able to recognize the intensity of his quest more fully than any of the other characters in the novel. She likes Harry, and when he presses her for a reason, she answers, "''Cause you haven't given up. 'Cause in your stupid way you're still fighting'" (91). Standing with Ruth at the top of Mt. Judge, Harry has a compassionate, Pisgah-like vision of death and suffering. He opens "the lips of his soul to receive the taste of the truth about it, as if truth were a secret in such low solution that only immensity can give us a sensible taste" (112).

Ruth is not wholly alone in recognizing this struggle in Rabbit. Eccles, the sympathetic Episcopal minister, also recognizes it, but the struggle is foreign to his orthodoxy, and "duty" demands that he reject it. Countering Rabbit's saintly declarations, Eccles says that Jesus taught "'that saints shouldn't marry'" (127). There is, of course, nothing about the high level of a saint's emotional experience which dictates the requirement of celibacy. Eccles has chosen to deny Rabbit's quest because it is foreign to the neat theological patterns into which the minister has organized his life. Rabbit's peculiar saintliness demands, in fact, that he not be celibate, for it is largely through sex that he is able to express his desire to comfort and heal; it is through sex that he is able to see Ruth's "heart." Updike reiterates this idea of salvation through sex in "Lifeguard," a monologue in which a young, devoted divinity student considers the advantages of his summer job as a lifeguard. He lusts after many of the women who parade before him, but he emphasizes that "To desire a woman is to desire to save her. Anyone who has endured intercourse that was neither predatory nor hurried knows how through it we descend, with a partner, into the grotesque and delicate shadows that until then have remained locked in the most guarded recess of our soul: into this harbor we bring her" (*PFe*, 216–217).

When Eccles chides Rabbit about his lack of celibacy he is being decidedly ironic, but as his knowledge of this dissenter increases, the seriousness and force with which Eccles attacks Rabbit also increase:

"Harry," he asks, sweetly yet boldly, "why have you left her? You're obviously deeply involved with her."

"I *told* ja. There was this thing that wasn't there."

"What thing? Have you ever seen it? Are you sure it exists?"

Harry's two-foot putt dribbles short and he picks up the ball with trembling fingers. "Well if you're not sure it exists don't ask me. It's right up your alley. If you don't know nobody does."

"No," Eccles cried in the same strained voice in which he told his wife to keep her heart open for Grace. "Christianity isn't looking for a rainbow. If it were what you think it is we'd pass out opium at services. We're trying to *serve* God, not *be* God."

They pick up their bags and walk the way a wooden arrow tells them.

Eccles goes on, explanatorily, "This was all settled centuries ago, in the heresies of the early Church."

"I tell you, I know what it is."

"What is it? What *is* it? Is it hard or soft? Harry. Is it blue? Is it red?
Does it have polka dots?"
It hits Rabbit depressingly that he really wants to be told. Underneath
all this I-know-more-about-it-than-you heresies-of-the-early-Church business he really wants to be told about it, wants to be told that it is there,
that he's not lying to all those people every Sunday. As if it's not enough to
be trying to get some sense out of this frigging game, you have to carry
around this madman to swallow your soul. The hot strap of the bag gnaws
his shoulder.
"The truth is," Eccles tells him with womanish excitement, in a voice
agonized by embarrassment, "you're monstrously selfish. You're a cow-
ard. You don't care about right or wrong; you worship nothing except your
own worst instincts." (*RR*, 132–133)

Rabbit is, of course, selfish after the manner of any man in search
of truth, and his life is a struggle for self-knowledge that is comically heralded by a television Mousketeer: "'Know Thyself, a wise
old Greek once said'" (9).
    In light of Rabbit's renunciation of traditional Christianity Up-
dike's choice of one of Pascal's fragments from the *Pensées* as an
introduction to the novel may seem somewhat enigmatic. It need
not seem so if we think of the *Pensées* as a testimony to the spiritual struggle of man and not as a testimony to the struggle of
Christian man. "The motions of Grace, the hardness of the heart;
external circumstances." In citing Pascal, Updike emphasizes the
spiritual nature of Rabbit's quest. It is, perhaps, only through the
action of something akin to the Christian concept of grace that a
voice calls to Harry that does not call to other men; his pursuit of
that voice demands a hardness of the heart and a definite oblivious-
ness to external circumstances. All of Pascal's religious writings rest
on the foundation of a personal religious experience of a peculiarly
intense nature. The *Pensées* themselves, as one of their best critics has noted, "reconstruct in logical terms—the speech of common mortals—a spiritual pilgrimage and a mystical experience."[5]
Eccles, to some degree, may be thought of as representing that
Reason which, for Pascal, would never alone be capable of achieving truth. Rabbit himself suggests Pascal's description of the man
who is seeking for Jesus but who has not found him: "Mais *ceux qui
cherchent Dieu de tout leur coeur*, qui n'ont de déplaisir que d'être
privés de sa vue, qui n'ont de désir que pour le posséder, et d'ennemis que ceux qui les en détournent, qui s'affligent de se voir
environnés et dominés de tels ennemis; *qu'ils se consolent*, je leur
annonce une heureuse nouvelle: il y a un Libérateur pour eux, je le
leur ferai voir, je leur montrerai qu'il y a un Dieu pour eux; je ne le

ferai pas voir aux autres."[6] This kind of seeker is *malheureux et raisonnable*, but in his very struggle to find essential truth (in Pascal's terminology, Jesus), he *has* found it. Rabbit is not a Christian saint precisely because Christianity is one of the unsuccessful environments which fail him and which he must reject. He has no taste for what Updike later calls "the dark, tangled, visceral aspect of Christianity, the *going through* quality of it, the passage *into* death and suffering that redeems and inverts these things, like an umbrella blowing inside out" (*RR*, 237). It is true that he is attracted to the church, but only so long as it promises to fulfill his needs. When it fails him, the stained-glass church window which had once "consoled him by seeming to make a hole where he looked through into underlying brightness" becomes "a dark circle in a stone façade" (306). There can be no doubt that Updike intends us to look upon Rabbit as a saint and to see his experiences as spiritual. Nonetheless, Rabbit is a saint who exists outside the Christian tradition. This exclusion is based, first of all, upon his own inability to conceive of a God in the traditional Christian sense, and secondly on the fact that Rabbit's "saintly" quest is a wholly solipsistic one. In discussing the novels of Ignazio Silone, R. W. B. Lewis finds it necessary to speak of a new kind of saint who is both rebel and outlaw, what he finally terms "the picaresque saint":

If we accept Silone's hints and speak of Spina as a kind of contemporary saint, we must add that he is a saint just *because* he is a martyr; he is a saint just *because* he is a man. His sanctity is manifested not in a private communion with God, but in an urgent communion with his fellow men: in his dedication of himself to assuaging a little the human sufferings of his time. That dedication requires of him that he be forever a wanderer, forever pursued and pursuing. It requires of him that, in the view of that much of the world that oppresses and hurts, he appear as a rogue.[7]

The world as Rabbit knows it is filled with nothing but oppressions and hurts, and this is the condition which dictates his peculiar kind of isolation; to everyone but Tothero and Mrs. Smith he is a perfect rogue. His absolute devotion to a quest for meaning dictates his absolute aloneness in a society which knows nothing of meaning. To these people he is not only an enigma, but he is destructive, even unto death, which he comes to represent for Ruth. Like Heller's *Catch-22*, *Rabbit, Run* emphasizes that man is victimized by life itself, and it remains for him to seek salvation alone—even when that means a rejection of human solidarity. Yossarian decides that self-preservation is more important than the insane commands and rituals of military life, but like Rabbit, he deserts only after he has tried all that can be expected of him as an individual.

Mrs. Smith, whose garden Rabbit has cared for and restored to beauty, says, "'That's what you have, Harry: life. It's a strange gift and I don't know how we're supposed to use it but I know it's the only gift we get and it's a good one'" (RR, 223). Harry has noted this quality in others and defined it as "force." Because Tothero represents a kind of spiritual force, Rabbit for a while thinks of him as the Dalai Lama, the object of his quest, but while Tothero has helped to inspire Rabbit with the sense of spiritual achievement, his realization of that impulse must come on a larger ground than that defined by a single individual.

Updike consistently avoids every opportunity to affirm the ethical values of Christian humanism. His most dramatic opportunity comes during the grave-side reunion of Harry with his family and with Eccles. The people are united at the funeral of Harry's infant daughter, who was drowned through the inattentiveness of her intoxicated mother. One would anticipate that this tragedy might finally give the family the common bond they have lacked, but for Harry reconciliation must be formed in truth, not in grief—a conviction his fellow mourners are unable to understand.

When faced with the loneliness and lack of values of the modern world, man can do one of three things. He can seek an escape through sensualism; he can attempt to find reconciliation with his fellows through some form of humanism; or he can break from all conventional ethics and systems and actively pursue new ones. It is the last category to which the absurd hero must be limited; and since his search is a search for values, his struggle is primarily religious. Any consideration of a religious system without God (or with only an irrelevant God) involves paradoxical inversions of values. Charles Glicksberg has pointed out that writers like Camus, in their stern negation of God, are more obsessively involved with God than writers who take Him for granted. God is present, then, even in the negation, for "even when a man denies God, he may in fact be affirming the existence of God."[8] If such a paradoxical inversion is involved in the writings of Camus or Updike, the God affirmed is not representative of traditional Christianity, which these writers see stripped of all power and significance. Nonetheless, Rabbit Angstrom does demand confirmation of a voice which calls to man and asks him to make life meaningful. Heroes like Rabbit reject formal Christianity because it is not religious enough. What they seek is not the consoling reinforcement of dogma or ritual but some transcendent inner vision of truth that will make life meaningful. Despite its secular origins there is something holy in such austere dedication to truth. Rabbit remains true to a standard of good by which he attempts to live, and the intensity of his loyalty to this standard can only be described as "religious." Everything in his world is in flux, but his intention is, in the presumed absence of God, to impose order and value on that flux.

Updike's characters occasionally claim the existence of a Divine Being, but their faith is intermittent, subjective, and often capricious, and the object of their belief is, in any event, rarely equatable with traditional Western concepts of divinity. As a group, Christians in Updike's stories emerge as "a minority flock furtively gathered within the hostile enormity of a dying, sobbing empire" (*PFe*, 250). David Kern, the hero of several Updike narratives, has a resurgence of faith when, after vindictively shooting pigeons who are covering the floor of his father's barn with their droppings, he is seized by the beauty of the dead birds: "As he fitted the last two, still pliant, on the top, and stood up, crusty coverings were lifted from him, and with a feminine, slipping sensation along his nerves that seemed to give the air hands, he was robed in this certainty: that the God who had lavished such craft upon these worthless birds would not destroy His whole Creation by refusing to let David live forever" (149–150). A later David Kern story, however, chronicles his profound disillusionment and his fear of the enormities and absurdities of life; he concludes that "the God who permitted me this fear was unworthy of existence. Each instant my horror was extended amplified God's nonexistence" (261). Earth packed by human feet becomes more meaningful to Kern than God, because this packing and the paths that it produces represent a spontaneous ritual of human beings giving shape to their lives. Like the packing of dirt, churchgoing (important even when faith is being drained away), acts of human kindness, and even driving an automobile are rituals which sustain man in a godless universe. Speaking to a sailor hitchhiker, Kern tries to explain his purpose as a writer: "We in America need ceremonies, is I suppose, sailor, the point of what I have written" (279).

In the descriptive outline for a story about Fanning Island, Updike pictures an island occupied solely by shipwrecked men. Doomed to extinction because there is no woman with them, the men make wives of one another and struggle to maintain remembered rituals. Updike took the theme for his Fanning Island outline from Pascal: "Qu'on s'imagine un nombre d'hommes dans les chaînes, et tous condamnés à la mort, dont les uns étant chaque

jour égorgés à la vue des autres, ceux qui restent voient leur pro-
pre condition dans celle de leurs semblables, et, se regardent les
uns et les autres avec douleur et sans espérance, attendent à leur
tour. C'est l'image de la condition des hommes" (243). Salvation
from this enslaved condition does not rest in the hands of an over-
seeing God, but in the hands of the man determined to live his life
meaningfully. There is no question that Updike intends Fanning
Island to stand as a microcosm of contemporary society, but the
story of its inhabitants is to be one of joy:

This is the outline; but it would be the days, the evocation of the
days . . . the green days. The tasks, the grass, the weather, the shades of
sea and air. Just as a piece of turf torn from a meadow becomes a *gloria*
when drawn by Durer. Details. Details are the giant's fingers. He seizes
the stick and strips the bark and shows, burning beneath, the moist white
wood of joy. For I thought that this story, fully told, would become without my willing it a happy story, a story full of joy; had my powers been
greater, we would know. As it is, you, like me, must take it on faith. (245)

Like Pascal's man in chains, Rabbit is a man without hope, cast up
on a deserted island of death, but his dedication brings the novel to
a conclusion which is almost paradoxically joyful. In part, we are
asked to take Rabbit's sainthood on faith even as we are asked to
take the joy of the Fanning Island story on faith.

   What alienates Harry from the world around him is his intention, and the disproportion of that intention to the reality which he
encounters is responsible for his absurd stance. "And meanwhile
his heart completes its turn and turns again, a wider turning in a
thinning medium to which the outer world bears decreasing relevance" (*RR*, 129). Since the saint's goal is to love absolutely and
entirely, he cannot give preference to any particular individual or
system. In order to be true to the quest he has assumed, Harry
must free himself from both the rationalism of the Springers and
the spiritual subjectivism of Eccles (in itself a kind of rationalism).
He is alone and an outcast, but he is still running, and now that all
ties have been broken there is hope of a sustained achievement for
him. Harry doubts that he can succeed, but Tothero has emphasized for us the fact that achievement can come even in defeat. For
the saint, it is the struggle, not the success of the struggle, which is
significant. At the thought of being unable to capture his goal, Rabbit panics, but the panic is "sweet," and the final words of the
novel, "he runs. Ah: runs. Runs" (307), are exultant.
   Responding to those inner voices which warn him that escape

from the pretensions and inconsistencies of the world is the only course by which he can maintain his integrity, Rabbit, like Huck Finn, lights out for the wilderness: escape becomes fulfillment and irresponsibility becomes responsibility. The child hero (or the childlike hero) is thus reiterated as one of the major devices in American literature, and again it is the socially disreputable hero in whom ultimate values reside. Updike portrays Rabbit as a contemporary saint who cannot resist the search for truth, even when the search ironically converts him into an ominous figure of death. The reader is constantly reminded that Rabbit has a gift to give to man—and not just a sexual one; at one point in the novel he himself jokingly defines his gift as faith. Strangled beneath the net of traditional Christian Humanism, Eccles, Janice, Ruth, and Rabbit's parents cannot recognize this gift. In fact, the love and integrity which Rabbit offers is so antithetical to their world that it appears poisonous.

In his third novel Updike illustrates the far-reaching significance of the modern saint's apparently solipsistic experience. *The Centaur* was originally conceived as a companion piece to *Rabbit, Run*. Its hero, George Caldwell, is in some respects merely an older and slightly more conventional Harry Angstrom; both men had once excelled as athletes, and both are enmeshed in a narrowly circumscribed world which repeatedly diverges from the principles they value. Updike has again chosen to represent this stultifying middle-class world by a small, mid-state Pennsylvania town. While Rabbit defends his values by running, George Caldwell maintains his intentions in the face of a hostile reality by retreating into a mythological kingdom in which Olinger, Pennsylvania, becomes Olympus. George's experiences are almost wholly psychological, but like Rabbit's they constitute a significant rebellion against the meaninglessness of life.

In his dreamlike, mythological world, George Caldwell becomes Chiron, the wise Centaur renowned among the Greeks as prophet, healer, and teacher of such famous heroes as Jason, Achilles, and Aeneas. Updike is by no means the only contemporary writer to have followed Joyce's lead in adapting ancient legend for purposes of exploring the modern milieu. Frederich Buechner depended heavily on the Philomela myth in *A Long Day's Dying*, Bernard Malamud wove the legend of Sir Percival into *The Natural*, and J. F. Powers drew obscure but interesting allusions to Arthurian legend in *Morte D'Urban*. Myth and legend would seem to serve two functions in modern literature: to suggest, after the manner of

Jung, universal, archetypal experiences; or to demonstrate, by comparison, modern man's decreased stature and relevance. Updike's use of the Chiron myth serves both functions.

The mythological Chiron, wisest and noblest of all the Centaurs, was accidentally wounded by a poisoned arrow while attending a wedding feast among the Lapithae of Thessaly. The famed healer was unable to heal himself and, tormented by his wound, begged to be permitted to give up his immortality. His death was finally accepted as atonement for the sins of.Prometheus. A loving, in many respects wise, public-school science teacher, George Caldwell is not entirely lacking in those qualities which distinguished Chiron, but unlike Chiron he is tormented by self-doubts, by feelings of persecution, and by the agonizing realization that his life is being expended in trivia. Physically he drives himself to the breaking point, giving his life up for his son, Peter, the "Prometheus" of the novel.

When *The Centaur* opens, Caldwell is standing before a characteristically unruly class attempting to impress upon them the immensity of the probable age of the universe. As he turns, an arrow strikes him in the ankle. "The class burst into laughter. The pain scaled the slender core of his shin, whirled in the complexities of his knee, and, swollen broader, more thunderous, mounted into his bowels" (*C*, 3). Struggling to retain consciousness, Caldwell moves painfully down the hall with the arrow scraping the floor behind him. "Each time the feathers brushed the floor, the shaft worked in his wound. He tried to keep that leg from touching the floor, but the jagged clatter of the three remaining hooves sounded so loud he was afraid one of the doors would snap open and another teacher emerge to bar his way" (4–5). It is a tribute to Updike's enormous skill as a literary craftsman that he can make the transition from Caldwell, the fifty-year-old science teacher, to Chiron the Centaur with such apparent ease. The result of these fluid transitions is that *The Centaur* is not merely a retelling of the myth of Chiron but a suggestion of the mythical dimensions of even the most ordinary contemporary experience.

George Caldwell fears that the arrow which has pierced his ankle has spread poison through his body—a poison representing the hatred he imagines his students feel for him. In fact, while they delight in baiting him and in parodying his mannerisms, Caldwell's students both love and respect him. Updike has included in the novel an "obituary" on Caldwell; written in maudlin journalese by a graduate of Olinger High School, it nonetheless indicates that the students' true feelings for their teacher are far from hatred. In his fears and his insecurity, Caldwell is a personification of modern man—worried about cancer, grocery bills, decaying teeth, and the power of authority as represented by Zimmerman, the high-school principal who plays Zeus to Caldwell's Chiron. Caldwell dresses in worn, ill-fitting clothes and seems a source of endless awkwardness and mediocrity.

The one redeeming quality which Caldwell has to offer is love. His gestures of affection, like Rabbit's, are often misunderstood in an age which sings "a material hymn to material creation" (10). While it finds its ripest expression in his relationship with his son, Caldwell's love spreads so widely that it even includes a degenerate hitchhiker whom he picks up against Peter's protests. "'You cook!'" he marvels. "'That's a wonderful accomplishment, and I know you're not lying to me'" (82).

The goal of Caldwell's life has been "to bring men out of the darkness" (94); the tragedy of his life is that he does not realize that it is as a man who loves and not as a teacher that he is best equipped to fulfill this challenge. He does, however, remind his Olympian students that "'Love set the universe in motion. All things that exist are her children'" (99). The scope of Caldwell's imagination and of his desire to give to his fellow man can be comprehended only in mythological terms, but he drily notes about the time in which he lives that "'It's no Golden Age, that's for sure'" (17). There is, in fact, virtually no difference between Olinger, Pennsylvania, and Rabbit Angstrom's home town of Brewer, Pennsylvania (and from the windows of the Olinger High School Caldwell can look out at the lane leading to the county poorhouse). In a world apparently devoid of meaning—even when he imagines himself dying of cancer, his money runs out, his car breaks down, and he and Peter become snowbound—he never ceases to believe that there is meaning. As Peter himself muses, "'And yet, love, do not think that our life together, for all its mutual frustration, was not good. It was good. We moved, somehow, on a firm stage, resonant with metaphor. When my grandmother lay dying in Olinger, and I was a child, I heard her ask in a feeble voice, "Will I be a little debil?" Then she took a sip of wine and in the morning she was dead. Yes. We lived in God's sight'" (50).

The metaphor through which the Caldwells move is the metaphor of love created by "Chiron" Caldwell, who maintains the ability not only to keep going, but also to keep on loving, in a world where no pleasant rewards encourage his struggles. Although he is finally mesmerized by the thought of death, he continues to radiate a quality of life and energy which affects even those who scorn him as an incompetent nuisance. The old enemies of rationalism and orthodoxy again emerge as the hero's major opponents. Rationalism is represented by Zimmerman, an authoritarian not unlike Conner, the poorhouse administrator; in a report to the school board Zimmerman suggests that Caldwell slights "humanistic values" in his presentation of the sciences. When he returns to his classroom after having the arrow removed from his ankle, Caldwell finds Zimmerman supervising his class: "Zimmerman's lopsided face hung like a gigantic emblem of authority, stretching from rim to rim of Caldwell's appalled vision. With a malevolent pulse, it seemed to widen still further. An implacable bolt, springing from the center of the forehead above the two disparately magnifying lenses of the principal's spectacles, leaped space and transfixed the paralyzed victim. The silence as the two men stared at one another was louder than thunder" (31). Spiritual subjectivism is suggested by the Reverend March, a handsome, arrogant minister who attends an Olinger basketball game and spends his time ogling the local Aphrodite, Vera Hummel, a sensual, middle-aged gym teacher. When Caldwell tries to question him about "god's mercy," March rebuffs him with meaningless aphorisms. Updike notes that despite the fact that March has been "tested" as a combat soldier, and "Though his faith is intact and as infrangible as metal, it is also like metal dead. Though he can go and pick it up and test its weight whenever he wishes, it has no arms with which to reach and restrain him. He mocks it" (237). Both Zimmerman and March instinctively recognize that Caldwell presents a threat to their systems of values.

Like Harry Angstrom, Caldwell represents both life and death, but the paradox is more successfully realized in Caldwell's case by an almost Whitmanesque vision of the significance of death. He outlines for his class the various stages in the formation of the earth and emphasizes the role of the microscopic volvox which theoretically introduced the phenomenon of death. There is nothing in the plasmic substance which forms the basis of life that should necessarily come to an end: "Amoebas never die." The volvox, however, pioneered in the idea of cooperation. "'. . . while each cell is potentially immortal, by volunteering for a specialized function within an organized society of cells, it enters a compromised environment. The strain eventually wears it out and kills it. It dies sacrificially, for the good of the whole. These first cells who got tired of sitting around forever in a blue-green scum and said, "Let's get together and make a volvox," were the first altruists. The first do-gooders. If I had a hat on, I'd take it off to 'em'" (42). Just as the cooperative cell dies sacrificially, so did ancient Chiron, by surrendering his immortality that Prometheus might be pardoned, die sacrificially for fire-stealing man. Like Chiron and the volvox, Hook, Rabbit Angstrom, and Caldwell all suggest Christ-figures, although in the intensity of his love Caldwell comes closer than any of Updike's other characters to something like a traditional concept of Christ. The mythological metaphor of the novel, however, continually reminds us that the principles Caldwell represents are far more ancient (and in many respects more universal) than those represented by Christ.

George Caldwell is the first of Updike's major protagonists to have joined hands with community; if Rabbit is a kind of Huck Finn, Caldwell is Updike's Tom Sawyer, but Caldwell's saintliness, moreover, is stripped of the romantic sentimentality for which Twain began to dislike Tom, more traditional than Rabbit's since it seeks social rather than asocial forms of expression. While George Caldwell's dedication to a ceaseless, exhausting struggle for value in a world from which value seems to have abnegated is "absurd," he lacks the awareness of absurdity which Camus asserts to be a crucial ingredient of the absurd experience. Dramatically, however, such awareness is provided by Peter Caldwell, who is often painfully aware of the disparity between his father's intentions and the reality which he encounters. While George Caldwell is clearly the narrative and philosophical focal point of *The Centaur*, the novel is also, and significantly, the story of Peter's education. When the boy has at last grasped the gravity of the threat of his father's death, "even at its immense stellar remove of impossibility" (93), he has begun to understand the significance of his father's life.

Both the modern Chiron and his son Prometheus are chained to the rock of mediocrity; the "curse" laid on Prometheus takes the form of adolescent awkwardness and psoriasis. The entire mythological structure is devaluated in its application to the modern environment. Chiron's conversation with "Aphrodite" Hummel in the girls' locker room of the school emphasizes this devaluation. Chiron attempts to defend the majesty of the gods, but Aphrodite answers that Zeus is "'A lecherous muddler'," Poseidon "'A senile old deckhand'" whose beard stinks of dead fish, Apollo an "'unc-

tuous prig'," and her husband Hephaestus simply a ditherer
(25–26). Ours is not, we are continually reminded, a Golden Age.
The mythological story of Chiron's pain and sacrifice defines the
significance of Caldwell's experience, and the value of his struggle
and of his ritualistic death is undimmed by this devaluation. What
the devaluation accomplishes is to serve as a reminder that the
experiences described in *The Centaur* are human experiences,
even though their significance may have mythological dimensions.
Updike prefaced his novel with a quotation from Karl Barth:
"'Heaven is the creation inconceivable to man, earth the creation
conceivable to him. He himself is the boundary between heaven
and earth'." As his mind shifts between Olinger and Olympus,
Caldwell continually reminds us of this boundary; he is lower than
the gods, but he transcends the physical through the intensity of
his struggle and transmogrifies the commonplace through the
power of love.

Mythological references in *The Centaur* therefore both illustrate
the narrowness and mediocrity of the modern environment and
suggest the overriding, universal significance of the human struggle. It is, however, on the level of Caldwell the man rather than
that of Caldwell the centaur that the novel has its greatest significance. The mythological level is provocative, but Updike quite
possibly took his mythological construct too seriously. The index
appended to the novel serves to make the reader too aware of a
narrative device which, in the hands of a less skillful writer, would
be little more than a gimmick. Any referential system of this kind
must be organic to the work of art which it serves; the description
of "Hephaestus" Hummel's garage and repair shop is possibly the
best example of Updike's success in achieving this unity. Caldwell
goes there to have the arrow removed from his ankle, and as he
moves tremblingly into the garage he descends into a kind of
underworld:

A deep warm blackness was lit by sparks. The floor of the grotto was
waxed black by oil drippings. At the far side of the long workbench, two
shapeless men in goggles caressed a great downward-drooping fan of
flame broken into dry drops. Another man, staring upward out of round
eyesockets white in a black face, rolled by on his back and disappeared
beneath the body of a car. His eyes adjusting to the gloom, Caldwell saw
heaped about him overturned fragments of automobiles, fragile and
phantasmal, fenders like corpses of turtles, bristling engines like disem-
bodied hearts. Hisses and angry thumps lived in the mottled air.
    . . . This tumble, full of tools, was raked by intense flashes of light

from the two workmen down the bench. They were fashioning what looked like an ornamented bronze girdle for a woman with a tiny waist and flaring hips. . . .

He walked toward the door but Hummel limped along with him. The three Cyclopes gabbled so loud the men turned. (7–8, 10, 17)

Even in his earliest poems and stories Updike was fascinated with that hallmark of twentieth-century American culture, the service station. He possibly sees in the trade of the mechanic the same chance of fulfillment, the vital contact between worker and product, which Paul Goodman saw there. Like the athletic field, the service station is an arena in which skill is rewarded and in which the individual can establish a vital contact with his world. Caldwell even envies George Hummel his craftsmanship, but this world too, as we are reminded, is being squeezed out by mass production and large national organizations.

Three days in the life of George Caldwell and his son are described in objective chapters told by Caldwell himself and retrospective chapters narrated by Peter. As Caldwell blunders his way through the Augean stables of Olinger High School searching for relief from the pain that has begun to gnaw at his entrails, we realize that the episodes of these three days are intended not merely to suggest the tediousness and frustration of his life, but also to foreshadow his death. The novel ends as it begins, with the figure of Caldwell merging with that of Chiron: "Chiron accepts death." According to one version of the Chiron myth, the centaur had begged for death not because of his pain, which was tolerable, but because (like the inmates of Updike's poorhouse) he was weary with life. It is weariness which leads Caldwell to the abyss and makes him yearn for death, but for all his longing, he never considers suicide as a solution. So long as he has strength, he continues the struggle; there is no more compelling requirement for any of Updike's characters than that of existing—no matter how essentially absurd the struggle for life may be, how remorselessly reiterant in its lessons of death and decay.

Though George Caldwell does not literally die in the novel, as Updike underscores in his *Paris Review* interview,[9] he accepts the fact of death's inevitability, and symbolically returns to the "deadly" routine of the classroom. Peter, recalling these events to his black mistress, mourns not only the death of the flesh but also the apparent demise of the spirit; thus, *The Centaur* anticipates a new variation on Updike's familiar figure of the spiritual resistance fighter—men like Joey Robinson and Piet Hanema who surrender to the quotidian rather than making the reflexive bolt for freedom celebrated in *Rabbit, Run*. Despite an underlying skepticism, a restless prodding of its own central hypotheses which Updike has described as the "yes, but" quality of his fiction,[10] *The Centaur* sustains its richly elegiac tone. Numerous critics have anatomized the novel's debt to the pastoral elegy,[11] but one aspect of formal pattern must be stressed again: the role of nature in assuaging the grief of the bereaved. While George Caldwell himself often seems alienated from his immediate natural environment, he accepts its ultimate regenerative lesson and passes it on to his son: "Yet even in the dead of winter the sere twigs prepare their small buds. In the pit of the year a king is born. Not a leaf falls but leaves an amber root, a dainty hoof, a fleck of baggage to be unpacked in future time" (*C*, 219).

Updike's lyric tribute to the redemptive power of nature is in keeping with the pastoral impulse that threads its way through classic American literature, weaving into a complex national fabric the writings of Cooper and Thoreau, Twain, Hemingway, Faulkner, Frost, Kesey, and Updike. In *Rabbit, Run* the hero's successful nurturing of Mrs. Smith's "ruined" garden is the proof of a gift of life, and in the collection *Olinger Stories* that Updike assembled and published immediately after *The Centaur*, "rural memories, accents and superstitions"[12] are assigned their special role in the development of the boy-hero. As Updike remarks, "He wears different names and his circumstances vary, but he is at bottom the same boy, a local boy,"[13] who grows up in the town of Olinger, Pennsylvania, and on the nearby farm that was the setting of "Pigeon Feathers." *Olinger Stories* was a kind of valediction to that corner of southeast Pennsylvania where Updike had spent his own childhood and adolescence; most of the writings that follow it focus on urban or suburban settings, and their heroes and heroines are the inheritors of a technological rather than a rural heritage. Nonetheless, before he began *Couples*, the controversial epic of suburban New England mores, Updike returned to the familiar Pennsylvania setting to compose the taut, intensely lyric novella, *Of the Farm*.

Of the Farm provides a kind of coda to *The Centaur*, exploring through a subtly shifted prism its central themes of freedom, identity, and mortality. This time they are perceived by Joey Robinson, a thirty-five-year-old Manhattan advertising director, who visits his widowed and critically ill mother on her Pennsylvania farm. With him are his second wife and her precocious eleven-year-old son Richard. Clearly Joey Robinson is a literary relative of the "lo-

cal boy" who grows up in the course of *Olinger Stories*, of Peter
Caldwell, and even of Harry Angstrom. Like the Caldwells, the
Robinsons move from Olinger at the insistence of the strong-willed
mother, and against the wishes of father and son, to a farm they can
never successfully manage. The ostensible purpose of Joey's visit to
the farm is to assist his ailing mother, but beyond that he wishes
her to know (and to approve) his new wife. While the two women
verbally fence and parry, Joey finds himself unexpectedly plunged
back through the layers of his past, each turning up like an archae-
ological stratum complex evidence—in pottery trinkets, photographs, faded books, a neglected family Bible—of the self once
resident there. Haunted by memories of his dead father, his divorced first wife, and their three children, Joey achieves release in
the simple rhythms of mowing a large field; and though he enthusiastically returns to New York at the end of the weekend, he and his
new family are subtly and significantly altered by their unidyllic
retreat.

Updike deftly sets the scene of pastoral withdrawal in the novella's opening sentence: "We turned off the Turnpike onto a macadam highway, then off the macadam onto a pink dirt road. . . . We
rattled down the slope of road, eroded to its bones of sandstone,
that ushered in our land" (*OF*, 3). As Larry E. Taylor has underscored, what we witness here is the familiar literary process of
leaving the sophisticated world of the court for the idyllic pastures
of Arcadia—or, perhaps more pertinently, escaping Duke Frederick's palace for the enchanted Forest of Arden.[14] Like the characters in Shakespeare's *As You Like It*, Updike's voyagers find in the
bucolic setting a curious blend of tranquility and conflict. Pointedly, Mrs. Robinson greets them as "'Pilgrims!'" and her voice
holds "a faint irony barely audible in the strange acoustics of the
engine's silence, as our Citroën hissingly settled through its
cushions of air" (*OF*, 7). For this strong-willed mother, who fought
to regain the property of her ancestors, the farm is a genuine arcadia, a place of freedom and rejuvenation; with Joey's stepson she
can even conspire to transform it to a "people paradise," despite
the unavoidable encroachments of taxes, housing developments,
superhighways, and garish shopping centers.

The vision to which Mrs. Robinson clings is made graphic in the
idyllic little landscape that hangs over the sofa, replacing the photograph of Joey's first wife Joan:

The pentagonal side of a barn was diagonally bisected by a purple shadow
cast by nothing visible, and a leafless tree of uncertain species stood

rooted in lush grass impossibly green. Beyond, I revisited, bending deeper into the picture, a marvelous sky of lateral stripes of pastel color where as a child I had imagined myself treading, upside-down, a terrain of crayons. The tiny black V of one flying bird was planted in this sky, between two furrows of color, so that I had imagined that if my fingers could get through the glass they could pluck it up, like a carrot sprout. This quaint picture, windowing a fabulous rural world, had hung, after we had moved to the farmhouse, in a room at the head of the stairs, where I had slept as an adolescent and where, when I had gone away, my father had slept in turn. (18–19)

The garish little reproduction acts as a kind of visual correlative to the novella's major themes. Most immediately, it clarifies for us Mrs. Robinson's sense of the pastoral ideal, even as the ironic language of the description shows us Joey's skepticism. The print had originally hung in his bedroom in Olinger when he was a child, then in the room where he slept as an adolescent, where his dying father slept, and where Richard sleeps during his weekend on the farm. And, indeed, Mrs. Robinson has tried, with only modest success, to communicate this vision to three generations. That the little picture has been exchanged for the image of Joan is a reminder that she was the "ideal" wife Mrs. Robinson chose for her son, the muse-like helpmeet for his poetic destiny.

In electing a career in "advertising dollar distribution," Joey embraces the very materialistic course that Peter Caldwell rejects in *The Centaur* when his father tentatively mentions the possibility of his taking a job in advertising. Here, as in other minor details, it is clear that we are not to read Peter and Joey as continuous figures—though the death of Peter's father is foreshadowed, that of Joey's father confirmed; though both schoolteacher fathers are named George; and though Mrs. Robinson clearly shares numerous traits of character with Cassie Caldwell. Mrs. Robinson has yearned for her son to be a poet, to consecrate his life to the ideal, as the print that hangs over the sofa is a testament to ideality; but Joey has resisted both her concept of vocation and her private version of pastoral. Speaking of the nature books his mother gave him as a child, he remarks, "'I could never match the pictures up with the real things, exactly'" (64). But while Updike is at pains to distinguish Peter and Joey, the artist and the artist *manqué*, the parallels in their histories and their reminiscences are prominent; the farm settings evoked in *The Centaur* and *Of the Farm* are the same, and hold clear autobiographical resonance for Updike. Furthermore, the span of present action in each work is three days, and while one contemplates the death of the father, the other seeks to come to terms with the impending death of the mother. In both books a young man struggles to assert his own identity, wavering between the lessons of a docile father and those of a dominating mother. And yet *Of the Farm* is far from being a simple reprise of *The Centaur*; nor are the contrasts fully encompassed by the differences in framing devices, the mythological and the pastoral, though here, at least, rests an important clue to Updike's shifting intentions. The pastoral mode exists not to suggest an alternative set of values for Joey, but as a way of testing and mellowing and confirming his election of an urban, middle-class destiny; while reminding him of certain essential, timeless values of the earth, it also confirms him in choices of career, divorce, and re-marriage made well before the novella opens. When he leaves the Arden of eastern Pennsylvania to return to the "court" life of New York, he does so without hesitation: "New York, the city that is always its own photograph, the living memento of my childish dream of escape, called to me, urged me away, into the car, down the road, along the highway, up the Turnpike. I was ashamed of my desire yet confirmed in it" (174).

The shame attaching to Joey's choice springs from the knowledge that he has betrayed, once more, his mother's vision, as surely as Peter Caldwell fulfilled the vision of Cassie in dedicating himself to his art; yet throughout *The Centaur* an older, reflective Peter contemplates his father's sacrifice and asks, in the fearful freedom of his creator role, whether or not his art can ever be worthy of that sacrifice. "Was it for this that my father gave up his life?" (*C*, 281). After the failures of theologist and scientist, the artist—a potent avatar of the absurd—must assume the heroic burden of producing meaningful shapes from the elusive and disordered fragments of modern life. Even if Peter is still struggling to penetrate the mysteries of his vocation, the struggle alone is ennobling, and the fire of vocation can cauterize many of the wounds of grief and guilt. In Joey Robinson, Updike sets himself a far more ambitious task: to suggest that in embracing the commonplace a man can make just as persuasive a declaration of identity and of personal freedom. Thus, Joey opts for "advertising dollar distribution" over poetry, and sets aside the perfect, stylish, "cool" wife in favor of a simple, earthy, vulgar woman. Broad and voluptuous, Peggy is the landscape that Joey embraces, choosing not the earth but the earth mother herself, hymned in one of the novel's most powerfully lyric passages:

My wife is wide, wide-hipped and long-waisted, and, surveyed from above, gives an impression of terrain, of a wealth whose ownership imposes upon my own body a sweet strain of extension; entered, she yields a variety of landscapes, seeming now a snowy rolling perspective of bursting cotton bolls seen through the Negro arabesques of a fancywork wrought-iron balcony; now a taut vista of mesas dreaming in the midst of sere and painterly ochre; now a gray French castle complexly fitted to a steep green hill whose terraces imitate turrets; now something like Antarctica; and then a receding valleyland of blacks and purples where an unrippled river flows unseen between shadowy banks of grapes that are never eaten. Over all, like a sky, withdrawn and cool, hangs—hovers, stands, *is*—is the sense of her consciousness, of her composure, of a noncommittal witnessing that preserves me from claustrophobia through any descent however deep. I never felt this in Joan, this sky. I felt in danger of smothering in her. (*OF*, 46–47)

In this passage is the key to Updike's portrayal, to the existential choices which Joey has made and which to the casual observer, as to his mother, so easily seem surrender rather than triumph. Putting aside vocation, the perfect wife, and three loving, dependent children, he would seem to have settled for compromise and mediocrity. But Updike would have us phrase those choices differently, would have us see Joey as a man who has resisted, like Harry Angstrom, the limiting versions of reality his society attempted to impose on his life; like the absurd men of Bellow's fiction, and in particular like the bumptious Augie March, he has developed a quality of "resistance," and a concomitant ability to decline limiting commitments.

As the book's epigraph from Sartre clearly states, the central theme in *Of the Farm* is the nature of freedom: "*Consequently, when, in all honesty, I've recognized that man is a being in whom existence precedes essence, that he is a free being who, in various circumstances, can want only his freedom, I have at the same time recognized that I can want only the freedom of others.*" Like many of Updike's boy-men, Joey Robinson struggles to free himself of an Oedipal burden; but even more central to the novel's intention is the problem of honoring the freedom of others. When asked what she gave her husband in exchange for Joey and the farm, Mrs. Robinson answers, "'Why, . . . his freedom!'" (31). Joey, however, recognizes that such a description of his father's frustration and restlessness is possible only in terms of the deceptive mythology his mother has made of her life as a complement to her pastoral vision of the farm itself. But what he has found with Peggy is, precisely, the joy of liberation from such self-delusion: ". . . with Peggy I skim, I glide, I am free, and this freedom, once tasted, lightly, illicitly, became as indispensable as oxygen to me, the fuel of a pull more serious than that of gravity" (47). (This choice of the earthy woman as a symbol of freedom will be explored more fully in *Couples* when Piet rejects the angelic Angela for Foxy; running through both works are variations on Tristan's reckless romance with Iseult.) Joey thus makes the initial step in fulfilling Sartre's hypothesis, intuitively grasping that one must first yearn for and achieve his own freedom before he can properly love others; then he must, in turn, desire *theirs*.

Although Joey can locate the center of his universe in the ample hips of his wife, Updike is firm in stressing that we are not concerned here with simple hedonism. Indeed, he devotes nearly six pages of the novella to the sermon Joey and his mother hear on Sunday morning; its subject is the creation of Eve, the text is from Genesis: "*And the Lord God said, It is not good that the man should be alone; I will make him an help meet for him*" (149–150). Twice during the course of his exposition, the young Lutheran minister learnedly alludes to Karl Barth, in quotations taken from a section of *Church Dogmatics* entitled "Freedom in Fellowship." The quotations thus acknowledge another link between *Of the Farm* and *The Centaur*, with its Barthian epigraph, and direct us toward an interpretation of Sartre's emphasis on "the freedom of others." In expounding the Genesis account of Eve's creation, Barth stresses that God calls his human creation not only to himself, but also to one another. Man is called in freedom horizontally as well as vertically, and Adam first understands his freedom on the horizontal, human level in relation to his helpmeet Eve.[15] Central to this relationship is respect for the helpmeet and her role; the man who plays the cruel tyrant violates the order commanded by God. The passages which the minister quotes from Barth stress that "'Successfully or otherwise, she is in her whole existence an appeal to the kindness of Man. . . . For kindness . . . belongs originally to his particular responsibility as a man'" (*OF*, 153). We must, of course, be wary of too literal or exclusive an interpretation of the sermon, for theologians and preachers tend to fare rather badly in Updike's universe; indeed, leaving the church, Joey comments on the minister's "limp and chill little hand" (154). Joey will, however, make his own interpretation of the sermon. The minister, for example, argues that an essential kindness "is implicit in the nature of Creation, in the very curves and amplitude of God's fashioning" (154). Later, frightened by his mother's heart attack, Joey instinctively reaches out to confirm similar curves and amplitude: "Peggy walked beside me and without breaking stride submitted to my caress when, hidden from the eyes of the house by the barn, I touched first the damp base of her neck and followed her spine with my fingers and went beyond to where the curve curved under the crotch of her pants" (162).

The sermon has other applications as well, for the "particular responsibility" of kindness, so essential to his manhood and to his freedom, has also been neglected by the younger Joey. Possessing what his mother terms "'this unexpected cruel streak'" (136), he had bullied his favorite dog in a way that Mrs. Robinson can only describe as "ungentlemanly." When he verbally bullies his second wife, she warns him not to treat her as he treated the puppy. But, in fact, part of the ritual function of the family's retreat to the garden is that they learn kindness to one another; and when Joey sees his wife assuming Eve-like tasks of nurture and cultivation, his heart is moved. Updike's growing confidence as a writer allows him to render these moments as burlesque without diminishing their spiritual resonance:

The broad white road, with one of those sweeping cloverleafs that seem histrionic, surrendered up the old black highway, and I turned onto the gray whirring surface of the township road, and then down our dirt road, and saw Peggy, and laughed, for she was on the garden ridge hoeing in her bikini.
The determination of her stance, the inexpert vigor of her blows at the ground, accented the width of her figure, which tapered to ankles that seemed to vanish in the earth. (88–89)

This latter-day Eve and vigorous earth mother seems literally rooted in the land, and Joey remarks, "The sight of her bare feet, the toenails painted, flat on the earth and caked to the ankles like the feet of a child or a gypsy moved me . . ." (89). Here, I believe, Updike shows us that his narrator is comprehending woman's existence as "an appeal to the kindness of man," and through this comprehension is better prepared to acknowledge the freedom of others. A growing sensitivity is revealed in Joey's troubled, solicitous feelings for the prematurely serious child Richard, and the honor he comes to pay to his mother's right to her pastoral dream. (In a typical but revealing gesture, seeing Peggy's embarrassment when she is discovered hoeing in her polka-dotted bikini, Joey seeks to distract his mother's attention.)

Later in the novel, when Joey panics after his mother's heart attack, he again discovers his wife in a comic-Edenic pose:

Peggy, bare-shouldered in her bikini, was up to her hips in brambles, serenely reaching toward those thickest and best berries closest to the sun-crumbled stucco of the old wall. She seemed a doe of my species, grazing immune in a thicket. My impression, of her beloved body immersed in thorns, was not mocked by the discovery that, though she wore above her waist only the little polka-dot bra, her bottom half was sheathed in the blue stretch pants that imitated dungarees; indeed she seemed in this centaurine costume more natural, more practically resolved to give herself—my city wife, my habituée of foyers and automatic elevators—to the farm. (161)

Making an Eve-like gesture to cover her "nakedness" from the men in a passing automobile, she does so by crouching amid poison-ivy bushes. As moments like these reveal, Updike handles his pastoral and Eden metaphors with the same dualism he brought to the myth of Chiron. While the farm represents no viable alternative for the self-created city man (or for his wife, though she grew up in Nebraska farm country), his three-day vigil there poses a series of significant tests; in this sense he is, as his mother declares in the novel's opening scene, a "pilgrim." Like the frog in the story he relates to Richard, Joey Robinson descends into himself in search of hidden treasure: one of the truths with which he returns is the declaration that "My wife is a field" (59); another is the recognition, through his mother's impending death, of "a thousand such details of nurture about to sink into the earth with her" (167).

In addition to the dualism which attaches to Updike's handling of literary metaphor, an essential dualism surrounds the problem of voice in the novel. While Joey has embraced literal, workaday ambitions, the language in which he describes his rural weekend repeatedly invokes a startling poetry of the commonplace. When we encounter phrases like "sere and painterly ochre" (46), "a rhomboid of sun" (50), or "potatoes dumbly odorous of earth" (115), do they indicate the intrusion of Updike's lyric sensibility, or can we take them as representative of Joey's apprehension of the external world? Since Updike, with his immense talent for literary ventriloquism, has consciously chosen (and for the first time in a novel) a first-person narrator, it seems unlikely that he would then disregard that formal choice. If the assumption is correct, then Joey clearly maintains the poet's enriching vision, though he has ceased to write poetry. Perhaps, indeed, we have a situation similar to that of novelist Henry Green, as described by Updike: "For sheer transparence of eye and ear he seems to me unmatched among living writers. Alas, for a decade he has refused to write, showing I suppose his ultimate allegiance to life itself."[16] Joey's allegiance to Madison Avenue, the impersonal city, a wife he calls "stupid," is also an allegiance to life, and here we have one measure of the absurdity of his position. We have it again in the paradox that his intention to be free of limiting commitments, of constricting mythologies, leads him precisely to the most conventional pieties of bourgeois society. What we witness in *Of the Farm* is the hero's growing awareness of this fundamental tension between intention and reality, his acceptance of it, and his lyric praise of that discrepancy. Revisiting the farm, Joey is revisiting an older self that stares out at him from the photographs he scarcely recognizes, reminding us of Camus's argument that "the familiar and yet alarming brother we encounter in our own photographs is also the absurd." [17]

Like Updike's earlier pilgrims, Joey Robinson poses fundamental questions about the nature of man's existence, and he declines to accept the conventional answers proffered by Einsteinian physics, Euclidian geometry, pulpit theology, selenology or vorticism, to name only a few of the systems of description and measurement that proliferate in the book. Through his helpmeet Joey is drawn away from preoccupation with infinity and death; through her he proclaims his humanity by striving to live with compassion and kindness, qualities traditionally awaited from the saint. That he should arrive at this stance only by denying vocation, divorcing his wife, forsaking his three children, and violating his mother's most treasured dreams: these roguish elements look back to the youthful Harry Angstrom of *Rabbit, Run*; in embracing and ultimately celebrating the commonplace, Joey anticipates the trials of Piet Hanema in *Couples*.

Of the Farm thus represents a major turning point in Updike's sense of the hero's struggle, even as it marks an end to his nearly exclusive concern with the austere small towns and farms of southeastern Pennsylvania as the setting for his fiction. In this respect, it is instructive to note the enthusiasm with which Joey Robinson returns to New York, which figures prominently as a setting in *The Music School*, the collection of short stories Updike published the year following the release of *Of the Farm*. There the shift of locales is further dramatized by the fact that "In Football Season," the last of the Olinger stories, becomes the first story in *The Music School*, where its sweet nostalgia is a counterpoint to the following tales of a complex, largely urban world. Here grief and adultery, professional struggle and discontent, adjustment and compromise hold sway, and in depicting them Updike moves away from the lingering romanticism that often tinted the earlier stories.

While *The Music School* is more varied in themes, moods, and settings than Updike's previous collections of short stories, certain motifs emerge which interestingly anticipate those explored in

Couples. Precisely half of the twenty stories are concerned with marriages threatened by the gathering storm clouds of adultery and, often, impending divorce. Two of those focus on Richard and Joan Maple, whose story begins on a snowy night in Greenwich Village in 1956, moves to suburban New England in the 1960's, and will eventually culminate in divorce in 1976; in 1979, Updike fused the stories together into a kind of episodic novel entitled *Too Far to Go.*[18] The decline and fall of marriages will become one of Updike's major themes in the following decade—in *Couples* (1968), *Rabbit, Redux* (1971), *Museums and Women* (1972), *Marry Me* (1976), *Too Far to Go* (1979), and *Problems and Other Stories* (1979); it even plays a minor role in Updike's African saga, *The Coup* (1978). As the narrator of "The Music School" prophetically observes, "My friends are like me. We are all pilgrims, faltering toward divorce. Some get no further than mutual confession, which becomes an addiction, and exhausts them. Some move on, into violent quarrels and physical blows; and succumb to sexual excitement. A few make it to the psychiatrists. A very few get as far as the lawyers" (*MuS,* 190).

In Updike's ongoing, monumental chronicle of bourgeois decline, we have thus witnessed the failures of the welfare state, of the church, of science, of marriage and the family, of politics and pastoralism and the arts, to provide the individual with a sense of worthy purpose, to assuage his fears of darkness and death. Metaphorically, the dilemma is explored in a terse, terrifying short story entitled "The Dark," in which a nameless man, incurably ill, battles insomnia. The story's title refers not merely to the room in which his vigil occurs, but also to the agonizing loneliness, the metaphysical *Angst* of his situation; the story, indeed, suggests more than coincidental parallels to Hemingway's "A Clean, Well-Lighted Place." Nonetheless, the Updike hero never surrenders his faith—often blind, often intuitive, sometimes nostalgic—in what Harry Angstrom identifies as "'something that wants me to find it'" (*RR,* 127). As Robert Detweiler has remarked of the Updike universe, "A faith in divinity lingers even in the efforts of self-consciously secular man."[19] And that yearning for divinity leads the fallen, adulterous narrator of "The Music School" to embrace the prolapsed world: "The world is the host; it must be chewed" (*MuS,* 190).

Two further leitmotifs of *The Music School* have a direct bearing on *Couples.* The first of them, represented by "Four Sides of One Story," Updike's updating of the myth of Tristan and Iseult, is in-

spired by the author's continuing fascination with Denis de Rougemont's *Love in the Western World*; it will be discussed in detail
below in an analysis of the Angela-Piet-Foxy triangle. The second
represents an ironic farewell to pastoralism in the pair of stories—
"The Family Meadow" and "The Hermit"—with which the collection concludes. In the former work, the brief record of a family
reunion, we not only see the urbanization of a family and its increasing estrangement from the land—as in "the White Plains people, who climb from their car looking like clowns, wearing red-
striped shorts and rhinestone-studded sunglasses" (235); we also
see the land itself surrendering to suburban blight:

The time has come for the photograph. Their history is kept by these
photographs of timeless people in changing costumes standing linked and
flushed in a moment of midsummer heat. All line up, from resurrected
Aunt Eula, twitching and snapping like a mud turtle, to the unborn baby
in the belly of the Delaware cousin. To get them all in, Jesse has to squat,
but in doing so he brings the houses into his viewfinder. He does not
want them in the picture, he does not want them there at all. They surround his meadow on three sides, raw ranch shacks built from one bas-
tard design but painted in a patchwork of pastel shades. Their back yards,
each nurturing an aluminum clothes tree, come right to the far bank of
the creek, polluting it, and though a tall link fence holds back the children who have gathered in these yards to watch the picnic as if it were a
circus or a zoo, the stare of the houses—mismatched kitchen windows
squinting above the gaping cement mouth of a garage—cannot be held
back. Not only do they stare, they speak, so that Jesse can hear them
even at night. *Sell*, they say. *Sell*. (237–238)

The jerry-built houses on the edge of the meadow duplicate those
that encroach on Mrs. Robinson's farm, and are echoed in the
ranch-style boxes Piet Hanema and his partner build on verdant
Indian Hill.

In "The Hermit," the concluding story of *The Music School*, a
middle-aged janitor seeks the Thoreauvian freedom and simplicity
of an old farmhouse surrounded by hundreds of wild, uncultivated
acres. Stanley's retreat into nature is no more successful than Rabbit Angstrom's; indeed, it becomes a parody of the transcendental
mysteries of Walden Pond. The ritualistic baths he takes are ironic
reductions of those described by Thoreau in *Walden* and Walt
Whitman in *Specimen Days*: "The stream was only inches deep
and a man's width wide; to wet himself Stanley had to lie on the
bed of red sand and smoothed sandstones and make of himself a
larger stone that the little stream, fumbling at first, icily consented

to lave" (256). Rising from such a sacramental bath, Stanley startles a local boy who bolts in embarrassment and fright. Stanley pursues him to offer reassurance, but his gesture is misinterpreted, and three days later he is taken away forcibly as a menace to society. Though Stanley has learned much from his pastoral retreat, the very intensity of his mystical absorption leads to the ultimate estrangement of madness. Rather than withdrawing, the Updike hero must accept the lesson that "The world is the host; it must be chewed" (190).

In the preceding pages I have more than once suggested the degree to which John Updike's increasing artistry and philosophical complexity anticipate his best-selling, sensational novel *Couples*, which either baffled or angered many reviewers, and more than a decade later is still wont to animate the critic's latent Calvinism. More generous detractors accused Updike of picking up the windfall in an orchard formerly tended by Henry Miller, Peter De-Vries, John O'Hara, and Mary McCarthy; those more acerb suggested his indebtedness to Grace Metalious and Jacqueline Susann. The novel's sexual explicitness is a prominent and essential aspect of the complex socio-political texture Updike creates, the dense web of manners and mores against which his characters act and react. As he himself has argued, the book, "in part, is about the change in sexual deportment that has occurred since the publication of *Rabbit, Run*."[20] As in the earlier work, the hero's priapic vigor is one measure of the life-drive with which he seeks to thwart death. Furthermore, sexual groupings and re-groupings are integral to the novel's examination of mythical and religious metaphor; but so, too, are Updike's recurrent allusions to contemporary events (the Cuban missile crisis, the space program, Kennedy's assassination); to concentrate on one activity to the exclusion of the others falsifies the novel's sumptuously baroque structure—elaborate, intricately textured, mythically resonant, and full of finely calibrated effects.

The omnipotence, the omnipresence, the insidiousness of death forms the dark undertow of the work, explicitly linking it to Updike's earlier fiction, though the motif has never before been so amply orchestrated. The sacrificial fall of the everyman Piet Hanema—"*me, a man, amen ah*" (*Cs*, 13)—can only be fully appraised in terms of the compulsive death anxiety that permeates *Couples*. The actual deaths of pets and other animals, of invented characters and of public personalities are threaded through the novel; sequentially, they include the crew of the *Thresher*, Ruth's hampster, the gutted mice in Ken Whitman's lab that lay "like burst grapes on a tray" (97), the trapped mouse "like a discarded swab in a doctor's office" (114) in the house where Frank and Marcia make love, Jackie Kennedy's premature baby, George Braque and Robert Frost, "a Pakistani mother bewailing the death of her child by earthquake" (283) in a photograph Piet discovers in his daughter's room, Jack Kennedy and Lee Harvey Oswald, a frozen bird Nancy seeks to restore to life, the fetus Foxy has aborted, and the Korean physicist John Ong. Punctuating this litany are Piet's recurrent memories of the deaths of his parents and, on one occasion, of his grandmother. In addition to these literal deaths, one repeatedly encounters—in what at first seem throw-away colloquialisms—phrases like "dead tired," "tired to death," "scared half to death," and "deadly serious."

The seasonal and religious motifs of the novel, whose time span stretches from early morning on Palm Sunday, 1963, to Easter, 1964, further stresses this dominant pattern. Images of the rank decay of nature recur in every season, and Whitmanesque lilacs that grow in the Whitmans' own dooryard stab Piet beneath one eye (402). At the first of the two dinner parties in the novel, on the Saturday preceding Easter Sunday, underdone "sacrificial" lamb is served; and at the second, on the evening of Kennedy's assassination, a mock *missa sollemnis* is performed. Ken Whitman, a biochemist who specializes in photosynthesis, comments that the specimens he uses all die: "'That's the trouble with my field. Life hates being analyzed'" (33). Bored with the "dead experiments" he supervises, Ken yearns to study the transformations of chlorophyll—"the lone reaction that counterbalances the vast expenditures of respiration, that reverses decomposition and death . . ." (95).

Freddy Thorne, Tarbox's Tiresias, its Lord of Misrule, cynical conscience, spoiled priest and anti-Christ, repeatedly points the group's attention to death. At the Easter dinner he describes meeting the Jew Ben Saltz as "'a fate worse than death'" (29), and Frank Appleby clumsily changes the subject to suggest that Tarbox's oldest inhabitant will soon be crushed to death by the accumulated back issues of *National Geographic*. Proposing a toast to the lost crew of the *Thresher*, Freddy remarks, "'We're all survivors. A dwindling band of survivors'" (32). When his sprained finger is splinted with a green plastic spoon, Freddy makes it into a death ray that he points at Eddie Constantine, Piet, and Foxy, saying,

"'Zizz. Die. Zizz. You're dead'" (71). Freddy's longest diatribe on death occurs at midpoint in the novel, in one of its most densely symbolic episodes, when he lectures a group of weary partygoers:

"Losing a tooth means death to people; it's a classic castration symbol. They'd rather have a prick that hurts than no prick at all. They're scared to death of me because I might tell the truth. When they get their dentures, I tell 'em it looks better than ever, and they fall all over me believing it. It's horseshit. You never get your own smile back when you lose your teeth. Imagine the horseshit a doctor handling cancer has to hand out. Jesus, the year I was in med school, I saw skeletons talking about getting better. I saw women without faces putting their hair up in curlers. The funny fact is, you don't get better, and nobody gives a cruddy crap in hell. You're born to get laid and die, and the sooner the better." (241–242)

While Piet protests that "'Things grow as well as rot'" (242), he secretly admires Freddy for having learned to live with "the antiseptic truth" (242). Here, as elsewhere in the novel, Freddy articulates in crude form Piet's most secret fears, acting as his comic-grotesque *Doppelgänger*, as anti-Christ to his Christ. Significantly, it is Freddy who arranges for Foxie Whitman's backstreet abortion, while an anguished Piet waits outside in the spring rain; for him, the unwanted pregnancy had been "a disaster identical with death" (345).

In exchange for arranging the abortion, Freddy claims a night with Piet's angelic wife Angela. Nervous and impotent, he seeks to distract her with further lessons derived from his dentistry:

"We die. We don't die for one second out there in the future, we die all the time, in every direction. Every meal we eat breaks down the enamel."

"Hey. You've gotten bigger."

"Death excites me. Death is being screwed by God. It'll be delicious."

"You don't believe in God."

"I believe in that one, Big Man Death. I smell Him between people's teeth every day . . ."

"Piet's terrified of death," she said, snuggling.

Freddy told her, "It's become his style. He uses it now as self-justification. He's mad at the world for killing his parents."

"Men are so romantic," Angela said, after waiting for him to tell her more. "Piet spends all his energy defying death, and you spend all yours accepting it." (370)

In a moment of genuine comic brilliance, Updike has the mismatched pair discuss Freud's *Beyond the Pleasure Principle* while Angela tries to coax Freddy into an erection. "'He says we, all

animals, carry our deaths in us—that the organic wants to be returned to the inorganic state. It wants to rest', " Angela adds (367).
The writings of Shakespeare are frequently invoked in *Couples*,
in part as a comic device suggesting Frank Appleby's intellectual
pretentiousness; but the clustering and patterning of images—of
death, light, dreams, carpentry, vegetation, the eucharist—also
achieve a cumulative effect reminiscent of Shakespeare's technique. A mere summary of recurrent images fails to convey their
intricate structure, the reinforcement they contribute to the elaborate narrative armature that supports this highly episodic work.
Two ski weekends, for example, contrast and define shifting al-
legiances among the couples; two ritual dinners show their hunger for ceremonies that will bring wholeness into a desacralized
world—and hence the embarrassed "bump of silence" (25) that
takes the place of grace at the Guerins' dinner. The death of the
Kennedy baby, "'born too tiny'" (212), is echoed in Foxy's abortion, and the aborted fetus is foreshadowed in the coughball Angela holds in her hand as she sits beside Foxy—"smaller than a golf
ball, a tidy dry accretion visibly holding small curved bones" (63).
For Ruth's new hamster, Piet constructs a minimal, parabolic cage,
to protect the animal from death, but later complains to Angela
that he feels himself to be in a cage. The sacrificial fall of the Jew
Ben Saltz (presumably the result of sexual license) is a prelude to
that of the symbolic Jew, Piet Hanema; seeing the man's archaic
profile, with its patriarchal beard, Piet thinks of Ben as someone
who "had touched bottom and found himself at rest, safe" (255).
    The first of the two epigraphs with which Updike precedes his
novel is from Paul Tillich's essay "The Effects of Space Exploration
on Man's Condition," in which the theologian stresses space travel
as the logical extension of Renaissance man's concentration on horizontal exploration of the physical world as opposed to the verti-
cal/spiritual understanding of the cosmos.[21] In Tarbox the space
program is a frequent topic of party talk; furthermore, Eddie Constantine is a jet pilot, and Ben Saltz has, supposedly, contributed to
the Mariner Venus probe. Angela Hanema, the "remote" and
heavenly female, is repeatedly associated with the stars, with
Venus, and, occasionally, with the moon; when the couples play a
new game called "Wonderful," she picks stars as the most wonderful thing she knows, and in fact was once taught the names of all
the first-magnitude stars by an astronomer uncle. On the night of
Kennedy's assassination, while the television set flickers with images of the President's coffin arriving in Washington, Angela and
Piet dance to "Stars Fell on Alabama," "Soft as the Starlight," and

then "It Must Have Been Moonglow." Later during the Thornes' "wake" for Kennedy, Piet is trapped in the upstairs bathroom with Foxy, and escapes through the window only to land beside Bea Guerin and Ben Saltz, who are hidden in the shadow of an elm. Bea explains, "'Ben brought me out here to watch a satellite . . .'" (*Cs*, 314), but all they have seen is a falling star. As they return to the house, Doris Day is singing "Stardust." In the opening scene of the novel, staring at his wife's nakedness, Piet had thought of the April night as "a blackness charged with the ache of first growth and the suspended skeletons of Virgo and Leo and Gemini" (10); as summer wanes and he sees the star patterns shifted toward winter, he thinks again of his own small mortality: "Vertigo affected him. Amid these impervious shining multitudes he felt a gigantic slipping . . ." (286). When, after separating from Angela, he takes their two children to a planetarium, his daughter Nancy—also obsessed by death—feels a similar vertigo: "'Mommy',", she cries hysterically, "'the stars went round and round and round'" (425).

Just as all the couples enjoy playing games, usually ones employing puns or "secret" identities, it is clear that John Updike, a brilliant wordsmith, thoroughly enjoys laying down the novel's ingenious verbal marquetry. If, at times, the entire performance borders on preciosity or archness (as when, during the showdown between the Whitmans and the Hanemas, Angela sips five-star Cognac), it more typically rewards the careful reader with a sense of the profoundly religious vision that characteristically illuminates Updike's craft. The clusterings of astrological images described in the preceding paragraph complement the Tristan and Iseult theme of the search for the pure white maiden, and parallel the allusions to Dante's Beatrice in the luminously pale and childless Bea Guerin, who is caught looking at the stars. Updike's quotation from Tillich's *The Future of Religions*, which incidentally anticipates the metaphor of the moon launch in *Rabbit Redux*, ties the theme of space exploration to the novel's central concern with the death of the church and man's hunger for eucharistic ritual. That hunger is parodied in both of the "last suppers" referred to above. In the latter Freddy and Georgene and Angela enter ceremoniously with salads and a ham; Freddy sharpens the carving knife "With a cruciform clashing of silver," intoning all the while, "'Take, eat'," and "'This is his body, given for thee'" (319). (The Eucharist is more tenderly parodied in the pregnant Foxy's gorging herself with cheap chemical bread in the early hours of Easter Sunday.) Tillich's argument about the exploration of horizontal rather than vertical space points us once more toward Updike's persistent concern with contemporary morality, whether reflected in jerry-built houses, wife-swapping, or athletic events. Each can have, frequently *does* have, in Updike's cosmology, its spiritual emanation. Even the sharp tabs on pop-top beer cans produce, according to Harold Little-Smith, "'the new stigmata'" (71).

In the world of Tarbox, loudly reiterant of death, to hear even the faintest intimations of immortality is extraordinary; to devote one's existence to a denial of death's supremacy is clearly absurd— in the fullest and noblest sense of the concept as Camus developed it. One should, perhaps, stress again Camus's concern with the very problems that have traditionally fallen within the province of theology:

the absence of God, the relationship of a God who is all powerful and all-knowing to the evil and the suffering that exist on earth, the contrast between the routine of life and the crisis of being lost and alone and doomed that the Existentialist hero experiences, the disruption of familiar, human reality by the knowledge of the inevitability and imminence of death, the search for the authentic life on this journey to the end of night.[22]

Piet's dogged desire, in an age of shoddy and planned obsolescence, to build houses of fine, enduring craftsmanship is already an indication of the essential conflict between intention and reality— the same conflict which prompts Angela's observation that "'Piet spends all his energy defying death . . .'" (Cs, 370). He is Sisyphus and Everyman, Christ, Noah, and a randy Don Quixote; by Updike's own interpretation, he is also Tristan and Don Juan, "Hanema/anima/Life," and "Lot, the man with two virgin daughters, who flees Sodom and leaves his wife behind."[23] He is, one might easily add, Peter, the rock on which a new church will be raised; and he is Piet—piety, *pietà*, *pietas*. In the structure and imagery of the novel, the Christian allusions are perhaps the most obvious; at the beginning of the novel, Piet leaves church with a palm frond in his hand, and gazes down the hill to see Foxy, dressed in white; only these two characters are regular church-goers, and at the end of the novel—when their commitment to each other is sealed—the physical church is destroyed by fire and the earth purified by torrential rains. Freddy Thorne speaks of the couples themselves as a "communion," a church, a magic circle to keep out the night. Piet, with the "cruciform blazon of amber hair" on his chest (Cs, 7), dreams of himself as "an old minister making calls" (10), and is mocked with signs of his mission—as by Bernadette's "crucifix hopping in the shallow space between her breasts . . ." (12). A carpenter in his early thirties, Piet is most at home "amid the holy odor of shavings" (197). It is he who laments that "'We've fallen from grace'" (200), and his own fate will leave the other couples "haunted and chastened, as if his fall had been sacrificial" (456). Foxy, whose first affair was with a Jewish artist, comes to think of Piet in terms of "a Jew she has refound in him" (204); the Saltzes remark after his separation from Angela that "'it's a pity you're not a Jew,'" and Ben sends him away with the words "'ain ben David ba elle bador shekulo zakkai oh kulo chayyav. The son of David will not come except to a generation that's wholly good or all bad'" (420). The austere office in which Piet spends the first three days of his separation from Angela, shortly before Easter, is described as a "tomb" (416); and he even develops physical hints of stigmata: "His side hurt; his left palm tingled" (432). Risen from the tomb, Piet finds himself a social outcast, ostracized by the couples who fear his failure will somehow prove contagious. Nonetheless, old friends stop him on the streets and begin to confess to him their secret hopes and fears—much as his frustrated and estranged tenants begin to open their troubled hearts to the Christ-like rent-collector in Edward Lewis Wallant's *The Tenants of Moonbloom.*

The Christ imagery of *Couples* is repeatedly fused with images of Eden, with allusions to Adam's sexuality and to the naming of the beasts,[24] to the sin of sexual knowledge and banishment from the garden. In a further parallel analogy, Foxy refers to Piet as her "*flying Dutchman*" (263), reminding us of Piet's curious aversion to the ocean, and of how the legendary Dutchman was condemned to sail the sea against the wind until Judgment Day, unless an innocent maiden should agree to share his exile. He is also the handsome prince who kisses Snow White back to life after her seven-year sleep.[25] Piet, furthermore, has indicated in playing "Wonderful" that for him the most wonderful thing on earth is a sleeping woman—that is, both the bewitched Snow White and the voluptuous female figure in William Blake's drawing of "Adam and Eve Sleeping," reproduced on the dust-jacket of *Couples.* Through the concatenation of figures—mythical, Biblical, operatic, fairytale—with whom Piet is associated in the novel, two dominant types emerge: the spiritual redeemer and the passionate lover. In fusing those dualistic roles, Piet emerges as one of the most intriguing, real, and "heroic" characters we have had in American literature for a great many years.

Above all, it is the recurrent image of the greenhouse which gives a three-dimensional embodiment to Piet's tangled, visceral plight. Recurrent memories of his gardener parents and their greenhouse evoke strains of innocence and Edenic simplicity. Yet when he is told of his parents' sudden death in an automobile accident, Piet has just returned from a vigorous sexual encounter— "his fingertips alive with the low-tide smell of cunt . . ." (318). Thereafter, the generative aspects of sexuality will be confused in his own mind with images of death, and he will be abnormally stunned and grieved by such commonplace events as the family cat's killing Ruth's hamster (in orange color and protuberant masculinity, another burlesque *Doppelgänger* for Piet himself); the cat's pouncing thus becomes "a thunderclap of death" (76–77). Piet digs a grave for the animal along the edge of the woods, where the children's pets have over the years composed a cemetery. Seeing the trees beginning to leaf, he feels "spring's terror" washing over him, and can only think, in echo of Eliot's *Waste Land*, of this "slow thronging of growth as a tangled hurrying toward death" (78). His thoughts shift ineluctably to his father's "green fond touch" (78), just as, later in the day, the sight of the local funeral home prompts a cluster of images that relate parents, sexuality, and death: "Growing up in odor of embalming oil instead of flowers, corpses in the refrigerator, a greenhouse better, learn to love beauty, yet might make some fears seem silly. Death. Hamster. Shattered glass. He eased up on the accelerator" (81). Sexual embrace is the gesture with which Piet seeks to ward off death, but sexuality also represents his imagined guilt for the death of his parents: had he been tending the garden instead of trying to slake his own sexual hunger, his parents might somehow have been spared. Hence, he has chosen an "angelic" wife who rarely experiences orgasm and maintains a certain virginal innocence—through her origins in Nun's Bay, her associations with Venus, Diana, and Eve, and her refusal to bear another child.

Angela Hanema is also Updike's most fully realized contemporary version of the legendary Iseult; indeed, in her fusion of passion and aloofness she is both Iseult the Fair and Iseult of the White Hands. Updike's interest in the story of Tristan and Iseult was first acknowledged in print in 1963, when his long, profound review of Denis de Rougemont's *Love Declared* appeared in the *New Yorker*, together with introductory comments on *Love in the Western World* which suggest he had for some time been familiar with the Swiss author's theories. Two years later, Updike included the review in his collection *Assorted Prose*, and at the same time published in the *New Yorker* a rather stilted quasi-modernization of the Tristan-Iseult legend entitled "Four Sides of One Story." The announced intention of *Love in the Western World* was to explore "the inescapable conflict in the West between passion and marriage" (*AP*, 284), and it provoked Updike to elaborate his own theories of passion, marriage, and death. De Rougemont concludes that Tristan and Iseult are, essentially, not in love with each other but with love itself; hence, as Updike paraphrases the argument, "their passion secretly wills its own frustrations and irresistibly seeks the bodily death that forever removes it from the qualifications of life . . ." (284). Passionate love, according to the Venus myth disseminated by the wandering troubadours, feeds upon denial, and both de Rougemont and Updike consequently stress the legendary episode in which Tristan and Iseult lay together in the wood of Morois with the "sword of chastity" between them—an image that perhaps accounts for the moment in *Of the Farm* when Joey Robinson, thinking of his pale first wife, remembers how "repeatedly she had taken me into her bed and her body as she might have taken an unavoidable sword . . ." (*OF*, 88).

The contrasts between chaste courtly love and the indulgence of physical passion, between pre-lapsarian innocence and the guilty, death-rendering knowledge of man after the fall, between images of light and of darkness, repeatedly thread their way through the fabric of the novel. Unlike the myth of Chiron in *The Centaur*, the legend of Tristan and Iseult is never rigorously applied to the plot; indeed, in a rigorous parallel, Angela should be Piet's mistress and Foxy his wife (though Foxy is also endowed with something of Iseult's luminosity, and as a married woman she is "unattainable"). Yet the legend is repeatedly evoked in imagery, theme, and individual incident; Piet's dangerous plunge from the bathroom window is the comic equivalent of the wounded Tristan's death-defying leap across the flour-strewn floor that protects his Queen's chastity. It is, however, in the recurrent intermingling of Eros and Thanatos that the novel shows its most profound indebtedness to Updike's readings of Denis de Rougemont. The twin narcissism of the lovers may disguise a death wish, but "A man in love," Updike argues, "ceases to fear death" (*AP*, 286); in the complementary myth of Don Juan, which de Rougemont and Updike acknowledge as an inversion of the Tristan story, "Don Juan loves Woman under the guise of many women, exhaustingly" (298). The two statements, taken together, help to focus the significance of Piet Hanema's seemingly inexhaustible sexual appetite. And hence, when Piet makes love to Bea Guerin, he experiences a "crisisless osmosis" in which "Death no longer seemed dreadful" (Cs, 336). As Robert Detweiler has argued in an extensive analysis of the role of the Tristan theme in *Couples,*

> Tristan seeks to avoid death by losing himself in the passionate love of a woman, and yet that effort, precisely because it has the flight from death as its object and not the true encounter with another being, only betrays the continuing intensity of the death wish. Don Juan attempts to outdo and overcome death by the conquest of many women, and yet the variety and exhausting athleticism of his seductions are in themselves death-dealing. Piet acts out both these roles, although he is a more thoroughgoing Tristan than a Don Juan, and embodies the different attitudes toward love and death.[26]

Central to Detweiler's thesis—and borne out by Updike's choice of a second epigraph from Alexander Blok's "The Scythians"—is the notion that pursuit of the Unattainable Lady is concomitant with the pursuit of death, though Piet's energies have allegedly been directed at defiance of death's dominion. This central and essential paradox of his stance becomes clear when he actively collaborates with death by helping to arrange Foxy's abortion; not only must he conspire with the priest of death, Freddy Thorne, but he must also sacrifice his own "virginal" wife in order to gain Freddy's compliance.

Standing in the Boston Common while Foxy is being aborted, Piet moves through meaningless mock-gestures of fasting, of charity and communion, yet he knows all along that he has "set a death in motion" (Cs, 375), and it is precisely this complicity which results in his redemptive fall. His suffering and entombment are balanced by three days of marathon love-making with Foxy, the sensuous and uninhibited woman of the earth, as opposed to the unattainable Venus-Virgin-Iseult who has, for centuries, dominated conceptions of romantic love in the West. A measure of Piet's progress is found in comparing the catalogue of death he draws up on an insomniac night and the reaction he feels, after his separation from Angela, when he reads of the death of John Ong. The earlier fantasies are almost all violent, from "The Chinese knife across the eye" and "The knotted silk cord" to "The splintered windshield. The drunken doctor's blunder shrugged away. The shadow of fragility on the ice, *beneath the implacably frozen stars . . .*" (259–260).[27] In dramatic contrast, Piet sees through

John Ong "how plausible it was to die, how death, far from invading earth like a meteor, occurs on the same plane as birth and marriage and the arrival of the daily mail" (428).

Until the concluding pages of *Couples*, Piet Hanema's struggle beneath the stars is highlighted and enriched by allusion to an entire galaxy of striving, quixotic, and absurd heroes. If *The Centaur* at moments seems constrictingly explicit in its mythological allusions, *Couples* may well strike many readers as too prodigal, even profligate, though here the allusions to myth, legend, fairy tale, and the Bible are considerably less intrusive. What is most remarkable about the performance is that, having carefully erected so many metaphorical waystations in the novel, Updike abandons them all in the concluding pages. In effect, he moves beyond myth, in a kind of leap of faith, a robust embrace of the quotidian that had been prefigured in *Of the Farm*. The stylistic equivalent of this existential choice is to be found in the sheer wonder with which Updike's prose can infuse the most banal objects, glorying in their mundane existence. If, as Sartre has argued, the ultimate evil consists in making abstractions of concrete things, Updike must be praised for attempting the opposite. That quality of "thingness," in which a jelly glass or a window sash is rendered with patient, radiant detail, links him to a tradition of realism that includes such great American poets as Walt Whitman and Robert Frost, as well as the Pennsylvania painter Andrew Wyeth. Indeed, in an article on Whitman, Updike cited the following declaration as a "thrilling" metaphysics of American realism:

"Whatever may have been the case in years gone by, the true use for the imaginative faculty of modern times is to give ultimate vivification to facts, to science, and to common lives, endowing them with the glows and glories and final illustriousness which belongs to every real thing, and to real things only."[28]

Through such a technique, Updike concludes, real things are assigned "the sacred status that in former times was granted mysteries,"[29] and one cannot resist the sense that he is speaking as much of his own art as of Whitman's.

So long as Piet Hanema is aware of the choice he makes at the end of his vigil—so long as he, like Joey, acknowledges the radical protest involved in opting for the earthy, the commonplace, he maintains the stance of an absurd hero; in this case the necessary "disproportion" is contained in the inevitable dialectical tension between what he desires and what the forces of myth and society esteem. But when the protest is succeeded by contentment, the tension slackens: Piet is then no longer a carpenter but a building inspector, no longer the Flying Dutchman but another landlocked husband. Or, one might suggest, he is a Sisyphus without a rock to push—hardly a figure to inspire wonder, except at the novelistic courage Updike shows in his creation. That Piet's hard-won knowledge should lead him to embrace the conventional was foreshadowed in *Of the Farm*; in turn, it anticipates the peace Harry Angstrom makes with his wife, Janice, at the end of *Rabbit Redux*, which ends in the equanimity of a husband and wife peacefully asleep together.

In 1970 Updike gathered together a group of stories concerned with a lovingly bumptious Jewish writer named Henry Bech; the earliest of them, "The Bulgarian Poetess," had first appeared in the *New Yorker* in 1965, and received first prize in the O. Henry Awards. Together, the linked stories emerge as a kind of episodic novel of self-realization structurally akin to Sherwood Anderson's classic *Winesburg, Ohio*; and like Anderson's work, *Bech: A Book* is a variation on the classic *Künstlerroman*. But unlike the impressionable young George Willard, Bech is middle-aged, Jewish, and urban—a first cousin of Saul Bellow's picaresque heroes; he is also a blocked artist, a disoriented voyager, and a frustrated lover: in short, the picaro as schlemiel. *Bech: A Book* is a surprising work, co-opting the mother-fixated, anguished intellectual boy-man who has become a staple figure in the Jewish novel of the postwar period. On the other hand, it is typical of Updike that he has never settled for a single predictable formula, that his work has shown a phenomenal capacity for both thematic and formal growth, and *Bech: A Book* is further welcome evidence of his prodigious talent.

Henry Bech is, for all his idiosyncrasy, a recognizable Updike figure in his quest for the divine woman, his fear of death, and his troubled relationship with the natural world. But the very themes which Updike tended to treat with high seriousness in the writings of the 1960's here become the subject of high comedy; and, indeed, Updike's comic voice becomes an increasingly resilient instrument in the works of the 1970's. Long accused by numerous critics of being a prototypic WASP, Updike triumphantly co-opts the philosophy and the mannerisms of the modern Jewish novel; he thus reverses the process whereby the Jewish novelist energetically appropriates and, in a sense, "masters" the dominant culture of the WASP—as in Philip Roth's *When She Was Good*, Bernard Malamud's *The Natural*, and Saul Bellow's *Henderson the Rain King*. The device also gives Updike the opportunity to respond, in a preface and appendices, to some of the more recurrent charges leveled against his own fiction, and through Bechian ventriloquism to protest against "the silken mechanism whereby America reduces her writers to imbecility and cozenage" (*B*, 6).

Though *Bech: A Book* is Updike's first extended work in the comic mode, the comic spirit has never been absent from his writing—even when it emerges solely in a puckish sense for ironic detail (as in Angela Hanema's drinking five-star Cognac from a Flintstones jelly glass). But one encounters it, too, in Piet's Tristan-like plunge from the Guerins' bathroom window, or in Joey Robinson's mowing in a costume that consists of Chaplinesque baggy pants and a beribboned coolie hat, or in his bikini-clad wife's crouching in a thicket of poison ivy. Often Updike's humor will consist of swift verbal put-downs, as when Joey, referring to his difficulty in matching real plants with the idealized pictures in botany books, describes this as "'an ancient philosophical problem'," and his stepson counters, "'Or else just lousy pictures'" (*OF*, 64). The variety and richly modulated function of comedy in Updike's writings (including his wittily epigrammatic verse) might easily be the subject of a book-length study in its own right. Such an inquiry goes beyond the province of this work, and yet it forms a major corollary of the absurd, as I suggested in the preceding chapter through Northrop Frye's description of romance, tragedy, irony, and comedy as linked episodes in a total quest myth. The disproportion inherent in the absurd is a stock formula for comedy, especially for the burlesque, as definitively exhibited in *Modern Times* when Charlie Chaplin repeatedly pits his intention against the reality of the machine. But the absurd, as Frye so persuasively suggests, also points to comedy of a different sort—to the transcendent self-fulfillment of "the divine comedy, the larger scheme of redemption and resurrection."[30] It is this which Camus signals when he writes, "One must imagine Sisyphus happy."[31]

Henry Bech never finds this ultimate transformation, and when he ascends into "heaven" in the concluding episode of the book, it is not choirs of angels but gossiping, back-biting literati who sing to him. Nonetheless, if Bech progresses no further along Frye's spectrum than the ironic, he ultimately makes ample testimony to the largesse of spirit and of talent with which Updike shapes this book. If the preceding works were concerned to mythicize modern man's struggles, *Bech: A Book* thoroughly and often poignantly demythicizes them. Like *Couples* and *Rabbit Redux*, the novels which precede and follow it, *Bech: A Book* draws one of its most

recurrent image clusters from the heavens—in particular, from allusions to the stars and to the exploration of space. With his pale,
flat-chested, and adoring Russian interpreter, Bech discusses space
travel, and she suggests he might someday return to her, à la Von-
negut, in a space-warp. On their last evening together, Kate remarks that

"It is strange . . . of the books I translate, how much there is to do with
supernature. Immaterial creatures like angels, ideal societies composed
of spirits, speeds that exceed that of light, reversals of time—all impossible, and perhaps not. In a way it is terrible, to look up at the sky, on one
of our clear nights of burning cold, at the sky of stars, and think of creatures alive in it." (B, 27–28)

Yet before Kate's reflections become too metaphysically inflated,
Bech counters with the remark, "'Like termites in the ceiling'"
(28). In "Bech Takes Pot Luck," the writer is spending a summer
vacation on an island with his mistress Norma, her sister Bea, and
Bea's children. There he encounters a worshipful former student
from a creative writing class. When Wendell beds the children
down on the porch, he points out the constellations and the area of
the sky where they might see shooting stars. When, after a session
of earnest pot-smoking, the student and Bech's girlfriend leave the
house, Bech is alone with Norma's sister Beatrice, a distant cousin
of Bea Guerin in *Couples*, who also looked for shooting stars. Together, Bea and Bech go outside and gaze up at the heavens: "The
stars overhead were close and ripe. What was that sentence from
Ulysses? Bloom and Stephen emerging from the house to urinate,
suddenly looking up—*The heaventree of stars hung with humid
nightblue fruit*" (108). Like Leopold Bloom, Henry Bech is a childless Jew, and just as Bloom has the voluptuous earth-mother Molly,
so Henry will now gravitate toward the heavy-breasted Bea with
her three children. But Bech's former student, the pot-smoking
Wendell, is no Stephen Daedalus, and the affair between Bech and
Bea will end in separation; there are, in such a universe, no epiph-
anies. Nonetheless, Bech continues to be haunted by the stars. At
a Southern girls' college which he visits as a distinguished writer,
he thinks repeatedly of his ineffectiveness, comparing his life with
the time it would take "the tail-tip star of Scorpio to crawl an inch
across the map of Heaven . . ." (129). Still later, in London, trying
to describe the beauty of his "swinging" companion, he thinks of
her perfectly spaced teeth as "*Stars with a talent for squad-drill*"
(178).

An urban man, most at home in the "cozy turf" of Manhattan, Bech accepts an invitation to lecture at the Virginia college where he finds his "urban nostrils" assaulted by the strong smell of horse manure that forces him to a moment of panic: "Along with the sun's reddening rays and the fecal stench a devastating sadness swept in. He knew that he was going to die. That his best work was behind him. That he had no business here, and was frighteningly far from home" (121). The intimations of mortality proliferate, underscored by the "massed fertility" of the adoring audiences that surround him. In a scene pointedly reminiscent of *Couples*, the growing sense of his own insignificance to the cosmic scheme mingles with images of Easter and of communion: "As Bech ate, mechanically offering votive bits of dead lamb to the terror enthroned within him, he saw that the void should have been left unvexed . . ." (129). Like Piet Hanema, Bech is obsessed by the cycles of growth and inevitable decay—"grass into manure, flesh into worms" (130–131), but in the comic language of the book, the dilemma can also be phrased (and distanced and, metaphysically, de-fused) as "some midnight meadow where manure and grass played yin and yang" (130).

What Bech himself describes as his "religious crisis" is accelerated on his second spring morning in Virginia when, stepping outside his room, he is "crushed by the heedless scale of outdoors" and "the inhuman mutual consumption that is Nature" (134). Trying to explain his fears to a Jewish professor at the college, he tells her, "'I can't describe it. *Angst*. I'm afraid of dying. Everything is so implacable. Maybe it's all these earth-smells so suddenly'" (137). The ultimate crisis comes during a walk in the woods when Bech, suffering "pantheistic pangs," falls to the ground to pray for mercy, experiencing a classic moment of transcendental vision that concludes, through a camera-swift change of focus, with superb comic deflation:

And now the silence of the created universe acquired for Bech a miraculous quality of willed reserve, of divine tact that would let him abjectly pray on a patch of mud and make no answer but the familiar ones of rustle, of whisper, of invisible growth like a net sinking slowly deeper into the sea of the sky; of gradual realization that the earth is populated infinitely, that a slithering slug was slowly causing a dead oak leaf to lift and a research team of red ants were industriously testing a sudden morsel, Bech's thumb, descended incarnate. (139–140)

When, in the scene that follows, Bech listens to the girls recite poems about nature and the "cold star" of earth, his eyes film with moisture, but it is "less full-formed tears than the blurry reaction pollen excites in the allergic" (141). Through just such picaresque fumblings and blunderings, Henry Bech does, indeed, gain "immortality" in the concluding story, "Bech Enters Heaven," as a new member of the modern literary pantheon. Allusions to such classics as *Ulysses*, Wordsworth's "I Wandered Lonely as a Cloud," and T. S. Eliot's *The Waste Land*, threaded throughout the work, establish his credentials as a literary voyager, even as the comic mode itself repeatedly undercuts his odyssey without diminishing Bech's own solid humanity. If *Bech: A Book* is a minor performance, it nonetheless shows a stylish virtuosity that will serve John Updike well in the variety of fictional landscapes he explores in the coming decade.

Until *Bech: A Book* all of John Updike's longer fiction, as well as many of his short stories, sustained an elaborate symbiotic relationship with traditional literary gesture—with the familiar modes of utopia and anti-utopia, pastoral and anti-pastoral, myth and legend, fairy tales and children's stories. The allusive superstructure of the fiction is, of course, most obtrusive in *The Centaur*, where the author supplies the ill-informed with an elaborate mythological index. Save for the concluding and curiously ineffectual story, "Bech Enters Heaven," *Bech: A Book* eschews this tendency to cast literary riddles; for the reader of modern fiction, there can scarcely be obscurity or arcanum in the figure of the schlemiel. Indeed, what Updike has done here, and will reinforce in much of his work in the 1970's, is to demythologize his own fictional universe. As Robert Detweiler has authoritatively argued,

It is apparent that from now on fiction for Updike can be composed free of the help and weight of archetypal models, of vague secondary stories from the collective past. This liberation is necessary because the old strategy has become too transparent; we have become overly self-conscious about our mythicizing epistemology and have rendered the narratation that depends on myth ineffective.[32]

What frequently replaces myth as an organizational module in the fiction is a growing awareness of contemporary history, an element always present in Updike's work, but one which in *Couples* becomes singularly resonant with implication for the entire imaginative embodiment of the novel. Updike has always been, preeminently, a novelist of manners, and his examination of contemporary mores and institutions has increasingly stressed the degree to which private conduct is shaped by public events. In his long poem

"Midpoint" and his single play, *Buchanan Dying*, Updike rings variations on this fundamental method of exploring history as metaphor; and in *The Coup* he adroitly "historicizes" fiction itself. Throughout *Rabbit Redux* allusions to contemporary events form "clusters" of the kind often composed in the earlier writings by images from the natural world, leading Robert Detweiler to refer to them as tropes.[33] The most prominent and the most determinant in the total orchestration of the novel are those of space travel, the Viet Nam war, race riots, and drugs; and these, in turn, are posed in intricate counterpoint to the fictional or "invented" tropes of angelic presences, mirrors, basketball, and fire, and to the overarching themes of the quest, death and rebirth, and redemptive sacrifice. As in *Rabbit, Run*, Updike underscores the novel's contemporaneity through the use of the present tense, but, far more than in the earlier work, real contemporary events thicken the very air through which Harry Angstrom moves. What is manifest here is not merely a shift in Updike's own novelistic vision, but a shift in the America he seeks to document; *Rabbit, Run* is set in 1959, at the end of a decade of conformity and political ennui, whereas *Rabbit Redux* seeks to come to terms with the stridulant and self-contradictory era of the 1960's. Appropriately, the absurdity of Harry Angstrom's intentions is also reversed. In the earlier novel, he had struggled to change when an entire society urged his conformity—Eccles to religion, the Springers to a mediocre but secure job, his parents to the responsibilities of marriage and family; only the half-mad Tothero, the senile Mrs. Smith, and the prostitute Ruth seemed to encourage the nascent nonconformity that Rabbit pitted—often ineffectually, painfully—against the Babbittry of Brewer, Pennsylvania. In the ten years separating the two novels, Harry's quality of resistance has been relentlessly eroded, together with the springy litheness of the young basketball player; he is left, instead, "with the thick waist and cautious stoop bred into him by a decade of the linotyper's trade, clues to weakness, a weakness verging on anonymity" (*RRx*, 4). Now, when an entire culture seems bent on sweeping, perhaps apocalyptic change, he struggles to remain the same, to defend his insufficient but easy suburban status quo. The events of the novel—a fusion of "real" and fictional occurrences—will lance this complacency, forcing a metamorphosis that restores his identity as "Rabbit." Indeed, references to details in the Beatrix Potter story become increasingly prominent in the final sections of the novel.

Harry Angstrom is literally "led back," is restored to health after disease, as the word "redux" signals, and as the author perhaps too coyly announces in having Harry and his father stop each workday afternoon at a bar called the Phoenix, where the opening scene takes place. Hawk, racist, suburbanite, he is radicalized—but not merely in the political sense; he is also radicalized in the sense of being taken back to his roots. The latter dimension is in part projected through the overly familiar device (to be repeated yet again in *A Month of Sundays*) of the confrontation with a dying parent; and Harry is literally returned to the safe haven of his parental home, to his own narrow childhood room, when his house is burned down by angry neighbors. He sleeps in the same bed he occupied as a teenager, and for a time his visiting sister Mim will complete the familiar family circle around the worn kitchen table. At the end of the novel, Rabbit even wedges himself into his old athletic jacket, the satin vestment of his former stardom, of what Tothero once identified as "the will to achieve" (*RR*, 61). Yet Rabbit has not merely reverted to the restless, inarticulately questioning young adult of the first novel; he is a man approaching middle-age who has discovered new and surprising capacities for suffering, for compassion, and for personal growth. The Camusian blow that breaks the spirit's sleep occurs when he learns that his wife Janice is having an affair with car salesman Charlie Stavros, a mirror version of Harry's own affair with Ruth in *Rabbit, Run*. It is this which abruptly shatters his complacency and redeems him from the anonymity Updike describes in the opening scene of the novel, when pale and ghostly workers file out of the Verity Press.

In the dense opening sequence of *Rabbit Redux* most of the major themes of the novel are sounded, as in a kind of overture. Harry's own death-in-life is accented by references to the dying city center of Brewer, to his mother's slow death by multiple sclerosis, to cancer, to the drowning of his infant daughter a decade before, and in the casual allusion to a co-worker who is "killing himself" with drink. Expressing concern that his son is alone in the house, Harry thinks he should hurry home, "In case it's burned down. In case a madman has moved in. These things happen all the time in the papers" (*RRx*, 9). And, in fact, the violence continuously reiterated by newspapers and television intrudes directly into his life when the "madman" Skeeter moves into his house and the neighbors set it ablaze, making a funeral pyre for the ethereal, enigmatic Jill. While Harry and his father exchange desultory remarks in the Phoenix Bar, a television set with the sound turned off shows the "jiggling star" of the Apollo moon launch as it lifts away from earth. "The men dark along the bar murmur among themselves. They have not been lifted, they are left here" (7), Updike remarks, but Harry—whether literally "spaced out" on grass or only figuratively in orbit—is destined to be lifted out of the stasis described in the novel's opening episodes. Following the rocket's blast-off, the television screen flashes the image of a housewife kissing a quiz-program m.c. and seeming to give him "a taste of her tongue" (7). The blending of images of space travel and of sexuality are frequent in the novel, heralded by the exchange between Soviet cosmonauts with which the section "Pop/Mom/Moon" is prefaced:

LIEUT. COL. VLADIMIR A. SHATALOV: *I am heading straight for the socket.*

LIEUT. COL. BORIS V. VOLYNOV, SOYUZ 5 COMMANDER: *Easy, not so rough.*

COLONEL SHATALOV: *It took me quite a while to find you, but now I've got you.* (2)

The space-docking maneuver underlies many subsequent scenes, including the novel's graphic sexual encounter between the runaway Jill and the angry Black Skeeter, as well as the concluding episode in which Rabbit and Janice strike a cautious peace and sleep together at the Safe Haven Motel. As Rabbit enters the bed with his wife, he feels "particles of some sort bombarding him," and "he and she seem to be slowly revolving, afraid of jarring one another away." They are "adjusting in space, slowly twirling . . . ," and "In a space of silence, he can't gauge how much, he feels them drift along sideways deeper into being married . . ." An abrupt answer from Janice seems to jar him, "but softly, an unexpected joggle in space." As Rabbit drifts into sleep, his hand loosens its grip on Janice's breasts, "lets them float away, radiant debris" (404–406).

In the concluding scene of the novel, Updike underscores Rabbit's new sense of self and wholeness in the image of coupled ships drifting through space, guided by attendant, perhaps angelic presences. But in the cosmonauts' dialogue quoted above, the implicit sexuality is mechanical, just as sex for modern women like Jill and Mim has become an automatic gesture stripped of emotional implication; and the cosmonauts' exchange is also comical, as it becomes again in the fragment quoted as introduction to the "Skeeter" section of the novel:

"We've been raped, we've been raped!"

                —BACKGROUND VOICE ABOARD SOYUZ 5 (205)

Yet the theme of rape will also become agonizingly real in this section, when an angry black militant rants and sobs about the rape of his people, when the television set broadcasts photographs of race riots, when Jill's body is violated by drugs, when the horrors of Viet Nam are graphically catalogued, and when even Jill's Porsche and her guitar are "ravished."

Thus, Updike richly orchestrates the tropes of the novel, evoking them as illustration of the self-consciously large themes of *Rabbit Redux*, but brushing them like grace notes, as well—when he describes the new trash cans in Brewer as having flying saucer lids, when Rabbit considers buying his mother a humidifier that "looks like a fat flying saucer" (90), or when Nelson reports that one of his classmates claims the inhabitants of the moon are so small humans inhale them "'and they make us think we see flying saucers'" (160). Even such incidental images reinforce the theme of exploration, the yearning for new worlds; they evoke the science-fiction fantasies of Harry's own youth, the collective fear of alien and atomic power, the hunger for mystery, and they suggest the degree to which spiritual and celestial presences are crowded out by those of technology. The label on the frozen dinner Rabbit heats for himself and his son seems to parody the kind of synthetics and concentrates fed to astronauts; and at the Burger Bliss he treats himself to a Lunar Special cheeseburger that flies an American flag. After seeing *2001: A Space Odyssey*, Harry compares his own house to a space ship, and notes that with its synthetic materials and its "gadgets designed to repel repair," his living room also has a "Martian" look (71–72). Returning from a baseball game that teases him with hints of an older America, he finds Janice gone and feels the house "silent, like outer space" (84). Reinforcing the analogies between astronaut, athlete, and traditional American hero, the movie theatre that had showed *2001* follows it with *True Grit*, then *Butch Cassidy and the Sundance Kid*; repeated allusions to the Lone Ranger and Daniel Boone further confirm the parallel.

Like an astronaut, Harry Angstrom sits within the complex mechanism of a linotype machine, setting a story about Brewer's role in the moon landing: "The machine stands tall and warm above him, mothering, muttering . . . The sorts tray is on his right hand; the Star Quadder and the mold disc and slug tray on his left; a green-shaded light bulb at the level of his eyes. Above this sun the machine shoulders into shadow like a thunderhead" (29). This splendid relic from the golden age of machinery will soon be obsolete, but Rabbit's command of its intricate mechanism gives him some of the old joy of the athlete; and the suggestion of a parallel to the astronauts is also clear. He is restored to his role as a questing man, as explorer, voyager, and pioneer—words officially annexed to the NASA lexicon; and there is one specific allusion to Harry as a Columbus figure. Like the early settlers of the New World, he is also inspired by the American Dream (absurdly, when a gathering stream of evidence testifies to the death or perversion of the dream); for him America is "something infinitely tender, the star lit with his birth" (47), and he clings to that faith however harshly reality instructs him to the contrary. As in *The Poorhouse Fair*, the values of an older America are suggested in hand-made artifacts of the past—for example, in the hand-painted signs, grindstones, and arrowheads unearthed during the razing of the city center that passes for Brewer's own "renewal" project; and those older values are parodied in the simulated antique cobbler's bench in the Angstroms' living room, which Harry rescues after the fire, together with the driftwood lamp that is a pathetic reminder of the natural world. The American heritage is evoked when the doped runaway Jill describes her visit to Valley Forge, and parodied when Mim the call-girl imitates the act she once performed showing Disneyland tourists through a replica of Mount Vernon.

As the painful process of his rebirth begins, Rabbit sits in a bar listening to nostalgic songs performed by a worldly, worn, clairvoyant black woman named Babe (in truth, another Beatrice, as we learn from the story of her arrest which Rabbit later sets); he thinks of these as "lyrics born in some distant smoke, decades when Americans moved within the American dream, laughing at it, starving on it, but living it, humming it, the national anthem everywhere" (124). He is not yet ready to consider the millions of Americans shut out from the dream, though references to Indians and blacks have been frequent in the preceding scenes; nor is he prepared to acknowledge that the conquest of space might represent a territorial fever and a militaristic zeal somehow related to American aggression in Viet Nam, or that the skies harboring astronauts can also shower napalm. Through Skeeter and Jill he learns to make some of these connections; the knowledge does not transform him from racist Hawk to liberal Dove, but it confirms and mellows the essential humanism that was central to his vision in *Rabbit, Run* as well. The runaway Jill reminds him of his own younger self, and Skeeter shows him that the black is "technology's nightmare" (234); the lessons they preach will be filtered through

Harry's own growing concern about his son Nelson's response to these unlikely visitors.

Here, as elsewhere, Updike is clearly treading a territory which Norman Mailer has far more daringly and provocatively charted; it is an act of courage (or of impudence, perhaps) not unlike that shown in his co-opting of the schlemiel figure in *Bech: A Book*. In the degree to which he represents the vitality and daring and potency the white middle classes have lost, the figure of Skeeter takes a pale page from Mailer's brilliant essay on "The White Negro" as existential hero; in the analogies between Viet Nam and the American Civil War, Updike evokes a theme far more adroitly represented in Mailer's *The Armies of the Night*; and the link between cowboys and gung-ho Viet Nam combat troops is brilliantly figured in Mailer's *Why Are We in Vietnam?*—complete with the homosexual overtones Updike also suggests. Above all, Mailer's nonfiction novel *Of a Fire on the Moon*, as a study of the symbiosis of science and magic, of the forgiveness and damnation inherent in technology, hovers behind numerous scenes in *Rabbit Redux*. Furthermore, there are echoes of the other ambitious "moon book" of this period, Saul Bellow's *Mr. Sammler's Planet*. Harry's direct confrontation with the latent violence and sexual aggressiveness of his time, like Mr. Sammler's, comes through a black criminal (and, similarly, Harry's first sense of threat occurs on a crowded bus); his sister Mim, who visits a dying mother, is a cousin of the flashily dressed and promiscuous Angela Gruner, who stands vigil at her father's deathbed; and the hassock stuffed with Mafia payoffs in Dr. Gruner's living room is no coincidental forerunner to that in the Angstroms' living room—"the very hassock that Rabbit as a child had once dreamed about: he dreamed it was full of dollar bills to solve all their problems" (353).

If, in such sly winks at the competition, Updike seeks to dazzle us with his cleverness, the analogies evoked are not always to his advantage. On the other hand, they help define his own distinctive fictional territory—in contrast to that of the urban Jewish intellectual—as the suburban world of the mortgage-holder and family man who feels most threatened, perhaps, by assaults on what he vaguely reverences as the American Dream. Furthermore, there is a unique ring of authenticity in Updike's portrayal of the Apollo-Saturn launch as a flickering, soundless background to Harry's first troubled dialogue with his father, in the degree to which the wonders of science and technology are suffused beneath the quotidian concerns of commonplace lives. Updike's fictional projection of the impact of the moon landing on middle America might almost be a conscious illustration of Mailer's sentiment that the horror of the twentieth century is "the size of each new event, and the paucity of its reverberation."[34] Television's continuous montages of fantasy, simulation, and reality frequently confuse Rabbit, as when the *Eagle* puts down on the moon and he thinks, "At last it happens. The real event. Or is it?" (*RRx*, 99). Speaking of the boredom that thickens around television coverage of the moon walk, Aquarius-Mailer says,

The event was so removed, however, so unreal, that no objective correlative existed to prove it had not conceivably been an event staged in a television studio—the greatest con of the century—and indeed a good mind, product of the iniquities, treacheries, gold, passion, invention, deception, and rich worldly stink of the Renaissance could hardly deny that the event if bogus was as great a creation in mass hoodwinking, deception, and legerdemain as the true ascent was in discipline and technology.[35]

What Mailer phrases conceptually, philosophically, Updike realizes in the brilliantly novelistic scene when Rabbit sits beside his invalid mother, herself sustained by the technology's latest wonder drugs, and watches the *Eagle* descend; his son Nelson dozes with his head against his thigh, and Harry's own father sleeps soundly in an armchair across the bedroom. While mother and son watch electronic letters spell out the historic announcement: MAN IS ON THE MOON, Mrs. Angstrom reaches out and lovingly strokes her son's head. When Harry responds he is, like his mother, thinking of the crisis in his own marriage, though his words apply equally to the shimmering silhouettes on the television screen: "'I don't know, Mom . . . I know it's happened, but I don't feel anything yet'" (*RRx*, 100). Mailer's "paucity of reverberation" is here made flesh.

Not all critics of Updike's fiction have been willing to read the concluding words of *Rabbit, Run* as a positive shout from the novelistic grandstand; but there can be no doubt that *Rabbit Redux* ends in a triumph, however banal, for the hero, a rebirth for which the black Skeeter is the primary agent. In the early pages of the novel, Updike repeatedly associates Harry with images of ennui and of death; only the author refers to him by the old, frisky nickname of Rabbit, and only the black characters will eventually adopt it again, though usually with irony. When Janice leaves him for Stavros, Harry seems to sink further into lethargy, until an encounter with a black colleague alters his life. Recalling Buchanan's invitation, Harry reflects, "He was lying down to die, had been lying down for years. His body had been telling him to. His eyes blur print in the afternoons, no urge to run . . ." (103). Furthermore, his own experiences have repeatedly stressed man's frail mortality; hence, he can see "dust accumulate, deterioration advance, chaos seep in, time conquer" (171). First through the runaway Jill, he will re-learn something of the exhilaration of running; and through her, too, he discovers a domesticity that was always a part of his dream, but that his wife Janice had never honored. While Jill cooks, the former part-time gardener leafs through the Garden Section of the Sunday paper, reading about flowers that, dried, *"will form attractive bouquets to brighten the winter months around the corner"* (153). Indeed, Harry now frequently works in his own suburban garden, often with the assistance of his son. When the new school year begins, he notes that "There is that scent in the air, of going back to school, of beginning again and reconfirming the order that exists" (192–193).

Such lessons are reinforced by Harry's dying mother, who urges, "'Run. Leave Brewer . . . Don't say no to life . . . Pray for birth. Pray for your own rebirth'," and he thinks, "Freedom means murder. Rebirth means death" (197–198). The painful, joyous process of Harry's private renascence assumes real impetus when Jill enters his life; but it receives its most important impulse when Skeeter moves into the suburban bungalow with Harry, Nelson, and Jill, making it a kind of "refugee camp" (226). Skeeter is precisely the "murderer" Rabbit's instinct has warned him of, but the death of the old self is also the prelude to joy, as laughter fills the house: "they are rejoicing in brotherhood, at having shared this moment, giggling and cackling; the house is an egg cracking because they are all hatching together" (213).

The cycle of death and rebirth which the novel charts is, to a considerable degree, dependent on the reader's acceptance of Skeeter as the savior who shows Harry the possibility of a new life. The phrase "black Jesus" occurs on three occasions in *Rabbit Redux*, Jill warns that the police will crucify Skeeter, and when a police officer spells the black man's name, it is as "'Sally, Katherine, double Easter—'" (329). Watching Skeeter strip off his shirt, Rabbit thinks he "has never seen such a chest except on a crucifix" (279). After the fire that destroys half of his house and kills the drugged Jill, Rabbit helps Skeeter escape, leaving him beside a highway sign pointing portentously toward "Galilee 2." He extends his hand to the black man and Skeeter spits in the open palm—a symbol of Baptism that verges unhappily on burlesque, leading to

Eugene Lyons's allegation that Updike has indulged in "gratuitous symbol mongering."[36] The charge would seem amply confirmed by the scene in which the virgin-whore Jill, Virgin Mary and Mary Magdalene, re-enacts the washing of Christ's feet: kneeling, she fellates Skeeter while Rabbit looks on in fascination. Afterwards, "A string as of milkweed spittle is on her chin; Rabbit wipes her chin and mouth with his handkerchief and, for weeks afterward, when all is lost, will take out this handkerchief and bury his nose in it, in its imperceptible spicy smell" (299). Even if the reader is prepared to accept this holy relic, this talismanic kerchief, as part of the metaphoric process shaping the novel's events, it is difficult to acknowledge its credibility within the dense and plangent air of contemporary reality which otherwise suffuses the book. That a middle-class suburban male, conventionally heterosexual and hostile to blacks, would carry this particular handkerchief in his pocket for weeks seriously strains the willing suspension of disbelief; that he would literally "bury his nose in it" baffles whatever credulity remains. Furthermore, such lapses seem the more gratuitous, the more obtrusive, in a book which otherwise largely eschews the reliance on external patterns. That Updike can project credible portraits of blacks is abundantly clear from the figures of Babe and Buchanan; in the context of *Rabbit Redux*, however, the anachronistic projection of a black Christ (or anti-Christ) dangerously unbalances the book.

Once Updike returns, in the final section of the novel, to the demythologized, commonplace realm in which the Angstroms move, *Rabbit Redux* begins to cohere again as a realistic work, though Rabbit's reunion with Janice at a motel called "Safe Haven" is an unhappy lapse. Similarly, the concluding paragraph of the novel must strain to incorporate images of space, sexuality, and fertility, the rabbit burrow, and the garden, but in doing so it confirms the willingness of Janice and Rabbit to begin a new life together with a new dimension of humanity and dignity and grace. Helping Stavros ward off death, Janice has absolved herself of guilt for the drowning of her infant daughter a decade before; in Stavros—Greek for "cross"—she too has found a redeemer. Thus, in the novel's final passage, the two unlikely pilgrims are at rest: "He. She. Sleeps. O.K.?" (407). However, in this total embrace of the commonplace, an essential tension flows out of the character and, as Updike himself said of Piet Hanema,

He becomes merely a name in the last paragraph: he becomes a satisfied person and in a sense dies. In other words, a person who has what he wants, a satisfied person, a content person, ceases to be a person . . . I feel that to be a person is to be in a situation of tension, is to be in a dialectical situation. A truly adjusted person is not a person at all—just an animal with clothes on or a statistic. So that it's a happy ending, with this "but" at the end.[37]

In the case of *Rabbit Redux* one might argue that the hero is not merely reduced to a name, but to a pronoun: "He."

With *Rabbit Redux* Updike would seem to have brought to a close not only a particular narrative impulse within his own work, but also the entire philosophical inquiry begun in *The Poorhouse Fair*, with the galaxy of absurd heroes who bore the weight of his argument. From the late 1960's onward, his writings become less daring, less radical, in their philosophical conclusions; the risk-taking is now focused on the formal plane. In the long auto-biographical poem "Midpoint," composed in the summer of 1968, Updike underscored precisely the note of acceptance of the imper-fect, the near-at-hand:

> Half-measures are most human; Compromise,
> Inglorious and gray, placates the Wise.
> By mechanistic hopes is Mankind vexed;
> The Book of Life is margin more than text.
> Ecclesiastes and our glands agree:
> A time for love, for work, for sleep, for tea.
> Organic music scores our ancient nerves:
> Hark to its rhythm, conform to its curves.[38]

It can, I think, be no coincidence that the word "curve" (or "curved") occurs three times in the brief concluding paragraph of *Rabbit Redux*, and that Harry Angstrom's triumph is measured precisely in his ability to recognize and conform to this curve. And if such a resolution signals a departure from the metaphysics of the absurd, the author is fully conscious of its implications. "Midpoint" concludes with the stanza

> Deepest in the thicket, thorns spell a word.
> Born laughing, I've believed in the Absurd,
> Which brought me this far; henceforth, if I can,
> I must impersonate a serious man.[39]

These are not the pages in which to consider the manifold im-plications of Updike's heightened interest in formal considerations, but it must be noted here that, even as his heroes have grown more conformist, Updike himself has taken ever greater technical risks. "Midpoint" itself, a visual collage of drawings, photographs, and typographic manipulations, is a prime example of an experimental tendency always present in Updike's work, but one which now achieves a new dimension, a new authority. Even *Couples*, a self-consciously old-fashioned novel that appeared in the same year "Midpoint" was written, amply demonstrates this innovative tendency. In a period when critics and sophisticated readers bayed the postulates of meta-fiction and fêted the birth of post-modernism, it was an act of considerable novelistic courage to construct this elaborate macrocosmic novel of suburban life, to endow a traditional form with contemporary validity. Updike even gives us, in a manner reminiscent of the "Finale" to George Eliot's *Middlemarch*, an epilogue in which he accounts for the characters' "after-years." Critics disturbed by the tidy resolution of Piet's marriage to Foxy are not unlike those who censure the final coming together of Dorothea and Will Ladislaw as too conventional, too much the clichéd "happy ending." Indeed, in many respects Updike's novel harks back to George Eliot's "Study of Provincial Life," with its intricately mingled concerns for contemporary history, complex social interrelationships, the role of the church, and the ambiguities of personal freedom. Furthermore, as David Daiches has argued about *Middlemarch*, "The world of moderate selfishness, moderate expectations, and realistic adjustment to things as they are, has its own attractions, its own validity, and its own norms."[40] In *Couples* as in *Of the Farm, Rabbit Redux, A Month of Sundays*, and *Marry Me*, Updike has returned the novel to Eliot's concern with the ordinary rhythms of life and work, and he does so with increasing confidence. Daiches's summarizing statement on the mode of *Middlemarch* might, I think, easily be transferred to *Couples* or to *Rabbit Redux*:

> The sense of the claims of ordinary life arises also from the abundant detail which fills the novel, forcing on the reader an awareness of the intersecting circles of activity which involve people with each other, individuals with the community, a given moment of time with history, and particular human ambitions and foibles with the human condition in general.[41]

Formally, *Rabbit Redux* also re-explores a fictional convention which has been virtually reduced to a pulp cliché—namely, that of the sequel. The phenomenon itself smacks of the kind of "return to" impulse of the best-seller, of Grace Metalious or—scarcely more tenable—Erich Segal; of serious contemporary novelists, only Gore Vidal has made significant use of the formula—with dubious results in *Myron* as sequel to *Myra Breckenridge*, but with brilliance in *1876*, the successor to *Burr*. Harry Angstrom, however, would scarcely seem a promising candidate for fictional resurrection, and Updike's formal coup is the greater since he manages to make the changes of a decade seem credible, his hero (despite his bristling prejudices) more empathetic, and the entire mechanism of the sequel a plausible device for dramatizing the moral crisis of America in the late 1960's. Continuing the formalistic probing of *Couples*, *Bech: A Book*, and *Rabbit Redux*, Updike presented *A Month of Sundays* in the form of diary entries composed by a lapsed minister, Tom Marshfield. In a series of running asides, Updike seems to ask how *The Scarlet Letter* might have developed had the minister and not Hester Prynne been pilloried. Tom Marshfield is sent to a desert retreat for seducing, among others, the church organist; and there he begins an increasingly passionate flirtation with the buxom, middle-aged matron who manages the penitential establishment—Mrs. Prynne. Marshfield's own wife is the daughter of Reverend Chillingworth. The diary records his trial in the wilderness, his ultimate conquest of Mrs. Prynne, and his own victorious renewal: "Last night after poker I went out under the dome of desert stars and was afraid, not afraid, afraid to be born again. Even so, come" (*MS*, 226).

Of all the writings that have followed the self-declared "midpoint" in Updike's literary career, *Marry Me* is the most conventional, the most prosaic in its narrative propositions and fictive manner. Nonetheless, it holds a key place in the ongoing cycle of marriage tales which form a continuous thread through Updike's work. It also extends the author's analysis of the absurd paradox at the heart of the Tristan-Iseult legend—what Updike refers to as "Tristan's Law," according to which "appealingness is inversely proportioned to attainability . . ."[42] As its subtitle "A Romance" stresses, Updike's eighth novel evokes that paradoxical tradition of courtly love according to which marriage, through restricting freedom, can only weaken love. As Updike remarks in his review of de Rougemont, "The heart *prefers* to move against the grain of circumstance; perversity is the soul's very life" (*AP*, 299). He then quotes, as an authority on the Court of Love, the Comtesse de Champagne:

We state and affirm, by the tenor of these presents, that love cannot extend its rights over two married persons. For indeed lovers grant each other all, mutually and freely, without being constrained by any motive of necessity, whereas husband and wife are holden, by their duty, to submit their wills to each other and to refuse each other nothing. (300)

In *Marry Me* a lover explains to his mistress that "'What we have, sweet Sally, is an ideal love. It's ideal because it can't be realized. As far as the world goes, we don't exist'" (*MM*, 46). While the guilty pair wait through a nightmare of delayed and cancelled and overbooked flights after a secret rendezvous in Washington, Sally is, appropriately, reading Camus's *The Stranger*; Jerry tries, repeatedly, to verbalize the existential dilemma in which they are caught, and for which the nightmare of their airport vigil is only a physical manifestation. "'I've figured out the bind I'm in', " he tells her. "'It's between death and death. To live without you is death to me. On the other hand, to abandon my family is a sin; to do it I'd have to deny God, and by denying God I'd give up all claim on immortality'" (55). Ultimately, Jerry will settle for mortal satisfactions, for the circumscribed if "sinful" joys of marriage to the woman he loves.

Like Piet and Rabbit, Jerry thus cedes his role as struggling "romantic" hero, as an absurd man pitting intention against reality. Similarly, beneath the political intrigues and manipulations of *The Coup* runs an almost constant domestic motif—particularly vivid, lovingly etched, in descriptions of the cluttered households of Colonel Elleloû's wives and mistresses; and he will finally abandon his messianic political ambitions for homelier pleasures: "She did still coo, when he spread her legs. The mats on the floor, once they cleared away the children's toys, seemed in their marital haste soft enough" (*Cp*, 296). The final surrender of the rebel's cause ends with an elegant, familial exile in Nice—"assiduous, economical, conjugal, temperate, optimistic, dynamic, middling, and modern" (298). Updike's African novel is a brilliant literary impersonation, full of incisively rendered detail, ingenious invention, and contagious wit; indeed, it compares favorably with Saul Bellow's *Henderson the Rain King*, though it lacks that novel's remarkable comic gusto.

In tracing the rise and fall of the dictator-rainmaker-messiah of a drought-ridden nation in sub-Saharan Africa, *The Coup* is an improbable novel to have been produced by the chronicler of small-town and suburban America—and improbably successful. One begins to feel that Updike is more and more motivated by the sheer delight of his own nimble virtuosity—as in the fables of microscopic organisms and prehistoric mammals that are among the stories collected in *Museums and Women*; or in his decision to write a closet drama about one of America's least celebrated statesmen, James Buchanan. Yet Buchanan was a logical subject for Updike, and not merely because he was a fellow Pennsylvanian: according to many observers (including James K. Polk and Henry Adams), America's fifteenth president represented many of the commonplace qualities of Updike's own fictional heroes. Furthermore, Buchanan coincidentally helped fulfill an ambition the author shared with Kierkegaard, who observed in his *Journals*, "I wanted to write a novel in which the chief character was to have been a man who had a pair of spectacles with one lens that reduced as powerfully as oxy-gas-microscope and the other that magnified equally powerfully; in his interpretation everything was very relative."[43] As a black servant girl responds in the play, when asked if she sees anything strange in the dying man's eyes, "Well, sah, one o' dem is blue, and de odder is more toward the color ob a frog half-hidin' hisself in de mud." Buchanan himself explains to her that "The blue one is farsighted, and the other is nearsighted."[44] The historic figure of James Buchanan thus gives us yet another model of Updike's own dualistic vision; significantly, both *Buchanan Dying* and *The Coup* explore this dualism through failed political leaders; indeed, the political dimension of Updike's writing has grown particularly dense ever since his farewell to pastoral in *Of the Farm*.

If Updike's concepts of the hero and of the milieu through which he moves have significantly shifted, one element of his prose remains constant—his command of the individual image and phrase, his ability to probe language to reveal an emotional truth in the most homely situations and objects. Recurrently, and often at the most unexpected moments, he prods us into a shock of recognition. In "Transaction," when a nervous married man brings a prostitute into his stylish hotel, the wait before the elevators deftly reveals his unease and embarrassment, without ever violating the object-centeredness of the passage; we are not told, intrusively, what he "thinks" or "feels," but are encouraged to experience it for ourselves in three brief sentences. "His eyes rigidly ahead, he crossed to the elevator doors of quilted colorless metal. He pushed the Up button. The wait built tall in his throat before an arriving car flung back a door."[45] If here the method is austere, it can also, of course, be luminous, lyric, epiphantic—as when Jerry Conant, having forgotten a corkscrew, smashes the neck of a wine bottle: "He swung firmly; a spatter of splinters glinted in his eyes before he heard the sound of broken glass; he plunged his startled gaze down through a jagged glinting mouth into a small deep cylindrical sea of swaying wine" (*MM*, 8). At times, to be sure, Updike's lyricism cloys, his symbols seem gratuitous, his plots implausible; and not only his own mannerisms, but also those of his characters, can become intrusive. It is a rare Updike novel when someone's speech is not emphasized by hands "chopping" the air, or when an errant husband does not seek to placate his wife with a back-rub. But Updike's lapses pale in comparison with his immense skills as a craftsman, and his generous gifts are particularly noteworthy in an age which ruthlessly devalues and dilutes language in the public sphere—as Updike, like Mailer, suggests in citing the bland technologese of NASA dialogues, the flaccid hyperboles of television commercials. If, at moments, Updike's own verbal elaborations seem to exist for their own sake, their exuberance can, I think, be taken as part of the author's general celebration of life, his exaltation of the quotidian and the fallible. With an increasingly meticulous, increasingly subtle, increasingly variable technique, he probes the great traditional themes of art—sex, mortality, and the nature of freedom. In his own words, "Domestic fierceness within the middle class, sex and death as riddles for the thinking animal, social existence as sacrifice, unexpected pleasures and rewards, corruption as a kind of evolution—these are some of the themes."[46] Such claims could scarcely be described as modest; neither, on the other hand, is the expanding fictional universe in which they are embodied.

The Absurd Man as Tragic Hero

During a *Paris Review* interview held in 1954, William Styron was asked whether he thought the current generation of American writers worked under greater disadvantages than their literary predecessors. He answered:

Writers ever since writing began have had problems, and the main problem narrows down to just one word—life. Certainly this might be an age of so-called faithlessness and despair we live in, but the new writers haven't cornered any market on faithlessness and despair, any more than Dostoevski or Marlowe or Sophocles did. Every age has its terrible aches and pains, its peculiar new horrors, and every writer since the beginning of time, just like other people, has been afflicted by what that same friend of mine calls "the fleas of life"—you know, colds, hangovers, bills, sprained ankles, and little nuisances of one sort or another. *They* are the constants of life, at the core of life, along with nice little delights that come along now and then. Dostoevski had them and Marlowe had them and we all have them, and they're a hell of a lot more invariable than nuclear fission or the Revocation of the Edict of Nantes. So is Love invariable, and Unrequited Love, and Death and Insult and Hilarity. Mark Twain was as baffled and appalled by Darwin's theories as anyone else, and those theories seemed as monstrous to the Victorians as atomic energy, but he still wrote about riverboats and old Hannibal, Missouri. No, I don't think the writer today is any worse off than at any other time.[1]

There are, Styron emphasizes, constants in life, day-to-day pleasures and perils which man can fasten to for their continuity, but even so, each age does have "its terrible aches and pains, its peculiar new horrors." Life in mid-twentieth-century Newport News, Virginia, where Styron was born, is not essentially different from Twain's life in Hannibal, Missouri. Love, Unrequited Love, Death, Insult, Hilarity are still the constants about which peculiar horrors or joys gather. In Twain's Hannibal as in Styron's Newport News there were the years of horror and anxiety in the face of mounting threats that the "world" would be blown apart. It matters little so far as the constants are concerned that it was a civil war which threatened Twain's world and, as the most obvious manifestation, submarines in Chesapeake Bay which threatened Styron's. For Henry Adams the threat of disintegration was posed ironically in the dynamo, an apparent symbol of power and progress which nonetheless threatened to make men "mere creatures of force around central powerhouses." The particular horrors of a new age do become significant, however, when we realize that they will dictate the terms of an artist's answers to the constant problems of life. In the same interview quoted above Styron goes on to point out that the "morbidity and gloom" of so many young writers today is the product of greatly increased knowledge about "the human self—Freud—that is, abnormal psychology, and all the new psychiatric wisdom. My God, think of how morbid and depressing Dostoevski would have been if he could have gotten hold of some of the juicy work of Dr. Wilhelm Stekel, say *Sadism and Masochism.*"[2] This knowledge is part of the *status quo*, but a *status quo* which, Styron concedes by analogy, makes the problem of the contemporary artist at least more deviously complex than that of, say, Dostoevski. While it is unquestionably true that young writers have cornered no market on despair, it is certainly equally true that they are frequently faced with unique difficulties in meeting the peculiar new horrors of their age.

In an article appearing in the *Saturday Review* in 1953, Maxwell Geismar attempted to look ahead to what might honestly be expected from such promising young talents as William Styron, outlining at the same time the peculiar amalgam of circumstances which seemed to surround the contemporary artist:

Pity the poor artist! The retreat either to the modes of personal sensibility, or those of religious and social authoritarianism may be a refuge for him. But it is hardly a source of great art anymore. The real drama and content of this period lie directly at the center of the chaos that surrounds him. It is there he must turn to come close to the spirit of the age, if he can only catch it. And surely no literary subject matter could offer him so many opportunities along with so many dangers. For our part we can only keep the boundaries of the middle way as wide as possible for him, preserve him from false orthodoxy, let him speak his mind without benefit of Congress—or even of captious critics.[3]

Lie Down in Darkness was indeed such a plunge into chaos, and like Updike's *Poorhouse Fair* it is a dismissal of more pervasive traditional "answers" to that chaos and an enumeration of contemporary absurdities. In the structure of this book is something of the baroque glory that abounds in Sir Thomas Browne's "Urn Burial," from which Styron took his title. Styron has admitted that the greatest problem which faced him in writing this first novel was the problem of "the progression of time,"[4] but the many complex episodes of the novel are so smoothly handled that the reader may tend to slight the enormous skill and concentration which were necessary to bring them off. A rereading of the book is clearly essential if the reader is to be conscious of Styron's exceptional technical virtuosity.

What we might call the centralizing action of *Lie Down in Darkness* occurs in the space of a few hours, beginning as Milton Loftis awaits the arrival of the train that bears the disfigured body of his daughter, and concluding shortly after her burial on the same day. With apparent casualness, the book manages to embrace all the events of more than a quarter century which bring Loftis, his estranged wife, and his mistress together for this tragic funeral. Styron's debt to the interior monologues of Joyce (especially in Peyton's final, frenzied, Molly Bloom–like soliloquy) and to Faulkner's experiments with time—most notably those in *The Sound and the Fury*—is obvious and tremendous. "I'm all for the complexity of Faulkner, but not for the confusion,"[5] Styron once commented, later extending those comments to include Joyce. That Styron is able to succeed so well and so personally with techniques that are associated with Faulkner and Joyce is in part, of course, a tribute to his enormous skill as a writer, but in part, too, the result of historical accident; for Styron is not essentially an experimenter, and therefore does not run the dangers which Joyce and Faulkner often ran of becoming overwhelmed by technique itself. Character and story are of immense importance to Styron, and his intense, fully drawn characters give the novel concentration and unity, just as such characters give substance to Faulkner's best work.

It is significant that Styron's greatest problem in writing this first novel should have been focused on "the progression of time," for even by arranging events on a merely temporal basis, man can begin to see in them some order or purpose. What Styron was forced to make orderly in this book was precisely what Geismar saw as the main challenge for the young writer: "the chaos that surrounds him." Emotionally, socially, and spiritually, *Lie Down in Darkness* is a painful chronicle of chaos, lightened only by the fact that the worst of the chaos is now relegated to the past, where it can be regarded with, if not calmness, at least objectivity.

The chief concern of this novel is with the efforts of Milton and Helen Loftis and their daughter Peyton to arrive at some sort of personal identification. At moments the book seems to verge on what might be classified as a Jungian integration of personality, except that psychoanalysis fails Peyton and would, we know, fail the other characters, too. For all his psychoanalytic inclinations, Styron tends to see his characters as figures from a Greek drama, as bared, tormented, and destined souls, in essence far removed from the aid of the analyst. That Peyton has an Electra complex and that much of the tension of the novel derives from repressed Oedipal desires is obvious, but it is equally obvious that all of the characters are somehow doomed to play out their fates without external interference. They do not, and Styron seems to say *cannot*, achieve any personality integration, can never reach full or complete identification because their incompleteness, like the writer's knowledge of "the human self," is part of the *status quo* of this first novel. Psychoanalysis can help to describe existing conditions, but it seems to offer no hope of resolving them. The fruitlessness of the quest for identification is most resounding in the case of Peyton, for she represents the promise of youth and sensibility; but rejected, unable to find the constant, Love, she continues a nymphomaniacal quest for peace and wholeness which is brought to an end only when she leaps, naked, briefly free, from the loft of a garment factory in Harlem. Unidentified for several days, her body is interred in a Potter's Field on Hart's Island, and even this temporary burial among unnamed dead suggests the horror of Peyton's frustrated quest for identity.

The first step toward the absurd is, according to Camus, the awakening that occurs when "the stage sets collapse" and man is forced to ask "Why?" It is then that he becomes conscious of the weary, enigmatic circles in which his life has run, and then that he has the chance to return gradually into the "chain" or to achieve a real awakening. It is at a somewhat dissipated but still youthful fifty years that Milton Loftis first comes to this absurd awakening: "At the age of fifty he was beginning to discover, with a sense of panic, that his whole life had been in the nature of a hangover, with faintly unpleasant pleasures being atoned for by the dull unalleviated pain of guilt" (*LDD*, 152). Suddenly Loftis knows himself to be a failure as a father, as a husband, and as a lawyer. He exists now in what Camus called "that weariness tinged with amazement."[6] "The stranger who at certain seconds comes to meet us in the mirror"[7] becomes for Loftis "a wasted, aging satyr" (*LDD*, 250), a mocking symbol of his hollow vanity. Loftis vacillates between a definitive awakening and being lulled back into the rhythmic chain of meaningless gestures from which he has only recently been aroused. His marriage is, perhaps, the most extreme example of the absurdity of his life, for he is in love with and married to a woman who is incapable not only of loving but even of being loved except in the make-believe, idealistic world of childhood which is kept alive for her in a demented daughter.

Beginning with consciousness of his failure as a husband, Loftis has made a primary absurd discovery, but it is the consequences of the absurd discovery which are of primary importance. For a year after the death of his retarded daughter, Loftis is reunited with his wife in something like a conventional marital relationship. He has totally rejected his mistress, and he even hopes that Helen may forget herself long enough to draw Peyton back into the family, for only Helen herself has the ultimate power to keep Peyton in the family circle or to drive her out. Loftis's intentions in this year of reconciliation are clearly opposed to reality. Helen and Peyton despise each other, partly because of their rivalry over Milton, partly because they are such wholly different creatures—Helen frigid and precise, Peyton sexual and flamboyant. Helen had had Maudie, the perpetual child, as the recipient of her own brand of sexless love, and Milton has had Peyton, has been stimulated by her sexuality, and has sought relief from sexual frustrations with his mistress, Dolly. It is inconceivable that the family, after so many years of harsh and agonizing separation, could suddenly draw together. By flaunting his intention against this reality, by refusing to be lulled to sleep again by alcohol and by the vulgar attentions of Dolly, Milton promises to emerge with something of the acuteness of the absurd hero; this promise is based not merely on the fact that Milton is involved in an absurd situation, but on the additional circumstance that he is aware of the absurdity. But when reality crashes down about him on the day Peyton returns home to be married, when he stands and watches the blood flow from the gouges which Peyton has made on Helen's cheeks, he reverts to alcohol and to Dolly, gladly sinking into a blurred mechanical chain and refusing to recognize any conflict in his life. After two years of this drugged existence, the stage sets collapse once more with the news of Peyton's suicide; Milton again rejects Dolly and pleads with Helen to take him back. They are standing with Carey Carr in the vestibule of the cemetery chapel waiting out a sudden rain storm. Loftis takes advantage of their refuge to draw Helen aside, and his pleading voice reaches Carey as "high, hysterical, tormented." Helen breaks away from Loftis and urges him not to make a scene. "'Scene! Scene!' Loftis shouted. 'Why, God damn you, don't you see what you're doing! With nothing left! Nothing! Nothing! Nothing!'" With a horror that causes him to moan to him-

self, "'Oh, my Lord, You shall never reveal Yourself'," Carey Carr
sees Loftis seize Helen and begin to choke her. "'God damn you!'
[Loftis] yelled. 'If I can't have . . . then you . . . nothing!'" (387–
388). The moment of violence ends as abruptly as it began, and
Loftis runs from the chapel in despair. Helen's final words echo
Milton's and express the meaninglessness and emptiness of their
lives: "'Nothing! Nothing! Nothing! Nothing!'" (389).

"The absurd is born," Camus says, of the "confrontation between the human need [for happiness and for reason] and the unreasonable silence of the world. This must be clung to because the
whole consequence of a life can depend on it. The irrational, the
human nostalgia, and the absurd that is born of their encounter—
these are the three characters in the drama that must necessarily
end with all the logic of which an existence is capable."[8] Milton
Loftis feels this longing and witnesses the dramatic confrontation
of his own needs with the unreasonable silence of the world, but he
lacks the strength to remain "awake" in the face of these contradic-
tions. His occasional isolated gestures against a life of chaos never
involve a thorough or sustained commitment.

Peyton, however, does achieve an awakening, and she is then
faced with the choice of suicide or recovery. She is too weakened to
struggle conclusively with the irrationality of the universe, and
since she cannot find a smooth, clean world like the inside of the
clock which she comes to worship, she has no choice but suicide.
Peyton has never really known the hypnotic rhythms of life which
lull Milton back to sleep, although she seeks them in the image of
the clock, knowing that she lacks the strength to come to grips
with the real world:

I went back to the windowsill and got the clock. I cupped my palms
around it, looking at the dots and hands, which shone with a clear green
light in the darkness: we have not been brought up right, I thought,
peering down into the alarm hole: there in the sunny grotto we could
coast among the bolts and springs and ordered, ticking wheels, riveted
to peace forever. Harry would like to know: rubies he'd love and cherish,
in that light they'd glow like the red hats of Breughel dancers. I could
hear the serene and steady whir, held it closer to my ear for the ticking, an unfitful, accomplished harmony—perfect, ordered, whole.
(LDD, 344–345)

Peyton is too sophisticated, knows too much of the inner self to be
able to escape through alcohol or sex, and when no other alternatives appear, she commits suicide.

Throughout *Lie Down in Darkness* there is a continuous stress on the return to childhood itself, as there is in much of the work of J. D. Salinger; this yearning for the experience of innocence may also be the attempt, neurotic or sentimental, to avoid coming to terms with the insuperable evils of the present. For Helen, Peyton, and even Loftis himself, recurrent urges toward the apparently uncomplicated world of childhood are efforts to avoid both the devastating complexities of adult life and—more importantly—the very absurdity of a loveless existence. The image of perfect innocence and uncomplicated love is given special vividness in the book by Maudie, whose "Mamadear" and "Pappadaddy" not only vividly recall the innocence of childhood, but also parody this innocence to a monstrous degree. Sitting in a Charlottesville hospital and waiting for Maudie's impending death, Helen tells Peyton and Loftis that Maudie "knows": "'I said, even if they don't know, well, Maudie knows, and that's enough. She knows! Want me to tell you about her, my dears?'" (217). Maudie had known how to love, and had actually been in love with a small, thin, half-Negro, half-Indian man who performed tricks for her. Although she had seen him only a few times, and then separated by a high fence, she could recognize love as a potential force. Helen revels in the idea of Maudie's knowledge, partly because of her intense desire that Maudie know some kind of happiness, but largely because the girl's love experience conformed to Helen's own romanticized, sexless view. Helen erred fatally in seeing Maudie's love as ideal and in failing to realize that an adult is incapable of living completely if such childhood perspectives are artificially retained.

What Styron has given the reader in this book is not a picture of an absurd man but rather a group of absurd situations: absurd marriage, absurd love, absurd death, brought into conjunction only through the passage of time. Helen, seeking order through the church, is frustrated by Carey Carr's primness and is aware that beneath his immaculate Virginia-Episcopal surface lies his own grief at the failure of personal revelation. Carey comments to his wife on the way to Peyton's wedding that a wedding ceremony "'is the symbolic affirmation of a moral order in the world'" (248), but the wedding itself, like all the Loftis reunions which begin with such high hopes, ends in a cataclysm of despair and violence. Loftis anticipates the wedding as a great victory, one which will somehow compensate for the uneventfulness of his life:

A man so unaccomplished, he reflected, might achieve as much as great men, give him patience and a speck of luck; though his road slopes off to a bitter sort of doom—and the wind, blustering down the night through chill acres of stars, suddenly made Loftis feel cold, and his life a chancey thing indeed—he has had his moment, a clock-tick of glory before the last descent. You know this man's fall: do you know his wrassling? *Bring home the bride again, bring home the triumph of our victory.* (260)

Like Sisyphus, Loftis is poised near the top of the hill, his shoulder bitten painfully by the enormous rock which he is attempting to lift, but unlike Sisyphus, he has reached such a point of decay that he is unable to "wrassle" it up even once.

The only figure in this novel who offers any real promise of completeness is Harry Miller, Peyton's Jewish husband. Harry is a painter, and the fierceness of his aesthetic intentions is suggested by the fact that he is able to create his most successful painting in the midst of Peyton's unfaithfulnesses and with the radio blaring the news of the atomic destruction of Nagasaki.

He was painting an old man. In grays, deep blues, an ancient monk or a rabbi lined and weathered, lifting proud, tragic eyes toward heaven; behind him were the ruins of a city, shattered, devastated, crumbled piles of concrete and stone that glowed from some half-hidden, rusty light, like the earth's last waning dusk. It was a landscape dead and forlorn yet retentive of some flowing, vagrant majesty, and against it the old man's eyes looked proudly upward, toward God perhaps, or perhaps just the dying sun. (374)

As she watches him paint, Peyton pleads for another chance, but Harry cannot understand the birds of guilt that torment Peyton and are driving her to her death. The picture we receive of Harry is never complete, but his speech to Peyton, recalled in her lengthy monologue, represents a major thematic climax: '

"There are a lot of things I'd like to talk about. Do you realize what the world's come to? Do you realize that the great American commonwealth just snuffed out one hundred thousand innocent lives this week? There was a time, you know, when I thought for some reason—maybe just to preserve your incomparable beauty—that I could spend my life catering to your needs, endure your suspicions and your mistrusts and all the rest, plus having to see you get laid in a fit of pique. I have other things to do. Remember that line you used to quote from the Bible, How long, Lord? or something—" "Remember how short my time is," I said. "Yes," he said. "Well, that's the way I feel. With your help I used to think I could go a long way, but you didn't help me. Now I'm on it alone. I don't know what good it'll do anyone but me, but I want to paint and paint and paint because I think that some agony is upon us. Call me a disillusioned innocent, a renegade Red, or whatever, I want to crush in my hands all that agony and make beauty come out, because that's all that's left, and I don't have much time—" (377)

Despite the heroic assertiveness of this statement, Harry Miller appears too infrequently to be the hero of the novel, although Styron clearly regards him as a symbol of hope. Since the figure of Harry is incomplete, the hope he offers cannot triumph over the despairing cries of "Nothing!" which Milton and Helen have uttered. There is no room in *Lie Down in Darkness* for the kind of positive, creative force which Harry represents. In sketching the heroic outlines of Harry's vision, Styron seems to be suggesting the direction which a later novel might take; it is, significantly, another painter who rises to tragic insight as the absurd hero of Styron's third book, *Set This House on Fire*.

Styron's second book, *The Long March*, was originally published in *Discovery* magazine. There is undoubtedly more than a passing note of subjective protest in this novella, for its indictment of the authoritarianism of military life followed shortly after Styron was himself recalled to the Marines. Stylistically, *The Long March* is in almost total contrast to *Lie Down in Darkness*. The book is a vivid and often savage trajectory covering approximately twenty-four hours in the life of a "peace-time" Marine company. Its central figure is Captain Mannix, a hulking Jew from Brooklyn, who finds first that he is too old to be a Marine but finally comes to wonder whether he could ever be anything else. A concentrated treatment of action and character provides emphasis for the day's two major events: the explosion of short rounds which causes the death of eight young recruits and the maiming of fifteen more, and the brutal, thirty-six–mile forced march which H&S Company undertakes.

Mannix's company was composed largely of men who had been in civilian life for six years and were recalled during the Korean War. Untrained, soft, they were in no condition for a forced march of any length. Colonel Templeton, however, demanded the march as proof of his battalion's readiness, and especially as a reminder to Mannix and his company that they were, above all else, Marines. The painful march through a hot Carolina night and morning, like the senseless death and crippling which occur when old ammunition is fired, is simply an extreme dramatic illustration of the "never-endingness of war" (LM, 420). Mannix and Culver, the latter being a kind of persona for Styron, have both known what they thought to be an enduring peace, but both have now learned that war is, after all, the human condition. Culver felt that "all of his life he had yearned for something that was as fleeting and incommunicable, in its beauty, as that one bar of music he remembered, or those lovely girls with their ever joyful, ever sprightly dance on some far and fantastic lawn" (419). Stripped of their illusions, Mannix and Culver nonetheless cling to something more fundamental, a vision of themselves. It is not as members of H&S Company or as Marines that they struggle to complete the long march, but as men who refuse to be intimidated by what they regard as a senseless authority. War has become, for the time at least, the reality of their lives, and with the last ounce of strength they cling to that intention which opposes the notion that war should be never-ending.

The Long March offers a bleak panorama, and at each turn Styron reminds his reader that this world whose aim is to keep alive the sufferings of war is, in fact, a world of absurdity. Unlike such professional Marines as Major Lawrence, Mannix refuses to be lulled to sleep by this world but determines instead to fight, regardless of the personal consequences. Mannix knows, as the true absurd hero always knows, that he has virtually no chance for victory, but he must be true to his intentions: "Born into a generation of conformists, even Mannix (so Culver sensed) was aware that his gestures were not symbolic, but individual, therefore hopeless, maybe even absurd, and that he was trapped like all of them in a predicament which one personal insurrection could, if anything, only make worse" (388). Challenging the absurd universe with such intensity and determination, Mannix becomes a true rebel, and as Camus emphasizes, "In every act of rebellion, the rebel simultaneously experiences a feeling of revulsion at the infringement of his rights and a complete and spontaneous loyalty to certain aspects of himself."[9] Mannix, like Camus's rebel, is prepared to support this rebellion precisely because he has been driven to the point where his most important loyalty—his loyalty to himself—has been challenged:

No, perhaps Mannix wasn't a hero, any more than the rest of them, caught up by wars in which, decade by half-decade, the combatant served peonage to the telephone and the radar and the thunderjet—a horde of cunningly designed, and therefore often treacherous, machines. But Mannix had suffered once, that "once" being, in his own words, "once too goddam many, Jack." And his own particular suffering had made him angry, had given him an acute, if cynical, perception about their renewed bondage, and a keen nose for the winds that threatened to blow up out of the oppressive weather of their surroundings and sweep them all into violence. And he made Culver uneasy. His discontent was not merely peevish; it was rocklike and rebellious, and thus this discontent seemed to Culver to be at once brave and somehow full of peril. (*LM*, 383)

The absurdity of the mock war maneuvers in which these Marines are engaged—"this new world of frigid nights and blazing noons, of disorder and movement and fanciful pursuit" (378)—reaches a dramatic climax in the march itself, one longer and more strenuous than most severe marches in actual wartime. Mannix's determination to complete the march and to drive his men to complete it as well is simply his way of scorning, through a kind of rebellion in reverse, the world which the Colonel represents. As the Colonel pushes out at the head of the vicious march, there comes from the rear the voice of the Captain, which reaches Culver as a huge force "dominating the night" (403).

Maxwell Geismar has called *The Long March* "a tour de force on the side of the angels, so to speak, and against the demons of industrial, scientific, and militaristic twentieth-century American life."[10] Certainly the movement from Milton Loftis's tentative, febrile gropings after rebellion (and his return to Helen is also a kind of "rebellion in reverse") to Captain Mannix's limited but successful rebellion is a very great step. In *The Long March* Styron demonstrated his ability to do more than simply enumerate the absurdities of the world; he suggested the possibility of a character who is capable of rising up against them. In *Set This House on Fire* Styron was to extend his view of the rebel and to place him in a background of stylistic and thematic richness comparable to that of *Lie Down in Darkness*.

In an article written for *Nation* in 1953 William Styron noted his peculiar inability to enjoy "practically any visually artistic representation": "I think this blindness of mine, though, has had its worthy effects, for if it has helped to keep me from understanding the more beautiful things about Europe it has also conspired with a sort of innate and provincial aloofness in my nature to make me more conscious of my *modern* environment, and self-consciously aware of my emotions as an American within that environment."[11] That Styron has italicized the word modern becomes particularly significant in light of the dramatically affirmative conclusion of *Set This House on Fire*. Again Styron has attempted to highlight the grotesqueries and frustrations of the contemporary environment, but in this novel he finds a unity and order infinitely more significant than the mere order of time which emerged from *Lie Down in Darkness*.

The very title of Styron's third book—and especially the source of the title—suggests the change which had come in his philosophical point of view. Both Peyton and Loftis had chosen to lie down in darkness, while Cass Kinsolving, his body shaken by fires and fevers, learns that such fires are preferable to exile from whatever power rules the moral universe. Thus, the fire of purgation cancels that of destruction and self-destruction, for as in T. S. Eliot's *Four Quartets* there is only one "discharge" from hatred and self-pity: "The only hope, or else despair / Lies in the choice of pyre or pyre— / To be redeemed from fire by fire." Styron took the title for his first novel from Browne's "Urn Burial"; for *Set This House on Fire* he went to Donne's sermon "To the Earle of Carlile, and his Company, at Sion," and specifically to a passage suggesting the horror of separation from God. Both metaphysicals, Browne and Donne had in common the interest in exploring experience by way of the intellectual excitements and preoccupations of their day. Despite their many resemblances, perhaps most striking in any comparison of Donne and Browne is the contrast in their prose styles and in the attitudes which those styles suggest. In Browne's prose the balance of the words and clauses, the leisurely spacing and punctuation, induce a slow, relaxed rhythm. The effect is to make the reader curious as to what might follow—but not excited, and the rhythms create neither pressure nor urgency. In contrast it is often difficult to cut across the constant jet of thought in Donne's prose; clause springs from clause and sentence from sentence with a complex criss-cross and overlay of ideas which demands a continual reference back and catching up with the sense. There is a similar contrast between the prose styles of *Lie Down in Darkness* and *Set This House on Fire*. In the former book Styron was largely concerned with a somewhat static enumeration and articulation of the various absurdities of modern life, while in the latter his involvement is direct and energetic. The two novels reflect stylistically the different impulses from which they were written. In *Lie Down in Darkness* Styron avoided any passionate moral commitment, but in *Set This House on Fire* his commitment was specifically and passionately an affirmation, through the attempted creation of a tragic hero, of the order of the universe.

In *Set This House on Fire*, as in his first two books, Styron has given considerable time to establishing the absurdity of the environment in which his characters are placed. Like his earlier work, this novel suggests an environment dominated by a profound desuetude of order and value, and again the action centers on the events of a single day. Unlike the day described in *Lie Down in Darkness*, that in *Set This House on Fire* does not simply *centralize* what would otherwise be the chaotic action of the book, but contains the *central* action of the novel. *Set This House on Fire* opens, several years after the tragic events which occurred in Sambuco, Italy, with the reminiscences of Peter Leverett, the fairly detached observer of the results of the two acts of horror which occurred on that day. Leverett serves much the same function in the novel that Nick Carraway served in *The Great Gatsby*, that of synthesizer and commentator. He does not, as did Nick, tell the story solely through his own reminiscences (the story is so much bigger and more complex that a single-narrator retelling would be virtually impossible), but he does provide the catalyst which induces Cass Kinsolving to fill in the gaps in his own knowledge of that day in Sambuco and offer a passive but critical commentary on the other characters. Peter Leverett further resembles Carraway in that he represents to some degree the older values of rural America and remains the only uncorrupted male character in the book.

Remembering, even with only the most vague knowledge, the events that had turned his day in Sambuco into one of almost unrelieved horror, Peter Leverett is tortured by dreams:

One of them especially I remember; like most fierce nightmares it had the habit of coming back again and again. In this one I was in a house somewhere, trying to sleep; it was dead of night, wintry and storming. Suddenly I heard a noise at the window, a sinister sound, distinct from the tumult of the rain and the wind. I looked outside and saw a shadow— the figure of someone who moved, an indefinite shape, a prowler whose dark form slunk toward me menacingly. Panicky, I reached for the telephone, to call the friend who lived nearby (my best, my last, dearest friend; nightmares deal in superlatives and magnitudes); *he*, somehow, I knew, was the only one dear enough, close enough, to help me. But there was no answer to all my frantic ringing. Then, putting the phone down, I heard a *tap-tap-tap*ping at the window and turned to see—bared with the malignity of a fiend behind the streaming glass—the baleful, murderous face of that self-same friend. (*STHF*, 5–6)

This first note of horror which the book strikes comes like a fearful prelude to the story, gothicly foreshadowing the violence which follows. Leverett knows that he will be haunted by such dreams until and unless he is able to find some order within the chaos of his day in Sambuco, and especially in the almost surrealistic episodes which occurred on the day of his arrival. He is fully confident that such an order exists if only he can find its key. Motivated by the desire to determine this order and to locate the moral responsibility for two inadequately related acts of violence, Peter Leverett journeys south, stopping briefly in Virginia, the source of those "older values" which he represents. His intention at this time is to visit Cass Kinsolving, the only person alive who might help him piece out a complete story: his stop is significant as an almost ritualistic preparation for the ordeal of discovery he is soon to undergo with Cass Kinsolving. As he prepares to leave Virginia, Peter thinks:

In times of stress and threat, I've heard it said, in times of terror and alarms, of silence and clinging, people tend to hold on to the past, even to imitate it: taking on old fashions and humming old songs, seeking out historic scenes and reliving old ancestral wars, in an effort to forget both the lack-luster present and a future too weird and horrible to ponder. Perhaps one of the reasons we Americans are so exceptionally nervous and driven is that our past is effaced almost before it is made present; in our search for old avatars to contemplate we find only ghosts, whispers, shadows: almost nothing remains for us to feel or seem or to absorb our longing. That evening I was touched to the heart: by my father's sweetness and decency and rage, but also by whatever it was within me— within life itself, it seemed so intense—that I knew to be irretrievably lost. Estranged from myself and from my time, dwelling neither in the destroyed past nor in the fantastic and incomprehensible present, I knew that I must find the answer to at least several things before taking hold of myself and getting on with the job. (18–19)

These thoughts, provoked by the idea of people who "tend to hold on to the past," recall John Updike's descriptions of the poorhouse inmates who struggle to maintain something of value in their lives by clinging to mementos of the American past.

From Leverett's point of view the disintegration of all apparent order began on the day he left Rome for a visit with his wealthy, oversexed, arrogant, but somehow gracious friend, Mason Flagg, whose name is perhaps suggestive of his flamboyant manner. Leverett dates the events which occur in Sambuco from the moment he left Rome. Setting out at night, he is forced to sleep in his car, fighting intense heat and swarms of mosquitoes. Later, almost driven off the road by a speeding Alfa Romeo, Leverett himself begins to speed, and he is doing over sixty miles an hour when he smashes into a motorscooter bearing a one-eyed, accident-prone Italian peasant. After being upbraided by the peasant's mother for wartime raping, stealing, bombing, and looting, Leverett, suffering from extreme nervous exhaustion, proceeds toward Sambuco in his wrecked car. The speedy building up of absurd incidents creates a tone of high comedy which finally becomes hysteria and ends only after sounding a note of total horror.

When Leverett reaches Sambuco, after a dreamlike encounter with Cass and his wife, it is only to blunder into the apparently serene village square to find himself in the middle of a movie set, intimidated by arc lights and cameras and outraged directors. Styron has achieved here a masterful comic tone, and with it has established the absurdity of this environment by introducing into the beautiful ancient village a movie crew engaged in the filming, in modern dress and with numerous unsuccessful scripts, of a costume novel about Beatrice Cenci. Assembled to work on the film is perhaps the greatest single collection of neurotics since Nathanael West's *Day of the Locust*. The Hollywood phantasmagoria offered Styron, as it offered West, a kind of microcosm of the world's distortions and illusions; and the description of the half-American, half-Italian cast brought together for the movie creates the nightmarish humor of the surrealist jokesmith without necessitating the manipulation of environment which surrealistic imagery usually presupposes.

It is Cass Kinsolving who forms the dramatic center of this novel, and Cass's only involvement with the movie crew is in the fact that Mason Flagg forces him to perform disgusting pantomimes for their amusement. Like John Updike's "Rabbit," Cass is continually running. Slotkin, a "kindly old Navy brain doctor," once told him, "'You will be running all your life'" (314). What Cass is running after is something "which had indeed flowed right on out of me, and which to save my very life I knew I had to recapture" (278). On the day he gratefully surrendered his chastity to a teen-age religious fanatic and nymphomaniac, she had referred to his orgasm as the loss of the "divine spirit"; Cass later accepts her description as one of particular significance. Commitment to an absurd marriage with a blissfully irresponsible, totally disorganized, and wholly devout Catholic (Cass comes from a staunch Episcopal family) hardly seems to have aided his search, and further agonized by his failures as a painter, Cass has become an alcoholic and acquired the added tortures of an ulcer. Cass had caught Mason Flagg in what was perhaps the only painful faux pas of his career, and the wealthy American embarked with such severity on a program of degrading and dehumanizing the young painter that he threatened to destroy him completely.

Largely as a result of Flagg's tortures, Cass has lost almost all touch with reality, a loss which would have been complete were it not for his intense love for an Italian peasant, Francesca, and his friendship with a semi-Fascist policeman, Luigi. It is chiefly Luigi who reminds Cass of his responsibilities—not necessarily to his family—but to himself as a man and, consequently, to life itself. Luigi's role in the novel and his emphasis on "force" are closely parallel to those of Tothero in *Rabbit, Run*. Trying to halt Cass's course of alcoholic annihilation, Luigi argues:

"I'm not a religious man . . . , and this you well know. However, I studied among the humanist philosophers—the Frenchman Montaigne, Croce, the Greek Plato, not to speak, of course, of Gabriele D'Annunzio—and if there's one thing of the highest value I've discovered, it is simply this: that the primary moral sin is self-destruction—the wish for death which you so painfully and obviously manifest. I exclude madness, of course. The single good is respect for the force of life. Have you not pictured to yourself the whole horrible vista of eternity? I've told you all this before, Cass. The absolute blankness, *il niente, la nullità*, stretching out for ever and ever, the pit of darkness which you are hurling yourself into, the nothingness, the void, the oblivion? Yet are you unable to see that although this in itself is awful, it is nothing to the moral sin you commit by willing yourself *out* of that life force . . ." (195–196)

Luigi's statement that "the primary moral sin is self-destruction" might almost have been taken from the pages of Camus's *Myth of Sisyphus*, for Camus's entire argument in that essay is eventually concerned with the problem of suicide and the subsequent affirmation of life itself. Sisyphus, it should be remembered, was sentenced to his unending task precisely because of his persistent commitment to life. Since Cass has lost virtually everything of value and since life appears to him to be hopeless, meaningless, and absurd, he has no desire to live; but through his very fall he is to realize the meaning of life, and through Luigi's intervention he will be given the chance to live it.

It is in Sambuco that Cass first begins to have the "visions" which will eventually assist him in rising to the heights of an absurd hero. The first of these visions is recorded in a diary kept fitfully during his early days in Sambuco: "'What saves me in the last analysis I have no way of telling. Sometimes the sensation I have that I am 2 persons & by that I mean the man of my dreams and the man who walks in daylight is so strong and frightening that at times I am actually scared to look into a mirror for fear of seeing some face that I have never seen before'" (361). This "stranger who at certain seconds comes to meet us in the mirror"[12] later reappears to Cass: "Then—wonder of wonders—he had withdrawn from himself. Standing aside, clammy and wet with horror, he saw his other self, naked now, step into the shower and, and with the numb transfixed look of one already dead, turn on all the faucets full blast" (STHF, 368). The "other self" has actually turned on jets of gas. This dream, like the vision of horror in the mirror, comes to Cass immediately before he meets Mason Flagg, and as Flagg begins to dominate him there is doubt that the visions will ever be productive of true rebellion; in fact, it is only the most severe circumstances which shake Cass out of the chain into which he has sunk. Without Luigi, he would long before have been crushed by the weight of his desire for "'a long long spell of darkness'":

He recovered himself momentarily, focusing upon me his hot drowned eyes. "Yes, I'll tell you how you can help old Cass," he said somberly. "Now I'll tell you, my bleeding dark angel. Fetch him the machine, fetch him the wherewithal—a dagger, see, a dirk, well honed around the edges—and bring it here, and place it on his breastbone, and then with all your muscle drive it to the core." He paused, swaying slightly from side to side, never removing his gaze from my face. "No bullshit, Pete. I've got a lust to be gone from this place. Make me up a nice potion, see? Make it up out of all these bitter-tasting, deadly things and pour it down my gullet. Ole Cass has had a hard day. He's gone the full stretch and his head aches and his legs are weary, and there's no more weeping in him." He held out his arms. "These limbs are plumb wore out. Look at them, boy. Look how they shake and tremble! What was they made for, I ast you. To wrap lovely ladies about? To make monuments? To enfold within them all the beauty of the world? Nossir! They was made to destroy and now they are plumb wore out, and my head aches, and I yearn for a long long spell of darkness." (238)

Camus stated that his aim in examining the absurd was ". . . to shed light upon the step taken by the mind when, starting from a philosophy of the world's lack of meaning, it ends up by finding a meaning and depth in it. The most touching of those steps is religious in essence; it becomes obvious in the theme of the irrational. But the most paradoxical and most significant is certainly the one that attributes rattonal reasons to a world it originally imagined as devoid of any guiding principle."[13] Cass Kinsolving's world was devoid of any guiding principle from the moment Mason Flagg came to Sambuco and tossed him the first bottle of whiskey—a bottle that was to enslave him; but even as he is losing all perspective, Cass is laying a firm basis for its re-establishment through his love for the peasant girl Francesca. He has walked with her back into the primitive, timeless valley where she was born, and has tried to save the life of her tubercular father. Helping Michele has given Cass something to live for, and while his mind is still too tormented to be able to realize fully the significance of this experience, the seeds of self-regeneration are planted:

On some wet black shore, foul with the blackness of death's gulf, he was searching for an answer and a key. In words whose meaning he did not know he called out through the gloom, and the echoed sound came back to him as if spoken in an outlandish tongue. Somewhere, he knew, there was light but like a shifting phantom it eluded him; voiceless, he strove to give voice to the cry which now, too late, awakening, he knew: "Rise up, Michele, rise up and walk!" he roared. And for the briefest space of time, between dark and light, he thought he saw the man, healed now, cured, staunch and upright, striding toward him. *O rise up Michele, my brother, rise!* (STHF, 425)

Cass knows that he has tried to give Michele something he does not really possess himself, that in rejecting life he has lessened his own ability to give life to others, and he thinks with sudden horror, "Michele will die because I have not given. Which now explains a lot . . . hell is not giving" (453).

Cass's nostalgia, his desire to give, and his blind rage for justice will, however, finally combine to cause him to break out of the weary chains in which Mason has bound him. "Every act of rebellion expresses a nostalgia for innocence and an appeal to the essence of being. But one day nostalgia takes up arms and assumes the responsibility of total guilt; in other words, adopts murder and violence."[14] Circumstances conspire to make all of Cass's "stage sets" collapse, and finally, jarred from his alcoholic chrysalis, he is able to perform a conscious, overt act in the name of order and value. Ironically, this act—the murder of Mason Flagg—is a profound moral wrong—not just because Cass has misjudged circumstances, but because he has a sudden realization of Flagg's humanness, and through that an insight into the meaning of life.

While the absurd hero may take many forms, underlying them all is the fundamental struggle with environment—the refusal to surrender personal ethics to environmental pressures. The tragic hero is perhaps the most intense example of the absurd, for his opposition is directed against the moral order of the universe itself. His "disproportion," while a strong affirmation of individual will, is nonetheless of such a nature that, at some point, it will be broken. This breaking or "fall" of the tragic hero is in itself an affirmation of the *logos* of the universe, of the fact that the world is governed by "rational reasons." Life may appear to be cruel to the tragic hero, but this apparent cruelty is necessary to affirm the existence of moral cause and effect in the world. In the fate of the tragic hero a pattern is given to experience, and that pattern is visible not alone to the hero himself, but also to the observer of his fall. The optimism inherent in tragedy is the result of this affirmation of a moral order and the assertion that man has not only sufficient power to challenge that order but sufficient nobility to achieve wisdom through his fall. It is absurd to come into collision with the universal law of righteousness (or, like Ahab, with the universal law of unrighteousness), but it is also the height of heroism. Perhaps the most significant reason for the failure of modern authors to create tragedy in its classical fullness is simply that tragedy demands for its full implementation a belief in a moral order superior to the individual. Without such a belief the ultimate tragic creation, the tragic hero, is inconceivable. In *Set This House on Fire* Styron has perhaps come closer than any other modern author to actualizing this creation.

One of the earliest facts which we learn about Cass is that he is a psychotic, dismissed uncured from a Navy hospital. He is frequently violent in public, he abuses his family, and he goes through the ritual of degrading songs and gestures whenever Mason Flagg demands this "payment." We also learn near the beginning of the novel that upon his discharge from the hospital Cass was presented with "a two-volume edition of Greek drama" (129). Cass refers at length to *Oedipus*, and in the course of the evening preceding his murder of Mason he quotes at length from the tragedy. Such passages alone suggest that Cass is meant to be compared to a classical tragic hero, and on the brink of his "fall" he seems to grasp the drama which he is now destined to play out:

"Hold on! Let me tell you what we'll do. Together you and me we'll pull a Prometheus on 'em. We'll bring back tragedy to the land of the Pepsi-Cola and the peanut brittle and the Modess Because. That's what we'll do, by God! And we'll make the ignorant little buggers like it. No more popcorn, no more dreamboats, no more Donald Ducks, no more wet dreams in the mezzanine. *Tragedy*, by God, that's what we'll give 'em! Something to stiffen their spines and firm up their joints and clean out their tiny little souls. What'll you have? *Ajax? Alcestis? Electra? Iphigenia? Hoo*-boy!" Once more his hand plunged into the neck of his T-shirt. "'I would not be the murderer of my mother, and of thee too. Sufficient is her blood. No, I will share my fortune, live with thee, or with thee die: to Argos I will lead thee . . .'" (118–119)

What Cass does not know at this time, but what he will learn as a participant in the tragedy of the following day, is a fundamental lesson of all tragedy: ". . . the harder you kite upward like that the harder you hit the ground when you fall" (267).

Cass, like Updike's Rabbit, had not only the opportunity but also the ability to become "a good family man, striving for the sunny ideal of *mens sana*," but he rejected this alternative in deference to "that necessary part of the self which saw the world with passion and recklessness, and which had to be flayed and exacerbated and even maddened to retain its vision" (296–297). It is because of this passion and recklessness that Cass finds himself in a situation in which he must sin, albeit unwittingly. W. H. Auden has argued that the tragic "situation" in which a character appears to have no choice but to sin is actually "a sign that he is guilty of another sin of hybris, an overweening self-confidence which makes him believe that he, with all his *arete*, is a god who cannot be made to suffer." Perhaps the most common instance of hybris is man's failure to recognize human limitations, in trying to operate with presumably complete knowledge and control when, of course, the effects of his actions can never be known in their entirety. Oedipus presumes to act as though he could totally control the results of his actions, and his final symbolic blinding is a recognition of his limitations, of what the Greeks would have recognized as *ate*.

Presuming to be godlike, the tragic hero often takes upon himself the responsibility of becoming a judge. Such was Oedipus' impetuous attack on his own father. Cass, too, demonstrates a lack of control, and we have, in his participation as a boy in the destruction of the Negro cabin, an example of the kind of hybris which we see when Oedipus strikes his father. Cass does not appear to know what made him participate in the willful destruction of all which this family owned or revered, but he suggests it in his observation that "all the clichés and shibboleths I'd been brought up with came rolling back—a nigger wasn't much more than an animal anyway" (378). It is the overweening, blind pride of a white Southerner which makes him strike the face of the humanistic moral universe. The tragic hero presumes to act like a god, sitting in judgment as Cass had done in his treatment of the Negro. Cass must bear the guilt and shame of this episode, must be half-smothered for his blind violation, and he later notes to Peter Leverett that "this figured in what happened to me there in Sambuco" (379). The essential, final ingredient of the tragic hero is that he must realize his own blindness, his own limitations, and accept the obligations of his guilt. At the point of Cass's recognition Styron becomes particularly specific:

Cass fell silent again. Then he said: "But to kill a man, even in hatred, even in revenge, is like an amputation. Though this man may have done you the foulest injustice in the world, when you have killed him you have removed a part of yourself forever. For here was so-and-so. Here was some swine, some blackguard, some devil. But what made him tick? What made him do the things he did? What was his history? What went on in his mind? What, if you had let him live, would he have become? Would he have stayed a swine, unregenerate to the end? Or would he have become a better man? Maybe he could have imparted to you some secrets. You do not know. You have acted the role of God, you have judged him and condemned him. And by condemning him, by killing him, all the answers to those questions pass with him into oblivion. Only *you* remain—shorn of all that knowledge, and with as much pain as if somehow you had been dismembered. It is a pain that will stay with you as long as you live . . ." (446)

It is through Peter Leverett that the scene in Sambuco is first set for tragedy. The macabre experiences of his trip lend the feeling of a surrealistic dreamscape to his arrival. The deserted square almost assumes the character of a stage awaiting its actors, and the personalities of the "movie folk clustered beneath the lights" (57), as they unfold in the following chapters, help to reaffirm the feeling that we are watching something performed in the theatre. From the moment of Leverett's arrival at Mason's palace, when he observes that "a confusing amber light played over the scene" (99) until his horrified viewing of the "act" that Cass performs for Mason, this theatrical feeling becomes increasingly frenzied and helps to prepare the reader for the scenes which follow.

Mason Flagg has raped Francesca, the graceful peasant girl who represents for Cass all the beauty and value which have gone out of his life. Cass knows of the rape and has determined to be revenged on Flagg, but before he can formulate a plan he learns that Francesca has been raped a second time, and that this time she has also been hideously, fatally mutilated. Never questioning Mason's guilt, Cass tracks and brutally murders the young American dilettante. This "justice" is executed against a classical setting: before a ruined villa with a "sagging façade and blasted columns" (463), a kind of temple bearing the inscription *DUM SPIRO SPERO*, the adopted

motto of Cass's home state, South Carolina. As if to illustrate and
support the argument of tragedy, Styron repeatedly suggests classical episodes and settings. Earlier in the novel, when Cass considered ways of breaking free of Mason, he had looked out to sea and
observed "above Salerno, aloft, unbelievably high in space . . . a
mist, a churning rack of cloud, terrible and only faintly discerned,
as of the smoke from remote cities sacked and aflame: he gave a
stir, touched on the shoulder by an unseen, unknowable hand"
(406).

The tragedy that takes place in Sambuco first comes to Leverett
through a series of wailing cries similar to those which might be
made by the chorus in a Greek play. The first words of explanation
which he hears are "'Quelle horreur! . . . Quelle tragedie'" (219).
Pressed for more details, the money-conscious hotel owner, Wind-
gasser, can only mutter, "'Overpowering twagedy, my God. It's
like the *Gweeks*, I tell you, but far worse!'" (220). Describing the
crowded square into which he runs, Leverett notes that "A squad
of carabinieri entered in a riot truck, stage right . . ." (221), and
when the horrifying events of the day are over, Cass comments to
Leverett, "*Exeunt omnes*. Exit the whole lousy bunch" (239).
Thus, as seen through Leverett's eyes, the tragedy which occurs in
Sambuco observes the unities of time, place, and action; it constitutes, in fact, a kind of play within the novel.

As a modern version of the tragic hero Cass has not challenged
the authority of a god or a group of gods, but he has challenged the
purposive ordering of the universe in which right action is somehow rewarded and wrong action punished, if only within the con-
fines of the individual conscience. Like Camus himself, Styron
avoids commitment on words like "god," but also like Camus he is
finally able to maintain that the world, which appears to lack all
vestiges of order, is in fact governed by "rational reasons." Camus
stated that the absurd does not lead to God because "the absurd is
sin without God."[15] What Camus undoubtedly intended to assert
was that the sense of sin must come from within, not from some set
of traditional rules handed down from an abstract higher power.
Perhaps it is sufficient to say that what Cass violates is Rabbit Angstrom's "something out there that wants me to find it." Important
to the creation of the modern tragic hero, as it is to the modern
saint, is the emphasis that there is, after all, *something* out there,
some convergence of individual consciousness in the formation of
transcendent values, even though none of the traditional defini-
tions of that "something" are acceptable. In terms of Cass's own

particular vision we might describe it as the humanistic order of the universe; even so, Cass must discover and shoulder his own sin, for there is no authority dictating punishment—least of all is there a threat of punishment after death. Even at the moment of killing Flagg, Cass is aware of his violation of this humanistic order as he had not been aware at the time of the destruction of the Negro cabin:

> Perhaps it was then that he drew back, understanding where he was, and what he had done. He does not recall. Perhaps it was only the "Doll-baby," echoing belatedly in his mind, that caused him to halt and look down and see that the pale dead face, which was so soft and boyish, and in death as in life so tormented, might be the face of almost anything, but was not the face of a killer.
>
> *Children!* he thought, standing erect over the twitching body. *Children! My Christ! All of us!*
>
> Then in his last grief and rage he wrestled Mason's body to the parapet, and wearily heaved it up in his arms and kept it for a moment close to his breast. And then he hurled it into the void. (*STHF*, 464–465)

What Cass learns after the murder is that Mason Flagg had not attacked and mutilated Francesca on the path outside the village, but that this atrocity was committed by Saverio, the village idiot who had earlier been apprehended in an almost identical crime. The authorities, however, are convinced that Flagg committed suicide after attacking Francesca; only Cass and his soul mate Luigi know the truth. In desperation Cass, who has had no use for religion, turns to a priest with the words, "Help me." The priest cannot help him any more than Slotkin, the psychiatrist to whom Cass once literally prayed, can help him to resolve this moral dilemma. Only the fundamentally humanistic Luigi can assist Cass by convincing him that he must, in order to achieve knowledge, not wallow in his guilt, but expiate it and eventually defeat it by living. Cass "'had come to the end of the road and had found there nothing at all. There was nothing. There was a nullity in the universe so great as to encompass and drown the universe itself. The value of a man's life was nothing, and his destiny nothingness'" (489). Despite this bitter pronouncement, Cass still feels "that old vast gnawing hunger," a hunger for order and meaning in the face of a meaningless universe. Luigi admonishes Cass to expiate his guilt, refusing him the right to sin in his guilt by cultivating it. He urges that Cass must, like Oedipus, become a penitent in life. Cass's choice now is the choice between suicide and life which Camus poses in *The Myth of Sisyphus*, and Cass chooses life.

Again there is the vagueness in terms and the refusal to accept traditional formulas characteristic of all the novelists considered in this study, but there is no doubt that the author sees Cass possessed of a kind of vision for which he had only groped tentatively before his "fall":

> "Now I suppose I should tell you that through some sort of suffering I had reached grace, and how at that moment I knew it, but this would not be true, because at that moment I didn't really know what I had reached or found. I wish I could tell you that I had found some belief, some rock, and that here on this rock anything might prevail—that here madness might become reason, and grief joy, and no yes. And even death itself death no longer, but a resurrection.
> "But to be truthful, you see, I can only tell you this: that as for being and nothingness, the one thing I did know was that to choose between them was simply to choose being, not for the sake of being, or even the love of being, much less the desire to be forever—but in the hope of being what I could be for a time. This would be an ecstasy." (500–501)

Styron sees Cass as a modern Oedipus, and Camus saw Oedipus as an example of the absurd man:

> Happiness and the absurd are two sons of the same earth. They are inseparable. It would be a mistake to say that happiness springs from the absurd discovery. It happens as well that the feeling of the absurd springs from happiness. "I conclude that all is well," says Oedipus, and that remark is sacred. It echoes in the wild and limited universe of man. It teaches that all is not, has not been exhausted. It drives out of this world a god who had come into it with dissatisfaction and a preference for futile sufferings. It makes of fate a human matter, which must be settled among men.[16]

"Oedipus gives," Camus says, "the recipe for the absurd victory," and suggesting the link between the classical Oedipus and Oedipus as the absurd hero, he adds, "Ancient wisdom confirms modern heroism."[17]

If the above speech, in which Cass announces his choice of being, makes no affirmation of the idea of knowledge, it does suggest hope that he will eventually achieve something like knowledge. Indeed he seems to demonstrate such an acquisition in one of the two letters appended to the novel, in which he writes, "Who was it in Lear who said ripeness is all. I forget, but he was right" (STHF, 506). As an artist he has turned social critic out of a desire for reform, and he thus demonstrates the increasing tendency of the existential hero to return to society. In triumphing over himself, in defeating his sense of guilt, in establishing a love for humanity, Cass has achieved a singular victory, and it is necessary to think of him as Camus intended that we think of Sisyphus, as "happy."

Despite its variations in setting and tone, Styron's work is consistently concerned with a rebel-hero outraged by the falseness, purposelessness, corruption, and banality of his society. With increasing resilience and ingenuity, those heroes do battle with the here-and-now, with the seemingly implacable *status quo* which prejudges their resistance as an aberration; hence, their opposition is fundamentally absurd, for the victory they seek will never be validated by the ruling establishment, whether it consist of middle-class propriety, the Marine Corps, or the shibboleths of nineteenth-century slaveocracy. Throughout Styron's writings we encounter tortured, divided characters yearning to be whole; increasingly, they learn the courage to be, to assert their humanness in the face of organizational absurdity. Styron's art validates this quixotic heroism of assertion, even though the hero's resistance typically creates fresh confusion. Peyton Loftis's anguished search for order ends in suicide, and the dogged Mannix suffers comic "exposure" at the end of his heroic march; only Cass moves beyond tragic recognition toward a new wholeness and ripeness, thus preparing a transition for Styron's most radical portrayal of the rebel-hero in *The Confessions of Nat Turner*.

Beneath the calm, affluent, often idyllic exterior which Styron's world characteristically projects, there exists a corrosive potential for violence—perhaps most aptly and awfully symbolized by the misfiring mortar shells in *The Long March*: "One noon, in the blaze of a cloudless Carolina summer, what was left of eight dead boys lay strewn about the landscape, among the poison ivy and the pine needles and loblolly saplings" (*LM*, 361). More poignantly than any other episode in Styron's writings, this senseless slaughter illustrates what Captain Mannix comes to recognize as the "never-endingness of war" (420), a persistent metaphor in Styron's writings for the condition of man. In *Lie Down in Darkness* Peyton leaps to her death on the day of the bombing of Nagasaki; in *The Long March* the Korean War is viewed as only another of an unbroken series of purposeless military conflicts; in *Set This House on Fire* Cass traces his own self-destructive impulses to the experiences in World War II which drove him to a psychiatric ward; military imagery and allusions to Biblical wars anticipate the bloody slave uprising in *The Confessions of Nat Turner*; Styron's play *In the Clap Shack* is set in the "charnel house" of a military hospital in

World War II; and the intricate narration of *Sophie's Choice* is repeatedly threaded through the nightmare of the Nazi holocaust.
(Significantly, Styron for some time gave *Sophie's Choice* the working title *The Way of the Warrior*.) Thus, life itself—irresistibly
shaped by wars and rumors of wars—seems purposeless, devoid of
meaning; and Styron's heroes, as metaphysical rebels, are struggling against a universe that again and again reveals itself as perpetually, irreversibly unjust. In this respect, they resemble those
fighters of the plague—Dr. Rieux, Tarrou, Rambert, Grand, and
Father Paneloux—who oppose the irresistible disease with medicine or heroism or prayer in Camus's *The Plague*. And just as
Camus used disease as a complex symbol existing both within and
outside historical time, so Styron treats war as both a symbolic and
a literal condition of man: slavery, Nazi death camps, the Korean
War are all manifestations of a deeper disorder. Like Camus in *The
Plague* Styron might well take an epigraph from Defoe's preface to
the third volume of *Robinson Crusoe*: ". . . it is as reasonable to
represent one kind of imprisonment by another, as it is to represent anything that really exists by that which exists not."

Nor is the parallel to Camus's method entirely coincidental, for
Styron has more than once acknowledged his indebtedness to
French literature—most fully and explicitly in a letter he wrote to
Pierre Brodin in 1963, when he was at work on *The Confessions of
Nat Turner*:

Of the moderns of any nationality, including the United States, Camus
has had the largest effect upon my thinking, and I have valued the quality
of his moral intensity more than anything I have found in any other contemporary. Consequently, I believe certain French attitudes have entered my writing, and last year in Paris—where, to my agreeable
surprise, my last book was greeted with such enthusiasm by French readers—I could not help but be pleased when I was told by an eminent critic
that it was hard for him to believe that I was not French.[18]

It would be false to Styron's own rich imaginative achievements to
regard Camus's influence as strictly programmatic; on the other
hand, Styron's acknowledged response to the "moral intensity" of
Camus's writings clearly played a major role in determining the
philosophical vision that underlies his novels. At the broadest
level, Camus obviously confirmed and shaped Styron's own feeling
for an absurd universe, and for the necessity of opposition to its
tyranny. Furthermore, suicide and murder as negations of the absurd dilemma are common to both writers' investigations, and in
both cases are rejected as untenable.

Beyond such thematic correspondence, Styron himself has noted a direct influence on the structure of *The Confessions of Nat Turner*—one which proves of enormous consequence for the novel's technique. Explaining first that the idea of writing about Nat Turner had haunted him for two decades, he recalls how Camus suggested a method for coping with such a tremendous theme:

. . . I had just read for the first time Camus' "The Stranger." It is a brilliant book, the best of Camus, and it impressed me enormously: there was something about the poignancy of the condemned man sitting in his jail cell on the day of his execution—the existential predicament of the man—that hit me. And so did the use of the first person, the book being told through the eye of the condemned. The effect of all this was so strong that I suddenly realized that my Nat Turner could be done the same way: that, like Camus, I would center the novel around a man facing his own death in a jail cell, which of course was true of Turner and how his life ended. And so there, suddenly provided, was the architecture of the book, its framework, along with the idea of telling the story in the first person.[19]

The decision had major ramifications both for the novel's symbolic structure and for its controversial reception. Nat Turner's is the most active, calculated struggle that Styron has recorded; not only is it dramatically more intense, but also the choice of a first-person narrator further concentrates the focus, which in Styron's earlier works had been deflected by the use of third-person or multiple narrative voices.

To attempt to narrate through the mind and the voice of a nineteenth-century slave was a hazardous decision, and one for which many commentators took Styron to task, but the result is that Nat's essentially tragic experience assumes an immediacy and authority missing from that of Cass Kinsolving. (Ironically, the choice also helped Styron throw off what remained of the rather insidious stylistic influence of William Faulkner, whose own moving portraits of Negro characters were constructed in the third person; Dilsey, alone of the quartet which presents the doomed story of the Compsons in *The Sound and the Fury*, is denied a narrative voice of her own.)

In concentrating on the final hours of Nat's life, Styron is also able to avoid the potentially Gothic melodrama of the slaughter of the whites; indeed, in the early pages of the novel we learn most of what there is to know about Nat Turner's uprising, its victims, and the fate of the rebels—thus leaving Styron free to shape the book according to the demands of meditation rather than those of con-

ventional straight-line narration. The technique obviously owes
much to Camus, who shows Meursault as he thinks back on the
events of his life in the shadow of impending death; and despite
the obvious differences between the murderers, the court brands
each a "moral monster" who has neither normal emotions nor any
sense of guilt or sin. Both refuse to offer the explanations or the
self-defensive justifications that society requires to label and effec-
tively shelve the individual acts of violence. Their seemingly un-
motivated acts of murder—of an Arab who meant no harm, of an
enlightened white girl who wished only good to those around
her—thus seem instances of classically "motiveless malignity," and
hence an indescribable threat to the very fabric of society (though
Meursault's ultimate reprehensible crime, of course, is his seeming indifference to the death of his mother). Nat Turner's embrace
of apocalypse shows the power of the human imagination to conceive—if only through violence—a new order of things, a new
scheme of identity. Here Styron's vision not only parallels Camus's
treatment of Meursault; it also recalls such classic works of American
literature as Melville's *Moby Dick* and "Benito Cereno," William
Faulkner's *Light in August*, Richard Wright's *Native Son*, Norman
Mailer's *An American Dream*, and Truman Capote's *In Cold*
Blood. One obvious advantage of the first-person technique (though
not its exclusive perquisite) is that it allows us to penetrate behind
the mask of motiveless malignity, to reveal the depths of anger or
indifference or despair that give the act of violence its ultimate,
murderous thrust.

The writings that precede *The Confessions of Nat Turner* all
show Styron pushing beyond the concept of *l'homme absurde* to
that of *l'homme revolté*, but only with the Virginia slave does he
explicitly portray the rebel-hero according to Camus's definition.
Previously, the revolt of Styron's heroes had been spontaneous,
uncalculated, but Nat Turner consciously and over a period of
years nurtures his scheme for a bloody revenge until the moment
is strategically right for his assault. He struggles to assert an essential humanity against a system that regards him as chattel. Camus's
own theory of the rebel is precisely developed with reference to
the slave uprisings of antiquity and the underdog's passionate
struggle against his oppressor. Of particular relevance to Styron's
portrait of Nat Turner is Camus's distinction between rebellion inspired by the wrathful Judaic God of the Old Testament and that
which takes Christ as its mediator; Nat Turner is directed by the
vengeful prophet Ezekiel, who commands him to "*Slay utterly old*

and young, both maids and little children, and women" (NT, 52); only at the end of the novel, in the shadow of his execution, does he begin to hear the pacific message of Christ.

Styron himself saw the novel's central conflict as between savagery and revenge on the one hand, charity and brotherhood on the other, and hence laid special stress on the single murder—of an innocent, liberal, compassionate young woman—which Nat himself commits. Thus, the novel's focus becomes the very paradigmatical act of murder with which the rising tragic curve of *Set This House on Fire* culminates; but in the later novel it assumes a far more central function. In a remarkable essay entitled "This Quiet Dust," Styron has described his own visit to Southampton County while he was researching *The Confessions of Nat Turner,* his discovery of the former Whitehead property, and his reflections on Nat's sole act of homicide. Though lengthy, those reflections are worth quoting in full for the light they shed on the novel's philosophical assumptions:

There was something baffling, secret, irrational about Nat's own participation in the uprising. He was unable to kill. Time and time again in his confession one discovers him saying (in an offhand tone; one must dig for the implications): "I could not give the death blow, the hatchet glanced from his head," or, "I struck her several blows over the head, but I was unable to kill her, as the sword was dull . . ." It is too much to believe, over and over again: the glancing hatchet, the dull sword. It smacks rather, as in *Hamlet*, of rationalization, ghastly fear, an access of guilt, shrinking from violence, and fatal irresolution. Alone here at this house, turned now into a huge corncrib around which pigs rooted and snorted in the silence of a spring afternoon, here alone was Nat finally able—or was he forced?—to commit a murder, and this upon a girl of eighteen named Margaret Whitehead, described by Drewry in terms perhaps not so romantic or farfetched after all, as "the belle of the county." The scene is apocalyptic—afternoon bedlam in wild harsh sunlight and August heat . . .
It is Nat's only murder. Why, from this point on, does the momentum of the uprising diminish, the drive and tension sag? Why, from this moment in the *Confessions*, does one sense in Nat something dispirited, listless, as if all life and juice had been drained from him, so that never again through the course of the rebellion is he even on the scene when a murder is committed? What happened to Nat in this place? Did he discover his humanity here, or did he lose it?[20]

In making the act of murder and its spiritual consequences his central focus, Styron aligns the novel with the central thesis of Camus's *The Rebel*. The logic of the absurd would seem to suggest suicide, murder, and medicine as equally legitimate, equally consistent in a universe apparently stripped of all moral consequence. In *The Myth of Sisyphus*, however, suicide is rejected in favor of the absurdist wager which confronts that universe with the will of the individual who judges it absurd; and this very act of resistance to a meaningless reality ends by giving individual existence a meaning—by emphasizing, therefore, the value of individual human life. The same reasoning that leads to the rejection of suicide must also lead to the rejection of murder. (Not surprisingly, both Camus and Styron are on record as firm opponents of any form of capital punishment, as well.) As John Cruickshank summarizes Camus's argument,

In the first place, to revolt against the absurd is to rediscover oneself. Rebellion reveals to a man the existence of a part of himself which he holds to be important, by means of which he identifies his essence as a human being, and in the name of which he confronts the absurdity of existence. The first value indicated is that of individual human worth, of potentialities that can only be expressed and fulfilled by such an attitude. But the individual has already seen that his worth is what identifies him as a human being, as a member of the race. It thus transcends his personal destiny and has to do with the nature of man in general.[21]

The rebel who resorts to murder has thus denied the very lesson of a shared humanity which has inspired his rebellion. Unfortunately, as Camus details through historical examples, the same concept of mutual dignity which inspires the rebellion against an oppressor may be distorted—particularly in modern revolutions—to the extent that it ends by negating those very values it set out to affirm. Thus, while revolt demands the renunciation of violence out of elemental respect for human life, revolution as a political expression of revolt commonly takes its definition from the principle of violence. This antinomy between the moral demands of revolt and the practical requirements of revolution is perhaps the quintessential instance of the conflict between theory and practice in Camus's portrayal of *The Rebel*. Of particular pertinence to *The Confessions of Nat Turner* is the passage in which Camus argues that

No doubt the rebel demands a certain freedom for himself; but in no circumstances does he demand, if he is consistent, the right to destroy the person and freedom of someone else. He degrades no one. The freedom which he demands he claims for everybody; that which he rejects he forbids all others to exercise. He is not simply a slave opposing his master but a man opposing the world of master and slave.[22]

Hence, Camus adds to his concept the value of moderation—precisely the value Nat Turner nullifies in his determination to "*Slay utterly . . .*"
In the struggle for recognition of his own humanity, Nat Turner denies the essential humanity of others; this is his tragic flaw, his blindness, of which he becomes aware in the novel's concluding pages when he renounces his own slaughter of the innocent: "*Yes, . . . I would have done it all again. I would have destroyed them all. Yet I would have spared one. I would have spared her that showed me Him whose presence I had not fathomed or maybe never even known. Great God, how early it is! Until now I had almost forgotten His name*" (NT, 428). The character we encounter here is entirely consistent with Styron's other heroes, who exorcise the devils of an oppressive system through violence to themselves or others. Such violence is perhaps a necessary concomitant of the desperate vision of such characters—as Camus judged it to be for the Marquis de Sade; but in Nat Turner more than any other character Styron shows the beginning of true awareness, of the self-knowledge which is the key to redemption and which gives the tragic peripeteia its ultimate philosophical consequence. And thus, though Nat Turner's rebellion is unsuccessful if viewed by the rigid measurements of history, it is triumphant in terms of the profound spiritual transformation the hero undergoes. Furthermore, as Camus himself argued, "Although apparently negative because it creates nothing, revolt is positive in a profound way since it reveals those elements in man which must always be defended." [23]

It seems to me necessary to underscore the philosophical background of William Styron's novel since the book was so persistently mis-read in the months immediately following its publication in the autumn of 1967. Long-awaited as the "big" novel Styron's talent amply promised, *The Confessions of Nat Turner* initially found a favorable critical response, but the second wave of reviews, oriented toward social and racial implication, charged Styron with being an unregenerate racist who had callously propagated "white southern myths, social stereotypes and derogatory literary clichés." [24] In the racially charged atmosphere of America in the late 1960's, it was no doubt inevitable that many would see Nat Turner as a forefather for the militant proponent of Black Power, and that the uprising he led would seem to find corollaries in the savage riots that erupted with such alarming frequency in cities across the United States. Above all, Styron's angriest critics charged that he was dishonest in his own claim, made in preface to the novel, that "I have rarely departed from the *known* facts about Nat Turner and the revolt of which he was the leader" (*NT*, ix). With that assertion, and his own description of the novel as "a meditation on history," Styron seemed to invite judgment by the kind of objective, external criteria Truman Capote had suggested two years before in subtitling *In Cold Blood* "A True Account of a Multiple Murder and Its Consequences." Thus, *The Confessions of Nat Turner* was implicated in the debate then raging over the self-proclaimed "nonfiction novel"—itself a vital chapter in the redefinition of contemporary aesthetics, but one largely peripheral to the real issues of Styron's book.[25] While the author frankly granted that he had allowed himself "the utmost freedom of imagination in reconstructing events" (*NT*, ix), many black readers could only see that freedom as producing the most outrageous and allegedly calculated distortions—particularly with respect to Nat Turner's family background, his sex life, and the role he played in the revolt itself. This is not the place to evaluate such indictments, which have already been exhaustively reviewed by other critics.[26] It is, however, worth noting that when *The Confessions of Nat Turner* appeared, there was a predictable if unhappily misguided desire—on the part of whites and blacks, literary critics and historians, boosters and detractors—to see the work as a manifesto or, at least, as a footnote to history rather than what it so memorably is: the compelling existential portrait of an agonist. As Frederick J. Hoffman observed, in *Set This House on Fire* Styron had already "assumed a larger risk, moved into a more competitive field, entered a tradition of psychological and moral analysis that has been occupied by Kierkegaard, Mann, Sartre and Camus before."[27] It is that tradition which Styron pursues in *The Confessions of Nat Turner*, using history solely as the springboard for the novelist's imaginative task, as he would do once more in *Sophie's Choice*.

For Camus the absurd begins with an unwaited shock of recognition which reveals the world as "suddenly divested of illusions and lights."[28] Such a shock occurs to Nat Turner when he is first confronted with the epithet "slave." As a child Nat overhears a discussion between Samuel and Benjamin Turner and two visiting Episcopal clergymen who glibly quote scripture in support of the benevolent and necessary subjugation of the Negro: "*Cursed be Canaan. A servant of servants shall he be unto his brethren*" (*NT*, 163). The drunken Benjamin defends slavery on economic grounds, and only the enlightened Samuel argues that it is "'the great cause of all the chief evils of our land. It is a cancer eating at our bowels, the source of all our misery, individual, political, and economic'" (159). Nat Turner has already been taken into the protective and nurturing custody of Samuel Turner, and has known few of the hardships of slaves compelled to toil in the fields; while the slavery debate proceeds he stands unwittingly by, tending a smudge-pot, until Benjamin points to him as an example of his brother's "saintly" but benighted vision.

Then Benjamin looked up and said: "You take a little slave like that one there—" And it was an instant before I realized he was speaking of me. He made a gesture toward me with his hand, turning about, and as he did so the others turned too and suddenly I could feel their eyes upon me in the fading light. *Nigger, Negro, darky,* yes—but I had never heard myself called a *slave* before. I remember moving uneasily beneath their silent, contemplative gaze and I felt awkward and naked, stripped down to bare black flesh, and a wicked chill like cold water filled the hollow of my gut as the thought crashed in upon me: *Yes, I am a slave.* (164)

It is from this moment of recognition, in which the young boy's "stage sets" collapse, that his vision as an absurd man is born; constantly reinforced by his readings from the Old Testament, it will finally be shaped into a murderous plan to slaughter all the whites in Southampton County, capture the arsenal at Jerusalem, and march to freedom in the Great Swamp. The fundamental absurdity of the scheme—the opposition between Nat's heroic intention and the reality of white self-interest and military superiority—was precisely what appealed to Styron as a novelist. "It was a scheme so wild and daring that it could only have been the product of the most wretched desperation and frustrate misery of soul; and of course it was doomed to catastrophe not only for whites but for Negroes—and for Black men in ways which from the vantage point of history now seem almost unthinkable."[29]

Nat's fierce opposition gains fresh intensity when Samuel Turner uses him as a go-between to sell four Negro youths to slave-traders—one of them the adored companion whom Nat had baptised shortly before. Later, as drought and tobacco-starved soil plunge Southampton County into depression, Samuel Turner is forced to sell all his property and move to Alabama, leaving Nat behind with the promise that he will eventually be freed. Beaten and exploited by the clergyman into whose custody he is given, Nat sharpens his hatred for Samuel Turner, the surrogate father of his privileged youth—thus recalling the Oedipal conflict thematically evoked in *Set This House on Fire.* That conflict, aggravating Nat Turner's hatred of all whites, is only resolved in the powerfully lyric moment near the conclusion of the novel when Nat imagines

sexual union with Margaret Whitehead. It is part of Styron's fundamental irony that this powerful union of tenderness and love is a
masturbatory fantasy; nonetheless, it is a powerful sign of Nat's
conversion to the lessons of Christ the mediator:

> I tremble and I search for her face in my mind, seek her young body,
> yearning for her suddenly with a rage that racks me with a craving beyond
> pain; with tender stroking motions I pour out my love within her; pulsing
> flood; she arches against me, cries out, and the twain—black and white—
> are one. (*NT*, 426)

It was, no doubt, in order to strengthen the dramatic impact and
the philosophical resonance of this revelation that Styron consciously suppressed earlier analogies to Nat Turner as a Christ figure—though the very suppression led to charges of misrepresenta-
tion from militant black critics. In the slim historical volume
entitled *The Confession, Trial and Execution of Nat Turner*, as
recorded by T. R. Gray, the convicted prisoner, in response to the
question whether or not he now feels himself mistaken, replies,
"Was not Christ crucified?"[30] Styron studiously—perhaps too studiously—avoids the remark in his reconstruction of Gray's interview with Nat Turner, as he avoids stressing other parallels to the
life of Christ: the fact that Nat was a trained carpenter, that his
rebellion against his oppressors occurred when he was in his early
thirties, that he hand-picked a group of passionately devoted disci-
ples for his work, and that their ultimate goal was the town of
Jerusalem. Perhaps Styron felt it necessary to avoid the allegorical
implications that would have undermined the multi-layered psychological portrait of a rebel he wished to draw. Further, Nat
Turner's struggle as absurd hero, his agonizing fall and subsequent
revelation are not the inspired sign of Mankind's redemption; in a
way that is at once more circumscribed and yet profoundly resonant with meaning, his triumph is that of a lone and lonely individual—the triumph of Man, not of Mankind.

Certainly, the Christ myth as an organizing literary device is all
too often reductive, and Styron may well have felt that its more
pointed evocation in the novel might seem to imply that Nat's sacrificial death had somehow redeemed his followers rather than
subjecting them (as, historically, it did) to even greater horrors and
deprivations than they had known before. Like Camus's Caligula,
Nat Turner revolts against the absurd, but his actions end by inten-
sifying it—and hence the dimension of historical absurdity which
hangs like a nimbus over the "real" events of his story. The motives
of Caligula's revolt clearly have Camus's approval, and there can be

no doubt that Styron is sympathetic with Nat Turner's loathing for the abomination of slavery. But in both cases the methods of revolt are utterly wrong. Caligula himself begins to realize this—in a moment uncannily parallel to Nat Turner's thoughts about the murder of Margaret Whitehead—after strangling his mistress Caesonia. Muttering that "murder is no solution," the ruthless emperor contemplates his other acts of cruelty and mayhem, finally concluding in the final act of the play that "I have not taken the right road, I have achieved nothing. Mine is not the right kind of freedom."[31]

In a note prepared for the original production of *Caligula*, Camus reflected on the nature of his hero's fatal error, and it requires no great transition to read his remarks as a gloss of the novel William Styron produced two decades later:

. . . his fault is to be found in his denial of men. One cannot destroy everything without destroying oneself. This is why Caligula depopulates the world around him and then, in keeping with his own logic, does what is necessary to arm against himself those who will ultimately kill him. Caligula's story is that of a high-minded type of suicide. It is an account of the most human and most tragic of mistakes. Caligula is faithless towards humanity in order to keep faith with himself. He consents to die, having learnt that no man can save himself alone and that one cannot be free by working against mankind. But at least he will have rescued some souls, including his own and that of his friend Scipio, from the dreamless sleep of mediocrity.[32]

In *The Confessions of Nat Turner* the friend redeemed from mediocrity is, of course, the noble and spirited Hark, whose piteous sufferings act as a tragic lament throughout the novel, but who achieves radiant nobility in the concluding pages: "Hark's bound and seated shape, like the silhouette of some marvelous black potentate borne in stately procession toward his throne, passes slowly by my door" (*NT*, 427). It is in this image even more than in the novel's concluding notes of Christian forgiveness, its swelling litany from Revelation, that Nat Turner's ultimate triumph can be measured.

Like embattled pilgrims wading the Slough of Despond, Styron's heroes and heroines struggle with defeat and despair, reenacting what Marc Ratner has described as "man's ancient feud with his own nature and destiny."[33] If Peyton Loftis succumbs to the desire to lie down in darkness, Mannix and Cass Kinsolving and Nat Turner achieve a vision which can accommodate the abyss of nothingness which opens before them. That such a vision can come only through violence to self or to others is one of the fundamental ironies of Styron's universe. In *The Clap Shack*, too, Magruder's stifled rage and helplessness in the face of medical and military authority burst full-blown into violence, but such eruptions typically signal the beginning of awareness, of self-affirmation, from which redemption can grow. The novelist Wright Morris has argued that precisely this combination of the destructive and the constructive is a hallmark of the modern literary temper:

If the modern temper, as distinct from the romantic, lies in the admission that men are mortal, this admission determines the nature of the raw material with which the artist must work. An element of despair, a destructive element, is one of the signs by which we shall know him—the other is the constructive use to which this element is put. It distinguishes this artist from the seriously hopeful, or the hopefully serious, who cannot bring themselves to admit of the contemporary facts. These men *know* better, almost without exception, but their hope lies in the refusal to admit what they know. This common failure of admission characterizes their work and blights their hope. The modern temper finds its facts, and its hope, in the statement by Albert Camus: "I want to know if I can live with what I know and only with that."[34]

Throughout his literary career Styron has stressed that this knowledge is primarily the knowledge of evil, decay, and despair, but that man must pass through the abyss if he is to achieve wisdom—a view he has cited as having obvious antecedents in Euripides, Dante, and Shakespeare.[35] What complicates Styron's treatment of this familiar theme is his sense of the fundamental absurdity of the universe, its lack of any transcendent system of "order"—natural or divine—which can be righted or redeemed by the hero's agony. Thus, whatever meaning attaches to the hero's struggle must be derived from the sheer force of his own rebellion against the destructive elements of his world. Increasingly, Styron has stressed the absurdity of that struggle by showing the individual pitted against institutionalized powers of destruction—against the military, against slavery, against the charnel-house atmosphere of a hospital ward, against the death camps of Nazi Germany. It was, perhaps, inevitable that Styron would finally turn to the Holocaust as the most devastating modern instance of the senseless cruelty of life, the most searing contradiction of the basic humanist assumptions underlying his work. The same brutal phenomenon had also engaged Camus, who in his series of four *Lettres à un ami allemand* attributed the rise of Nazi *Realpolitik* to the moral void created by a growing sense of the fundamental absurdity of existence. The Nazi revolt failed, according to Camus, for reasons not unlike those underlying Nat Turner's failure—namely, the inability to distinguish between self-sacrifice and mystification, energy and violence, strength and cruelty. Thus, Camus's *Caligula* has often been read as a comment on Hitler, on the betrayal of revolt which logically concludes in the suicide of the two fanatical but brilliantly charismatic rebels.

There is not only an external, historical logic to the subject on which Styron focuses in *Sophie's Choice*; there is also an internal and literary continuity which lends the theme particular novelistic urgency. Having focused his portrayal of evil on the institutional, on the heartless and conscienceless exercise of absolute power, Styron could scarcely avoid the death camp as an ultimate metaphor. Just as Samuel Turner had compared slavery to a deadly cancer, so Sophie's lover Nathan analyzes the rise of Fascism:

Wasn't it possible, he asked Sophie once—and, he added, speaking as a cellular biologist—that on the level of human behavior the Nazi phenomenon was analogous to a huge and crucial colony of cells going morally berserk, creating the same kind of danger to the body of humanity as does a virulently malignant tumor in a single human body? (*SC*, 323)

The analogy between slavery and the concentration camp is repeatedly stressed in the novel—dramatically accented by the fact that Sophie's two admirers are a paranoid Jew and a Southern writer living, ironically, on the inheritance from the sale of a slave, and obsessed by the figure of Nat Turner. Still further analogies are derived from the parallels which Styron's autobiographical narrator draws between the American South and the Poland in which Sophie grew up—both poverty-ridden, agrarian, feudal, and proud, both shadowed by "the abiding presence of race . . ." (247).

Analyzing the theses of Hannah Arendt and Richard L. Rubinstein, Styron underscores that the form of human society developed by the Nazis was directly evolved from the institution of chattel slavery which found its despotic apotheosis at Auschwitz and achieved there a barbaric dimension uncharacteristic of old-fashioned plantation slavery—namely, "the simple but absolute *expendability* of human life" (235). Styron then explores the implications of such a concept:

It was a theory splintering all previous hesitancies about persecution. Bedeviled as they may have been at times by the dilemma of surplus population, the traditional slaveholders of the Western world were under Christian constraint to avoid anything resembling a "final solution" to solve the problem of excess labor; one could not shoot an expensively

unproductive slave; one suffered with Old Sam when he grew superannu-
ated and feeble, and let him die in peace. (This was not entirely the case.
There is much evidence, for instance, that in the West Indies in the
mid-1700s the European masters for a time felt no compunction about
working slaves to death. In general, however, what I have said is applicable.) With National Socialism there came a sweeping away of leftover
pieties. The Nazis, as Rubenstein points out, were the first slaveholders
to fully abrogate any lingering humane sentiments regarding the essence
of life itself; they were the first who "were able to turn human beings into
instruments wholly responsive to their will even when told to lie down in
their own graves and be shot." (235–236)

The distinction which Styron makes here does not, however, fundamentally alter his dominant thesis: that the evil of chattel slavery
and the evil of the concentration camps are philosophically equal.
The grotesque racist murder of Bobby Weed, referred to on several occasions in the novel, is "'as bottomlessly barbaric as any act
performed by the Nazis during the rule of Adolf Hitler!'" (70), as
Nathan argues. What is false in his argument is the assertion that
all white Southerners share guilt for this outrage; in fact, it is mankind that is indicted by such atrocities, and only through sharing
and acknowledging man's fundamental, recurrent inhumanity can
such guilt ultimately be purged.

    Styron would thus seem to argue that, while the concentration
camp, through its concept of expendability and its technological
refinements, represented new extremes of inhumanity, it could simultaneously be seen as a metaphor in much the way he had previously viewed war and slavery. Further, he variously suggests that
the modern city has a similar capacity to degrade and destroy, a
penchant for senseless cruelty illustrated in the quarrel between
Stingo's father and an irate taxi driver. More pointedly, Styron creates an episode in which Sophie is trapped between two uniden-
tifiable human shapes on a crowded subway train when the lights
suddenly go out. As she feels a hand probe beneath her skirt, she
knows "that no cry or protest would avail her" (92), and that she
must submit to digital rape. (The anonymous violence, the sexual
outrage, are analogous to Bellow's presentation of the city in *Mr.
Sammler's Planet.*) Later, as Sophie recalls the train that took her
to Auschwitz, the atmosphere of threat and of panic, the desperation and utter hopelessness, are drawn in clear parallel to the
Brooklyn episode. And when Stingo and Sophie take a bus to the
beach, finding themselves in a dense crowd of deaf Jewish children, the journey again has diabolical overtones: ". . . our con-

veyance had been rented by the devil. Heaving and rocking its way through the bungalow barrens of Queens and Nassau, clashing gears, exuding fumes, the decrepit bus seemed likely to imprison us forever" (352). Indeed, wherever the motif of a journey is evoked, it is likely to suggest a grotesque journey to the end of night. The motif reaches a crescendo in the panicked train ride south, when Stingo and Sophie, like Hawthorne's Clifford and Hepzibah, attempt to escape the guilty torment of the past. Sophie deserts her sleeping rescuer in a Washington hotel room, and his own anguished pilgrimage reaches new depths of despair: "In addition, the carnal, raw-nerved discomfort of my hangover had become a crucifixion . . . There was also an extravagant nightmarishness about the passing moonscape that aggravated my depression and fear" (504). While he returns to New York, Stingo reads compulsively from the Bible, and his agony is witnessed—like that of Mannix in *The Long March*—by an ample black woman whom Stingo describes as "my fellow pilgrim" and "the dark priestess" (505, 506). Later, he locks himself in the toilet and scrawls apocalyptic messages in his notebook, and when he returns to his seat his companion asks, "'Why you cryin', sonny? . . . Somebody done hurt you bad?'" (506). Once more, the scene echoes the moment when a black maid asks the beaten Captain Mannix, "'Do it hurt? . . . Oh, I bet it does. Deed it does'" (*LM*, 421). The black witness, schooled in suffering and in faith, thus becomes another intricate link between North and South, Poland and Virginia, the concentration camp and slavery, between "the grand old Hebrew woe" (*SC*, 506) of the Book of Job and the sweetness of the Sermon on the Mount.

Such devices belong to the elaborate and often somewhat strained mechanism by which Styron attempts to suggest the universal dimension of the Nazi experience. The point is also stressed in repeated reminders that Jews had no monopoly on the incinerators of Auschwitz and Belsen. Gypsies and homosexuals and other undesirables were also systematically destroyed, together with the ill and the feeble and the very young. Sophie herself, of course, is not Jewish, but she too bears the chilling registration numbers tattooed onto her arm. Her husband, her virulently anti-Semitic father, and her daughter all die in the camps; all are Gentile, and none could be labeled a political enemy. As Sophie's best friend in Warsaw argues, "'I despise the idea of suffering being precious. In this war everyone suffers—Jews, Poles, Gypsies, Russians, Czechs, Yugoslavs, all the others. Everyone's a victim. The Jews are also the victims of victims, that's the main difference. But none of the suffering is precious and all die shitty deaths'" (474).

Styron thus attempts to present the Holocaust both as a unique and devastating instance of rampant evil and as a complex, universal metaphor for the condition of man in a universe stripped of value. The transition between those extremes of implication is one he attempts to bridge with a variety of narrative devices, dramatic parallels and allusions—as in the various diabolical journeys of the novel, which are themselves given literary authority through references to Dante's *Inferno*. Stingo, the aspiring young writer who reassembles the fragments of Sophie's tragedy, notes in introduction to the story that "I had traveled great distances for one so young, but my spirit had remained landlocked, unacquainted with love and all but a stranger to death" (24). His "voyage of discovery" will be inspired by the unattainable Sophie, as Dante's focused on his lost love Beatrice. When first exposed to the bizarre rituals of violence and tenderness that link Nathan Landau and Sophie Zawistowska, Stingo observes that they "had quite simply laid siege to my imagination . . . like Paolo and Francesca" (59), whose piteous tale causes Dante to fall to the ground as though dead. Dante encounters Paolo and Francesca in the second circle of hell where carnal sinners are punished, and if there is no suggestion of sin in the relationship of Nathan and Sophie, there is a recurrent, often clumsily comic stress on their unbridled carnality. "Love led us to one death,"[36] Francesca tells Dante, and Nathan and Sophie end their lives in joint suicide. Similarly, Sophie is associated with Dido and with Cleopatra, tragic queens who killed themselves for love, and who also appear in the second circle of Dante's *Inferno*.

Through the use of pastoral and temporal devices, Styron further attempts to suggest, sometimes ironically, the universal dimensions of his story. *Sophie's Choice* opens in the early summer of 1947, a time "which was sunny and mild, flower-fragrant, almost as if the days had been arrested in a seemingly perpetual springtime" (*SC*, 3). It is, as well, the "springtime" of the young novelist's sexual and literary aspirations. From the cheap Manhattan boarding house where Stingo lives as a junior editor at McGraw-Hill, he spends most of his time reading pastoral classics like "The Bear" or "gazing down into the enchanted garden" (13) of a neighboring house. Later, in Brooklyn, he has a recurrent sense of "a place remote, isolated, almost bucolic" (41), and most of his meetings with Sophie take place in the park or by the sea. When they walk together through Flatbush, "the bourgeois blocks rimming Prospect Park seemed dazzling, ethereal, almost Mediterranean, like a flat leafy Athens" (306). Such pastoralism underscores Stingo's Southern heritage, clarifies his latent hostility to the city, but also recurrently reminds us of the blight on that heritage: his own exhilarating freedom to create is the result of the sale, generations before, of a family slave. Another, later inheritance provides him with the possibility of a pastoral retreat on a peanut farm a few miles from "the ancient habitat of 'ole Prophet Nat,' that mysterious negro who so frightened the pants off or (if you will pardon the more accurate expletive) the s—t out of an unhappy slave-holding Virginia so many years ago" (109).

When Stingo learns that Sophie had arrived at Auschwitz on April 1, 1943, he reconstructs his own movements on that day, remembering "a lovely spring morning in Raleigh, North Carolina . . ." (217). Speculating on this grotesque coincidence, Stingo quotes George Steiner:

"This is where my imagination balks. The two orders of simultaneous experience are so different, so irreconcilable to any common norm of human values, their coexistence is so hideous a paradox—Treblinka *is* both because some men have built it and almost all other men let it be— that I puzzle over time." (216)

One recalls the elaborate time motifs in *Lie Down in Darkness*, and how the despairing Peyton Loftis (like Faulkner's Quentin Compson) is obsessed by clocks in the hours preceding her suicide: "Could we not get one wound up forever? Suppose as we soared dozing across the springs the wheels, the cogs and levers, all these should give way, run down; then our womb would fall, we'd hear the fatal quiet, the dreadful flutter and lurch earthward instead of the fine ascent" (*LDD*, 349). Later, Peyton thinks of her alarm clock in terms of "the glow of rubies and diamonds, shining with a self-luminous light, flawless and divine" (356), comparing their perfection to Dante's Beatrice, and still later remembers, "Yet the clock first, in the hall . . . And so it would be just that way: globed from the atoms in the whirling night, among the springs and jewels and the safely operating, bright celestial wheels" (361). In a strikingly similar passage, Sophie Zawistowska recalls the clock tower of St. Mary's in Cracow, how she would lie awake listening to its music

"and I would wonder about time—this mystery, you know. Or I would lie there and think about clocks. In the hallway there was a very old clock on a kind of stand that had belonged to my grandparents, and once I opened the back of it and looked into it while it was running and saw a whole lot of levers and wheels and jewels—I think they were mostly rubies—shining in the reflection from the sun. So at night lying there I would think of myself *inside* the clock . . . where I would just float around on a spring and watch the levers moving and the various wheels turning and see the rubies, red and bright and as big as my head." (*SC*, 80)

For Styron's devotees, part of the intrigue of *Sophie's Choice* rests precisely in such recapitulations of his earlier writings, and in Stingo's reflections about his novelistic intentions, which at times lend the work the fascination of a palimpsest. What is worth noting here, however, is that in *Sophie's Choice* Styron gives his most elaborate orchestration of motifs of time, pastoralism, and music, using them as recurrent devices which suggest both harmony and the disruption of harmony. The motifs are drawn tautly together in the paragraph that describes Stingo's reaction to the sight of the dead lovers, who in their last hours have listened to part of the Pastoral Symphony, the lament for Eurydice from Gluck's *Orfeo*, and a Mozart piano concerto that always reminded Sophie of "children playing in the dusk, calling out in far, piping voices while the shadows of nightfall swooped down across some green and tranquil lawn" (508). Styron's intentions in such passages, for all their noble humanistic passion, are too self-consciously literary. Sophie has been repeatedly associated with figures from the *Inferno*, and the gates of the camp at Auschwitz are "the gates of hell" (217). Neither Nathan nor Stingo can lead this latter-day Eurydice out of the underworld, though the young writer (who on one occasion literally saves Sophie from death) can perhaps give her new life through his art, in the manner of Dante apotheosizing his beloved Beatrice. Styron makes specific allusion to that process in linking the concentration camp, the murder of Bobby Weed, and lines from Revelation that he had memorized as a boy: "*And God shall wipe away all tears from their eyes. And there shall be no more death, neither sorrow nor crying, neither shall there be any more pain . . .*" (73). When Beatrice first appears to Dante in *The Divine Comedy*, she wears the colors of Revelation.

Allusive devices in literature typically serve to give resonance and dimension to the particular, but the particular reality of the Holocaust is at once so vast and so absolute as to make virtually any metaphor reductive. The Nazi horror is re-enacted in the suicide pact of Nathan and Sophie, paranoid schizophrenic Jew and concentration-camp survivor, who die from cyanide poisoning, as countless Nazi victims died of cyanide gas. And while this grimly ironic historical re-enactment is being set in motion, Stingo is writing a novel about the suicide of a young Southern girl whose lover is a Jew—an episode that is, in turn, allegedly based on the "real" suicide of Stingo's (or Styron's) childhood sweetheart. This bravura interplay of foreshadowing/echoing/paralleling unhappily does not add up to illumination but to manipulation; it bears to the art of fiction the same relationship that good journeyman carpentry bears to fine cabinet-making. The horror of Auschwitz, made graphically clear in Sophie's tortured memories, clearly has to be distanced, for it is so absolute, so desolating, as to defy any conventional or direct presentation; its caustic power threatens to burn through the vessel of art that contains it. Hence, Styron resorts to allusive techniques and multivalenced symbols; even more questionably, he creates an elaborately distanced fictional apparatus that combines the oblique multiple narration of Faulkner's *Absalom! Absalom!* and the embedded narration of Emily Brontë's *Wuthering Heights.*

At the center of this narrative puzzle stands Stingo, the randy and idealistic young writer who struggles to come to terms with his art; thus, at the outermost layer of the narrative shell, *Sophie's Choice* is both *Künstlerroman* and *Bildungsroman*, a portrait of the artist as a young man confronted with pain and horror that outstrip the resources of the creative imagination. On this level, the novel is also about the problem of story-telling. Styron, through the autobiographical Stingo, attempts to relate the life of Sophie Zawitowska, but Sophie's own narration unfolds obliquely and with little attention to chronology; furthermore, the guilt-ridden survivor is "not quite straightforward in her recital of past events . . ." (146), and we are thus presented with what amount to "approximations" of her story. As in *The Confessions of Nat Turner*, Styron again speculates on the relationship between history and story-telling as versions of reality, and on the entire problem of narration as an attempt to order the chaos of the world. Stingo's personal struggle to distinguish between reality and illusion has a bumptious comic parallel in his struggle to lose his virginity; misinterpreting the liberated monologue of an alluring Jewish beauty, he provides an important clue to his early "misreading" of Sophie and Nathan. As Stingo confesses, he is "too often weakly misguided by the external masquerade" (68), a theme further elaborated in Sophie and Nathan's fondness for expensive costume—one of the novel's least plausible devices.

As voyeur and voyager, naive observer and budding novelist,

Stingo inevitably recalls the "Mr. Ishyvoo" of Christopher Isherwood's *Berlin Stories*. Furthermore, *Sophie's Choice* duplicates the boarding-house device of that work and again presents us with a zany, enchanting, sexually liberated, tormented, potentially suicidal heroine who casts her spell over the narrator; and Landau, Nathan's family name, echoes that of one of the more prominent families in Isherwood's chronicle. Both writers concern themselves with the horrors of Fascism—Isherwood with its threat and Styron with its consequences; but what the latter clearly lacks is Isherwood's lightly ironic touch, the perspective of his sophisticated wit. There are, to be sure, moments when Styron's prose shows a new capacity for surrealistic humor, as in the following passages:

How vividly there still lingers on my palate the suety aftertaste of the Salisbury steak at Bickford's, or Riker's western omelette, in which one night, nearly swooning, I found a greenish, almost incorporeal feather and a tiny embryonic beak. (12)

In the shadows her face was so close to mine that I could smell the sweet ropy fragrance of the sherry she had been drinking, and then her tongue was in my mouth. . . . Plunged like some writhing sea-shape into my gaping maw, . . . it wiggled, it pulsated, and made contortive sweeps of my mouth's vault: I'm certain that at least once it turned upside down. (168)

As in the latter passage, much of the novel's humor focuses on Stingo's sexual frustration: the absurd as priapic denial. There are also fine dramatic instances of Nathan's compulsive clowning, his mock-Jewish "spieling," but ultimately these are only a prelude to a plunge into paranoia.

The comic self-mockery with which Stingo views his adventures and aspirations (or with which the middle-aged Styron regards his own younger self) is too infrequent to determine the tone of the novel, which repeatedly returns to the "high serious" mode appropriate to its monumentally somber theme. As Stingo admits, "In my career as a writer I have always been attracted to morbid themes—suicide, rape, murder, military life, marriage, slavery" (110), and he has a tendency toward overwrought language ("immemorial," "perdurable") and other effusions of style calculated to express the consequence of such subjects. It is this quality which critics have tended to regard as an unhappy inheritance from Southern fiction. As John Gardner complained when *Sophie's Choice* appeared, "It is no longer just the South that is grandly decayed, morally tortured, ridden with madmen, idiots and weaklings socially enfeebled by incest and other perversions; it is the

world." Gardner also found Styron's plot to suffer from "the help-
less groaning and self-flagellation of the Southern Gothic novel."[37]
Stingo's self-confessed morbidity, whether a hallmark of Southern Gothic or not, is clearly borne out by the novel's obsession with
death. *Sophie's Choice* opens with a gratuitous anecdote about the
death of a promising young writer shot through the head by a Japanese sniper. A letter from Stingo's father informs him of the suicide of Maria Hunt, which becomes the inspiration for a novel
about Peyton Loftis's suicide, and in turn foreshadows Sophie's suicide attempts—one thwarted, the other successful. The news of
Maria Hunt's death even intrudes into Stingo's recurrent pastoral
dreams: "I peered out the window of the room at home in which I
was still sleeping and caught sight of the open coffin down in the
windswept, drenched garden, then saw my mother's shrunken,
cancer-ravaged face twist toward me in the satin vault and gaze at
me beseechingly through eyes filmed over with indescribable torture" (*SC*, 46). In a fit of rage, Nathan screams at Sophie, "'I need
you like *death*'" (47), and later cries out "in a tone that might have
been deemed a parody of existential anguish had it not possessed
the resonances of complete, unfeigned terror: 'Don't . . . you . . .
see . . . Sophie . . . we . . . are . . . dying! *Dying!*'" (77). It is
Emily Dickinson's poem "Because I could not stop for death" that
brings the star-crossed lovers together, and Nathan temporarily
restores Sophie to life, but his latent capacity for rage and disorder
will bring them a joint death through the "nothing" pill. Stingo
receives a second legacy when his father's friend Frank Hobbs dies;
the letter announcing the event also reminds Stingo that the lonely
widower was "still mourning the death of his only child, Frank Jr."
(108). As Stingo frets over the difficulty of presenting his heroine's
suicide, the radio broadcasts news of Göring's suicide in a Nurem-
berg prison. These allusions to death all occur within the outermost sphere of the narration; as layers are peeled away to reveal
Sophie's tormented past, an agonized litany swells out of the book,
with deaths too numerous, too hideous, too bizarre, too senseless
to suggest anything but the patterns of nihilism and despair. Of all
these, of course, it is one of the last revealed that is the most anguished—the gassing of her daughter at Auschwitz when Sophie's
"choice" falls on her son as the child who should be permitted to
live. The bereaved mother's further, ultimate "choice" is her own
suicide.

Thus, on every level of this multi-layered narrative, Styron confronts us with the two existential phenomena on which Camus had
focused his philosophical explorations: murder and suicide. Be-

cause the compelling figure of Sophie stands at the center of this complex matrix, it is she who has the power to make Stingo "aware of the meaning of the Absurd, and its conclusive, unrevocable horror" (466). In coming to terms with that horror, Stingo must also recognize his own "murderous" capacities, his own guilt. In part, this is the inherent racial guilt of a white Southerner, but it rests as well in his own potential anti-Semitism, revealed when his small inheritance is stolen and he immediately suspects the caretaker Morris Fink. Sophie, raised in a family of professional Jew-haters, can only reinforce this feeling; indeed, she had tried to barter for her freedom in Auschwitz by boasting that her own father had first proposed the "ultimate solution." The following exchange occurs at the beginning of Sophie and Stingo's visit to Jones Beach:

> "Nathan had everything that is bad in Jews," Sophie said, "nothing of the little bit that's good."
> "What's good about Jews at *all*?" I heard myself say loudly, querulously. "It was that Jew Morris Fink that stole the money from my medicine cabinet. I'm *certain!* Money-mad, money-greedy Jewish bastard!"
> Two anti-Semites, on a summer outing. (354)

A more thorough indictment of Stingo's guilt occurs in an episode he recalls from his childhood, when he goes joy-riding after school rather than hurrying home to tend the fire for his invalid mother. When he finds her later, suffering from cold and fear, she averts her eyes from his face: "It was the *swiftness* of that turning away which would thereafter define my guilt; it was as swift as a machete dismembering a hand" (297). Many years later, he will similarly feel that he had "copped out" (428) in not tending properly to the drug-crazed Nathan, and that he was thus in part guilty for his death and for Sophie's; his defection, furthermore, is connected to unfulfilled sexual lust—and hence to one of the most classic, primal sources of guilt. This constellation inevitably recalls Cass Kinsolving's raging guilt over the murder of Mason Flagg, with its dense sexual innuendos, and the parallel is italicized when a hotel clerk describes to Stingo the call Sophie made to New York before her hasty departure: "'She was talkin' to someone—a man, I guess. She began to cry a lot and told him she was leavin' here right away. Kept callin' to him—she was real upset, Reverend. Mason. Jason. Something like that'" (499). If we press the parallel further, there is also correspondence between Cass's youthful guilt in the destruction of the Negro cabin, the first incidence of his tragic blindness, and Stingo's desertion of his mother.

Like the hero of *Set This House on Fire*, Stingo must ultimately come to terms with his own murderous potential—with the universal capacity for evil made manifest in the Nazi death camps. Art itself, the shaping of Sophie's story into a novel, becomes a kind of expiation, as well as a potent instance of the absurd. Camus himself described the artist as the most absurd of all men, for he struggles against the fundamental verity that both intellectual explanations and aesthetic re-creations of the world are vain. As John Cruickshank has described Camus's position,

L'homme absurde is sealed off from transcendence and rooted in the world of immediate appearances. Now this, according to Camus, is the world of particularity in which the artist must work. This is the source from which he takes the materials of his art. Thus the outlook and activity of the artist, in their basic forms, direct attention to the fact of the absurd. The artist joins Don Juan as an exemplar of absurdism. It is clear, at the same time, that Camus does not romanticize art as an escape from the absurd. He sees it as being, in its own way, a conscious or unconscious acceptance of the evidence by which l'homme absurde is faced. The work of art is situated at a point where the desire for transcendence and the impossibility of transcendence conflict. . . . Art, for Camus, is imaginative confirmation of the absurd.[38]

Such a hypothesis neatly describes Stingo's dilemma as an artist, determined as it is by the Camusian need to revolt against the known and knowable "facts" of the world and the desire to replace it by some better alternative. The artist rebels finally against the limitations of physical existence and the fact of death.

Such rebellion cannot destroy the world it is seeking to reject, but it can at least create a world of forms and ideas that corresponds more closely to its own aspirations. One of the mysteries and triumphs of art is its role in enabling the eternal human prisoner to create, from the conditions of his imprisonment, the image of a free life that he has never known. Camus therefore regards art not only as an aspect of revolt but as the creation of a universe of replacement. It gives positive substance to revolt against the absurd.[39]

The narrator of Sophie's Choice is thus consistent with a remark Styron made at the time he published The Confessions of Nat Turner: "I realized all my work is predicated on revolt in one way or another."[40] The statement finds its necessary corollary in Camus's insistence that "The novel is born at the same time as the spirit of revolt and reflects, on the artistic level, the same aim."[41] Those twin assertions describe both the ambitiousness of Styron's novel and its ultimate failure. We see Sophie only through Stingo's eyes, and her tragedy is thus oddly displaced—both by her own groping, fragmentary recitations, and by Stingo's love-crazed, guilt-ridden remembrances of them. And Stingo in turn is denied complete heroic status by the fact that he, too, is seen through a kind of veil—in this case that of the middle-aged, established writer looking back on his own younger self. When one compounds this problem with structural and stylistic infelicities of the sort that mar *Sophie's Choice*, the novel must fall short of the genuinely tragic status it might otherwise have achieved. Nonetheless, it remains a work of extraordinary power, even when the power is raw and unassimilated; and Sophie Zawistowska joins a distinguished band of romantic, mercurial, blighted but eternally captivating literary heroines—Camille, Emma Bovary, Sister Carrie, Sally Bowles—though she perhaps deserved a more accomplished chronicler than Stingo.

The young writer does, however, succeed in recording a single line to stand against the horrors of Sophie's life and her death, one of the thoughts scribbled in his notebook on the desperate journey back to New York: "*Let your love flow out on all living things*" (*SC*, 513). Even though Auschwitz would seem to have blocked forever the flow of that love, like some fatal embolism in the bloodstream of mankind, he clings to his absurd vision. With it this "grail-tormented Christian knight" (358) finds his own improbable transcendence, awakening on the beach on the day after Nathan's and Sophie's double funeral to stare up at the morning star. "Blessing my resurrection" (515), he inscribes the following words in his mind: "'*Neath cold sand I dreamed of death / but woke at dawn to see / in glory, the bright, the morning star'*" (515), an echo of the concluding lines of *The Confessions of Nat Turner*, with its dream of the ocean: "*Oh how bright and fair the morning star*" (*NT*, 428). Once more, Styron's rebel hero has made his private peace, conquering the urge to lie down in darkness; and yet again the vision of the abyss of suffering is the beginning of wisdom.

The Absurd Man as Picaro

In his first two short novels Saul Bellow presented heroes who served as acutely impressionable centers of consciousness reflecting the dislocations of metropolitan life. In both *Dangling Man* and *The Victim* distortions of contemporary values and victimization by environment are greatly simplified, but the simplifications are fruitful in delineating the milieu in which later Bellow characters are to function.

Paul Levine has noted that "In its style, philosophical content, and hypothetical nature, *Dangling Man* stands in a unique place in our contemporary literature, more closely resembling a novel by Albert Camus than one by any American novelist writing today."[1] Certainly the Camus novel to which *Dangling Man* is a counterpart is *The Stranger*, and the similarity goes far beyond the incidental fact that Camus avowedly adopted for that book certain stylistic techniques from the American novel. Both *Dangling Man* and *The Stranger* describe the absurd experience rather than suggest a specific absurd metaphysics, and Meursault and Joseph ultimately arrive at absurd stances as a result of the same ironic, although apparently indiscriminate, clustering of circumstances. These experiences seem to fit no logical pattern: they are simply there, and their presence announces itself with the same apparent lack of reason to both reader and participant. An effect of immediate involvement is achieved in both novels through the use of narrators who observe without attempting to analyze; Bellow accomplishes this sense of involvement through the device of Joseph's journal, and Camus through having Meursault tell his own story directly to the reader. Both writers have taken a form usually intended to reach profound depths of introspection and have used it in a way that is predominantly objective.

Like Meursault, Joseph is a petty clerk who suddenly finds himself a metaphysical outsider, dangling between commitments and value systems. Also like Meursault, Joseph is initially caught up in the stifling ritual of daily activity and is highly susceptible to external stimuli; living empirically in a prolapsed world, he grows from philosophical innocence to a state of aggravated consciousness in which he questions the very nature of human existence. Neither Joseph's nor Meursault's reaction to his environment is wholly negative. Sitting in his room writing his journal, Joseph is given a chance to derive a personal value system to oppose (without denying) the "real" world, just as Meursault, shut away in prison, at last drafts a personal code which both scorns the ministrations of the church and rejects the consolation of death as an escape from human misery.

The shock which destroys the monotonous routine of Joseph's daily life comes in the form of a draft notice. His life interrupted, he can finally look upon it for what it is really worth, and he finds it devoid of all significant meaning. In the face of this meaninglessness Joseph develops the intention to spin a life out of his own spirit, having the opportunity to do this as he "dangles" between a regular job and induction into the army. His temporary dislocation at first suggests that a hostile universe deprives contemporary man of all significant inner life. Looking out the window before he begins his journal, Joseph surveys the run-down buildings, dingy warehouses, and smoking chimneys which make up his physical as well as his spiritual horizon, and concludes:

> It was my painful obligation to look and to submit to myself the invariable question: Where was there a particle of what, elsewhere, or in the past, had spoken in man's favor? There could be no doubt that these billboards, streets, tracks, houses, ugly and blind, were related to interior life. And yet, I told myself, there had to be a doubt. There were human lives organized around these ways and houses, and that they, the houses, say, were the analogue, that what men created they also were, through some transcendent means, I could not bring myself to concede. There must be a difference, a quality that eluded me, somehow, a difference between things and persons and even between acts and persons. Otherwise the people who lived here were actually a reflection of the things they lived among. (DM, 24–25)

Pressing his forehead against the glass, Joseph looks out on the reality of his life, and confronts a barren insignificance to which he refuses to concede his belief in some transcendent meaning. It is Joseph's intention to affirm the basic humanity of man in a universe which speaks to him largely through "taverns, movies, assaults, divorces, murders." So far as metaphysical progression is concerned, Dangling Man moves in an inverse direction to that of The Stranger; Joseph begins with a stance remarkably similar to that which Meursault is able to strike only in the last moments of his life. The final test of the absurd hero, however, rests in his ability to live the conflict between intention and reality; Meursault is not asked to submit to this test, and Joseph is unsuccessful in maintaining his intention; thus neither character wholly qualifies as an absurd *hero*, although at the most intense point of his rebellion Joseph is as close to Camus's concept of the absurd man as is any other character in American fiction.

Joseph adopts none of the minor badges of social defiance which often denote the rebel, for the small arenas of nonconformity do not interest him; he conserves his strength and his energies so that he can give "all his attention to defending his inner differences, the ones that really matter" (28). Just as he refuses the socially obvious representation of his differences, so too he refuses obvious philosophical positions; life is neither good nor bad, but an experience, and his anxiety stems from the desire to see that experience as a reflection of forces which are ultimately compassionate and creative. The vision which he requires is frequently thwarted, however, by what he calls "treasons": "There were so many treasons; they were a medium, like air, like water; they passed in and out of you, they made themselves your accomplices; nothing was impenetrable to them" (56). Everywhere he turns Joseph finds these treasons and betrayals, which constantly hammer at the life he is struggling to define. At a cocktail party they reveal themselves in an intensely personified form as Joseph watches a friend torture a hypnotized woman whose body is incapable of registering the indignities to which she is subjected. The state of hypnosis itself is perhaps the most successful single representation of that spiritual drowsiness and emotional lethargy which Camus described in *The Myth of Sisyphus* as the almost universal condition of modern man. The figure of the hypnotizer becomes for Joseph a representation of all the cruelties and injustices which the world imposes:

> This was only the beginning. In the months that followed I began to discover one weakness after another in all I had built up around me. I saw what Jack Brill had seen, but, knowing it better, saw it more keenly and severely. It would be difficult for anyone else to know how this affected me, since no one could understand as well as I the nature of my plan, its rigidity, the extent to which I depended on it. Foolish or not, it had answered my need. The plan could be despised; my need could not be. (57)

Joseph finds the same frustration of this need in his pompous, money-oriented brother, in the spoiled niece who accuses him of

attacking her, and eventually in his own wife, and his own stance is
continually refined as life presents him with one disappointment
after another. His consciousness of a divorce from the world becomes more intense as the novel progresses, and while he had
once envisioned the possibility of deriving some strength through
recourse to friends and relatives, he becomes increasingly aware
that his struggle is to be a lonely one. Like Camus's Meursault, he
finds no meaning in the social life, and he rejects the order of men
when he suddenly realizes that his friends band together for mutual protection, behaving the way the group expects them to behave, asserting group values, and ridiculing anything that threatens their mutual definition. Joseph's disillusionment with people is
the prelude to a total deracination characterized by a "feeling of
strangeness, of not quite belonging to the world" (30). An indifferent world precludes belief in a beneficent personal God, and
Joseph asserts that "there are no values outside life. There is
nothing outside life" (165).

"What, in fact, is the absurd man?" Camus asks. "He who, without negating it, does nothing for the eternal. Not that nostalgia is
foreign to him. But he prefers his courage and his reasoning. The
first teaches him to live without *appeal*, to get along with what he
has; the second informs him of his limits."[2] It is when Joseph has
the revelation of the necessity of living without appeal and within
narrowly circumscribed limits that his original intention becomes
sufficiently refined to suggest his possibilities as an absurd hero; he
is, in this moment of revelation, at least an absurd *man*. Joseph's
revelation comes while he is listening to a Haydn *divertimento* for
the cello. The sober opening movement of Piatigorsky's performance convinces him that he is yet an apprentice in suffering and
humiliation, and that he is foolish to imagine avoiding further indignities; it was not among human privileges to be exempt from
them:

What I should do with them, how to meet them, was answered in the
second declaration: with grace, without meanness. And though I could
not as yet apply that answer to myself, I recognized its rightness and was
vehemently moved by it. Not until I was a whole man could it be my
answer, too. And was I to become this whole man alone, without aid? I
was too weak for it, I did not command the will. Then in what quarter
should I look for help, where was the power? Grace by what law, under
what order, by whom required? Personal, human, or universal, was it?
The music named only one source, the universal one, God. But what a

miserable surrender that would be, born out of disheartenment and chaos; and out of fear, bodily and imperious, that like a disease asked for a remedy and did not care how it was supplied. The record came to an end; I began it again. No, not God, not any divinity. That was anterior, not of my own deriving. I was not so full of pride that I could not accept the existence of something greater than myself, something, perhaps, of which I was an idea, or merely a fraction of an idea. That was not it. But I did not want to catch at any contrivance in panic. In my eyes, that was a great crime. Granted that the answer I was hearing, that went so easily to the least penetrable part of me, the seldom-disturbed thickets around the heart, was made by a religious man. But was there no way to attain that answer except to sacrifice the mind that sought to be satisfied? From the antidote itself another disease would spring. It was not a new matter, it was one I had frequently considered. But not with such a desperate emotion or such a critical need for an answer. Or such a feeling of loneliness. Out of my own strength it was necessary for me to return the verdict for reason, in its partial inadequacy, and against the advantages of its surrender. (*DM*, 67–68)

Joseph's emphasis on courage, reasoning, and lack of appeal might have been drawn directly from Camus's own answer to the question, "What, in fact, is the absurd man?"

In the first part of the novel, Joseph, like Meursault, has an acute awareness of the passage of time, but also like Camus's hero, he eventually begins to lose all sense of time's regular passage. Metaphysically, this distorted time sense emphasizes an attitude of indifference to the physical and "withdrawal from temporal existence in the world of sense into more speculative and timeless self-awareness."[3] Joseph and his wife spend a lonely New Year's Day in their drab apartment, and feel "set aside" by the absence of any celebration or diversion. "But what such a life as this incurs [Joseph comments] is the derangement of days, the leveling of occasions. I can't answer for Iva, but for me it is certainly true that days have lost their distinctiveness" (*DM*, 81). Joseph's absurd intention takes him increasingly farther out of life, and his contacts with the world become little more than open hostilities. He comes to envy an artist friend, John Pearl, who is able to carve for himself a life of the imagination in which he sustains a "real world" of "art and thought."

Realizing that he lacks the resources of imagination which sustain John Pearl, Joseph is cast into a yet deeper state of despair, and as the novel progresses he is eventually faced with the idea of suicide as a solution to his acute loneliness; even while he doubts his own ability to live a life of curtailed expectations, he is yet unable to accept the obliteration of expectation which death entails. "The sense in which Goethe was right: Continued life means expectation" (148).

With the possible exception of Asa Leventhal in *The Victim*, all of Saul Bellow's heroes are consciously questing figures, and Joseph introduces this gallery of contemporary knights when he says:

> The quest, I am beginning to think, whether it be for money, for notoriety, reputation, increase of pride, whether it leads us to thievery, slaughter, sacrifice, the quest is one and the same. All the striving is for one end. I do not entirely understand this impulse. But it seems to me that its final end is the desire for pure freedom. We are all drawn toward the same craters of the spirit—to know what we are and what we are for, to know our purpose, to seek grace. And, if the quest is the same, the differences in our personal histories, which hitherto meant so much to us, become of minor importance. (154)

Joseph's quest is not wholly successful, and he must confess that he has not done well "alone" in the world. Thus, in the final pages of the novel he gives himself up to the regulation of army life with shouts of joy for regular hours, "supervision of the spirit," and regimentation. His idiopathic freedom has isolated him so painfully that he at last seeks social accommodation within the ranks of the army. While our final view of Joseph is not essentially heroic, it is of a sympathetic character who possesses all the sensitivity of spirit prerequisite to the creation of an absurd hero, and his return to the world ironically foreshadows the more successful reconciliations of Henderson and Moses Herzog. Joseph has purposely committed himself to the mechanistic universe which was once so repulsive to him, but he leaves us with the hope that "the war could teach me, by violence, what I had been unable to learn during those months in the room. Perhaps I could sound creation through other means. Perhaps. But things were now out of my hands. The next move was the world's" (191).

At the heart of Bellow's work rests the conviction that man's problems derive from a profound dislocation of his social and political universe. While *Dangling Man* opens with the vision of a character intensely determined to put such dislocations to rights, *The Victim* opens with the inverse picture of a middle-class magazine editor who appears unaware of any fundamental disharmony in his universe; Asa Leventhal's greatest concerns seem to be an illness in the family, a vacationing wife, and a dirty apartment. Despite his apparently contented surface, we soon learn that Asa has come perilously near falling spiritual prey to the same grey environment which Joseph was regarding when *Dangling Man* opened: "He occasionally said to Mary, revealing his deepest feelings, 'I was lucky. I got away with it.' He meant that his bad start, his mistakes, the things that might have wrecked him, had somehow combined to establish him. He had almost fallen in with that part of humanity of which he was frequently mindful (he never forgot the hôtel on lower Broadway), the part that did not get away with it—the lost, the outcast, the overcome, the effaced, the ruined" (*V*, 20). Because he has enjoyed some measure of success, Asa feels that he has been able to overcome the tragic destiny which usually awaits modern man, and in the complacency that results from this judgment, he falls into a lethargy as deadening as that which surrounds "the overcome, the effaced, the ruined."

It is through Kirby Allbee that Asa will achieve an awakening that will allow him "to know what we are and what we are for, to know our purpose, to seek grace" (*DM*, 154). Several years before the novel opens, Kirby Allbee had secured Asa Leventhal an interview with his employer. Whether at Allbee's instigation or from natural maliciousness, Mr. Rudiger mercilessly attacked the young man, and Asa, in turn, flew back at him with all the stored-up vehemence of weary, fruitless months of job seeking. Shortly after this encounter, Kirby Allbee was fired. Years later, having exhausted his dead wife's insurance money, Allbee returns as a kind of *alter ego* antagonist to remind Asa of his "guilt." At first Allbee seems only a hopelessly degenerate anti-Semite, but he becomes a significant catalyst, forcing Asa to break out of his complacent mold and to admit, if only on the Conradian level of potentiality, the fact of his guilt.

Asa, who has always prided himself on the position he has won in the literary jungle, is repulsed by Allbee's suggestion that the individual has no responsibility in the world. "'The day of succeeding by your own efforts is past'," Allbee argues. "'Now it's all blind movement, vast movement, and the individual is shuttled back and forth. He only thinks he's the works. But that isn't the way it is. Groups, organizations succeed or fail, but not individuals any longer'" (*V*, 70–71). Often when he paints such pictures of human insignificance Allbee reasons speciously, and indeed, his accusations against Asa are a clear indication of the fact that he believes in individual responsibility. But as he manipulates for an advantage with Asa, Allbee is revealing to the incredulous Jew the very face of the absurd universe, which is clearer, as delineated in this novel, to Allbee's vision than it is to Asa's.

Kirby Allbee had been at best a questionable employee who was always subject to alcoholic evasions. In the face of this reality, his intention of touching Asa for a new start in life appears absurd, and Asa turns to his friends for confirmation of "the absurdity, the madness of the accusations" (86). But when Asa has reconciled himself to the tentative but significant validity of Allbee's social absurdity, he himself will be better equipped to understand metaphysical absurdities. "There was something in people against sleep and dullness, together with the caution that led to sleep and dullness. Both were there, Leventhal thought" (99). His first defense is to assume a guise of sleep and dullness, until Allbee begins to antagonize a sense of values which refuses sleep, and Asa's recognition of those values also entails an admission of his guilt.

Gradually, as his conflicts with Allbee increase in number and intensity, Asa begins to see himself in a new light. After an especially painful encounter with Allbee, Asa takes his young nephew to the zoo, where he is maddened by the fear that Allbee is hiding somewhere in the crowd: "He tried to put him out of his thoughts and give all his attention to Philip, forcing himself to behave naturally. But now and then, moving from cage to cage, gazing at the animals, Leventhal, in speaking to Philip, or smoking, or smiling, was so conscious of Allbee, so certain he was being scrutinized, that he was able to see himself as if through a strange pair of eyes: the side of his face, the palpitation in his throat, the seams of his skin, the shape of his body and of his feet in their white shoes. Changed in this way into his own observer, he was able to see Allbee, too" (107). Later in the novel Leventhal has "an unclear dream in which he held himself off like an unwilling spectator; yet it was he that did everything" (168). This shifting of perspective in which Asa becomes both pursuer and pursued alarms him, and he strives against "countering absurdity with absurdity" (108).

Asa Leventhal is not totally unaware of the suffering and evil which dominate the modern world; he knows something of what it is to be a "victim." He merely chooses not to concern himself with this aspect of life, and the isolation into which he recedes is not unlike that glacial, betraying hardness of the heart which characterized many of Nathaniel Hawthorne's characters. Allbee accuses him of keeping his spirit "under lock and key," where it is unnecessary to have to make the kind of reconciliations which Joseph tried to make in *Dangling Man.* "'It's necessary for you to believe'," Allbee argues, "'that I deserve what I get'."

"It doesn't enter your mind, does it—that a man might not be able to help being hammered down? What do you say? Maybe he can't help himself? No, if a man is down, a man like me, it's his fault. If he suffers, he's being punished. There's no evil in life itself. And do you know what? It's a Jewish point of view. You'll find it all over the Bible. God doesn't make mistakes. He's the department of weights and measures. If you're okay, he's okay, too. That's what Job's friends come and say to him. But I'll tell you something. We do get it in the neck for nothing and suffer for nothing, and there's no denying that evil is as real as sunshine. Take it from me, I know what I'm talking about. To you the whole thing is that I must deserve what I get. That leaves your hands clean and it's unnecessary for you to bother yourself. Not that I'm asking you to feel sorry for me, but you sure can't understand what makes a man drink." (146)

Against his will, Leventhal is at last convinced that it is no longer possible to think in the old dichotomous terms, and later, at the funeral of one of his nephews, he rejects the consolation which the chapel and its crucifix seem to offer. "Prompted by an indistinct feeling, he thought to himself, 'Never mind, thanks, we'll manage by ourselves. . . .'" (180). Leventhal is learning to live without appeal either to the neat patterns with which he had once regulated his life or to any kind of supernatural consolation. His former evasions had been perpetrated with a kind of innocence, but as he gradually moves toward consciousness, he realizes that innocence itself can often be maliciously destructive. "'Wake up!'" a friend urges him. "'What's life? Metabolism? That's what it is for the bugs. Jesus Christ, no! What's life? Consciousness, that's what it is. That's what you're short on. For God's sake, give yourself a push and a shake. It's dangerous stuff, Asa, this stuff'" (264).

Leventhal moves closer to consciousness as Allbee comes to occupy an increasingly intimate role in his life. The climax to both consciousness and intimacy occurs when Leventhal returns home from a night at a friend's house to find Allbee making love to a prostitute in Leventhal's bed. After driving the couple from his apartment, he reflects on the look of terror in the woman's eyes, and "Both of them, Allbee and the woman, moved or swam toward him out of a depth of life in which he himself would be lost, choked, ended. There lay horror, evil, all that he had kept himself from" (277).

Kirby Allbee helps Asa to learn that "Each man is responsible for his actions because he is accountable for their consequences" (166), and at the same time Asa's eyes are opened to suffering and evil which he had never felt strong enough to reckon with. But he does not become a perpetually suffering martyr as does Nathanael West's Miss Lonelyhearts, whose vision of suffering and responsibility are in many ways similar to Asa's. He now knows the meaning of responsibility, but he also knows its limitations. When Allbee tries to involve Asa in a dual suicide without first getting his permission, Asa is at last able to break the bonds that have joined them, and in the moment when he struggles with Allbee in the gas-filled apartment, he casts his vote with life, despite all the horror and evil which have just been revealed to him. Allbee is to some degree the victim of Asa's narrowness, but both are victims of a world which at every turn warns that man may be "lost, choked, ended."

Asa Leventhal had feared extending his consciousness to include humanity as a whole because he doubted his own ability to live with the vision that would await him. At the conclusion of the novel he is, after a symbolic reunion with his wife, not only able to live with this vision but also able to live happily. Life apparently holds out empty promises to most men, turning them away when they present themselves to make their claims, but Asa doubts that this is the final picture. "For why should tickets, mere tickets, be promised if promises were being made—tickets to desirable and undesirable places? There were more important things to be promised. Possibly there was a promise, since so many felt it. He himself was almost ready to affirm that there was. But it was misunderstood" (286). While Asa's vision is only fragmentary, this undefined "promise" which he derives from it brings *The Victim* to a conclusion more significantly, if as vaguely, affirmative as that of *Dangling Man*.

Both *Dangling Man* and *The Victim* are brief, arresting trajectories written in a terse prose which, after two novels, readers came to expect from Saul Bellow. *The Adventures of Augie March*, therefore, appeared to many to be more of a departure than it really was. Its flowing, demotic language, its bumptious hero, and its mammoth episodic structure make it a modern picaresque, and it has in fact been compared to all the great picaresque novels of the past. As the story of a young boy cast adrift in life and gradually proceeding toward a defined system of values, it is perhaps closer to *The Adventures of Huckleberry Finn* than to any other picaresque novel. As an analysis of rebellion and of man's lonely attempt to spin a life of his own, the book grew logically from the themes of Bellow's first novels. While in his earlier works Bellow saw this spinning concentrated in a single dramatic episode, he now sees it in its full organic process. From his earliest recollections as a fatherless child in the Chicago slums, Augie has had, like Huck Finn, to improvise, to live by his wits and his instincts, and often to travel incognito. Both Huck and Augie have a profound and premature knowledge of human depravity, and yet both approach the world with a remarkable tenderness; their resilient good humor is perhaps their best defense against nihilism and self-pity.

Through the episodic structure of this novel Bellow has done far more than reveal a single state of mind; he has re-created an era and peopled it with an enormous and varied fictional population. One of the most significant early influences in Augie's life is Grandma Lausch, an eccentric old Russian Jew with a vaguely romantic past who is taken in by the March family as a boarder and comes to rule over them as a semibenevolent tyrant. It is Grandma Lausch who teaches Augie the values of expedient lying, as when she sends him with a trumped-up story to the Public Health Department in order to get glasses for his half-blind mother. Given a mission and given credit for understanding the "set up" behind it, Augie is easily persuaded to play an appropriate role. He warns, however, that he is not trying to create the impression that, because of his willingness to rise to such challenges, he might have been a Cato or "a young Lincoln who tramped four miles in a frontier zero gale to refund three cents to a customer. I don't want to pass for having such legendary presidential stuff. Only those four miles wouldn't have been a hindrance if the right feelings were kindled. It depended on which way I was drawn" (AAM, 23).

Augie is drawn many ways in the course of this novel—to deceit, sacrifice, love, theft, and pain. At moments he seems to have some of the qualities and a measure of the fate of Nathanael West's parodic Lemuel Pitkin—another picaresque "voyager"—but something always brings Augie back to a middle ground, and he says no—though often at the last minute—before he is drawn over the brink. He flirts with every kind of radicalism which a big city offers, but such digressions never stir "the right feelings," and Augie drifts away from them. As a young boy he spends one summer with a group of enterprising relatives who are able to give him odd jobs, and Cousin Anna undertakes a comically macaronic program of religious instruction based on the Hebrew calendar and her own vague knowledge of the Old Testament. "I have to hand it to her," Augie comments, "that she knew her listener. There wasn't going to be any fooling about it. She was directing me out of her deep chest to the great eternal things" (27). The entire episode is written in a high comic style, but somehow Augie's life does become vaguely directed "to the great eternal things."

Even while he is learning from such people as Cousin Anna and Grandma Lausch, Augie is continually saying "no," refusing to be limited by loyalties which threaten his independence. It is Einhorn, his shadily but monolithically powerful employer, who first notices this quality in Augie when he confronts him about his role in a petty neighborhood theft:

". . . were you looking for a thrill? Is this a time to be looking for a thrill, when everybody else is covering up? You could take it out on the roller coasters, the bobs, the chute-the-chutes. Go to Riverview Park. But wait. All of a sudden I catch on to something about you. You've got *opposition* in you. You don't slide through everything. You just make it look so."

This was the first time [Augie notes] that anyone had told me anything like the truth about myself. I felt it powerfully. That, as he said, I did have opposition in me, and great desire to offer resistance and to say *"No!"* which was as clear as could be, as definite a feeling as a pang of hunger. (116–117)

Like so many picaros, Augie is singularly "adoptable." Almost everyone he meets wants either to adopt him or at least to plan his life. The first people to demonstrate this inclination are Grandma Lausch and Cousin Anna. When Augie begins to work for the Einhorns they continually emphasize the fact that he will not be remembered in their will, but that their entire commercial empire will go to their son—almost as a defense against Augie's adoptability. Mrs. Renling, a wealthy carriage-trade shopkeeper, takes control of Augie's life, teaches him how to dress, how to handle himself socially, and finally tries to begin formal adoption proceedings. Augie is perhaps the most adoptable character in American literature since Huckleberry Finn, but it is essential that the opposition in him arise in time to leave him absolute control over his own spirit. His persistent refusal to become involved or to conform to the will of others is positive criticism of things as they are. Even when he falls in love with women who try to "adopt" him, he refuses to be wholly recruited to their views of reality. What Augie fears when such overtures are made is the destruction of the self, and to him the contemporary world seems awesomely resourceful in the techniques of destruction.

Augie's brother Simon cultivates the very kind of emulation

which Augie resists. Having lost everything his family owns as the result of his infatuation for a bosomy neighborhood blonde, Simon determines to marry a wealthy commercial heiress. In a short while he has so thoroughly indoctrinated himself to the tastes and mannerisms of Charlotte Magnus's family that he becomes virtually their most representative member. On his way to becoming a commercial tycoon, Simon plans a similar course for Augie, setting him up as an ideal husband for Lucy Magnus, Charlotte's cousin. Since his love for his brother is so great, Augie plays Simon's game with thoroughness if not with enthusiasm, but he eliminates himself as a matrimonial candidate when he becomes involved with the efforts of a neighbor, Mimi Villars, to get an abortion. The child is not Augie's, but circumstances are against him, and Simon gives up all hope of being able to reform Augie's life, rejecting him as a *schlemiel*. Mimi, meanwhile, as one of the few people who do not want to adopt Augie, becomes a significant influence on his life. Her view of the world is statically fatalistic, and life for her is only a malicious joke through which man must suffer. In his rebellion against her morbid vision, Augie first begins to formulate his own impressions of life: "Me, I couldn't think all was so poured in concrete that there weren't occasions for happiness that weren't illusions of people still permitted to be forgetful of permanent disappointment, more or less permanent pain, death of children, lovers, friends, ends of causes, old age, loathsome breath, fallen faces, white hair, retreated breasts, dropped teeth; and maybe most intolerable the hardening of detestable character, like bone, similar to a second skeleton and creaking loudest before the end" (255).

It is this intense determination to see life as eventually meaningful which makes Augie realize "the shame of purposelessness" demonstrated by the WPA crew to which he belongs for a short while. He is suddenly aware that he is no longer a child, and that it is no longer sufficient for him merely to believe; he must implement his beliefs. There is never hope that Augie will be able to escape from reality into a world of childish innocence, even though his own innocence is perhaps his most outstanding characteristic. As in *Lie Down in Darkness*, the uncomplicated world of childhood is given an overtone of horror in being represented by a demented child—in this case Augie's brother Georgie, whose simple-minded song foreshadows Augie's efforts to find love:

> Georgie Mahchy, Augie, Simey
> Winnie Mahchy, evwy, evwy love Mama. (3)

From the moment of his realization of the shame of purposeless-ness, we see Augie's picaresque humor in a new light, as he himself reminds us that "Even the man who wants to believe, you some-times note kidding his way to Jesus" (302). If Augie is to succeed in his quest for a metaphorical Jesus he must maintain the defenses which have protected him from invasion by an adoption-minded world. The greatest single crisis of his life comes when he falls in love with the eccentric socialite Thea Fenchel, whose romantic, adventurous view of life threatens to strip Augie completely of the liberty which has always protected him. In Simon as well as in his own mother, Augie has an example of a family tendency toward surrender of freedom, and he has, in fact, become involved in so many "schemes" that he imagines himself as the family's least sta-ble member. As he prepares to leave for Mexico with Thea, Augie visits his mother, who instinctively fears that this new involvement will make her son unhappy. "And what lay behind this, I believe, was that if Simon hadn't helped me to choose, if I had picked for myself, my mother thought me to be sufficiently like her to get myself in a bad fix. I said nothing of the hunting to her, but it did occur to me how it was inevitable for the son of a Hagar to go chase wild animals at one time or another" (322). Having committed him-self to Thea's almost monomaniacal plan to hunt giant iguanas with an eagle, Augie begins to assume a more than casual parallel to Melville's Ishmael, that other son of Hagar.

There is no Queequeg to guide this modern Ishmael as he sets out on his mysterious voyage to Mexico (although there is such a figure in Bellow's *Henderson the Rain King*). It seems Augie's spe-cial fate to face the world alone, just as Joseph and Asa Leventhal faced it alone. If there is promise of a kind of rebirth in this pil-grimage to Mexico and in Caligula, the savage eagle which Thea and Augie carry with them to hunt the prehistoric lizards, the promise is quickly dispelled. The cul de sac which Augie encoun-ters in Mexico is foreshadowed in the novel by the experience of Eleanor Klein, who goes to Mexico for the ostensible purpose of marrying a well-to-do cousin but finds herself exploited as part of a sweatshop labor system. Rather than fulfillment and promise, Augie finds sordidness and infidelity in Mexico, and even Calig-ula—whom he fears, abhors, accepts, and finally in some respects admires—proves to be a failure; he is afraid of reptiles. As the bizarre life they have created begins to disintegrate around them, Thea and Augie gradually resume their individualistic poses. Augie strives vainly to reconstruct their romance, but gradually turns to alcohol and gambling in the hope of making his anxious days pass more quickly. Somehow Augie has managed to maintain his inno-cence, a quality which makes him a natural success at poker, for the people with whom he plays can never tell whether he is bluff-ing. "'Nobody can really be as innocent as all that'," an opponent scoffs, and Augie admits, "This was true, though I would have said I actually did intend to be as good as possible" (369). Even when he learns of Thea's affair with another man (and, ironically, when he makes love to Stella, a young movie starlet), he still maintains his intention to be as good as possible, although reality has taught him that it is those people who try to be good (his mother, his brother Georgie, Sophie Geratis) who somehow always end by being cheated. Augie's point of view—the maintenance of an intention which is opposed at almost every turn by reality—begins gradually to define him as an absurd man, even an absurd man with a specifi-cally practical idea of his own intention: "Everyone tries to create a world he can live in, and what he can't use he often can't see. But the real world is already created, and if your fabrication doesn't correspond, then even if you feel noble and insist on there being something better than what people call reality, that better some-thing needn't try to exceed what, in its actuality, since we know it so little, may be very surprising. If a happy state of things, surpris-ing; if miserable or tragic, no worse than we invent" (378). In re-fusing to succumb to the grimness of reality Augie becomes a re-bel, and he invents for himself "a man who can stand before the terrible appearances" (402) of external life. This instinct, Augie notes, is characteristic of inventors and artists and leaders of men, and is almost always used to recruit followers and therefore sustain the individual in his make-believe. Just as Augie refuses to be re-cruited to others' defenses against external life, so he initially de-clines to proselytize for his own creation, an image which "wanted simplicity and denied complexity" (402). Since Augie is a lone pil-grim by necessity rather than by choice, it becomes evident that he does not play the role of recruiting officer himself, for the sim-ple reason that the object of his quest lacks sufficient definition; Augie's experiences are not intended to be programmatic, pre-cisely because such a straightforward conception of experience— the presumption life can be arranged on a taut line—is foreign to Bellow's feeling for the vagaries of life. Augie's goal is similar to that of Rabbit Angstrom, since, although it is vague and elusive, its value comes from the fact that it repeatedly denies external reality as a final or total expression of human potential.

In his pilgrimage after what his friend Clem Tambow refers to as "'a worth-while fate'," all that Augie seems to have achieved is a fractured skull, lost teeth, and a broken heart. Because he continues to pursue his vague goal with such determination, Clem accuses him of having "'a nobility syndrome. You can't adjust to the reality situation. I can see it all over you. You want there should be Man, with capital M, with great stature'." "'Tell me, pal, am I getting warm or not?'" Clem asks. "'You are, yes you are'" (434–435), Augie answers. Clem argues that Augie must reconcile his vague goals with reality, and Augie refuses. "'I'll put it to you as I see it. It can never be right to offer to die, and if that's what the data of experience tell you, then you must get along without them'" (436). In refusing to reconcile himself to an adverse reality and in rejecting the idea of death as a solution to his dilemma, Augie increasingly asserts his position as an absurd man. Gradually, too, his conception of the general nature of his goal begins to come clear. He aims, he says, for the "axial lines of life, with respect to which you must be straight or else your existence is merely clownery, hiding tragedy" (454). In the painful struggle against reality man will suddenly come into harmony with these lines, and his life will be filled with joy, just as Sisyphus himself will suddenly be flooded with happiness as he shoulders the impossible weight of his stone. "'I have felt these thrilling lines again'," Augie explains. "'When striving stops, there they are as a gift. . . . Truth, love, peace, bounty, usefulness, harmony!'"

"At any time life can come together again and man be regenerated, and doesn't have to be a god or public servant like Osiris who gets torn apart annually for the sake of the common prosperity, but the man himself, finite and taped as he is, can still come where the axial lines are. He will be brought into focus. He will live with true joy. Even his pains will be joy if they are true, even his helplessness will not take away his power, even wandering will not take him away from himself, even the big social jokes and hoaxes need not make him ridiculous, even disappointment after disappointment need not take away his love. Death will not be terrible to him if life is not." (454–455)

What Augie has described is a life lived without appeal, a life in which, other truths being denied, pain and disappointment not only become something to live for; they may even be a source of joy. Augie has paraphrased, in this vision of "axial lines," the absurd formula embodied in the figure of Sisyphus. Augie's greatest desire is to be no more and no less than human, retaining a moral vision in terms of the axial lines he has discovered. In rejecting the temptations of wealth and success to which Simon yields, he becomes a rebel, but deflection from society is, as Camus argues, "profoundly positive in that it reveals the part of man which must always be defended." It was his failure to realize the positive aspects of Augie's revolt which led Robert Penn Warren to refer to him as "a man with no commitments."[4] While it is true that Augie resists limiting commitments to society, he does so in order to protect his commitment to himself.

Although this positive aspect of his quest—his belief in the presence of axial lines—is slow in achieving definition, through it Augie envisions founding a home where he can board and teach orphaned children. The height of his fervor for this project becomes almost comic, and the reader sees him as a kind of overgrown "catcher in the rye." Augie's adoption scheme—an ironic and to some degree philosophically inconsistent reversal of his own earlier independent position—fades as he becomes carried away with the idea of the Second World War: "Overnight I had no personal notions at all" (*AAM*, 457). Through the war and his hasty marriage to Stella, Augie becomes again the peripatetic hero. Torpedoed at sea, he climbs into a life boat with the only other survivor of the shipwreck—a monomaniacal biologist who claims to have discovered a process for creating life. Bateshaw, who does all he can to recruit Augie to his schemes, becomes a tragic and bitter parallel to Augie's own struggles against reality:

"The shoving multitude bears down, and you're nothing, a meaningless name, and not just obscure in eternity but right now. The fate of the meanest your fate. Death! But no, there must be some distinction. The soul cries out against this namelessness. And then it exaggerates. It tells you, 'You were meant to astonish the world. You, Hymie Bateshaw, *Stupor mundi!* My boy, brace up. You have been called, and you will be chosen. So start looking the part. The generations of man will venerate you as long as calendars exist!' This is neurotic, I know—excuse the jargon—but to be not neurotic is to adjust to what they call the reality situation. But the reality situation is what I have described. A billion souls boiling with anger at a doom of insignificance." (503)

Bateshaw speaks with more insight into the boredom of the human spirit and the need to resist the "reality situation" than anyone Augie has ever known before, and it is an essential irony of the novel that this man who seems to speak so wisely of "unused capacities" is a hopeless neurotic.

As the novel closes we have a view of Augie playing what, on the surface at least, is the most conventional role of his life. He is involved in selling (often in blackmarketing) surplus goods in Europe, and his wife Stella is working in Paris as a movie actress. War has tempered Augie, and a relatively successful marriage has helped to smooth down some of his rough edges. The experience with Bateshaw has affected his ideas of opposition to reality, but he still maintains the belief that "Death is going to take the boundaries away from us, that we should no more be persons. That's what death is about. When that is what life also wants to be about, how can you feel except rebellious?" (519). He is still affirmative, even though hope, as represented by the idea of a home for children where he can unite his mother and demented brother, is now transferred to his unborn children.

It seems essential to the picaresque structure of *The Adventures of Augie March* that we leave the hero as we found him—a wanderer. Saul Bellow has at least shown us a moment of absurd vision which, however transitory, offers a promise not enjoyed by Leventhal or Joseph and only exceeded in *Henderson the Rain King* and *Herzog*. In the laughter which concludes the novel, however, we are inevitably reminded of the man "you sometimes note kidding his way to Jesus." Augie has gone out of his way to drive Stella's maid, Jacqueline, to Normandy, where she will visit her family. When his car breaks down, Augie hikes with her across the frozen winter fields, singing to keep warm. As they near her home, he learns that the dream of her life is to go to Mexico, and remembering how the same dream had once seemed to be the hope of his own life, he begins to laugh. But he realizes that, after all, it is no more laughable that Jacqueline should hope to find fulfillment in Mexico than that Augie now sought the same fulfillment in her native France. Later,

I was still chilled from the hike across the fields, but, thinking of Jacqueline and Mexico, I got to grinning again. That's the *animal ridens* in me, the laughing creature, forever rising up. What's so laughable, that a Jacqueline, for instance, as hard used as that by rough forces, will still refuse to lead a disappointed life? Or is the laugh at nature—including eternity—that it thinks it can win over us and the power of hope? Nah, nah! I think. It never will. But that probably is the joke, on one or the other, and laughing is an enigma that includes both. Look at me, going everywhere! Why, I am a sort of Columbus of those near-at-hand and believe you can come to them in this immediate *terra incognita* that spreads out in every gaze. I may as well flop in this line of endeavor. Columbus too thought he was a flop, probably, when they sent him back in chains. Which didn't prove there was no America. (536)

And Augie, trying to beat the dark to Bruges to close an illicit deal for purchasing nylon, with his movie starlet wife awaiting his return in a moldy Paris apartment, nevertheless does not disprove the existence of "axial lines."

In *Seize the Day*—a collection consisting of a novella, three short stories, and a one-act play—Saul Bellow returned to the terse prose and muted action which characterized *Dangling Man* and *The Victim*. In the novella which gives this book its title, we are presented with a painful picture of a morbid gerontocracy obviously intended to represent the same oppression and dehumanization which Bellow constantly endeavors to expose in his work. Tommy Wilhelm, the pathetic failure who is the hero of "Seize the Day," seems to have wandered up almost every dead end which the world has to offer. His early career as a screen star was a hopeless joke; his marriage has ended in a torturous separation; a once rejuvenating love affair has simply faded away; and he has resigned, out of pride, a lucrative and well-established sales position with a large Eastern manufacturing company. Like Bellow's Joseph, Tommy Wilhelm is a dangling man, suspended between jobs and between loves; and like Leventhal he is a strange kind of victim-victimizer.

The action of this novella is concentrated in a single day in the life of Tommy Wilhelm, an impulsive, in many respects childlike, man. During that day Wilhelm is compelled to review the course of his life in an effort to comprehend his needs as well as his weaknesses. In the figure of his father, Wilhelm has a constant reminder of the demands which the external world makes on a man, and Dr. Adler has measured up to those demands with great vigor. He is distinguished, moneyed, respected, neat, "sensible," and his son (who has maintained the "stage" name he was given years before) is a perpetual source of disappointment. Wilhelm's pursuit of mercy and tenderness is unrelenting, but these are not qualities to be found in Dr. Adler, or in the aging residence hotel to which the father has retired, or in the indifferent, fast-paced city about which Wilhelm blunders.

If Dr. Adler is intended to suggest the superficialities of the urban system, Dr. Tamkin, a shady psychiatrist, represents its corrupting influences. Tamkin is the only person to whom Wilhelm can talk, and while he seems at first to represent a kind of salvation, he turns into the same deceitful but distinctly comic maniac as Bateshaw in *The Adventures of Augie March*. Winning Tommy's confidence with free psychiatric "advice" and a willing ear, he enlists him in a stockmarket scheme which seems Tommy's last hope for recouping his dwindling resources. Tamkin tries to teach Wilhelm that the real universe is "'the present moment. The past is no good to us. The future is full of anxiety. Only the present is real—the here-and-now. Seize the day'" (SD, 66). He emphasizes to the younger man the necessity of distinguishing his "real" soul from his "pretender" soul. Much of what Tamkin argues seems true to Wilhelm—especially the psychiatrist's description of the human soul as something "howling from his window like a wolf" when night comes (67), and Wilhelm momentarily accepts his line of reasoning and agrees to cooperate in his schemes. The charlatan-psychiatrist draws a picture of the world as "'a kind of purgatory'" populated by "'poor human beasts'" (71), a description which seems tailored to Wilhelm's experience, but it presupposes a nihilism which he cannot accept. Even while he is cringing beneath the blows which life is delivering him, Wilhelm maintains his intention to find tenderness and kindness. His quest amounts simply to an effort to reaffirm man's humanity, to restore an idea of dignity to the human race, and his intention is both reflected and parodied in one of Tamkin's poems:

MECHANISM VS FUNCTIONALISM
ISM VS HISM

If thee thyself couldst only see
Thy greatness that is and yet to be,
Thou would feel joy-beauty-what ecstasy.
They are at thy feet, earth-moon-sea, the trinity.

Why-forth then dost thou tarry
And partake thee only of the crust
And skim the earth's surface narry
When all creations art thy just?

Seek ye then that which art not there
In thine own glory let thyself rest.
Witness. Thy power is not bare.
Thou art King. Thou art at thy best.

Look then right before thee.
Open thine eyes and see.
At the foot of Mt. Serenity
Is thy cradle to eternity. (75)

The quest which this poem ambiguously describes has been encouraged by something like an absurd vision which had occurred to Wilhelm several days before the novella opens. As he passed through an underground corridor he suddenly imagined himself embracing and blessing all mankind, and the memory of that vision returns to him as he sits in the stock exchange waiting for Tamkin:

A queer look came over Wilhelm's face with its eyes turned up and his silent mouth with its high upper lip. He went several degrees further—when you are like this, dreaming that everybody is outcast, you realize that this must be one of the small matters. There is a larger body, and from this you cannot be separated. The glass of water fades out. You do not go from simple *a* and simple *b* to the great *x* and *y*, nor does it matter whether you agree about the glass but, far beneath such details, what Tamkin would call the real soul says plain and understandable things to everyone. There sons and fathers are themselves, and a glass of water is only an ornament; it makes a hoop of brightness on the cloth; it is an angel's mouth. There truth for everybody may be found, and confusion is only—only temporary, thought Wilhelm. (84)

As these thoughts pass through Wilhelm's mind Tamkin is in the process of losing the rest of their money on the stock exchange, and in the crowded room in which Tommy Wilhelm sits men are frantically worshipping the golden calf of speculation. In this environment his deepening convictions seem increasingly absurd.

Tamkin vanishes, and Wilhelm is left alone to contemplate his complete financial ruin. Turning to his father in a final, desperate plea for grace, Wilhelm is rejected more bitterly than ever before. His vision of truth and of brightness seems to have faded completely, but in the final moments of the story crowds force him into a funeral procession, and before he knows what is happening he is standing over a coffin looking down into the face of a total stranger. Suddenly he begins to cry for this man, "another human creature," who comes to represent everyone he had ever loved, everyone from whom he had wanted kindness. Like the true Christian knight, Wilhelm has cast off the burden of pride, "bending his stubborn head, bowing his shoulders, twisting his face" (117–118), and achieving at last the feeling of oneness with humanity which has been the object of his quest. As the funeral music comes to his ears he sinks "deeper than sorrow, through torn sobs and cries toward the consummation of his heart's ultimate need" (118). As one of Bellow's critics has commented, "This is a vision . . . that transcends defeat, transcends, in fact, both love and death because it fastens on the means of their reconciliation."[5] The Bellow hero can run no longer; beaten and exhausted, Wilhelm is forced in his extremity to find a meaning to life or to die. In his final, desperate adventure he finds himself moving "toward a consummation of his heart's ultimate need," a need for existence itself. The movement from isolation to affirmation of existence in the world is reiterated in *Henderson the Rain King* as "Grun-tu-molani." Henderson himself is able to carry the principle farther because his energies and ambitions demand to know the form and the goal which existence should adopt. All Bellow heroes begin by trying to throw off responsibility and the chaotic weight of the world, but love for mankind finally brings them back to the business of living in the real world, even when the real seems chaotic and destructive.

Throughout Bellow's work there is an increasingly modulated emphasis on the almost Jamesian notion that the lack of money will enslave the individual to the artificialities of contemporary life; in a world which typically measures success by the material, it becomes increasingly difficult for the individual to escape the dehumanizing marketplace. Only in the wealthy (three million dollars after taxes) Henderson do we have a successful Bellow "knight" completely free of financial pressures. In the three short stories which accompany "Seize the Day," as well as in the one-act play "The Wrecker," Bellow continues to crystallize his comments on reality around society's compulsion for material success. Rogin, the central character of "A Father-to-Be," realizes that "Money surrounds you in life as the earth does in death" (*SD*, 123). He has a sudden feeling of hope, however, in the idea that all men are similarly enslaved, and while we know that Rogin's elated feeling can be only temporary, Bellow's last view of him is of a man overwhelmed by "his own secret loving spirit" (133), as his anger at his spendthrift mistress gradually fades away.

Like Henderson, Clarence Feiler in "The Gonzaga Manuscripts" has sufficient financial independence to pursue an economically undisturbed quest, but his very financial independence eventually leads him to bitter disappointment. Feiler travels to Spain in search of the mysterious manuscripts which give this story its title. That he is related to all of Bellow's other heroes is clear from the fact that he chooses to devote himself to the obscure Spanish poet Gonzaga rather than to modern English history, which to him "'doesn't express much wish to live'." He is in touch, he feels, with "'a poet who could show me how to go on, and what attitude to take toward life'" (163). Gonzaga becomes an *in absentia* Sancho Panza or Queequeg, and by locating the lost manuscripts Feiler hopes to make a gift to the world as well as to give shape to his own life. "He was becoming an eccentric; it was all he could do with his good impulses. As yet he did not realize that these impulses were religious" (163–164). Bringing to light the testimony of a great man is to be his gesture both against a superficial world and in behalf of it. Clarence Feiler is led through a minor peccadillo of mistaken identities and tweaked noses, almost always looked at askance as the boorish, insensitive caricature of the American tourist. At last, however, he seems to have found the object of his quest. Standing beneath "a harshly crowned Christ" (189) in a Segovian church, Clarence reaches out to his contact man for the long-sought manuscripts. The moment has all the solemnity and ecstatic expectation of a communion service, a mood which is broken only when the American looks down to discover that he is holding mining stocks. The great symbol of life which he sought has been replaced by stock in a pitchblende mine—"*Para la bomba atómica*" (190), as his guide explains.

"Looking for Mr. Green" chronicles the lonely search of a Chicago relief worker for an elusive Mr. Green. It is George Grebe's duty to see that the man receives his relief check, and as he wanders through the Negro district he begins to learn something of the distrust which poorer people feel for the person who claims to have something to "give" them. He comes "as an emissary from hostile appearances" (160), but finding Mr. Green becomes more than just the opportunity to perform well in his new job. For George Grebe the search becomes a symbolic opportunity for expressing his desire to reach out and help his fellow man. Even though the circumstances under which he delivers the check are humiliating, he is nevertheless elated by the knowledge that Mr. Green "'*could* be found!'" (160).

In the one-act play "The Wrecker" a man is determined to destroy the dingy apartment that represents his enslavement to the city, and to emphasize the relationship between contemporary slavery and the drive for material success. Bellow has his "wrecker" turn down a $1,000 bonus in order to remain in his apartment after other tenants have vacated the building and have the pleasure of destroying it himself. He is able to defeat his wife's appeal to the joys of lovemaking which the bedroom represents for her, and in the end she joins him in the destruction of their home. While the play is nonsensical and often frivolous, it is not an inappropriate conclusion to a volume which emphasizes the idea of money as the image of an oppressive public world. The wrecker's gesture of defiance is dramatically satisfying, and the contrast between his destructive intention and the reality of the massive stone walls he has vowed to destroy is a clear example of the absurd.

All of the variety of Bellow's earlier work and all of his concern with the individual who is able to maintain his intention in the face of an opposing reality come together to form an intense and unified testament to the absurd hero in *Henderson the Rain King*. Joseph dangles and drops; Leventhal is only partially awakened; Augie's vision wavers with the buffetings of fate; and Tommy Wilhelm's consummation comes as the result of a push from the crowd. Only the prodigious Henderson is a consistently and devotedly conscious seeker, and the consummation of his quest creates a feeling of magnificence unknown in Bellow's other novels—even in the more complex resolution of *Herzog*. But Henderson is closely related to Joseph, Leventhal, Wilhelm, Augie March, and Moses E. Herzog in that they are all faced by the crossroads where "one path leads to the society, the other away from the community." Henderson is able to rejoin society on satisfactory terms, reinforcing Richard Lehan's observation of the tendency for the new existential hero to take the path toward society, as in the case of Camus's Rieux, Tarrou, and D'Arrest, and Bellow's Leventhal and Wilhelm.[6] Like Camus's later heroes and like Tommy Wilhelm and Asa Leventhal, Bellow's Henderson is an example of the contemporary absurd hero's possession of a new and strangely ennobling compassion.

Much of *Henderson the Rain King*—especially the opening description of Henderson's bizarre life as the pig-raising, law-breaking, violin-playing scion of an ancient and distinguished American family—is clearly reminiscent of the picaresque tradition. But when Henderson journeys into the heart of a symbolic Africa, the novel—while maintaining all the elements of a picaresque—also moves into what might be called the grail tradition. In bringing rain to the dry land Henderson has lifted the curse from the realm of the Fisher King, and he flees to safety with the risen King. The wasteland which he cleanses is Biblical and Shakespearian as well as contemporaneous with the wasteland of T. S. Eliot. The novel is filled with references to fertility myths, and Henderson is a pilgrim in progress. In the faithful guide Romilayu, he has his Sancho Panza, Queequeg, Virgil, and Hopeful. While all of these ingredients are significant to the structure of the novel, it is well to heed Bellow's own advice to "symbol hunters"[7] and to avoid taking such obvious analogies too seriously. Henderson *is* a questing figure, a clumsy knight-errant, and finally a Rain King, but Bellow repeatedly urges us to see him as a human being rather than the embodiment of myths. We can, and invariably must, approach his character through the mythological suggestions which surround him, but we must always see Henderson as an archetype in his own right, a character with sufficient substance and importance to stand alone.

The comic turn which Bellow often introduces should remind us of the danger of becoming overly serious when dealing with his work. Henderson himself keeps us aware of the ridiculousness of the serious when, as the "Sungo," he runs about an African village in great ballooning green silk pants and sprinkles water on the grateful natives; everyone awaited this blessing from the Sungo. The women were especially eager for the dole of water, Henderson comments, "as the Sungo was also in charge of fertility; you see, it goes together with moisture" (HRK, 242). By lacing Henderson's picaresque voyage with suggestions of grail legends, Bellow suggests the former as a comic inversion of the latter, and emphasizes not only the ridiculousness of the serious, but the seriousness of the ridiculous.

Bellow warns us that the quest myth does not totally explain Henderson's experience, and it in large part fails to do so because Henderson does not have recourse to the same spiritual absolutes available to the grail-seeking knight; just as Updike showed us a saint without God, so Bellow shows us a knight without God. To emphasize this quality of the hero Bellow has interjected into the myth and fantasy of his novel tones of what one critic has called *dire realism* and *significant modernity*.[8] Henderson's modernity is emphasized in the opening chapters of the novel, when we see him blundering through the contemporary frustrations and enigmas faced by all Bellow heroes. Trying to explain why he suddenly left for Africa, Henderson comments that "Things got worse and worse and pretty soon they were too complicated."

When I think of my condition at the age of fifty-five when I bought the ticket, all is grief. The facts begin to crowd me and soon I get a pressure in the chest. A disorderly rush begins—my parents, my wives, my girls, my children, my farm, my animals, my habits, my money, my music lessons, my drunkenness, my prejudices, my brutality, my teeth, my face, my soul! I have to cry, "No, no, get back, curse you, let me alone!" But how can they let me alone? They belong to me. They are mine. And they pile into me from all sides. It turns into chaos. (HRK, 3)

His trip to Africa, Henderson assures us, at last provided an end to this chaos. But it is not merely his dislocation and frustrations which make Henderson a questing man; for inside him is a voice— much like that which haunts Rabbit Angstrom—which says "*I want*," and it is through his voyage into the Africa of his own soul that he will finally satisfy this cry.

Like many absurd heroes, Henderson considers suicide as a salvation from the pains of his life, but suicide must be rejected as a denial of one of the essential terms of the absurd confrontation. After several painful months in Paris, when he tries to adjust to new dental work and a disintegrating marriage, Henderson meets Lily, an eccentric American opportunist with whom he had once had an affair. He runs away with her to visit the famous cathedrals of France, but becomes so disgusted with her sloppiness and lying that he sends her back to Paris alone. He has threatened her with suicide unless she ceases to annoy him, and his threat is not wholly comic. After leaving Lily, he drives to Banyules, and in a marine station there he has a vision of death which he instinctively rejects. Pressing his head against the glass of an aquarium, he looks in at an octopus, "and the creature seemed also to look at me and press its soft head to the glass, flat, the flesh becoming pale and granular— blanched, speckled. The eyes spoke to me coldly. But even more speaking, even more cold, was the soft head with its speckles, and the Brownian motion in those speckles, a cosmic coldness in which I felt I was dying. The tentacles throbbed and motioned through the glass, the bubbles sped upward, and I thought, 'This is my last day. Death is giving me notice'" (19).

Repulsed by this vision of death, Henderson devotes himself even more intensely to life. The savage, loony gusto with which he attempts to live is certainly unparalleled in contemporary litera- ture; the nearest approximation is Papa Cue Ball, the tormented, rumbustious hero of John Hawkes' *Second Skin*. Everything which he does—including raising pigs in all the handsome old buildings on the estate which he has inherited—is executed with a fierce energy compatible with his enormous body, but every life-seizing gesture seems to end in destruction or frustration. Even the pigs warn him of his alienation from life, as he continually recalls Daniel's admonishment to King Nebuchadnezzar, "'They shall drive thee from among men, and thy dwelling shall be with the beasts of the field'" (21). While his ponderous body often makes his aloneness seem comical, it also frequently gives his isolation a poi- gnant significance. Such is the case in the crossroads incident which Henderson recalls from the war. After reporting that he has crabs, Henderson is stripped, soaped, and shaved by four army medics, who leave the naked, hairless man standing in the middle of a crossroads near the waterfront at Salerno. "They ran away and left me bald and shivering, ugly, naked, prickling between the legs and under the arms, raging, laughing, and swearing revenge. These are things a man never forgets and afterward truly values. That beautiful sky, and the mad itch and the razors; and the Medi-

terranean, which is the cradle of mankind; the towering softness of
the air; the sinking softness of the water, where Ulysses got lost,
where he, too, was naked as the sirens sang" (22).

Even after he has divorced his first wife and married Lily, Henderson is still naked and alone in the world, and as well as the
significant physical pains which he suffers from dental work, fights,
and accidents, he is continually and increasingly tormented by the
voice which cries "*I want.*" He tries every kind of cure he can think
of, meanwhile realizing that "in an age of madness, to expect to be
untouched by madness is a form of madness. But the pursuit of
sanity can be a form of madness, too" (25). Henderson's particular
"mad" pursuit of sanity will eventually reveal itself as the pursuit of
order or meaning lying behind the madness and suffering of the
world. He attempts to ease the strangulation in his heart by learning to play his father's violin, hoping also to make spiritual contact
with a man whose life was one of quiet order and whose beard was
"like a protest that gushed from his very soul" (25). "I played," he
says, "with dedication, with feeling, with longing, love—played to
the point of emotional collapse. Also down there in my studio I
sang as I played, 'Rispondi! Anima bella' (Mozart). 'He was despised and rejected, a man of sorrows and acquainted with grief'
(Handel)" (30). But the violin and the singing do not relieve his
frustrated feeling that he is only another of the countless displaced
persons without a station in life.

Henderson opposes reality, which reveals itself to him as suffering, loneliness, madness, with the intention that human life can be
made meaningful, that the spirit can be satisfied. He never hides
from reality and is in fact, as he argues to Lily, "'on damned good
terms with reality'" (36), but it offers no fulfillment of his spiritual
needs, a fulfillment which will be consummated only through what
King Dahfu will reveal to him as a "higher reality." Like Tommy
Wilhelm's frustrations, many of Henderson's stem from pride. It is
pride which leads him to a pig-raising career and which also causes
him to commit "an offense against my daughter" (37) by parting her
from the abandoned Negro baby which she finds and brings home
to raise. When he sees the despair in his daughter's eyes, he realizes that he has helped to displace at least one other person in the
world, and that Ricey's belief that she is the baby's mother is a
corollary to his own desire to love man. Bound home after leaving
the inconsolable Ricey with an aunt in Providence, Henderson sits
alone playing solitaire and is in such a state of nervous exhaustion
when he leaves the train that he has to be carried off, swearing

continually, "'There is a curse on this land. There is something bad going on. Something is wrong. There is a curse on this land!'" (38). Henderson will lift this curse when he raises up the ponderous figure of Mummah in an African rain ceremony.

Horrified by what he has done to Ricey and by his possible involvement in the death of the old woman who helped Lily in the kitchen, Henderson leaves for Africa. The dedication with which he attacks this new mission is indicated by the fact that he buys only a one-way ticket, and in fact, the Henderson who leaves Idlewild Airport never returns—but is sloughed off somewhere in the heart of an imaginary Africa. His break with civilization is not complete, however, so long as he merely accompanies the honeymooning friends who have formed the photographic expedition he joins. Promising him a jeep in return for his services, Henderson convinces the often laughably dedicated native guide, Romilayu, to take him to places "off the beaten track," and in the primitive, isolated villages which they visit Henderson stills the voice that cries inside him. His long trek into the heart of Africa begins with a kind of purification in which he leaves his old troubles behind him: ". . . it was all simplified and splendid, and I felt I was entering the past—the real past, no history or junk like that. The prehuman past. And I believed that there was something between the stones and me. The mountains were naked, and often snakelike in their forms, without trees, and you could see the clouds being born on the slopes" (46).

· Henderson's first peccadillo in Africa occurs among the Arnewi, a cattle-worshipping people whose gods are dying because of the drought and whose emergency water system, a cistern, is poisoned by "unholy" frogs. One of Henderson's first announcements to these people is that "'I am really kind of on a quest'" (65). As he comes to grips with an Arnewi warrior in a wrestling match that is intended to introduce strangers to the tribe, Henderson thinks, "'I do remember well the hour which burst my spirit's sleep'" (67). And this breaking of his spirit's sleep—like the absurd man's shaking off the routine of "Rising, streetcar, four hours in the office or the factory"—is the beginning of consciousness and identification. Confronted by the Arnewi queen Willátale, Henderson is compelled to review his own life before telling these people who he is: "Who—who was I? A millionaire wanderer and wayfarer. A brutal and violent man driven into the world. A man who fled his own country, settled by his forefathers. A fellow whose heart said, *I want, I want.* Who played the violin in despair, seeking the voice of angels. Who had to burst the spirit's sleep, or else. So what could I tell this old queen in a lion skin and raincoat . . . ?" (76–77). He is at last able to confess to someone about the voice inside him, and Willatale helps him to break his spirit's sleep by describing that voice as "grun-tu-molani," the desire to live as a whole man. Henderson becomes convinced that the Queen can show him the mysteries of life and determine precisely what his voice wants. She understands that Henderson has "'never been at home in life'" (84), and is therefore in many respects still a child. Overcome with the discovery of someone who can understand him, Henderson raises his helmet in salute to all the members of the court. "'Grun-tu-molani'," he shouts. "'God does not shoot dice with our souls, and therefore grun-tu-molani'" (85).

In hopes of striking a kind of exchange with the Arnewi through which they will lead him into the secrets of grun-tu-molani, Henderson sets about ridding their cistern of frogs. Using his wartime training, he rigs a bomb out of gunpowder and a flashlight case, but the bomb destroys the cistern as well as the frogs, and Henderson leaves the Arnewi in disgrace. While it might prove interesting to speculate on the degree to which Bellow intended to parody American lend-lease programs in this episode, the real significance rests in the fact that as soon as Henderson calls upon the devices of "civilized" man, he blunders into the same blind alleys that characterized his life in America.

After weary days of walking, Henderson and Romilayu reach the Wariri, a more aggressive tribe whose first act is to strip the white man of all his civilized possessions, leaving him only the clothes he wears as a reminder of the world he has come from. Like the Arnewi, the Wariri are troubled by drought, and it is Henderson's special privilege to be given a seat of honor by their king in order to watch the rainmaking proceedings. His longing to do something for people prompts him to volunteer to try to move the giant wooden goddess Mummah, who must be propitiated if rain is to come, and whose bulk has overwhelmed all contestants. Henderson moves the statue even though, as the unbeliever, he has made a bet with the king that the ceremony will not produce rain. The contest offers Henderson an opportunity to demonstrate his physical power and therefore to make some payment to nature for the gift of strength which he feels he has abused. The challenge of the stolid wooden goddess becomes his opportunity to make a gesture against the "law of decay" (190) by which he has always lived, and his success in lifting the idol fills him with joy:

I stood still. There beside Mummah in her new situation I myself was
filled with happiness. I was so gladdened by what I had done that my
whole body was filled with soft heat, with soft and sacred light. The sen-
sations of illness I had experienced since morning were all converted into
their opposites. . . . And so my fever was transformed into jubilation.
My spirit was awake and it welcomed life anew. Damn the whole thing!
Life anew! I was still alive and kicking and I had the old grun-tu-molani.
(192–193)

As if to remind us that Henderson's zeal for living and the free-
ing of his spirit are not the consummation of his quest—that he
must also learn *how* to live—Bellow follows this ecstatic monologue with a farcical tour of the village in which the new Sungo or
Rain King, stripped naked by the native women, is chased through
the village, dropped into muddy water holes that they may be
blessed with water, and finally overwhelmed by a shouting, whip-
flailing group of his worshippers. But rain does come from what
had only a few hours before been a cloudless sky, and Henderson at
last has a "sign."

Only one character in this novel is untouched by the comic sense
which emerges in Bellow whenever there is danger of overserious-
ness, and that is King Dahfu, the elegant, graceful, resplendent,
slightly rebellious monarch who tries to show Henderson how he
can move from what appears to be an arrested state of "becoming"
into a state of "being." Dahfu is charmed by Henderson's almost
childlike insistence that the world can and should be something
other than a location for suffering.

Henderson's fascination with Daniel's prophecy to Nebuchadnezzar comes back to him when he agrees to become a pupil of
Dahfu's philosophy, for this means entering the den of a massive
lion imprisoned beneath the palace and, through emulation of the
lion's movements and sounds, recapturing the dignity and humility
which nature intended her higher creatures to demonstrate.
Weakened by fever, by his duties as Rain King, by trying to understand palace intrigues and Dahfu's intricate philosophy, Henderson begins again to think of reality as an unbearable complex of
pressures. His point of view is understandable to the king, who
argues that

"Men of most powerful appetite have always been the ones to doubt reality the most. Those who could not bear that hopes should turn to misery,
and loves to hatreds, and deaths and silences, and so on. The mind has a
right to its reasonable doubts, and with every short life it awakens and
sees and understands what so many other minds of equally short life span

have left behind. It is natural to refuse belief that so many small spans should have made so glorious one large thing. That human creatures by pondering should be *correct*. That is what makes a fellow gasp. Yes, Sungo, this same temporary creature is a master of imagination. And right now this very valuable possession appears to make him die and not to live. Why? It is astonishing what a fact that is." (232)

Through his contact with the vital and sympathetic king, Henderson comes to believe with increasing strength that there is a force which rules the world and to which man can appeal in his need. He appeals to that still undefined force when he prays for Dahfu's safety, for the young king must capture the soul of his father wandering the bush in the form of a massive lion. Each night since his arrival in Africa, Henderson has watched, with increasing interest, Romilayu kneeling at his prayers; carried away by his anxiety for the king's safety, Henderson kneels beside the native and prays: "'Oh, you . . . Something,' I said, 'you Something because of whom there is not Nothing. Help me to do Thy will. Take off my stupid sins. Untrammel me. Heavenly Father, open up my dumb heart and for Christ's sake preserve me from unreal things. Oh, Thou who tookest me from pigs, let me not be killed over lions. And forgive my crimes and nonsense and let me return to Lily and the kids'" (253). This appeal to a supernatural power is not, of course, consistent with Camus's description of the absurd man, but insofar as Henderson's prayer emphasizes an order to the universe in opposition to almost everything which reality has revealed to him, its substance correlates with the absurd stance he has begun to take; the successful conclusion of his quest will eliminate Henderson's need for such appeals.

Through the influences of Dahfu, the lion, and Romilayu, Henderson is being purified and prepared for the consummation of his vision. Dahfu tells him of all the things which he can now learn from the lion: "'She will make consciousness to shine. She will burnish you. She will force the present moment upon you. . . . You fled what you were. You did not believe you had to perish. Once more, and a last time, you tried the world. With a hope of alteration'" (260). The lion's den now becomes the scene of a massive and often comical therapy, in which Henderson renounces the tendency of his consciousness "'to isolate self'" (267). When he roars he gives up everything in his soul which has ever wanted to come forth, and at last he even brings forth, as a "hot noise," all of his human longing. His most supreme moment of roaring summarizes the entire course of his life, "from birth to Africa; and certain words crept into my roars," he says, "like 'God,' 'Help,' 'Lord have mercy,' only they came out 'Hooolp!' 'Moooorcy!' It's funny what words sprang forth. 'Au secours,' which was 'secooooooor' and also 'De profoooondis,' plus snatches from the 'Messiah' (He was despised and rejected, a man of sorrows, etcetera)" (274).

Despite his fear of the lion and the fever which makes his "exercises" painful and draining, Henderson's persistence in the ritual to which Dahfu has introduced him is not simply the result of his feeling of friendship for the king. The ritual of the lion's den is part of the larger picture of man's search for hope, of his insistence that the world can be changed for the better.

Part of the wisdom that Henderson finds is in the knowledge that he cannot raise himself into any other world, that no matter how much a prison his life and his deeds seem, he must live in the world, and while he admits, "*I don't think the struggles of desire can ever be won*" (285), he continues to reap the profits of the struggle itself. Dahfu has warned him that there is no issue from the dreary circles of fear and desire unless man is willing to take life into his own hands. Freed by his new realizations, he concludes, "I must begin to think how to live," and among other things he knows that he "must break Lily from blackmail and set love on a true course" (288). Despite the apparent ridiculousness of his decision—its *social* absurdity—he determines to enter medical school and learn to serve humanity by healing. The role of healer (like that of Dr. Rieux in *The Plague*) seems to be a logical one for the absurd man who has returned to society.

The most dramatic expression of Henderson's opposition to reality comes when he witnesses Dahfu's attempts to capture the savage lion that presumably bears the soul of his father. The voice of this monstrous beast threatening his friend jars Henderson's mind from any hope of escape from reality through dreams or "unreal" constructs. When Dahfu falls from his slight perch above the enclosure into which the lion has been driven, Henderson leaps down with him. As the king lies dying, Henderson throws himself on the "bitch" of reality and makes it fast with a rope. But when he escapes from the scheming Wariri politicians who plan to make him their puppet king, he takes with him the small lion cub decreed to contain the soul of the dead Dahfu; as the feverish Henderson stumbles his way back to civilization, he also has a reminder that life is not always harsh or cheap. The cub reminds him that something is promised to man, that he is intended, at least occasionally, to have justice.

Henderson's voice has demanded reality, and there is no doubt to what accomplishments its demands have driven him. His "quest is a successful one since he returns from his symbolic Africa in presumed possession of the selfhood he went to seek. But what success means here and how he has achieved it can best be understood by what his symbolic adventures and misadventures achieve. An actual process and method, akin to a religious experience, must be undergone."⁹ Through the symbolic prophet Dahfu, Henderson enters a new world of the self, and after becoming naked before the Wariri he is reclothed in Rome. On the journey home he is attracted by a small orphan who is being sent to live with relatives in Nevada. When the plane lands in Newfoundland to refuel, he gathers the boy up in his arms, trying to give him something of the warmth and joy which he now feels for life. Slipping on the ice, he runs around the plane exultantly:

I held him close to my chest. He didn't seem to be afraid that I would fall with him. While to me he was like medicine applied, and the air, too; it also was a remedy. Plus the happiness that I expected at Idlewild from meeting Lily. And the lion? He was in it, too. Laps and laps I galloped around the shining and riveted body of the plane . . . The great, beautiful propellers were still, all four of them. I guess I felt it was my turn now to move, and so went running—leaping, leaping, pounding, and tingling over the pure white lining of the gray Arctic silence. (*HRK*, 340–341)

Ihab Hassan has appropriately commented that "for once the American hero does go back home again," and he goes home with the knowledge that "chaos does not run the whole human show."¹⁰

What Henderson has found is the way back to the world and to a life of service, and his victory comes suddenly after he has dedicated himself to a struggle which seems hopeless but which he must maintain in order to be true to himself. Camus described happiness and the absurd as inseparable, for the absurd teaches "that all is not, has not been, exhausted. It drives out of this world a god who had come into it with dissatisfaction and a preference for futile sufferings. It makes of fate a human matter, which must be settled among men."¹¹ Out of an absurd, chaotic, fragmentary world in which loneliness and pain seem the only constants, Henderson achieves a vision which permits him to take hold of his own fate. In this process he becomes a model for what Leslie Fiedler regards as the most successful contemporary hero, the man who learns that "it is the struggle itself which is his definition."¹²

At first glance, Saul Bellow's *Herzog* would appear to be a return to an earlier narrative mode, recalling Joseph's digressive journal and his long dialogues with self, or even the tormented but essentially static trials by conscience to which Asa Leventhal is subjected. *Herzog* owes much to those early exercises in what Bellow himself has called "victim literature," but it owes an equal debt to the picaresque structures and optimistically assertive conclusions of *The Adventures of Augie March* and *Henderson the Rain King*. Moses Herzog is both victim and victimizer, whose own worst enemy is his "narcissistic, masochistic, anarchic personality" (*H*, 4), but he is also the comic hero—bumptious, often self-contradictory, occasionally roguish. Like Augie March, he is "a sentimental s.o.b." in an unsentimental and selfish world; like Henderson, a dedicated opponent of the wasteland mystique and a comic champion of extreme emotional versatility. Augie's picaresque wanderings through Montreal, Chicago, Mexico, Rome, and Paris were presented in a realistic manner which owes much to the American naturalists who have influenced Bellow; Henderson's voyage was the stuff of romance—more fantastic and more highly charged with symbolic nuances. Like Conrad's Marlowe or Hemingway's African hunters, Henderson moved into an Africa of the heart which exists without relationship to time and space. Herzog is a wanderer in the mind as well as the heart—the picaro flat on his back; his actual travels to Europe, the abortive trips to Martha's Vineyard and Chicago, the retreat to the ruined house in the Berkshires—these are sharply detailed and memorable episodes, but the real pilgrimage is more internalized even than that of Henderson, for whom Africa was a subsuming metaphor. In *Herzog* there is no metaphorical representation of the quest; there is only the quest itself.

   Thus, Bellow unites the two traditions in which he had formerly worked—the meditative, highly ratiocinative but essentially impotent victim, and the comic, instinctual rebel. Though the fusion is not entirely successful, the effort itself makes *Herzog* Bellow's most ambitious novel to date. He himself has described the process as

a break from Victim literature . . . As one of the chieftains of that school I have the right to say this. Victim literature purports to show the impotence of the ordinary man. In writing *Herzog* I felt I was completing a certain development, coming to the end of a literary sensibility. This sensibility implies a certain attitude toward civilization—anomaly, estrangement, the outsider, the collapse of humanism. What I'm against is a novel of purely literary derivation—accepting the canon of Joyce and Kafka. With Dostoevsky, at least, his eyes are turned freshly to the human scene. This view of life as literature is the modern disease—a

French infection. Inevitably, it puts all hope into the performance, into virtuosity.[13]

Herzog becomes the extreme extension of all Bellow's earlier themes and devices—beginning with the victim, morose, almost paranoid, consumed by self-pity, tottering on the brink of nihilism and alienation, but clinging (like Augie and Henderson) to a transcendent view of man's fate, though all life seems to negate that vision; and finally mastering the courage to live in terms of the resulting tension. If there is fault in the execution, it is that Herzog's determination to fasten himself to the real in life-giving combat is heavily dependent on that very "virtuosity" which Bellow ironically cites as a false source of hope.

Augie's quest was pre-eminently emotional, despite his philosophical reverence for "axial lines," and it was often supported chiefly by the rhetoric which Bellow admits he did not have under consistent control in that book. For Henderson the quest began with a sense of emotional vacancy, gradually and dynamically—especially in the dialogues with Dahfu—assuming an enriched spiritual significance. What Herzog calls "my vague pilgrimage" (*H*, 17) is charted not only in emotional and spiritual terms, but in intellectual terms as well. Though the final form of his resolution seeks its references in the heart, Herzog must also do battle with the windmills of philosophy, law, psychology, biology, and political theory.

Bellow is the only contemporary novelist who can speak repeatedly of sincerity (indeed, he rarely speaks about anything else) without sounding maudlin, clichéd, or merely irrelevant. The subject is given flesh in Moses Elkhanah Herzog, the man of "*Herz* (n., neut.), heart; breast, bosom; feeling, sympathy; mind, spirit; courage; center; vital part; marrow; pith; core, kernel . . ." He is "*Herzog* (n., masc.), duke"—as one critic has suggested,[14] the man of "noble heart," who has given his adult life to a study of "the importance of the 'law of the heart' in Western traditions, the origins of moral sentimentalism and related matters" (*H*, 119). But he studies these laws *in vacuo*, detached from the objective external world, a profound dilettante at last undermined and "awakened" by the unfaithfulness of his wife and his best friend. Thus, Herzog's "stage sets" collapse; when they do so he samples various alternatives of conduct—indiscriminate "potato love," the nihilism of Reality Instructors, the final and unredeemable retreat into self, only to find each one lacking. Herzog must learn to live with reality without sacrificing heart, without crippling the "vital part," with-

out denying "Spirit; courage; center." Only contact and engage-
ment can keep the law of the heart alive; only brotherhood can
legitimatize feeling. In a world dominated by "actors" who depress
and exploit and distort this law, such an intention is as absurd as
loving Seymour Glass's Fat Lady; it is also as essential.

Herzog's compulsive letter writing offers a brilliantly versatile
conceit for the absurd predicament: these letters are the calling
cards by which he attempts to revisit the world from which he had
once abdicated, and they also chronicle the absurd conflict of his
intention (heart) with the hostile reality which he encounters.
Nonetheless, so long as Herzog maintains the conflict only on paper, until he is willing to engage it fully and consciously in life, he
is only an absurd man—not an absurd hero. Only when he has
learned to live in terms of the conflict does he earn the name
Moses, archetype of prophets, or Elkhanah, the one whom "god
possesses." The names are, of course, richly allusive. Tony Tanner
displayed acrobatic zeal in suggesting a possible relationship between the hero of Bellow's novel and Maurice Herzog, who led a
famous mountain-climbing expedition into the French Himalayas;
Maurice is a possible derivative of the Biblical name Moses. Discussing his dangerous expedition, Maurice Herzog argued that

in overstepping our limitations, in touching the extreme boundaries of
man's world, we have come to know something of its splendour. In my
worst moments of anguish I seemed to discover the deep significance of
existence of which till then I had been unaware . . . The marks of my
ordeal are apparent on my body. I was saved and I had won my freedom.
This freedom, which I shall never lose, has given me the assurance and
serenity of a man who has fulfilled himself. It has given me the rare joy of
loving that which I used to despise. In this narrative . . . we bear
witness.[15]

So broad and sensitive is Bellow's literary experience that his
knowledge of Maurice Herzog's narrative is not unlikely, and indeed, the passage which Mr. Tanner cites might almost have been
drawn from the concluding pages of *Herzog*. But even if Bellow is
acquainted with this source, its discovery would have been little
more than coincidence, for Herzog's final peace, in which he too
can accept that which he used to despise, and in which he wins his
freedom despite the marks of ordeal etched in his face, is the logical conclusion of the quest on which all the author's earlier heroes
have embarked.

Indeed, if there is a specific literary source for Bellow's intense
hero, it is to be found in Joyce's *Ulysses*, though here, too, any

possible literary derivation must be thought of in terms of syntactic convenience—at best, a reinforcement of Bellow's own nominal shorthand—rather than as a direct source of imitation or even of inspiration. The sole reference to the Jewish merchant Moses Herzog occurs near the beginning of the Cyclops episode in *Ulysses*. The unnamed, garrulous narrator encounters Joe Hynes "dodging along Stony Batter," and the following is part of the dialogue between them before they decide to visit Barney Kiernan's:

—What are you doing round those parts? says Joe.
—Devil a much, says I. There is a bloody big foxy thief beyond by the garrison church at the corner of Chicken Lane—old Troy was just giving me a wrinkle about him—lifted any God's quantity of tea and sugar to pay three bob and said he had a farm in the country. Down off a hop of my thumb by the name of Moses Herzog over there near Heytesberg street.
—Circumcised! says Joe.
—Ay, says I. A bit off the top.[16]

Then follows shortly a statement of Michael Geraghty's legal transaction with Herzog, who is clearly fated never to collect that debt, due to be repaid in weekly installments of three shillings; similarly, Joe Hynes is unlikely to repay the three shillings borrowed from Leopold Bloom.

The opening section of the Cyclops episode contains various parodies of public rhetoric, of which Herzog's legal agreement (quoted in full) is the first example—and singularly appropriate to a public house favored by the legal profession. In examining the possible significance which this passage in *Ulysses* may have had for Saul Bellow, however, it is necessary to note the degree to which Bloom himself is not only a complex, but also a composite character; he is every older man (ultimately every man) in search and in need of mature resolution; he is many-sided and, as Homer said of Odysseus, "polytropic." Thus, in Bloom, Joyce fuses a complex set of literary and historical personalities in addition to Ulysses: "Jesus, Elijah, Moses, Dante, Shakespeare, Hamlet, and Don Giovanni" are among the antecedents noted by Tindall.[17] Similarly, many of the occasional figures who appear or are referred to in *Ulysses* also represent aspects of Bloom's polytropic experience. Thus, in light of Bellow's novel, Tindall's analysis of the parallel figures incorporated in Bloom takes on enriched significance: "That Jesus gets along with Ulysses is not so surprising as it seems; for allegorical fathers of the Church had found Ulysses a moral prototype of Jesus, who is, of course, a kind of Everyman. Moses is another exile seeking home and leading others there. Jesus and Moses are analogues for Bloom, and, since Stephen is a potential Bloom, for Stephen, too." Tindall then settles on an examination of the four most significant parallels: "Ulysses, Jesus, Moses, and Bloom again."[18] The text of *Ulysses* contains many references to Moses, usually in association with Bloom himself, though occasionally with Stephen. Thus, Bloom's thematic relationship to Moses Herzog is strongly reinforced: both are aliens, Jewish exiles in Irish Dublin, and both are owed "debts" by society which it is therefore unlikely they will ever collect.

In speculating about the Moses/Leopold Bloom/Moses Herzog parallel, one finds in Joyce's Cyclops episode numerous arguments and devices which would seem to foreshadow the method and the themes of Bellow's novel. One must, to be sure, keep in mind Bellow's own prejudice against the novel of literary derivation and his warning to "symbol hunters," although the latter is essentially a contemporary translation of Mark Twain's famous notice to critical poachers in *Huckleberry Finn*. The critic would perhaps be well advised to think of Moses E. Herzog as a collateral descendant (via the force of Bellow's imagination) of Joyce's Herzog-Bloom. Certainly Bellow is familiar with *Ulysses*, whereas his knowledge of Maurice Herzog's story—however tantalizing to the critic—is highly speculative, and would, in any event, have proved far less germinal than the Cyclops episode in Joyce's novel. While an understanding of *Herzog* is in no way dependent upon literary sources and hence not what Bellow would condemn as "the novel of literary derivation," the reader, without violating Bellow's belief in the independent integrity of the work of art, can look to *Ulysses* for the themes and motifs which would have reinforced his own examination of the limitations, the strengths, and the significance of the contemporary hero. In terms of the Cyclops episode, the major reinforcement would seem to rest in three closely related areas: Bloom (the composite hero) as an outcast whom society greets with stony incomprehension, dramatized by the characters who surround him at Barney Kiernan's bar; Bloom's external lassitude, contrasted with his vitally active attempts to understand the world about him—woman, the Citizen, friendship; and Bloom's statements about love, which Bellow's Herzog occasionally seems to be echoing. To his cynical fellow drinkers (Reality Instructors, all), Bloom responds,

—But it's no use . . . Force, hatred, history, all that. That's not life for men and women, insult and hatred. And everybody knows that it's the very opposite of that that is really life.

—What? says Alf.

—Love, says Bloom. I mean the opposite of hatred.[19]

We know that Bloom maintains this belief despite his own failed marriage, and even though his literal-minded companions make him an object of grotesque ridicule. In addition to such thematic parallels to Joyce, there are stylistic correspondences in Bellow's skillful juxtaposition of legal terminology, philosophical jargon, and historical formulations with a vigorous, often bawdy conversational tone, as well as in his kaleidoscopic narrative manner.

The immediate and present action of Bellow's novel describes the period of extreme crisis when Moses E. Herzog's fears that he is not only unable but unworthy to live according to "the law of the heart" which he has expounded; though his withdrawn condition can be psychologically described as depressive and occasionally paranoid, he himself best identifies it as "*Heartsore*" (*H*, 17). This intellectualized Leopold Bloom sums up his despair when, after temporarily losing radio contact while on maneuvers with the Army, he manages to croak asthmatically (and so that the entire fleet hears him), "'We're Lost! Fucked!'" Dressing to visit Ramona, Herzog summarizes for himself the factors which collaborate to give him this profound feeling of alienation:

Well, for instance, what it means to be a man. In a city. In a century. In transition. In a mass. Transformed by science. Under organized power. Subject to tremendous controls. In a condition caused by mechanization. After the late failure of radical hopes. In a society that was no community and devalued the person. Owing to the multiplied power of numbers which made the self negligible. Which spent military billions against foreign enemies but would not pay for order at home. Which permitted savagery and barbarism in its own great cities. . . . On top of that, an injured heart, and raw gasoline poured on the nerves. (201)

The description is a microcosm of the absurd world in which many modern heroes are compelled to function, but to the harshness and impersonality of external reality is added "an injured heart," injured not only by those who have betrayed him, but injured by its very owner, for "he, Herzog, had committed a sin of some kind against his own heart, while in pursuit of a grand synthesis" (207). That heart is finally healed by Ramona's love and by the self-analysis which Herzog undergoes while writing his interminable, unmailed letters.

Herzog's violation consisted in believing that life was a "subject" which could be looked at with intellectual detachment (hence his apparent indifference to his mother's death) and counted on to

yield itself to logical principles, to be encompassed in "systems."
This fault is not simply the result of misguided and overstimulated
intellect; it also grows from Herzog's fear of "the depths of feeling
he would eventually have to face, when he could no longer call
upon his eccentricities for relief" (10). Like most of Bellow's heroes, Herzog must learn to face both inner and external reality; he
must rejoin the world. The result of his failure to do so is spiritual,
emotional, and intellectual sickness. In the critical interim, he becomes masochistic and depressive; he experiences "the sickness
unto death" (105); he is "'no better than any other kind of addict—
sick with abstractions'" (123); and in this condition, when an air-
line stewardess offers him a drink, he feels "incapable of looking
into the girl's pretty, healthful face" (241).

Herzog chronicles this agonized man's attempt to rejoin the
world without sacrificing the principles of heart for which his integrity demands defense. This entails not only a new understanding of the world which surrounds him, but also a purification and
revaluation of self. Herzog's most immediate parallel in this regard
is Bellow's Bummidge, the hero of *Last Analysis*, whose comical
autotherapy is similarly motivated though executed with a greater
flair for the burlesque. As Bummidge's harassed agent describes
this self-analysis, "He recaptures the emotions. He fits them into a
general framework. He thinks and thinks, and talks and talks, and
the girl takes it all down, and types it in triplicate, in leather bind-
ers." Herzog's syndrome is not unlike Bummidge's "Humanitis":
"It isn't that I don't like people. I need 'em, I even love 'em. So
why can't I bear 'em?"[20] And Bummidge's lament is precisely that
of Herzog: "Oh, how can I pull the plug and let the dirty water out
of my soul. Value, value, give me value. Oh, for some substance."[21]

With a variety of intentions—most of them selfish—Herzog's
friends suggest therapy for his condition, offering two major alternatives to his intellectual retreat. Sandor Himmelstein is a part-
time exponent of Potato Love, that "Amorphous, swelling, hungry,
indiscriminate, cowardly potato love" (*H*, 91) which shields man
from reality by enveloping him in emotional fantasies. Far more
insidious are the Reality-Instructors, whom Sandor himself joins
with brutal intensity when the irrational potato love fails him. The
teacher of reality denies heart entirely, emphasizing that "'We're
all whores in this world, and don't you forget it'" (85). Simkin is
another of the Reality-Instructors who love "to pity and poke fun at
the same time" (30), and all of them point the way to a pessimism,
even a nihilism, which Herzog cannot in honesty accept, however
much such a principle might simplify his own dilemma. He must

come to terms with reality, but first he is compelled to understand it, and for Herzog (as for Bellow's other heroes) reality cannot be encompassed by "*the commonplaces of the Wasteland outlook, the cheap mental simulants of Alienation, the cant and rant of pipsqueaks about Inauthenticity and Forlornness. I can't accept this foolish dreariness. We are talking about the whole life of mankind. The subject is too great, too deep for such weakness, cowardice . . .*" (75). Similarly, he writes testily to Heidegger: "*I should like to know what you mean by the expression 'the fall into the quotidian.' When did this fall occur? Where were we standing when it happened?*" (49). He is repulsed that "The very Himmelsteins, who had never even read a book of metaphysics, were touting the Void as if it were so much salable real estate" (93), that despair is almost a voting requirement, that an entire generation imagines "that nothing faithful, vulnerable, fragile can be durable or have any true power" (290), and that "*comfortable people playing at crisis, alienation, apocalypse and desperation*" dominate the fashionable magazines (316–317).

Herzog searches not for rest or escape or illusion, but for that state in which he can exercise the intentions of his heart in full knowledge and presence of reality—however antagonistic the latter may seem. He can deny neither term—unlike the Potato Lovers, who deny reality, and the Reality-Instructors, who deny heart. Herzog himself has been an intellectual Potato Lover, and the results of this sort of abstracted humanism include an unhealthy absorption with the past, to which the scholar looks "with an intense need for contemporary relevance" (5), writing many of his letters to the dead because "He lived with them as much as with the living—perhaps more . . ." (181). Herzog's intellectualized emotionalism, without anchor in reality, is shown at its most perverted extreme in Lucas Asphalter, who humanizes his animals to a grotesque degree: "Now Herzog had to consider some strange facts about Asphalter. It's possible that I influenced him, my emotionalism transmitted itself to him. . . . I suspect Luke may be in a very bad way" (45–46).

Through his meetings with Asphalter, the sordid courtroom trials which he observes, the bizarre automobile accident, the healing love of Ramona, and his questioning, argumentative letters, Herzog finally achieves an objective view of his absurd predicament: "He too could smile at Herzog and despise him. But there still remained the fact. *I* am Herzog. I have to *be* that man. There is no one else to do it. After smiling, he must return to his own Self and see the thing through" (67). Herzog learns to "be," and his

progress is recorded in the letters, through which he phrases his
lover's quarrel with an essentially unloving world; he is schooled in
the absurd tension between intention and reality and is at last content to exist in terms of the tension: *"'But what do you want,
Herzog?'"* he asks himself at the conclusion of the book. *"'But
that's just it—not a solitary thing. I am pretty well satisfied to be,
to be just as it is willed, and for so long as I may remain in occupancy'"* (340). Thus, he is prepared to renew what he calls "universal connections," the equivalent of Augie's "axial lines," but defined now in more specific humanistic terms. First, he conceives of
his struggle as being significant in terms of "the human condition"
(107) as a whole: "The progress of civilization—indeed, the survival of civilization—depended on the successes of Moses E.
Herzog" (125). This is not simply narcissism or a distinctive lunacy;
it is an index of Herzog's struggle for a stance which will allow him
existence in terms of mankind—not merely in terms of intellect, of
the exacerbated self, or of a hostile, external reality. Without this
broader significance Herzog loses all sense of time and space: he
glances at his watch without being able to fix the time in his mind;
he tries to orient himself in space, but from his apartment window
he can see "Nothing in particular. Only a sense of water bounding
the overbuilt island" (159), and all he can fix firmly in his mind is
his own face in the mirror.

The central paradox of Herzog's experience is that only through
self can man renew universal connections, but too much involvement in self may cancel out the universal: "If ever Herzog knew
the loathsomeness of a *particular* existence, knew that the *whole*
was required to redeem every separate spirit, it was then, in his
terrible passion, which he tried, impossibly, to share, telling his
story" (157). Thus, he becomes increasingly aware of the gro-
tesquerie of his own peccadilloes, and becomes the subject not
only of the author's comic sense, but of his own as well. As comic
detachment grows, Herzog becomes aware that the letters themselves, though crucial in helping him to resist the Potato Lovers
and the Reality-Instructors, are a means to an end which can be
fully experienced only when he no longer needs to write them. As
he explains to Asphalter with grim humor: "'I must be trying to
keep tight the tensions without which human beings can no longer
be called human. If they don't suffer, they've gotten away from me.
And I've filled the world with letters to prevent their escape. I
want them in human form, and so I conjure up a whole environment and catch them in the middle. I put my whole heart into
these constructions. But they are constructions'" (272). Herzog

sees the average intellectual as a "Separatist"—hence he himself has hoarded food in the Ludeyville house in a scheme for solitary self-sufficiency, which seems ludicrous to him once he has become "a specialist . . . in spiritual self-awareness" (307), for that very awareness teaches him that no definition of the self is complete unless it embraces other people—even such actors as Gersbach and Madeleine.

Madeleine is essential in forcing the crisis through which Herzog comes to terms with reality, and Ramona is the crucial counterbalance which saves him from insanity and gives him strength to keep his absurd intention alive. He confesses to Simkin that he is not a realist (convinced now of the necessity of confronting reality but uncertain how to interpret it), and his ultimate vision embraces all the ambiguities of the world about him, resisting both romanticism and nihilism:

The air from the west was drier than the east air. Herzog's sharp senses detected the difference. In these days of near-delirium and wide-ranging disordered thought, deeper currents of feeling had heightened his perceptions, or made him instill something of his own into his surroundings. As though he painted them with moisture and color taken from his own mouth, his blood, liver, bowels, genitals. In this mingled way, therefore, he was aware of Chicago, familiar ground to him for more than thirty years. And out of these elements, by this peculiar art of his own organs, he created his version of it. Where the thick walls and buckled slabs of pavement in the Negro slums exhaled their bad smells. Farther West, the industries; the sluggish South Branch dense with sewage and glittering with a crust of golden slime; the Stockyards, deserted; the tall red slaughterhouses in lonely decay; and then a faintly buzzing dullness of bungalows and scrawny parks; and vast shopping centers; and the cemeteries after these—Waldheim, with its graves for Herzogs past and present; the Forest Preserves for riding parties, Croatian picnics, lovers' lanes, horrible murders; airports; quarries; and, last of all, cornfields. And with this, infinite forms of activity—Reality. (278)

Madeleine had hampered such an inclusive vision by driving him, through her own ambition, further onto the shoals of intellectualism, and by giving him additional evidence to support the nihilists' conclusion that man is by nature whorish. As a bitch goddess who coolly applies lipstick after a meal by looking at herself in a knife blade, Madeleine has a polite and morally rigid ancestress in James' Madame de Mauves, a frivolous one in Fitzgerald's Daisy Fay Buchanan, and a serious competitor in West's Faye Greener, with her "long, sword-like legs." Herzog's spirit is too active, too resilient, to be completely dominated by this woman (though she does give him cause to question his own potency); she appropriately chooses a one-legged lover named Valentine: a paper imitation of the real man of heart, an *ersatz* Herzog, though physically more powerful, as his name implies.

Ramona, on the other hand, offers regeneration through love: "She, Ramona, wanted to add riches to his life and give him what he pursued in the wrong places. This she could do by the art of love, she said—the art of love which was one of the sublime achievements of the spirit. . . . What he had to learn from her— while there was still time; while he was still virile, his powers substantially intact—was how to renew the spirit through the flesh (a precious vessel in which the spirit rested)" (184–185). And Ramona can succeed because she knows not only how to produce sensual gratification (as cook, florist, lover), but because she, too, has been tested and tempered: ". . . she knew the bitterness of death and nullity, too" (185). In the conclusion of the novel Herzog offers Ramona not one of the letters he has written for months, but a bouquet of wildflowers.

Ramona, the friendship of Asphalter, his two children, the rich memories of Napoleon Street—all reinforce the man of heart as he passes through this crisis of consciousness. They reaffirm his belief that man only *seems* lost, remains alienated only when he blindly accepts the fashionable stance of alienation as a condition of existence. Despite the new barbarisms of a machine age, well known to Herzog as a moral historian, he can reaffirm that *"Civilization and even morality are implicit in technological transformation"* (164); that *"there are moral realities"* as well as physically unstable, destructive ones (178); and even as he scents the odor of decay rising through a waste pipe, he notes "Unexpected intrusions of beauty" (218).

Herzog's Jewishness, a matter on which many reviewers of the novel peremptorily turned their backs, seems a vital factor insofar as it gives Herzog a sense of the significance of family ("He could be a patriarch, as every Herzog was meant to be. The family man, father, transmitter of life, intermediary between past and future, instrument of mysterious creation . . ." [202]); a richness and complexity of experience, heavy with love as well as deprivation, which causes him to rebel against the simplistic clichés of popular nihilism ("much heavy love in Herzog; grief did not pass quickly, with him" [119]); and an almost dauntless compassion (". . . we had a great schooling in grief. I still know these cries of the soul" [148]). It is true that he possesses these traits in greater degree than the other members of his family; that he himself feels that modern experience has made much of the traditional Jewish experience inapplicable; and that other backgrounds might have resulted in a constitution similarly resistant to nihilism, dedicated to children and the principle of family. Nonetheless, the relevant fact remains that such values as Herzog embodies are not, at least in this degree, the common stock of modern industrialized America. Herzog *is* a Jew, and many of his values grow directly from his Jewish-immigrant background rather than from his adult experiences as a liberal intellectual. Though he was brought up in an eccentric and only erratically "religious" family, he himself repeatedly refers to his Jewishness. The critic who urges that this "Jewishness" is unimportant to the novel is correct to the same degree that Leopold Bloom's Jewishness is unimportant; he is right if he intends to suggest that the character is a symbolic alien whose struggle has significance for all of us. But he is clearly wrong if he intends to suggest that a Jewish background is irrelevant in terms of the particular character's dramatic development. Similar arguments apply to all of Bellow's Jewish heroes.

In Moses E. Herzog, Saul Bellow presents the richest and most diverse of his band of questing men who dissipate their powers and energies in fruitless, often comic quests for salvation which are resolved only through the character's realization that man's triumph comes when he has learned to sustain the vital equilibrium between intention and reality. One need only recall Joseph's remarks in *Dangling Man* to observe the consistency of Bellow's heroes while, at the same time, appreciating the mature development which these concepts are given in the person of Herzog: "We are all drawn to the same craters of the spirit—to know what we are and what we are for, to know our purpose, to seek grace. And, if the quest is the same, the differences in our personal histories, which hitherto meant so much to us, become of minor importance" (*DM*, 154).

In *Herzog* the struggle to externalize, to escape the trap of self and renew universal connections, depends on the hero's seeing his own dilemma in an objective light: that he cannot do so consistently is indicated by the shifting narrative voice, which moves erratically between first and third persons until Herzog has formulated his resolution, "*I am pretty well satisfied to be, to be just as it is willed, and for so long as I may remain in occupancy*" (340). From this point, the third-person triumphs, as though the objective narrative voice were a further indication of Herzog's restoration to life, a proof that he is now truly "confident, cheerful, clairvoyant, and strong" (1). Perhaps Herzog's victory is only temporary, but we leave him in the conclusion of the novel a wiser man than any of Bellow's earlier heroes, one who has affirmed and legitimized the absurd struggle on all levels of experience—emotional, spiritual, and intellectual.

As the record of a picaro in stasis, a mental voyager, *Herzog* looks back to the monologuist, ratiocinative tradition of *Dangling Man* and its journal device; it also anticipates Bellow's growing commitment to the intellectual hero who has developed mind at the expense of heart. The structural consequence for Bellow's fiction is that plot atrophies further, reduced to a series of encounters with urban chaos or with memory, and curiously lacking in imaginative vitality. Increasingly, Bellow seeks to animate his fictional landscape with comedy, attempting to break with victim literature in *Herzog* through the "comic use of complaint." [22] The device has even more varied consequence for *Mr. Sammler's Planet* and *Humboldt's Gift*, where coincidence and parallel action might almost be read as a parody of Victorian novelistic conventions. If Bellow's central drama of the movement from alienation to affirmation has become clichéd, there can be no doubt that his comic gifts have matured—as has the zestful blend of slang, Biblical cadence, and erudition which characterizes his language at its best.

Bellow has always had a unique talent for deft cameo portraits of the mad and the half-mad who populate the modern urban world, as in the brief description of figures Sammler observes in Stuyvesant Park:

He noted a female bum drunkenly sleeping like a dugong, a sea cow's belly rising, legs swollen purple; a short dress, a mini-rag. At a corner of the fence, a wino was sullenly pissing on newspapers and old leaves. Cops seldom bothered about these old-fashioned derelicts. Younger people, autochthonous-looking, were also here. Bare feet, the boys like Bombay beggars, beards clotted, breathing rich hair from their nostrils, heads coming through woolen ponchos, somewhat Peruvian. (*MSP*, 110)

Before *Mr. Sammler's Planet* Bellow's Hogarthian eye was most apparent in *The Adventures of Augie March*, but there the ever-swelling cast of eccentrics often bordered on the burlesque. In *Mr. Sammler's Planet* character is treated more integrally: the half-mad Shula-Slava, for example, is a passionate collector of things, but no more passionate than the deceased Mrs. Gruner with her Westchester mansion packed with the elegant detritus of conspicuous consumption; or the beneficent Dr. Gruner, stuffing undeclared income into his leather hassock; or Angela, who collects men.

Shula's family name, Sammler, itself means "collector," and her father collects experiences and impressions and (above all) memories as hungrily as his daughter collects pamphlets and coupons. Like most of Bellow's heroes, Artur Sammler is more acted upon than acting: he is recipient, not agent; collector, not inceptor.

Perhaps the most impressive quality about *Mr. Sammler's Planet* is the way in which motifs are provocatively intertwined: madness, violence, impersonation, avariciousness, and predatory sexuality thread themselves through almost every episode of the novel. Each major image or incident is either echoed or counterpointed elsewhere in the work: both the exotic pickpocket and the spare Dr. Sammler are rather dandified, and both wear sunglasses; the burst pipe in the Westchester mansion is a corollary to Dr. Gruner's aneurism; Mr. Sammler's rudely aborted lecture has its counterpart in the theft that follows Dr. Lal's lecture; the trapped pickpocket is struck a vicious blow on the head, as Sammler had been struck by his would-be executioners; Sammler and Gruner are both widowers with unmarried daughters; Margotte cultivates a jungle of tortured, largely unidentified plants, and Wallace schemes to establish a plant-labeling business. Such parallels are reinforced on the level of plot by a series of coincidences which flower into the *opera buffa* of the episode in the Gruner house in Westchester.

Such formal elaborations help give the novel its comic momentum, even though they cannot entirely correct the lassitude that increasingly plagues Bellow's fiction. Similarly, the novel's greatest asset, Artur Sammler, often proves a liability, especially when Bellow uses him as a ventriloquist's dummy for expressing his own somewhat crabby dis-ease with the contemporary world. Nonetheless, Sammler remains a unique and often moving character, a spiritual witness of far greater authority than can be found elsewhere in Bellow's writings. A septuagenarian Polish Jew whose intellect was shaped on the fringes of the Bloomsbury group and whose soul was tempered by the horrors of the Holocaust, he is a particularly complex embodiment of the Bellovian craving for order. Whatever "treasons" Bellow's other characters may have encountered, they can only seem pale in comparison to Sammler's witnessing of his wife's death, his own resurrection from a mass grave, and the zombie-like state in which he was then compelled to live. Half-starved and clad in rags, he had taken sudden, sweet pleasure in murdering a Russian soldier. Even though the modern city in which he ultimately finds refuge seems intent on repeating such desperate gestures, Sammler remains firm in his belief in an ultimate human decency. Despite the absurdity of existence, Sammler notes that "almost daily" he has "strong impressions of eternity" (240), and reasons that one must conduct his life in terms of those impressions. Thus, even more consciously and more persistently than any of Bellow's other heroes, he pits his intentions against a hostile reality.

To create this aged hero in the 1960's, when the classic American emphasis on youth was at its most strident pitch, was itself an act of novelistic courage; it was a decade top-heavy with self-congratulatory novels, films, and sociological studies concerning the young. The classic American hero, as D. H. Lawrence observed, is the beardless youth who embodies our faith in the renewed innocence of a second chance, and who has become one of our most treasured clichés. The only other American writer to have created so moving and authentic a portrait of old age is Edward Lewis Wallant; the hero of Wallant's *The Human Season* is, like Sammler, a widower who struggles to make a life of dignity for himself amid the rootlessness and violence of the American city. Bellow's description of Sammler's lonely morning ritual, sipping grapefruit juice from a container and mechanically grinding coffee, is a direct echo of the sparse but poignantly detailed language with which Wallant described Berman's rituals:

He put the kettle on to boil and sat down to wait for it. He brushed at some microscopic crumbs on the table's oilcloth, fussed at the frayed edge for a moment until he recognized the gesture with horror as not being his own.

He got up and looked out the window. The next house was only about fifteen feet away. The white siding was overlaid with five years' accumulation of soot.[23]

There are even closer parallels between *Mr. Sammler's Planet* and Wallant's second novel, *The Pawnbroker*; its hero, like Sammler, was a former professor at the University of Cracow who survived the concentration camps where his wife was raped and murdered. *The Pawnbroker* concludes with the weary survivor leaving to help his mistress pray over the body of her dead father, just as *Mr. Sammler's Planet* culminates in the idiosyncratic Kaddish that Sammler chants in the hospital dissecting room. In both novels the specific horrors of the concentration camp seem to be repeatedly echoed in the violent realities of the city—as they are similarly echoed in William Styron's *Sophie's Choice*.

Bellow first presented an elderly protagonist in two stories which were published shortly before *Mr. Sammler's Planet*—"The Old System" (1967) and "Mosby's Memoirs" (1968). Both depict older intellectual characters who think back on their lives in an attempt to create a perspective on the present; in this respect, Dr. Samuel Braun and Willis Mosby are related to the lonely old woman in the earlier story "Leaving the Yellow House" (1957), who remembers the events of her life as she formulates her last will and testament. As he sits drinking his morning coffee, Dr. Braun reflects on the old values of love and passion and anger, of family piety and religious zeal, that had organized the lives of his immigrant ancestors; comparing those with the present leads this Samuel to Sammleresque conclusions:

> But every civilized man today cultivated an unhealthy self-detachment. Had learned from art the art of amusing self-observation and objectivity. Which, since there had to be something amusing to watch, required art in one's conduct. Existence for the sake of such practices did not seem worth while. Mankind was in a confusing, uncomfortable, disagreeable stage in the evolution of its consciousness. Dr. Braun (Samuel) did not like it. It made him sad to feel that the thought, art, belief of great traditions should be so misemployed. (*MM*, 44)

A scientist who fears he has never loved properly, Dr. Braun is moved to tears by the memory of his passionately contending ancestors with their hearts filled with love and injury. The tears lead him to hope he has approached some new level of understanding, but then he realizes he has understood nothing: "It was only an intimation of understanding. A promise that mankind might— *might*, mind you—eventually, through its gift which might— *might* again!—be a divine gift, comprehend why it lived. Why life, why death" (83). The same theme is central to *Mr. Sammler's Planet*, most focused and pointed in the lengthy dialogue between Artur Sammler and the scientist Dr. Lal. "The Old System" and "Mosby's Memoirs" are both important in the evolution of ideas Bellow would explore more fully in his novel; they are also instructive in that both take the form of reminiscences, so that the primary action occurs entirely in the mind. Even when Willis Mosby ventures out from his writerly retreat to explore the historic ruins at Mitla, the suffocating tomb into which he descends is the tomb of memory; it is also the symbolic destination of an intellect that has "disposed of all things human" (184).

Every Bellow hero is spiritually a displaced person, but only Mr. Sammler is both literally and figuratively so; age, education, and

sophistication set him apart from the modern urban world, which
he moves through with eager curiosity but an essential air of detachment. From hospital windows, a moving bus, or the windows
of his own cramped room, he gazes with his single good eye at the
sterile landscape of the modern city. The violence and disorder he
witnesses are familiar elements of Bellow's urban settings, but here
there seems a new note of frenzied madness:

Because of the high rate of speed, decades, centuries, epochs condensing
into months, weeks, days, even sentences. So that to keep up, you had to
run, spring, waft, fly over shimmering waters, you had to be able to see
what was dropping out of human life and what was staying in. You could
not be an old-fashioned sitting sage. You must train yourself. You had to
be strong enough not to be terrified by local effects of metamorphosis, to
live with disintegration, with crazy streets, filthy nightmares, mon-
strosities come to life, addicts, drunkards, and perverts celebrating their
despair openly in midtown. You had to be able to bear the tangles of the
soul, the sight of cruel dissolution. You had to be patient with the stu-
pidities of power, with the fraudulence of business. Daily at five or six
a.m. Mr. Sammler woke up in Manhattan and tried to get a handle on the
situation. He didn't think he could. Nor, if he could, would he be able to
convince or convert anyone. (*MSP*, 78)

For Sammler, this urban madness finds confirmation in sexual excess, crime, and the mindless radicalism of the unwashed young.

We witness less than two full days of Mr. Sammler's life in New
York, yet that time is sufficient for Bellow to reiterate all the major
themes of dislocation and dread presented in his previous fiction.
His hero survives the pain and indifference of the New World as he
had survived mass shooting, anti-Semitic Poles, and literal entombment. Risen from the dead, he offers the authentic voice of
the past—a voice that speaks out for reason, order, tradition, and
self-respect, and he clings to those values against the hostility of
his environment, the indifference of many of his acquaintances,
the aggression of strangers, and the perversity of circumstance.
What Bellow celebrates in his hero is what Faulkner identified in
his magnificent portrait of Dilsey as the quality of "endurance," but
here refined by intellectual self-awareness. Robert Frost stressed
similar virtues in his declaration that "The best way out . . . is
THROUGH; we must live in this confusion as if it were the salt of
existence, before any saving clarity can even be imagined."[24] As
Bellow has repeatedly stressed, however hostile the world appears, it is the only world we have, and definition comes not
through estrangement from reality but through accommodation;
hence, he can see no hope in other worlds—in the colonizing of

distant planets or in neurotic retreats into the remote territories of the interior, such as Angela, Shula, and Wallace variously undertake.

Through the extraordinary device of this kindly, eccentric, dignified old survivor, Bellow attempts to reckon with modernism in some of its more grotesque manifestations—with student radicalism, Mafia activities, sexual experimentation, the invasion of privacy, indifference to public violence, and the cult of narcissism. Sammler witnesses crime in a crowded city bus and later discovers it in his own family—in his obsessive daughter and in his gentle benefactor, Dr. Gruner, and if such events lead him to doubt that his planet has much future, they do not invalidate his belief in institutions and constraints, in charity and self-esteem, for he has clearly learned well the lesson of survival against apparently insupportable odds. And despite the cruel lessons life has taught him, he cherishes his faith in "Trying to live with a civil heart. With disinterested charity. With a sense of the mystic potency of humankind. With an inclination to believe in archetypes of goodness. A desire for virtue was no accident" (*MSP*, 140).

Sammler is the reader's touchstone, and though we should be wary of identifying him too exclusively with Saul Bellow, the old man nonetheless voices opinions strikingly like those the novelist has expressed in fiction and forum. It is this congruency, perhaps, which makes some of Sammler's crankiness seem particularly disturbing. In any case, we must be cautious about accepting his judgments at face value. Some of them are obsessive, like his repeated references to the rank odors and sexual degradation of the radical young, whose males are "Hairy, dirty, without style," and whose females have "a bad smell" (40). Sammler's opportunistic nephew Wallace is similarly characterized by "a slightly unclean odor from the rear" (91). Sammler also frequently criticizes the dress of the young, a kind of slovenly uniform which to him merely signals their essential conformity. He also deplores "this imitative anarchy of the streets—these Chinese revolutionary tunics, these babes in unisex toyland, these surrealist warchiefs, Western stagecoach drivers . . . They sought originality. They were obviously derivative. And of what—of Paiutes, of Fidel Castro? No, of Hollywood extras" (152–153). Quite apart from the fact that Nathanael West made similar observations with more stylistic verve and far more consequence in the 1930's, we must qualify our reading of such passages with the reminder that Sammler himself is an arch-conformist in his dress. His own epicene costume, the furled umbrella, and carefully cultivated British accent are the inheritance of his Bloomsbury days, of his lengthy, meticulous cultivation of elegant Anglophilia. There are, in short, distinctions and discriminations to be made in judging what Sammler calls "the sovereign youth-style" (12), though they are not, in fact, made in the novel. Similarly, Mr. Sammler is distressed by Angela's baroque tales of sexual exploits, but he does not discourage her recounting them; nor does he seek to stem the painful sexual confessions of Walter Bruch. Hence, when Sammler attends a Picasso exhibition and marvels that "Old Picasso was wildly obsessed by sexual fissures, by phalluses" (70), one might legitimately question whether the obsession is Pablo's or Artur's. When Sammler professes astonishment at the poverty of radical student jargon, he temporarily forgets his own affection for clichés: "He had other irons in the fire, he had other fish to fry" (130). He flatly denounces the picaresque misadventures of Wallace Gruner, yet Wallace's exploits are distinctly reminiscent of Bellow's own favorite creation, Eugene Henderson. This lack of compassion is even more clearly etched in Sammler's lack of understanding for his daughter Shula, who is as sweetly, consistently filial as she is batty; his equation of her with the black pickpocket as yet another thief unhappily obscures the roles of both characters.

The black pickpocket—princely, predatory, ubiquitous—is one of Bellow's most ingenious fictional creations. A kind of Nietzschean *Übermensch*, he exists outside the law—as does Raskolnikov, to whom Sammler more than once compares him (and hence the pickpocket is more closely parallel to Dr. Gruner, grown rich through Mafia-financed abortions, than to Shula-Slava, whose "crime" is motivated by a welter of misguided romantic intentions). Working the downtown buses, the pickpocket preys almost exclusively on unwitting elderly victims; hence, he becomes a vivid embodiment of the coolly, callously predatory nature of big-city life, and the animal imagery with which he is repeatedly characterized becomes part of the total projection of New York as an asphalt jungle. As Sammler describes even the more opulent sections of town: "You opened a jeweled door into degradation, from hypercivilized Byzantine luxury straight into the state of nature, the barbarous world of color erupting from beneath" (11). When Sammler tries to report the crime he has witnessed, he finds only phone booths that have been vandalized, used as urinals; and when he finally gets through to the police, they are indifferent. It is the sense of the individual's powerlessness that dominates Sammler's reflections on urban crime, and that relates this contemporary episode to the historical slaughter of Jews in Nazi concentration camps.

In addition to the role he plays in the novel's exploration of criminal and victim, the black pickpocket is central to Bellow's examination of the Dionysian motif. Aware that he has been observed, the thief follows Sammler home, traps him in the foyer of the building where he lives, and exposes himself to the old man. The moment focuses the novel's recurrent associations of sexuality and power; it also provides focus for the random sexual energy, bordering on anarchy, which Sammler feels all around him. This is no deflected Freudian symbol of aggressive virility—knife, club, or revolver—but the thing itself, revealed in a majestical fashion to the half-blind survivor:

> He was never to hear the black man's voice. He no more spoke than a puma would. . . . The pickpocket unbuttoned himself. Sammler heard the zipper descend. Then the smoked glasses were removed from Sammler's face and dropped on the table. He was directed, silently, to look downward. The black man had opened his fly and taken out his penis. It was displayed to Sammler with great oval testicles, a large tan-and-purple uncircumcised thing—a tube, a snake; metallic hairs bristled at the thick base and the tip curled beyond the supporting, demonstrating hand . . . (53–54)

Such a portrait belongs within the complex tradition of the "dark companion" in American literature—one Leslie Fiedler has described as fundamentally "ambiguous, a dream and a nightmare at once."[25] He is, on the one hand, the initiatory companion, Chingachgook; on the other, he is the savage Injun Joe, committing murder in a graveyard, seeking the slaughter of the innocent in a forbidding cave. He is the sweetly nurturing Nigger Jim, but he is also Babo, the apparently docile servant of Melville's "Benito Cereno" who literally holds a razor to his effete master's throat; or he is Styron's Nat Turner, an obedient slave plotting murder and mayhem. As Fiedler concludes, "finally the dark-skinned companion becomes the 'Black Man,' which is a traditional name for the Devil himself."[26]

Mr. Sammler, obscurely but persistently attracted to this outlaw, admits a kind of Miltonic fascination in the figure, though he ultimately rejects this interpretation as too simplistic. Clearly the pickpocket does represent the city's depravity, its predatory evil; on the other hand, like many of his fictional predecessors, he projects an energy and grace that few of the novel's white characters possess, inevitably recalling Norman Mailer's thesis of "The White

Negro" as psychic outlaw.[27] (Perhaps, too, the reader associates with this displaced African prince something of the inherent wisdom and dignity of King Dahfu, whose most intimate companions were beasts of prey.) While Sammler initially reports him to the police, he declines to condemn the thief, even when he has watched him victimizing a pathetic old man, and in an outrageously contrived scene near the conclusion of the novel, Sammler actually saves the pickpocket's life. On the way to his dying nephew's bedside, Sammler is distracted by a violent street scene, at the center of which are the pickpocket and Sammler's own reader and disciple, Jules Feffer, locked in deadly embrace while the black man tries to wrest away the camera with which Feffer had photographed him. Once more Sammler is reminded of his own helplessness:

To be so powerless was death. And suddenly he saw himself not so much standing as strangely leaning, as reclining, and peculiarly in profile, and as a *past* person. That was not himself. It was someone—and this struck him—poor in spirit. Someone between the human and not-human states, between content and emptiness, between full and void, meaning and not-meaning, between this world and no world. (*MSP*, 293)

Bellow thus establishes Sammler as another "dangling man," but his passive, watchful, impotent status will soon be materially altered. When the old man begs his crippled son-in-law, an artist *manqué*, to stop the fight, Eisen strikes the pickpocket with a baize bag containing his clumsy sculptures. "Everything went into that blow, discipline, murderousness, everything," and Mr. Sammler thinks, "What have I done! This is much worse! This is the worst thing yet!" (294). It is at this point that Sammler physically intervenes, blocking the murderous arm and saving the black man's life. Later he thinks,

The black man? The black man was a megalomaniac. But there was a certain—a certain princeliness. The clothing, the shades, the sumptuous colors, the barbarous-majestical manner. He was probably a mad spirit. But mad with an idea of noblesse. And how much Sammler sympathized with him—how much he would have done to prevent such atrocious blows! (297)

The passage recalls the dialogue between Eugene Henderson and his black mentor, King Dahfu, who explains to him about the "continuity-matter" of the chain of revenge: "'All wish to rid themselves and free themselves and cast the blow upon the others'" (*HRK*, 213). The message of compassion which Dahfu teaches is that someone must eventually break the chain: "'A brave man will try to make the evil stop with him. He shall keep the blow. No man shall get it from him, and that is a sublime ambition. So, a fellow throws himself in the sea of blows saying he do not believe it is infinite'" (214). Sammler realizes the truth of Dahfu's teaching, and in reaching out to arrest Eisen's murderous blow, helps redeem that moment in the Zamosht Forest when he himself had murdered with deliberate pleasure. He also ends his passive, impotent role as aging Prufrockian observer.

Sammler thus opposes his will to reality, answering the chain of aggression with a sweet compassion that clearly outlines his role as absurd hero. On the other hand, the fact that he should protect the thief and reflexively forgive his criminal nephew even while he condemns his daughter and Wallace is an inconsistency Bellow never resolves. For these and similar inconsistencies, Bellow allows himself the symbolic irony of Mr. Sammler's blind eye, and in suggesting his hero's limitations as well as his wisdom and compassion, he succeeds in creating a character who is humanly believable in both his weaknesses and his strength. "His friends and family," Bellow remarks, "had made him a judge and a priest" (*MSP*, 95), but Sammler wishes to be only a man, and as such he emerges from the novel that bears his name—with all his prejudices, his blindness and crankiness and obsessions, but also with his pride and dignity intact.

While Mr. Sammler makes it clear that he does not wish to be treated as a symbol, that is, in fact, what Bellow ultimately and somewhat inconsistently makes of him: like Shula and Dr. Gruner, the author finally asks the old survivor to assume a burden of meaning he cannot sustain, and in the fifth chapter of the novel Bellow's manipulations of his hero badly strain the imaginative fabric of the work. Bellow's characters all engage in lengthy discussions with Reality-Instructors; those discussions are a crucial part of their ritual preparation to reaffirm the values of life. Thus, Joseph has his lively debates with *Tu As Raison Aussi*; in *The Victim* Asa Leventhal and Kirby Allbee carry on a continuous debate; Augie March sharpens his values against the worldly Einhorn or the psychopathic Bateshaw; Tommy Wilhelm listens to Dr. Tamkin's nihilistic sermonizing in "Seize the Day"; Henderson engages in lengthy philosophical dialogues with King Dahfu; and Herzog assails the Reality-Instructors in a series of unmailed letters. The terms of these dialogues differ, but their dramatic function is the same: to allow the hero the opportunity to define and assert his private philosophy and to prepare him for the climactic gesture whereby he will reaffirm a basic and sacred humanity. Perhaps Mr. Sammler's dialogue with Dr. Lal seems so painfully contrived only because Bellow has now repeated the device too often; Sammler's statement of his philosophy contains some of Bellow's most effective lyrical-metaphysical prose, and few reviewers could refrain from quoting at length from his monologue. But, dramatically, Bellow has manipulated his hero as a kind of ventriloquist's dummy and has exploited him as surely as Angela or Wallace or Feffer had wished to exploit him. At this point in the novel it becomes painfully apparent that the work suffers from a dissociation of sensibility—that the narrative, the individual incidents, the carefully drawn characters do not directly support the burden of intellectual meaning Bellow wishes to ascribe to them.

It is not the first time that Bellow's work has demonstrated a fundamental disparity between action and idea or between image and symbol, but the disparities become more apparent with each successive novel. Because the idea of order, of human solidarity and community, is so important to Bellow, he must make some symbolic reaffirmation of that idea in the conclusion of his works, and because his plots do not always consistently support such gestures, he must attempt to persuade by the sheer force of his remarkable rhetoric. Only *The Victim* is an exception to this pattern. The following is the prototypic Bellow conclusion:

I was still chilled from the hike across the fields, but, thinking of Jacqueline and Mexico, I got to grinning again. That's the *animal ridens* in me, the laughing creature, forever rising up. So we were let out, this kid and I, and I carried him down the ship and over the frozen ground of almost eternal winter, drawing breaths so deep they shook me, pure happiness, while the cold smote me from all sides through the stiff Italian corduroy with its broad wales, and the hairs of my beard turned spiky as the moisture of my breath froze instantly. And inside—something, something, happiness . . . "Thou movest me." That leaves no choice. Something produces intensity, a holy feeling, as oranges produce orange, as grass green, as birds heat. Some hearts put out more love and some less of it, presumably. For that is the truth of it—that we all know, God, that we know, that we know, we know, we know. The next move was the world's. I could not bring myself to regret it.

This Bellovian conclusion is, of course, a pastiche of the endings of five separate novels; its fabrication is mere critical gamesmanship, but the facility with which such a mock-conclusion can be compiled points, at a serious level, to the central problem in Bellow's novels: the imaginative structure fails to provide adequate support for the intellectual structure, so that at crucial moments the author's ideas cease to be organically embodied in character, action, or image. At these moments Bellow is not making novels; he is making arguments. The problem can be further explored by comparing the rhetorically weak ending of *Mr. Sammler's Planet* as it appeared in the *Atlantic* with the no more resolved but verbally more persuasive version of the published novel.

Bellow himself has made a similar criticism of the writings of William Faulkner, arguing that "The symbology of certain of his novels, for example 'Light in August,' is just too pat not to believe that it wasn't written under the influence of critical literature. There is a difference between 'culture-making' and the writing of a novel. The deliberate attaching of symbols to actions or characters is 'culture-making'."[28] Bellow's argument is interesting for several reasons—not least of which is the fact that Faulkner is the American writer whom he most admires. Despite the vast difference in the milieus of their fiction, there are interesting parallels between the Southern writer and the Jewish one—in their emphasis on tradition, their concern with family, with racial injustice, religion, guilt, and the mongrelization of values in the modern world. However, Bellow's reflections suggest either a misunderstanding of Faulkner or an odd transference of creative experience. First of all, Bellow suggests that Faulkner fell prey to "critical canons" that filtered down to him "through academic culture," and hence composed *Light in August* under the self-conscious influence of critical literature. While it is possible to argue that Faulkner's symbolic devices are particularly obtrusive in that novel, there is no indication that he had, at the time of its composition, any particular awareness of academic criticism. No major study of his own work had been published in 1932, and he never evinced any particular interest in critical literature. Saul Bellow, on the other hand, is on record as being "a close reader of criticism of his own work"[29]—a fact which may be more than coincidentally related to the intellectual top-heaviness of his fiction. Not only is he a reader of criticism; he has also been a teacher of literature.

Even if the lapses in technique can, to some extent, be identified as the excess of Bellow's considerable virtues, the fact remains that Bellow relies more and more in his fiction on heavily manipulated patterns of confrontation and accommodation. John W. Aldridge has argued that before *Herzog* Bellow had assailed "the commonplaces of the Waste Land outlook," and readers had come to expect from his writing "some departure from the fashionable drapery of alienation." According to Aldridge, however, "our trust is grievously misplaced, for Bellow slyly slips Herzog into the breach left by the banished Waste Land cliché. Herzog emerges, in fact, as the Waste Land cliché irrigated and transformed into the Promised Land, while the platitude of Alienation is converted into the even hoarier platitude of Accommodation and Togetherness."[30] Aldridge's philosophical objections find their corollary in the strained mechanism of Bellow's plots, the woodenness of his symbols, as Gilbert Porter has argued in an otherwise sympathetic analysis of *Mr. Sammler's Planet*:

With Sammler's prayer the novel ends, thus bringing to a conclusion the movement from actions to reflections—involving sexual madness, crime, distortions of the self, technology in a void, and death—that has constituted the basic narrative strategy. Sammler agrees to refer to his discourse in the long philosophical scene . . . as a recital, and the novel itself, at least formally, has something of that quality, a staged performance. Animal imagery is employed appropriately, though perhaps heavy-handedly, to depict human bestiality, savagery, and grotesqueness. Water imagery is used skillfully to suggest overpopulation, immensity, turbulence, mystery, death, and the influence of the moon on the earth. There is an imbalance, however, between reflections and actions: the novel is heavy on ideas, light on fictional concretions, thematic embodiments. Characterization, for example, is weak. With the exception of Mr. Sammler, the characters are merely walk-on functionaries, as though they are bearing signs declaring their thematic significance . . . The novel lacks the vital characterization and the density of texture that enriches, say, *The Adventures of Augie March*. The plot, too, is very loose. Despite occasional strategic juxtaposing of parallel scenes, there is no clearly established relationship between the pickpocket plot, the stolen-manuscript plot, and the death-of-Gruner plot. And the book reveals a paucity of the usual Bellow wit, perhaps because wit and indignation mix well only in satire.[31]

While the rich motifs and parallel plots of *Mr. Sammler's Planet* seem to be far more intricately related than Porter's analysis concedes, the novel indeed remains a curiously stilted performance. Throughout his career Bellow has had, essentially, one story to tell—in Joseph's words, that of the struggle "to know what we are and what we are for, to know our purpose, to seek grace" (*DM*, 102). When a great writer reiterates the same story we term it consistency; in a lesser one it is known as repetitiousness. Through *Herzog* it seemed clear that, if Bellow persisted in rewriting the same novel, it was better in each new reincarnation, however badly the machinery of confrontation and affirmation creaked beneath the thin skin of his plots. *Mr. Sammler's Planet*, however, and despite its distinctive touches of genius, ultimately shows the bankruptcy of Bellow's novelistic imagination. Bellow himself has unintentionally underscored this phenomenon in citing a joke which, he argues, is one of those which distill "the wisdom of life":

An American tenor was performing, making his debut at La Scala. He sings his first aria early in the first act. The applause is tremendous and people shout "Ancora, vita, vita." So he sings the aria once more. The second time the applause is even more tremendous; the Scala roof seems to go off with everybody shrieking "Ancora, vita," so he sings the aria a third. After he's sung it a third time, they call for it a fourth time. He holds up his hands and, with tears in his eyes, he makes a little speech. He says he never hoped for anything like this, that this is the greatest hour of his life, that his mother is a poor laundress in Kansas City and that his father decamped early and left them alone and after a cheap, rotten start he'd studied at the Juilliard, and he'd studied in Paris, and in Rome, and in Milan, and this was an unforgettable night for him, it justified a belief in himself, justified himself to his mother. But, the cast is waiting, the Maestro is waiting, the orchestra is waiting, we must go on with the performance. But the crowd shouts—"No, no!" and he says "how many times must I sing this aria?" Someone shouts, "you gonna sing until you get it right!" I know we all often feel like that.[32]

Whether he has "got it right" or not, perhaps the time has come for Bellow to tell another joke.

Not only does *Mr. Sammler's Planet* seem weak in terms of formal development; it also fares badly in a comparison with contemporary works that employ similar themes and devices—namely, John Updike's *Rabbit Redux* and Norman Mailer's *An American Dream*, both of which use the moon as a complex central image, both of which contain extraordinary black men—symbols of violence and sexual potency, but also, like Sammler's pickpocket, with a mysterious and princely aura about them. All three novels contain sexually liberated females of incredible sensuality.[33] Indeed, Updike's description of Mim as near-parody of the sexual liberation of the 1960's might well be applied to Angela:

She appears to wear no makeup, no lipstick, except for her eyes, which are inhuman, drenched in peacock purple and blue, not merely outlined but re-created, and weighted with lashes he expects to stick fast when she blinks. These marvellously masked eyes force upon her pale mouth all expressiveness; each fractional smile, sardonic crimping, attentive pout, and abrupt broad laugh follows its predecessors so swiftly . . . In the style of the Sixties her clothes are clownish: bell bottom slacks striped horizontally as if patched from three kinds of gingham; a pinstripe blouse, mannish but for the puff sleeves; shoes that in color and shape remind him of Donald Duck's bill; hoop earrings three inches across. (*RRx*, 352–353)

Together, Rabbit and his sister wait out the slow dying of his mother, as Sammler and Angela stand vigil while Dr. Gruner dies, and in both instances the talk is of the young women's lonely, exploitative sexual lives. Updike's novel is set in the summer of 1969, and telecasts of the Apollo moon flight filter through the book's complex action. Bellow's novel is set a few months earlier, and Dr. Lal is nervous that he might miss the publicity the moon landing will give his book. Rabbit Angstrom confronts black radicalism, an unwashed hippie drop-out, and a decaying marriage while the television plays an ironic recitative for his misadventures—ironic because so clearly unrelated to the human problems of being a particular man in a particular place with particular needs and fears. Bellow's use of the coming Apollo expedition is not dissimilar, but in comparison to Updike's vital dramatic structure, the contrived dialogue between Mr. Sammler and Dr. Lal seems even more clumsily wooden.

Bellow's novel precedes Updike's, but there are similarly interesting parallels between *Mr. Sammler's Planet* and Mailer's *An American Dream*, as well as *Of a Fire on the Moon*, both of which were published before Bellow's novel. In *An American Dream*, Stephen Rojack hears whisperings of Mafia connections and is haunted by memories of the German soldier he killed; like Mr. Sammler, Rojack is an intellectual, a spiritually displaced person, and a man fascinated by evil, by the powers of the moon, by the violence of the city. Such parallels might be extended almost indefinitely, but ultimately one is impressed by the extraordinary differences between Mailer and Bellow and, at a more muted level, between Updike and Bellow, for both Mailer and Updike have demonstrated a remarkable capacity for growth. Mailer, in particular, has more than any other living American novelist asked fundamental questions about the form of the novel itself, about the novelist's responsibility to his audience, and about the role of the imagination in an age when the documentary is "the bleeding heart of television land." In *Why Are We in Vietnam?* he has even brilliantly co-opted the mythology of Protestant America. Bellow refrains from asking such questions in his fiction, although he occasionally addresses himself to them in lectures and articles.

Mailer has remarked that when initially invited to chronicle the Apollo mission,

He felt as if he had begun the study of a new world so mysterious to his detective's heart (all imaginative novelists, by this logic, are detectives) that he could only repeat what he had said on the day the assignment was first offered to him: it was that he hardly knew whether the Space Program was the noblest expression of the Twentieth Century or the quintessential statement of our fundamental insanity.[34]

Such concern echoes the terms of the Lal-Sammler discussion, but it also parenthetically points toward an interesting phenomenon in contemporary fiction—the use of the mystery story as a metaphor for the creative process itself and for man's search through largely irrelevant clues for the key to metaphysical truth. As such, the device has been used by such *nouveaux romanciers* as Alain Robbe-Grillet, Michel Butor, Nathalie Sarraute, and, of course, Mailer himself. *Mr. Sammler's Planet* contains numerous detective-story ingredients—the mysterious pickpocket, the hidden treasure, the insidious manipulations of organized crime, the twice-purloined manuscript, but Bellow fails to exploit these as structural devices to support the larger themes of his novel, and not surprisingly so, perhaps, when we consider his disdain for the *nouveau roman*. Bellow need not be a proponent of avant-garde experimentation, yet every great artist asks consequential questions about the form in which his vision is contained; one sign of Bellow's decline as a novelist is his disinterest in formal experimentation or, to put it another way, his apparent satisfaction with a narrative formula which dangerously constricts his vision. One begins to sense in him something Sammleresque—a contentment with the ways of the past, a dis-ease with the present, an avuncular superiority over unwashed radicalism. In the process, insight solidifies into banality, as in Bellow's own remarks about the city:

As a matter of fact, the characteristic life of the city today, as drawn by Joyce in *Ulysses* at the latest, is not really visible in America at this moment. People are not out in the streets as Leopold Bloom was in 1904, they're in the suburbs. The inner city is blighted, the scene of violence, crime and horror. People there are not reading books.[35]

It not only remains questionable whether the characters who make up, say, the vigorous Night Town life of *Ulysses* are dedicated readers (many, one suspects, are only semiliterate, and Joyce found Dublin no congenial home for the artist). It also becomes clear that stereotypes of the decaying inner-city blur historical memory, obscuring the urban blight revealed by Hogarth and Dickens and Zola, the tenement horrors exposed by Jacob Riis, the brutalizing anonymity observed by Upton Sinclair, Dos Passos, and Dreiser. Here, as elsewhere, the reader not unfairly expects that Bellow will probe the cultural assumptions on which his fiction stands; but he seems increasingly at ease with the one-eyed and hence dimensionless vision of Mr. Sammler.

Just as he declines to explore the detective-story metaphors that abound in *Mr. Sammler's Planet*, so Bellow seems reluctant to probe for structural implications the device of the literary legacy central to *Humboldt's Gift*. Indeed, Bellow made far more ingenious use of the device in "The Gonzaga Manuscripts," with its rich echoes of Henry James's "The Aspern Papers." In *Humboldt's Gift* the legacy is encased in a multi-layered tissue of meaning, implication, and double entendre, but such complexities are reflected solely through the inheritor's monologuist perceptions; the novel itself remains, technically, as wooden, old-fashioned, and full of clumsy coincidence as *Mr. Sammler's Planet*. Charlie Citrine's interminable ruminations and his vigorous monologues on spirituality—aimed, usually, at deafly diehard materialists—often recall the tendentious qualities of Mr. Sammler's voice; and he expresses similarly crabby judgments on the contemporary scene, as in the description of an "insignificant Picasso sculpture with its struts and its sheet metal, no wings, no victory, only a token, a reminder, only the *idea* of a work of art" (*HG*, 218). The novel suffers from such intrusions, and its authority is further eroded by a sloppiness in detail—the ex-wife first met casually (and intentionally) wearing a velvet jumpsuit during an August heat-wave in New York, a needlepoint pillow produced by embroidering. Roger Shattuck, reviewing the novel for the *New York Review of Books*, objected that entire episodes and individual characters seemed superfluous, whereas the nature of the story should have imposed "a basic narrative economy."[36]

Again, one senses that many of Bellow's vices represent the excess of his virtues. The same superabundance, the dense detail, the sensuous and spiritual plenitude which characterized *The Adventures of Augie March* are poured forth again in a novel whose superfluities are at least partially redeemed by Bellow's decision to return to the high comic mode with which the peccadilloes of Augie and Eugene Henderson were presented. As another of Bellow's bumbling seekers after truth, Charlie Citrine often travels through the world of memory and ideas, like Moses Herzog and Artur Sammler; indeed, he shares with Herzog a natural preference for the horizontal, and when assailed too harshly by the Reality-Instructors, his instinct is to darken the windows and to retreat to his green plush sofa: "I now lay there grieving. Again!" (*HG*, 168). But Citrine is also a physical voyager, a picaro whose wanderings crisscross Chicago and then take him to New York, Coney Island, Corpus Christi, Madrid, and Paris. The explicitly spiritual nature of his quest is underscored by his own comparison of his wanderings to those chronicled in Bunyan's *Pilgrim's Progress*; both carry their heroes away from family on "the soul's journey past the gates of death" (176). There is even a tribute to Henderson's earlier pilgrimage in the minor, throw-away incident of the quixotic search for a beryllium mine in East Africa, and in the presence of an "orphan" whom Citrine patiently nurtures near the conclusion of the novel.

Humboldt's Gift is, in fact, studded with reminders of Bellow's earlier writings. Like Tommy Wilhelm, Citrine is trapped, flailing, in the intricate commercial nexus of his society; and like Tommy he ceremonially ends his estrangement at a funeral. As in "The Gonzaga Manuscripts" the hero's picaresque journey takes him to a pension in Madrid; Clarence Feiler's abortive search for lost manuscripts that are buried in a grave brings him repeated encounters with death. Like Joseph and Augie, Charlie is constantly wary of being conscripted to the versions of reality his friends and acquaintances try to thrust upon him—Yoga, Rosicrucianism, primitivism, criminality, radical chic, sensualism, callous commercialism; like Augie, he samples all the alternatives, but ultimately says no to "limiting commitments." With Artur Sammler, another bookish man, he shares the conclusion that "This planet was still the base of operations" (405). The contrast between Chicago's decaying but still nourishing old immigrant neighborhoods and the glittering, exploitative high-rise institutions of the new city look back to *The Adventures of Augie March* and *Herzog*. In a telling juxtaposition, Charlie sits in the opulent semidarkness of the Playboy Club and remembers how as a child he had come by streetcar from the slums and learned to swim a few blocks away from the luxurious skyscraper. Like Herzog, Citrine is a man of letters who has been celebrated by the establishment but now finds himself blocked, stalled by the seeming disproportion between his intentions and the disarray of his life; whose troubled present is molded by a calculating, castrating ex-wife and an almost primitively sensuous mistress; and whose reflections reveal the comic pathos of a vain intellectual's efforts to age with style and dignity. Both men des-

perately yearn for order, and yet both seem perversely determined to sabotage their dreams with acts of division, separation,
miscalculation.

Humboldt's Gift achieves its primary unity through Bellow's ex-
uberant, inventive comic voice, which floats us over many of the
novel's inconsistencies and narrative infelicities. It is united further by the orchestration of four central metaphors: death, sleep,
cannibalism, and money, all of which point back to *Henderson the
Rain King*. Both novels, like Updike's *Couples*, are permeated by
death anxieties, and both heroes devote much of their energy to
evading reminders of death's dominion. Still, Henderson realizes
that "All the major tasks and the big conquests were done before
my time. That left the biggest problem of all, which was to encounter death. We've just got to do something about it" (*HRK*, 276). In
a similar vein, Charlie Citrine reflects, "But nothing had been
done about the main question. The main question, as Walt Whitman had pointed out, was the death question" (*HG*, 332). Charlie
Citrine's thoughts range from the death of his parents and the "sacrificial" death of the American poet Von Humboldt Fleischer to the
fatal plane crash in which his fiancee Demmie Vonghel was killed
and a heart-attack victim at the Downtown Club. He thinks of his
parents' graves, which tie him to Chicago, but also reflects that it is
"slaughter-city," and that "billions of animals had died here" (114).
During the present action of the novel Citrine learns that his
brother faces dangerous open-heart surgery and that the second
husband of Humboldt's wife Kathleen has been killed in a hunting
accident. His voluptuous mistress has divorced a salesman of
crypts, and will finally marry a prosperous mortician: in the manner of fairy tales, death once more ensnares beauty. Citrine's widowed childhood sweetheart, Naomi Lutz, sums up the events with
unintentional comedy shortly after her own father's death: "'Isn't
all this dying something, Charlie!'" (301).
    Charlie Citrine vacillates between fascination with death and an
instinct to flee from its incessant reminders—as Henderson had
fled from the corpse on his own kitchen floor. He cannot bear to
attend funerals, shudders at the thought of seeing the lid screwed
down on the coffin, and yet as a biographer he has made the deceased his "bread and brother." Unable to face the dying Humboldt, he subsequently feels a ponderous burden of guilt for the
poet's death—and for his own luxurious survival. He wonders
"why I feel such loyalty to the deceased. Hearing of their deaths I

often said to myself that I must carry on for them and do their job, finish their work" (107). Like Harry Houdini, Charlie Citrine was born in Appleton, Wisconsin, and he feels deep affinities with the great escape artist, whom Von Humboldt Fleischer had celebrated in a ballad called "Harlequin Harry." Houdini and Citrine are examples of men who "'struggle so hard with the problem of death'" (435), and Charlie Citrine repeatedly reflects on this affinity. Humboldt, Charlie, and Harry Houdini are all the sons of Jewish immigrants, and Charlie particularly admires Houdini's defiance of "'all forms of restraint and confinement, including the grave'" (435). Furthermore, when Houdini returned from his triumphal tours, he always visited the grave of his mother, telling her in whispers about his adventures and spending a fortune exposing spiritualists who promised him contact with her spirit. Of Houdini's death from peritonitis, Charlie reflects, "'So you see, nobody can overcome the final fact of the material world. Dazzling rationality, blazing of consciousness, the most ingenious skill—nothing can be done about death. Houdini worked out one line of inquiry completely. Have you looked into an open grave lately . . . ?'" (436). After he is deserted by Renata, Charlie spends his days reading to the dead, trying to draw near them as Henderson had tried to commune with his father by playing the violin; and in the novel's concluding episode, resonant with echoes of pastoral elegy, Charlie will himself finally be able to look into the open grave of his re-buried idol Von Humboldt Fleischer. Both literally and figuratively, he ultimately succeeds in burying the dead.

Closely intertwined with the dominant theme of death is the leitmotif of cannibalism. It first occurs when an expansive Von Humboldt Fleischer explains to Charlie Citrine, his eager young apprentice, about the rituals of the Cannibal Society of the Kawkiutl Indians: "'The candidate when he performs his initiation dance falls into a frenzy and eats human flesh. But if he makes a ritual mistake the whole crowd tears him to pieces'" (14). For Humboldt, the savage ritual is a model for the relationship between the poet and his public—in particular, for the poet and his critics, but the eat-or-be-eaten philosophy is not one which the young idealist can accept. Nonetheless, Charlie Citrine goes on to "cannibalize" his friend for the successful Broadway play and film *Von Trenck*, and the renowned dead for his subsequent biographies. In a parody of that role, he will be tricked by Rinaldo Cantabile into playing the part of a Chicago hit-man—"a dummy impersonating a murderer . . ." (277). Musing on the cynicism with which society regards the martyred artist—Edgar Allan Poe, Hart Crane, Randall Jarrell, John Berryman—Citrine is amazed at "how successful bitter hard-faced and cannibalistic people exult" (118). When the plane carrying his fiancee and her father crashes in the Venezuelan jungle, Charlie goes in search of the wreckage and finds himself in a tribe of cannibals: "'They had eaten the first group of missionaries that came there. As you sang in the chapel [you] saw the filed teeth of somebody who had probably eaten your brother—Dr. Timothy's brother was eaten, and he knew the fellows who had done it . . .'" (301). The ruthless lawyer who represents Citrine's ex-wife is repeatedly referred to as "Cannibal Pinsker," and the whole rapacious, exploitative climate of the business and legal worlds is viewed in terms of cannibalism.

Just as Charlie had cannibalized Humboldt's spirit for a Broadway play, so Humboldt cannibalizes Charlie's in a ludicrous film scenario about a successful writer who becomes spoiled by luxury and is blocked in his work until he journeys to a lush tropical island with his mistress and converts their adventures into a book that cannot be published for fear of a jealous wife's wrath; subsequently, the writer takes his wife to the same island and repeats all the physical steps of the idyll. When the book appears, his wife divorces him because it is clear that she is not the heroine of the tender love scenes, and the mistress rejects him because he has betrayed her by repeating the trip with another woman. The scenario is part of Humboldt's legacy to Charlie; the other part is a copy of a scenario the two had written together many years before, and it is explicitly a story of cannibalism. Opening with the crash of Umberto Nobile's lighter-than-air ship in the Arctic, it ultimately focuses on one of the survivors rescued from an ice floe—an Italian who had lived by consuming the body of a companion. Signor Caldofreddo, a kindly old ice-cream salesman in a Sicilian village, has managed to escape his earlier notoriety, but a Danish journalist who arrives to interview him threatens to destroy his own peace and the happiness of his beautiful daughter. Ultimately driven to confess his sins to the entire village, Caldofreddo finds forgiveness and acceptance in the lines "'Think of what our ancestors ate. As apes, as lower animals, as fishes. Think what animals have eaten since the beginning of time. And we owe our existence to them'" (182). In short, cannibalism belongs to the natural order of things earthly.

The two scenarios improbably serve to restore Charlie's dwindling fortunes; they also variously warn of the danger of the artist's reckless plundering of reality, of the attempt to convert the fruits of the imagination into commercial "properties." Here there are clear overtones of Hawthorne's concern for the artist figure as someone inclined to tamper with and thus pervert the natural order of things—as in "Ethan Brand," "Rappaccini's Daughter," "The Birthmark," or "Dr. Heidegger's Experiment." (Hepzibah, the name of the wife in Humboldt's exotic paradise-island scenario, is in fact borrowed from Hawthorne's *The House of the Seven Gables.*) The artist may have a certain liberty to plunder, exploit, cannibalize, but the price for such freedom is that he owes a tremendous debt to life; it is the debt which Charlie has not paid, and which is temporarily obscured by the more literal debts and debentures, damage suits and claims, stocks and alimony payments, publishers' advances and poker losses and elegant investments in carpets and automobiles, the talk of leases and bagmen and unnumbered Swiss accounts, of tax audits and mortgages, retainers and options, the money-grubbing of Renata's mother, bond swindles, ransom demands, wills and gouging lawyers' fees. The confusion of spiritual and material values is persistent in the world through which Charlie moves. Even in Humboldt's filmscript of romantic escape and lyric apostrophe, the writer's agent sees the island only as "the investment opportunity of a lifetime. He is already planning to build the world's greatest resort here. At night he sits in his tent with a map, laying out a pleasure dome. The natives will become waiters, cooks, porters, and caddies on his golf course" (346). Similarly, when Charlie visits his brother Ulrich—a figure strongly reminiscent of Augie March's brother Simon, the self-styled commercial tycoon—he finds him less concerned with the open-heart surgery that awaits him than with the rocky peninsula he plans to convert into an extensive resort complex.

Humboldt had once lectured that "in the unconscious, in the irrational core of things money was a vital substance like the blood or fluids that bathed the brain tissues" (242), and Charlie himself later extends the analogy. Not only does he draw his own associations between money and blood, but he also sees both reflected in the rich red leather seats in Cantabile's ostentatious Thunderbird; commercial machinations, in turn, become linked to cannibalism in the total metaphoric structure of *Humboldt's Gift.* These threads are all drawn together in Charlie's determination "to investigate, to satisfy myself that death *was* final, that the dead *were* dead" (263), and he accepts this charge as an urgent imperative. Otherwise,

You could simply assume that they had been forever wiped out, as you too would one day be. So if the daily papers told of murders committed in the streets before crowds of neutral witnesses, there was nothing illogical about such neutrality. On the metaphysical assumptions about death everyone in the world had apparently reached, everyone would be snatched, ravished by death, throttled, smothered. This terror and this murdering were the most natural things in the world. And these same conclusions were incorporated into the life of society and present in all its institutions, in politics, education, banking, justice. (263–264)

It is precisely Charlie Citrine's denial of such self-evident metaphysical "assumptions" that marks him as an absurd hero.

Given Bellow's vision of the world of commercial cannibalism, it at first seems ironic that Von Humboldt Fleischer's legacy to his former disciple brings him hard cash, but with the money Charlie re-buries his dead, makes a home for two lonely old men, and spends a month in meditation and study at the Goetheanum—the Rudolf Steiner Center near Basel. Many readers of *Humboldt's Gift* have found it difficult to accept Charlie Citrine's absorption with Steiner as an entirely serious element of the novel, but Bellow's own essays and lectures have made it clear that he himself feels a growing commitment to the Austrian social philosopher and Goethe scholar who, in 1902, founded the German Theosophic Association. Steiner's writings, furthermore, play a central role in reconciling the evidence of mortality with which Citrine is bombarded and "the incessant hints of immortality" (356) which repeatedly well up in his heart. Steiner eventually moved beyond theosophy to create an occultist doctrine he called anthroposophy; it rejected conventional scientific and theosophical views alike, in favor of a "spiritual science" that involved the study of the human spirit through disciplined "scientific" inquiry. Anthroposophy posited the existence of a spiritual world comprehensible to pure thought and fully accessible to the individual who properly cultivated his own inherent faculties. Steiner argued for the transmigration of souls—a concept to which Charlie Citrine frequently refers—and advocated self-discipline of mind and body to promote cognition of the spiritual world. Charlie's own explorations of Steiner's philosophy are guided by a Chicago anthroposophist, Dr. Scheldt, with whom he discusses his own growing tendency "to deny that so extraordinary a thing as a human soul can be wiped out forever. No, the dead are about us, shut out by our metaphysical denial of them. As we lie nightly in our hemispheres of sleep by the billions, our dead approach us. Our ideas should be their nourishment" (141).

However one evaluates Steiner's spiritualist doctrines, which have often encouraged a kind of superficial cultism, they are clearly central to Citrine's probing of theories of transcendence, to the fundamental "change in my attitude toward death" (328). When he remarks that "I had begun to entertain other alternatives" (328), they are at the intellectual level alternatives derived in great measure from the teachings of anthroposophy, though in Bellow's universe the theoretical must always find ratification in the private sphere. Thus, the metaphor of sleep is theoretically explored in terms of Steiner's pamphlet *The Driving Force of Spiritual Powers in World History*, with its argument that mankind has lost the ability to sleep fruitfully. According to Steiner, in true sleep the soul is released from the body to enter the "supersensible world" where it mingles with "the invisible forces which were known by initiates in the ancient world in their Mysteries" (264). In this state, according to the pamphlet, the words one has spoken all day vibrate and echo about the sleeper, forming the basis of his communication with higher beings. Hence, the debasement of language and feeling automatically robs the sleeper of his transcendent powers:

"But now, our daily monkeyshines are such, our preoccupations are so low, language has become so debased, the words so blunted and damaged, we've said such stupid and dull things, that the higher beings hear only babbling and grunting and TV commercials—the dog-food level of things. This says nothing to them. What pleasure can these higher beings take in this kind of materialism, devoid of higher thought or poetry? As a result, all that we can hear in sleep is matter creaking and hissing and washing, the rustling of plants, and the air conditioning. So we are incomprehensible to the higher beings." (264–265)

What Citrine is describing, within the context of Steinerian thought, is the decline of the imagination, which becomes a recurrent lament in the novel. But his reflections are also directly pertinent to the characterizations of Von Humboldt Fleischer and Demmie Vonghel, both of whom suffer from insomnia, prefer late-show horror films to the horrors of their own nightmares, and sleep only with the aid of drugs. Insomnia itself thus becomes a sign of spiritual malaise.

Charlie Citrine reflects on Steiner's theories of sleep in two key passages of the novel—in both cases when he is particularly aware of the predatory aspects of his urban surroundings.[37] There is, however, another and more pervasive use of sleep that is both more pertinent to the hero's own spiritual crisis and more familiar to readers of Bellow's earlier fiction. This is the equivalent of the numbing chain of mechanical gestures which characterize Camus's portrait of the "unawakened" man who moves like a somnambulist through the cycles of "Rising, streetcar, four hours in the office or factory, meal, streetcar, four hours of work, meal, sleep, and Monday Tuesday Wednesday Thursday Friday and Saturday according to the same rhythm . . ."[38] It is only when this rhythm is broken that the fundamental question of "Why?" arises, and man achieves his first significant awareness of the absurd. Eugene Henderson spoke of his determination "to burst the spirit's sleep" (*HRK*, 76); while chopping wood, he is struck in the face—the first of the blows that gradually awaken him. The blows that startle Citrine awake are from the baseball bats with which Cantabile ravishes the sleek skin of his Mercedes 280-SL. From this point, he will no longer be able to view the violence of the streets from the intellectual detachment and the oblique high-rise angles he has carefully cultivated; he now enters the life of the streets, the marketplace, the courtroom, and the blows descend almost without pause.

When Cantabile first demands that Charlie pay his gambling debts, he warns that "'You don't know what you're into. Or who I am. Wake up!'" (*HG*, 46). Charlie himself thinks, "I often said 'Wake up!' to myself, and many people also have cried, 'Wake, wake!' As if I had a dozen eyes, and stubbornly kept them sealed. 'Ye have eyes and see not.' This, of course, was absolutely true" (46). The passage is echoed, much later in the novel, when Charlie visits his entrepreneur brother, who argues, "'I can't read the crap you write. Two sentences and I'm yawning. Pa should have slapped you around the way he did me. It would have woken you up'" (384). Charlie has a particularly strong identification with Rip Van Winkle, and often uses metaphors like "Sleeping at the switch" (306). Again, he struggles to relate such ideas to the problem of imagination, and to his own blocked state:

"The true poise, that of contemplation or imagination, sits right on the border of sleep and dreaming. Now, Naomi, as I was lying stretched out in America, determined to resist its material interests and hoping for redemption by art, I fell into a deep snooze that lasted for years and decades. Evidently I didn't have what it took. What it took was more strength, more courage, more stature." (306)

Sleep thus becomes doubly symbolic—of Citrine's arrested spiritual development and of his literary decline. In part, his with-

drawal is calculated, the result of a classic Bellovian dis-ease with
the modern world, as revealed in remarks that "the lessons of
jungle guerilla tactics were being applied in all the great cities of
the world" (36) or that "mania and crime and catastrophe were the
destiny of mankind in this vile century" (166). He thus becomes "a
fanatical reader, walled in by his many books, accustomed to look
down from his high windows on police cars, fire engines, am-
bulances, an involuted man who worked from thousands of private
references and texts . . ." (280). Cultivating a Rip Van Winkle
slumber, the writer increasingly loses touch with the reality which
should nurture his work. Ironically, it is the small-time Mafioso
Rinaldo Cantabile who prods Citrine awake; Cantabile becomes
his nemesis, but also his alter ego, initiating the first of a series of
bizarre, mystifying events that intrude on the writer's luxurious
withdrawal. "'All you people are soft about the realities'" (173),
Cantabile lectures him, echoing Humboldt's observation many
years before that "'The actual world can kiss your ass'" (122). Later
the petty mobster reiterates, "'You're an isolationist'" (256), and
Charlie himself must recognize that "I had used the conditions of
life to test my powers of immunity" (267). Sleep, immunity, isolation, death: all are familiar concepts in terms of the description of
the existential malaise; all must be combatted if the spirit and its
manifestations through the creative imagination are to flourish.
Hence, Charlie comes to recognize that Cantabile "seemed to have
a spiritual office to perform . . . to move me from dead center"
(287–288).

There are two instructors who guide Charlie Citrine through his
spiritual awakening—the street-wise Cantabile and the artist *manqué* Von Humboldt Fleischer, who, through his legacy and a long,
rambling letter, speaks literally from beyond the grave. The failed
poet was in great measure inspired by Delmore Schwartz, who for
Bellow as for many of his intellectual generation was symbolic of
the difficulty of being an artist in America; but the characterization
also owes something to Bellow's intimate friend John Berryman,
whose life ended in suicide. In this sense the entire novel is a kind
of elaborate Kaddish; through it Bellow-Citrine makes a gift to the
dead just as he receives one, and hence the double-entendre of the
novel's title. More important than the biographical references en-
coded in the figure of Humboldt is the fact that, even when rejected by the critical establishment as a "burnt-out case," reduced
to absolute penury, and neglected by his friends, the poet can still
plead for the life of the mind and for the concept that "we are not

natural beings but supernatural beings" (347). If Cantabile shatters Citrine's isolation, it is Humboldt who instructs him on how to live with his new awareness; only when he has accepted this lesson can he repay his debts to the dead—debts revealed in his awareness "that I had sinned against Humboldt" (112). Such lessons would, however, be irrelevant if they found no naturally responsive chord within Charlie Citrine; but, in fact, the intimations of spiritual dimensions have long seized him—only to be suppressed in his materialistic embodiment of the successful establishment artist. Even as a child, bed-ridden with tuberculosis, he had felt a rapture for the world; "'Oh, I loved them all terribly, abnormally. I was all torn up with love'" (74); he is also a sentimentalist whose heart aches "at the destruction of the past" (76).

Such instincts and intimations will be tested and strengthened by the series of trials Charlie endures in the novel, as Eugene Henderson was tempered by his African peccadilloes. Gradually he perceives a kind of "light-in-the-being" which balances his image of contemporary decline:

I had experienced it briefly, but it had lasted long enough to be convincing and also to cause an altogether unreasonable kind of joy. Furthermore, the hysterical, the grotesque about me, the abusive, the unjust, that madness in which I had often been a willing and active participant, the grieving, now had found a contrast. I say "now" but I knew long ago what this light was. Only I seemed to have forgotten that in the first decade of life I knew this light and even knew how to breathe it in. But this early talent or gift or inspiration, given up for the sake of maturity or realism (practicality, self-preservation, the fight for survival), was now edging back. (177–178)

In this passage as in numerous others, there are distinct echoes of Wordsworth's ode "Intimations of Immortality from Recollections of Early Childhood."

Only when he is able to respond to the imperatives of his own inner voices is Citrine able to burst the spirit's sleep, to claim his spiritual prerogatives as an absurd hero by living in terms of the disparity between his intentions and the reality he encounters—a polarity suggested early in the novel in the contrast between musicians performing "pious and beautiful cantatas on ancient instruments" (66) and the ruined windshield of the Mercedes, smashed into crystalline blossomings by Cantabile. Slowly Citrine acknowledges that "life was a hell of a lot more bounteous than I had ever realized. . . . It rushes up also from within" (331), and he accepts the Herzogian necessity "to put metaphysics and the conduct of life together in some practical way" (357). In a series of symbolic actions that test his new-found resolve, Charlie Citrine begins to meet his spiritual obligations—in a visit to his ailing brother, in nurturing Renata's abandoned child, in providing a home for Uncle Waldemar and Menasha Klinger, in re-burying Humboldt in a grave adjoining that of his mother. As a symbolic act, the traditional Jewish burial becomes the novel's culminating affirmation of order, an illustration of the conviction that human beings "held permanent membership in some larger, more extended human outfit . . ." (332). *Humboldt's Gift* thus becomes a complex articulation of what Bellow has described as the writer's most urgent task: "to remind people of their common stock of emotion, of their common humanity—of the fact, if you will, that they have souls."[39]

The confrontation with death has been a recurrent motif in Bellow's fiction—the ultimate absurd hypothesis that must somehow be accounted for outside conventional systems of religious consolation. In an interview he gave in 1964, Bellow described the dilemma of Eugene Henderson in terms that might well be applied to Charlie Citrine: "What Henderson is really seeking is a remedy to the anxiety over death. What he can't endure is this continuing anxiety: the indeterminate and indefinite anxiety, which most of us accept as the condition of life which he's foolhardy enough to resist."[40] In his most memorable and persuasive treatments of the death anxiety, it is comedy—in its broadest contours of affirmation and redemption—which characterizes Bellow's approach. Hence, he could term *Humboldt's Gift* "a presumptuous book which attempts to make a comedy of death."[41] The comic voice becomes more definitive in the novel's concluding scene, when Charlie Citrine watches Humboldt's new grave fill with earth. Strains of pastoral elegy are threaded through the episode, which teeters on the verge of sentimentality—only to be relieved by the aged Menasha rising on his toes, with Adam's apple thrust forward, to sing "In questa tomba oscura" from *Aïda*. Similarly, crocuses thrust up through rotted leaves; their promise is real, but the danger that they seem too archly poetic is undercut by Menasha's anecdote: "'They used to tell one about a kid asking his grumpy old man when they were walking in the park, "What's the name of this flower, Papa?" and the old guy is peevish and he yells, "How should I know? Am I in the millinery business?"'" (487). Though Bellow, like Charlie Citrine, maintains his "Tolstoyan" appetite for serious, big ideas which at times threaten to scuttle the novel, comedy helps to keep it afloat.

In the short story "A Silver Dish" it is again the comic that tempers a long meditation on death. The hero, Woody Selbst, contemplates the recent death of his aged father and wonders how, without a religious framework, the matter of mourning should be approached. Furthermore, thinking of the murderous impulses revealed by the daily papers, he questions what meaning the death of a single, feeble old man can possibly have: "And still others shoot others, or shoot themselves. That's what you read in the press, see on the tube, mention at dinner. We know now what goes daily through the whole of the human community, like a global death-peristalsis."[42] Woody's reflections on mourning include the memory of a scene he had witnessed near the Murchison Falls in Uganda, when a buffalo calf stepped into the water and was suddenly dragged to its death by a crocodile. The parent cattle, meanwhile, stood dumbly by, as though trying to comprehend what had happened, and clearly unable to do so. Woody, a professional loner but a man of great charity and compassion, also struggles for meaning, and eventually finds it in his own childhood faith that "this world should be a love-world, that it should eventually recover and be entirely a world of love."[43]

Such messages in Bellow's writings are always moving testimonials to man's spiritual resourcefulness, to the irrepressible muscularity of his soul. As John Cruickshank has remarked about the absurd, "The myth of Sisyphus means for Camus that the most appaling of truths can lose their power over us once we have absolutely recognized and accepted them."[44] Among those appalling truths, clearly, is the truth of death. Despite the richness of the message Bellow has to deliver, the mission he feels as a spokesman for what fellow Nobel Prize winner William Faulkner termed "the old verities and truths of the human heart,"[45] there remains a disturbing disparity between philosophical assertion and fictional demonstration—particularly in the later work. This is true of *Humboldt's Gift*, even though the novel contains brilliantly conceived episodes, characters that are richly fleshed, fine passages of lyrical prose, and a sense of operatic extravaganza. Nonetheless, Bellow often seems to exploit his own characters, using them as excuses to push forward his central thesis, and hence neglecting their autonomous life within the novel. Thus, Von Humboldt Fleischer is reputed to be a brilliant, dynamic "Mozart of conversation" (*HG*, 13), but most of what we hear of that conversation is pompous, overbearing, diffuse; Charlie Citrine, obsessed by the role of boredom in the modern world, is in turn one of the greatest bores in Bellow's fictional universe—a man woefully in love with the sound of his own voice; and Renata, the sensual, opportunistic mistress, is a clumsy reprise of Ramona in *Herzog*.

Here, as in *Mr. Sammler's Planet*, Bellow's noble philosophical assertions are inadequately illuminated by imaginative energy, and this seems a particularly obtrusive failure in a book which repeatedly argues that "The imagination must not pine away" (112) and that "Mankind must recover its imaginative powers" (250). As Roger Shattuck concluded in his review of *Humboldt's Gift*, "the fictional impulse is out of adjustment. The spark is unsteady."[46] But however faulty the voice, the values it proclaims are clearly and forcefully on the side of the angels, of man's absurd but ennobling struggle to grasp what Camus termed the "superior meaning" of life. "The world," he continued, "has at least the truth of man, and our task is to give man his justification against fate itself."[47] It is Bellow's task as well.

The Love Ethic

Few heroes of contemporary literature have aroused so much devotion, imitation, or controversy as J. D. Salinger's Holden Caulfield, the disaffiliated adolescent whose lost weekend in New York is chronicled in *The Catcher in the Rye*. As an impressionable adolescent making his first tentative movements into an adult world, Holden becomes a sensitive register by which the values of that world can be judged. From the opening pages of this novel the world is seen to be fragmentary, distorted, and absurd—in Holden's own special vernacular, "phony." It is an environment in which real communication on a sensitive level is impossible, and when Holden unsuccessfully tries to explain his spiritual pain to Sally Hayes, there is certainly more than a coincidental suggestion of Eliot's "J. Alfred Prufrock" in the frustrated cry, "'You don't see what I meant at all'" (*CR*, 173).

Holden does not refuse to grow up so much as he agonizes over the state of being grown up. The innocent world of childhood is amply represented in *The Catcher in the Rye*, but Holden, as a frustrated, disillusioned, anxious hero, stands for modern man rather than merely for the modern adolescent. He is self-conscious and often ridiculous, but he is also an anguished human being of special sensitivity. Even though he is often childishly ingenuous, and his language is frequently comic, Holden must be seen as both a representative and a critic of the modern environment, as the highly subjective tone of the novel suggests.

As a misfit Holden has literary predecessors in such early Salinger stories as "The Hang of It," "The Varioni Brothers," "Soft-Boiled Sergeant," "This Sandwich Has No Mayonnaise," and "The Stranger." Holden is not unlike Rabbit Angstrom or Augie March in seeking the environment in which he can perform at his best, and the result is a painful contemporary odyssey. As the novel opens, Holden is in the process of rejecting yet another uncongenial environment, Pencey Prep. There he feels surrounded by phonies, just as he had felt surrounded by them at Elkton Hills, his previous school: "One of the biggest reasons I left Elkton Hills was because I was surrounded by phonies. That's all. They were coming in the goddam window" (19). That "Goddam Elkton Hills" is far more than an example of the social snobbery of an Eastern prep school. It comes to stand for a world in which values and perspectives have become so distorted that there seems little if any room for the sensitive individual who attempts to order the flux of human existence or to bring it into the light of a consistent aesthetic perspective. To this significant degree, the milieu in which Salinger heroes function is "absurd." Like Camus's absurd man, the Salinger hero tries to live by ethical standards in an indifferent, often nihilistic universe. An important distinction, however, must be drawn between Camus's absurd man and the absurd man in Salinger's fiction. This distinction is primarily one of consciousness, for Camus's heroes consciously acknowledge the absurdity of their struggle against reality. While the reader is in a position to see the absurdity of Holden's quixotic gestures and of Zooey's ultimate, transcendent "love" stance, he is never entirely certain that the characters themselves see their own struggles as absurd, though Zooey at least approaches this essential awareness. These characters, however, do demonstrate "disproportions" on the level of values which make the myth of the absurd applicable to their struggles. The context of the absurd does not perhaps explain as much about Salinger as it did about Updike, Styron, or Bellow, but it does help us to see what Salinger has tried to accomplish in his writing and to understand his relationship to other contemporary novelists.

Few areas of modern life escape Holden Caulfield's indictment. Among those most severely challenged are the movies (to which his brother D. B., a writer, has prostituted himself) and religious enthusiasm. Holden explains that the children in his family are all "atheists" because his parents are of different religious persuasions (foreshadowing the Irish-Jewish Glass family). Thus Holden's biting but revealing point of view is not clouded by specific religious commitments, and he can love the nuns whom he meets in Grand Central Station even though he feels that Catholicism usually throws up insurmountable barriers to communication. Just as he loves the nuns for their simplicity and honesty, he sees through the selfish religious pose of "this guy Ossenburger," an undertaker who contributes a dormitory wing to Pencey.

The phoniness of Hollywood and of religion as it is often practiced in the contemporary world come together to form a dramatic whole in the Christmas pageant which Holden attends at Radio City. Following the Rockettes and a man who roller-skated under tables, "they had this Christmas thing they have at Radio City every year": "All these angels start coming out of the boxes and everywhere, guys carrying crucifixes and stuff all over the place, and the whole bunch of them—*thousands* of them—singing 'Come All Ye Faithful!' like mad. Big deal. It's supposed to be religious as hell, I know, and very pretty and all, but I can't see anything religious or pretty, for God's sake, about a bunch of actors carrying crucifixes all over the stage" (178). The blatant, graceless *kitsch* of the movie which follows the stage show (and which has been identified as James Hilton's *Random Harvest*) is an equally commercial deception, an artificial substitute for the love and generosity which Americans have forgotten how to express. After his experience with a Radio City Christmas, Holden feels yet more agonizingly frustrated and alone. "I'm sort of glad they've got the atomic bomb invented," he comments. "If there's ever another war, I'm going to sit right the hell on top of it. I'll volunteer for it, I swear to God I will" (183).

Wherever Holden turns, his craving for truth seems to be frustrated by the phoniness of the world. From his hotel window he looks out upon scenes of perversion and distortion; in bars and night clubs he hears only the laconic accents of shallow supersophisticates or self-satisfied intellectuals. When he finds innocence or purity it is always jeopardized by evil or apathy, and he searches desperately for something to sustain him. An answer seems to come from Mr. Antolini, a former English teacher who explains to Holden that the fall he is riding for is "'a special kind of fall, a horrible kind. The man falling isn't permitted to feel or hear himself hit bottom. He just keeps falling and falling. The whole arrangement's designed for men who, at some time or other in their lives, were looking for something their own environment couldn't supply them with. Or they thought their own environment couldn't supply them with. So they gave up looking'" (243–244). Mr. Antolini urges Holden to continue to search in humility for a cause worth living for. Such a search, he assures Holden, has been chronicled by educated and scholarly men, and he promises to guide the boy into an intellectual channel that will both stimulate and comfort him. Whatever consolation there may have been in this message is destroyed when Holden awakens to find Mr. Antolini petting him—and he flees from yet another example of the world's perversion.

What prompts Holden's quest is his desire for unity, a desire that is expressed in the comfort and safety which he always felt in the Museum of Natural History:

The best thing, though, in that museum was that everything always stayed right where it was. Nobody'd move. You could go there a hundred thousand times, and that Eskimo would still be just finished catching those two fish, the birds would still be on their way south, the deers would still be drinking out of that water hole, with their pretty antlers and their pretty, skinny legs, and that squaw with the naked bosom would still be weaving that same blanket. Nobody'd be different. (157–158)

That such a reassuringly ordered universe is an impossible dream is emphasized by the fact that, when Holden visits the Museum near the conclusion of his New York odyssey, he sees the words "'Fuck you' . . . written with a red crayon or something, right under the glass part of the wall, under the stones" (264). Holden wishes to erase the interminable "Fuck you's" on all the alley walls and school corridors and sidewalks in the world, and this intention to cancel out vulgarity and phoniness is a poignant if naive example of the absurd.

The Catcher in the Rye is an important articulation of one of the possible responses which man may make to an essentially destructive life experience. Since, Holden reasons, there is no fulfillment in the adult world, since all it can offer man is frustration or corruption, the only worthwhile task to which he can devote himself is that of the protector who stops children before they enter the world of destruction and phoniness and keeps them in a state of arrested innocence:

"Anyway, I keep picturing all these little kids playing some game in this big field of rye and all. Thousands of little kids, and nobody's around— nobody big, I mean—except me. And I'm standing on the edge of some crazy cliff. What I have to do, I have to catch everybody if they start to go over the cliff—I mean if they're running and they don't look where they're going I have to come out from somewhere and *catch* them. That's all I'd do all day. I'd just be the catcher in the rye and all. I know it's crazy, but that's the only thing I'd really like to be. I know it's crazy." (224–225)

Holden's reiteration of the word "crazy" reminds us that his ambition is also "absurd," for his Christ-like intention (suffering the little children to come unto him) is opposed to the reality in which children like his own sister, Phoebe, are carted off to the Lister Foundation to see movies on euthanasia and move along grimy school corridors which flaunt the words "Fuck you!" at them. While Holden has a vision of his role in the world, he is unable either to live the absurdity he has outlined or to develop an absurd faith. The reasons for this failure on his part are simple and obvious. First, even though we are clearly intended to see him as a representative of modern man, Holden is an adolescent, and both his experience and his perspectives are too limited for him to offer any kind of finalized "answer" to the phoniness of the world. Second, and perhaps most important, his vision carries within itself a destructive contradiction. While Holden's intention is absurd in its opposition to reality, the goal of his intention is to help innocent children to *avoid* reality. His conclusion negates his premise insofar as it eliminates one of the two crucial terms of the absurd confrontation and offers no formula by which man can live in and with his world. Holden's intention is moving and vaguely saintly, but it involves a nostalgia which, according to Camus, the absurd man must reject. (Indeed, Holden himself rejects it when he decides that he must not attempt to protect Phoebe during her final ride on the carousel.)

What Salinger leaves us with in this novel is an often biting image of the absurd contemporary milieu. The idea of perpetuating the innocence of childhood is a philosophically untenable position, and the only other unrejected proposals in the novel are so vague that their full importance can be seen only in Salinger's later work. The first of these proposals for a stance at once self-protective and humanistically fulfilling is made by Carl Luce, who suggests a vague mystical discipline derived from Eastern philosophy as a solution to Holden's spiritual agony, but Luce's approach to this discipline seems supersophisticated and "phony." In the epilogue to the novel Holden suggests the possibility of re-entering society when he says, "I sort of *miss* everybody I told about. Even old Stradlater and Ackley, for instance. I think I even miss that goddam Maurice" (277). Holden misses even the phonies of the world because his experience has taught him something about the necessity of loving, and here Salinger sounds what is to become his major and most complex theme.

After *The Catcher in the Rye* Salinger wrote several stories examining the mystical process, and even though his mystically inclined heroes are engaging and at times inspiring, their stance must be rejected, too, in favor of a position that leads man to the world rather than to an intense but isolating subjective experience. Like efforts to recapture the innocence of childhood, mysticism (which Salinger usually considers in terms of Zen Buddhism) is finally seen as an evasion and contradiction of Western man's spiritual quest. In Zen Buddhism, the life of the mystic is only temporarily one of isolation, for after the achievement of *satori*, the state of total enlightenment and consciousness that is the goal of Zen Buddhism, the enlightened man re-enters the world to perform good works. Thus, Salinger's rejection of the transitory, unearned mystical *experience* is understandable in terms of its failure to provide a program which the individual can follow in order to give his life meaning, but his rejection of mysticism itself is more difficult to understand—especially in light of his own involvement with Zen Buddhism. Mysticism is treated as a "fever" in Salinger's writings, an isolating and therefore unfruitful discipline that inevitably leads Western man away from the paths of significant human involvement. Furthermore, while *satori* may eventually guide the Buddhist back into his world, the good works which he is prepared to perform are not necessarily those works which a spiritually enlightened Westerner should be prepared to perform. It is not through mysticism but through love that the Salinger hero at last re-enters the world.

From 1945 until 1951, J. D. Salinger published sixteen short stories, several of the same slick, predictable character as the stories he wrote for popular magazines during the Second World War. Five of those stories, however, were concerned with Holden Caulfield and his family, and three of them represented the beginning of his largest and most serious body of work—the "saga" of the Glass family. The first of these stories centers on an elusive character named Seymour Glass, whose suicide is the subject of the first story in Salinger's second book, *Nine Stories*. Little in this brief account indicates the scope of the Glass series, but it sets the stage for the rejection of mysticism as a solution to the contemporary spiritual dilemma. In order to appreciate the strength of Salinger's rejection, one must understand his fascination with the mystical process itself. Two of Salinger's *Nine Stories*, "De Daumier-Smith's Blue Period" and "Teddy," chronicle, respectively, the mystical vision and the mystical faith.

De Daumier-Smith is the fanciful pseudonym adopted by a somewhat typical Salinger *isolatoe* who brashly attempts to create a new image of himself with which he can confront a world from which he suddenly feels disaffiliated. De Daumier-Smith's rebellion resembles Holden's in that he too is hypersensitive to the phoniness of the world, but the origin of his disaffiliation is more specifically identified as the absence of love. Jean narrates his own story, and the most pertinent fact about his childhood is that he had never truly loved anyone but his mother. Shortly after her death, he moves to New York with his stepfather. Having drawn some slight attention as an artist when his family lived in Paris, Jean embroiders his experiences, draws up an imaginary list of professional credentials and friends (including Picasso) and applies for a job as an instructor at "Les Amis Des Vieux Maîtres," a correspondence art school in Montreal. What prompts him to make this sudden "quixotic gesture" is the realization that he and his father "were both in love with the same deceased woman" (*NS*, 98). This knowledge forces him out of the innocent private world in which he had formerly lived, and the very telling of his story is an attempt to give order to the experiences which greet him in the public world—a world which at first seems no more complete or fulfilling than the Oedipally narrow world in which he had previously functioned. The isolation which De Daumier-Smith suffers is underscored by the fact that we never learn his real name; he adopts a bogus identity and a preposterously contrived set of credentials in order to teach students whom he will never see in a French art school run by two Japanese. When Jean reveals to the Yoshotos that he is a student of Buddhism, they inform him that they are Presbyterians. However ambitiously ingratiating he becomes to his employers, his loneliness only increases.

What seems to offer Jean consolation is his discovery of naive beauty in the crude but talented paintings of Sister Irma of the Order of St. Joseph. In Jean's wild daydreams about the nun, she comes to represent his last chance to communicate with another sensitive spirit, and he yearns for a moment of truth and love with her which will make him spiritually whole and effect his conversion into a great healer.

When her Superior severs Sister Irma's relationship with the art school after reading Jean's passionate letter to her, the boy is cast into a painful and almost total despair; but from that dark night of the soul he passes into a period of illumination. Like the precocious members of the Glass family, Jean has been a student of comparative religions, and his study has at least partially prepared him for the epiphany which greets him and flashes like the sun into his dark night. Les Amis Des Vieux Maîtres is located over an orthopedic appliances shop, and as Jean pauses before the window, he seems to see it as a *collage* representing all of the crippling inhumanity of the world: "The thought was forced on me that no matter how coolly or sensibly or gracefully I might one day learn to live my life, I would always at best be a visitor in a garden of enamel urinals and bedpans, with a sightless, wooden dummy-deity standing by in a marked-down rupture truss" (116). Later,

however, he has what he calls an "Experience," in which everything in the window is transformed: "Suddenly (and I say this, I
believe, with all due self-consciousness), the sun came up and sped
toward the bridge of my nose at the rate of ninety-three million
miles a second. Blinded and very frightened—I had to put my
hand on the glass to keep my balance. The thing lasted for no more
than a few seconds. When I got my sight back, the girl had gone
from the window, leaving behind her a shimmering field of exquisite, twice-blessed, enamel flowers" (121).

"De Daumier-Smith's Blue Period" offers a strong suggestion
that a mystical experience may help man to alter his vision of the
world so significantly that he will be able to live in it. Jean de
Daumier-Smith does return to the world after his dark night of
despair to spend a "normal" summer of girl-watching on the beach.
While Jean has something closely related to a mystical revelation,
he is not a mystic: "I'd like, if possible, to avoid seeming to pass it
off as a case, or even a borderline case, of genuine mysticism"
(120). While his experience offers the promise of a degree of spiritual fulfillment he had not known before, his story suggests
no code by which the individual can oppose a world made up of
"enamel urinals and bedpans" and ruled over by a "wooden
dummy-deity." His discovery of an order and transcendent meaning in a sterile and hostile world is rather a product of chance, than
the climax of experience. This situation is typical for the modern
hero, to whom revelation or epiphany comes as a sudden intuitive
flash, suggesting in part that visions of order or meaning are not
available through reason.

In "Teddy" Salinger concerned himself with the realized mystic
Teddy McArdle, a precocious ten-year-old who has achieved the
enlightened consciousness of *satori*. Teddy's mysticism frees him
from the grossness of his parents, but Salinger treats his mystic
lyrically and impressionistically, never attempting to describe the
process by which Teddy arrives at *satori*, other than by referring to
the boy's intense periods of meditation, but in "A Perfect Day for
Bananafish" he allegorically demonstrates that mysticism is not a
solution to man's dilemma.

As we learn from later stories about the Glass family, Seymour
Glass has traveled to Florida with his wife in order to "recover"
from a state of acute depression. In the first half of "A Perfect Day
for Bananafish," through a telephone conversation between his
wife and her mother, we are given some insight into the causes of
his depression. Muriel comes from a world whose main concerns
are with "normalcy" and whose emotional outlets are found in the

kind of melodramatic movie which to Holden Caulfield seemed a puerile commercial sham. The hotel room in which Seymour commits suicide is characterized by the smell "of new calfskin luggage and nail-lacquer remover" (18). Without the bananafish allegory the reader might see Seymour's suicide as merely a rejection of this world of crass superficiality, but it is also—and more significantly—a rejection of the mystical life itself.

While Muriel is talking to her mother and trying to reassure her that Seymour has had no more destructive urges, Seymour is on the beach with Sybil Carpenter. He catches the young girl's attention with a variety of fantasies, the most complex of which involves the bananafish. Pushing Sybil out into the water on a rubber float, he explains to her the inherent fatalism of bananafish: "'Well, they swim into a hole where there's a lot of bananas. They're very ordinary-looking fish when they swim *in*. But once they get in, they behave like pigs. Why, I've known some bananafish to swim into a banana hole and eat as many as seventy-eight bananas.' He edged the float and its passenger a foot closer to the horizon. 'Naturally, after that they're so fat they can't get out of the hole again. Can't fit through the door'" (16).

Seymour's life has been filled with erratic spiritual experiences, and to his brothers and sisters he stands as a kind of Christ-figure. Like the bananafish, however, he has become so glutted with this experience that he can no longer participate in the real world outside himself. This inability, which accounts for what he calls the "very tragic life" which the bananafish leads, is emphasized by the fact that he cannot bear the eyes of the world. After leaving Sybil on the beach, Seymour walks into the hotel elevator along with a young woman:

"I see you're looking at my feet," he said to her when the car was in motion.
"I beg your pardon?" said the woman.
"I said I see you're looking at my feet."
"I *beg* your pardon. I happened to be looking at the floor," said the woman, and faced the doors of the car.
"If you want to look at my feet, say so," said the young man. "But don't be a God-damned sneak about it." (17)

Following this episode, Seymour enters his hotel room, takes a pistol from his suitcase, and fires a bullet through his head.

Salinger rejects the mystic's experience as a solution to man's alienation in an absurd universe because mysticism ("banana fever") removes man from reality. While Seymour is never a fully

realized mystic like Teddy, it is inconsistent to explain away his
suicide as despair over the idea of achieving *satori*. Seymour has
already rejected *satori* because it leads him out of the world in
which he feels he must live, and his rejection is overt and conscious. His life has been filled with one transcendent experience
after another, with visions and intense spiritual moments which
affirm his ability to achieve *satori*. Among the reminders of such
experiences, Seymour notes, "I have scars on my hands from
touching certain people."

"Once, in the park, when Franny was still in the carriage, I put my hand
on the downy pate of her head and left it there too long. Another time, at
Loew's Seventy-second Street, with Zooey during a spooky movie. He
was about six or seven, and he went under the seat to avoid watching a
scary scene. I put my hand on his head. Certain heads, certain colors and
textures of human hair leave permanent marks on me. Other things, too.
Charlotte once ran away from me, outside the studio, and I grabbed her
dress to stop her, to keep her near me. A yellow cotton dress I loved
because it was too long for her. I still have a lemon-yellow mark on the
palm of my right hand. Oh, God, if I'm anything by a clinical name, I'm a
kind of paranoiac in reverse. I suspect people of plotting to make me
happy." (*RHRB*, 88)

As we learn in "Raise High the Roof Beam, Carpenters," Seymour
was so happy over his marriage to Muriel that he was unable to
attend his own wedding. Seymour's wedding-day happiness came
from the thought that he might at last emerge from the spiritual
"hole" into which he had begun swimming as a child. Unable to
resign a quest for a miraculous spiritual perfection, and simultaneously unequipped to join the world of mere possibility, Seymour chose suicide. As Dan Wakefield has noted, suicide and miracle are the extremes between which many of Salinger's characters
fluctuate, but the author's primary concern is with the alternatives
which exist between those extremes. No appeal to a spiritual absolute (and no transcendent spiritual experience) is a wholly successful alternative. In his later stories Salinger turns his attention to
other stances which man can make in an absurd world to give his
life meaning.

Salinger would certainly agree with Dan Wakefield's observation
that ours is a time in which men are "'no longer feeling within
themselves the idol but still feeling the altar,' and the questions of
what replaces the idol which once provided a set of answers for
human conduct; the question of how men act with morality and
love if there is no idol which prescribes the rules, is a central and

vital question."[1] Salinger begins to define his answer in "For Esmé—with Love and Squalor." The narrator of this story—who is never more fully identified than as "Sergeant X"—writes his story as a kind of epithalamium after receiving an invitation to Esmé's wedding. He had met the girl while stationed in England for special D-Day training, and the loneliness which he experienced before their meeting is idiomatic to the Salinger hero.

On a free Saturday afternoon at the end of his training course Sergeant X walks into Devon and almost by accident enters a church in which a children's choir is rehearsing. There he becomes enchanted by Esmé, a young girl of "about thirteen, with straight ash-blond hair of ear-lobe length, an exquisite forehead, and blasé eyes that, I thought, might very possibly have counted the house" (NS, 68). Later Sergeant X meets the girl in a tea room, and Esmé tries to comfort and entertain the lonely G.I. When she leaves the tea room, it is with the request that X someday write her a story "about love and squalor."

X's experience with squalor comes in Bavaria, where he is trying unsuccessfully to recover from his encounter with undefined battlefield horrors. His recovery is not aided by the loutish insensitivity of his companion, Clay, or by his own brother's request for wartime souvenirs: "'. . . how about sending the kids a couple of bayonets or swastikas . . .'" (79). X is quartered in a house recently confiscated from a family whose daughter was an official in the Nazi party; among the books which she has left behind is Goebbel's *Die Zeit Ohne Beispiel*, a title ironically descriptive of X's condition. He opens the book to find the words "'Dear God, life is hell'" written on the flyleaf. With a sudden energy X writes under this a passage from Dostoevski, "'Fathers and teachers, I ponder, "What is hell?" I maintain that it is the suffering of being unable to love'" (79). It is in this inscription that the inability to love is specifically articulated as the curse that visits Salinger's pilgrims. Later X is saved by a small package lying among the clutter of his desk, for the package represents a gesture of love which directly opposes the squalor of his world. In the package is an "extremely water-proof and shock-proof" watch which had belonged to Esmé's dead father, and which she now sends X as a lucky talisman. X sits for a long while with the watch in his hand, and "Then, suddenly, almost ecstatically, he felt sleepy. You take a really sleepy man, Esmé, and he *always* stands a chance of again becoming a man with all his fac—with all his f-a-c-u-l-t-i-e-s intact" (85). The story which X writes for Esmé is itself a gesture of love (similarly, Salinger wrote one of his most important stories, "Franny," as a wedding present for his wife). The love which saves Sergeant X comes from an inno-cent child, but the idea of love as man's salvation, unlike the sug-gestion of mysticism, is not rejected, and it finally becomes devel-oped into an absurd gesture which Salinger offers as the answer to an idol-less altar.

The absurd love gesture is chronicled in the two interrelated stories, "Franny" and "Zooey," which were originally published in the *New Yorker* and later combined and published as a book. Franny and Zooey are the youngest brother and sister of Seymour Glass, and part of the urban menagerie of sensitiveness and ti-tanesque idiosyncrasy around which Salinger is constructing his contemporary saga. To understand how Franny and Zooey offer a resolution which Seymour and other mystically inclined heroes could not accomplish, it is necessary to know something of the relationships of this sprawling family.

There are seven Glass children—in order of birth, Seymour, Buddy, Boo Boo, the twins Walt and Waker, Zachary (Zooey), and Franny. Les and Bessie Glass, the parents, were once a famous vaudeville team (billed as "Gallagher and Glass") on the old Pan-tages and Orpheum circuits. Les is Jewish and Bessie Irish, and they are descended "from an astonishingly long and motley double file of professional entertainers." The public life of their parents has helped to give the Glass children an especially acute sense of the public world, and this sense is accented by the fact that all seven children began life as child prodigies on a radio quiz program called "It's a Wise Child." (Salinger is almost certainly aware of Telemachus' consciously cryptic reply to Athena when she ques-tions him about Odysseus: "It's a wise child that knows its own father." This oblique reference to *The Odyssey* emphasizes the quest for identity on which each of the Glass children has at some point embarked.)

The story of Seymour Glass (1917–1948) is told directly through "A Perfect Day for Bananafish" and indirectly through "Raise High the Roof Beam, Carpenters," "Seymour: An Introduction," and "Zooey." Buddy Glass is a shy, sardonic creative-writing teacher who occasionally takes upon himself the task of narrating his fam-ily's spiritual history. In "Seymour: An Introduction" he emerges as a *persona* for Salinger himself. In spiritual training Buddy was closer to Seymour than any other member of the family, and while he hardly seems well adjusted, he is less clearly psychotic than Seymour. Boo Boo first appears in the Glass saga as Boo Boo Tan-nenbaum, the mother of Lionel, the sensitive child hero of "Down at the Dinghy." In this story Salinger suggested the brutality of the world in the specific guise of anti-Semitism. Lionel has isolated himself from the world because he has overheard the family cook refer to his father as a "kike." Even though Lionel believes that a kike is "'one of those things that go up in the *air*'" (*NS*, 65), he is horrified that his father should be considered such an obscurely unnatural phenomenon. Boo Boo's involvement with Zen Buddhism does not seem significant, and she is perhaps more down-to-earth than any of the other children, preferring to be thought of as a "Tuckahoe homemaker." Our only other encounter with Boo Boo is through the Sapphic scrawl which she leaves on a bathroom mirror on the day of Seymour's wedding: "'Raise high the roof beam, carpenters. Like Ares comes the bridegroom, taller far than a tall man. Love, Irving Sappho, formerly under contract to Elysium Studios Ltd. Please be happy happy *happy* with your beautiful Muriel. This is an order. I outrank everybody on this block'" (*RHRB*, 76).

Of Waker we know no more than the fact that he has presumably found peace through becoming a Roman Catholic priest. In "Zooey," however, we learn that his answer offers no promise to the other children in the family. Walt never directly enters any of the Glass stories, although he seems to have certain qualities in common with an earlier Salinger creation, Sergeant Babe Gladwaller, the hero of "The Last Day of the Furlough" and the friend of Vincent Caulfield, Holden's older brother. We do learn, however, that Walt was killed in the Army of Occupation in Japan following the explosion of a Japanese stove which he was packing for his commanding officer. Walt is a symbol of innocence and tenderness for the heroine of "Uncle Wiggily in Connecticut." When she thinks of the innocence she has lost, Eloise has an alcoholic vision of the sophisticated squalor of her life and a moment of visionary love with her escapist daughter, Ramona. Eloise, who was once engaged to Walt, feels she has been destroyed by the exurbanite world her husband Lew represents (and when she refers to his favorite author as the unheard-of L. Manning Vines, she identifies him as the company commander who grudgingly gave Buddy leave to attend Seymour's wedding in "Raise High the Roof Beam, Carpenters"). Through the innocent love of a child Eloise achieves a moment of salvation similar to that which Sergeant X achieved, and, while like his salvation, hers is temporary and unstable, it nonetheless suggests the future development of Salinger's love theme.

When Salinger first introduces Franny Glass, she is a twenty-

year-old college girl and summer-stock actress; and her older
brother Zooey, who guides her through a religious crisis to the
absurd love stance, is a television actor in his late twenties who
suffers from an ulcer and, like Holden Caulfield, from profound
disgust with the world of shams in which he lives. It is Zooey who
gives the final *coup de grâce* to the idea of mysticism as an answer
to the absurd universe.

"Franny" opens on a brilliantly lit Yale-game Saturday with Lane
Coutell, Franny's date for the weekend (and her sometime lover, as
we later learn), waiting on a railroad-station platform. He is rereading a letter from Franny which creates for the reader the impression of a typical college girl enthusiastically if somewhat vaguely in
love. She hopes there will be an opportunity for dancing, that the
weekend will not involve tiresome receiving lines, and that her
spelling is improving. When Franny steps from the train the picture given by her letter seems to be elaborately confirmed:

> Franny was among the first of the girls to get off the train, from a car at
> the far, northern end of the platform. Lane spotted her immediately, and
> despite whatever it was he was trying to do with his face, his arm that
> shot up into the air was the whole truth. Franny saw it, and him, and
> waved extravagantly back. She was wearing a sheared raccoon coat, and
> Lane, walking toward her quickly but with a slow face, reasoned to him-
> self, with suppressed excitement, that he was the only one on the plat-
> form who really *knew* Franny's coat. He remembered that once, in a
> borrowed car, after kissing Franny for a half hour or so, he had kissed her
> coat lapel, as though it were a perfectly desirable, organic extension of
> the person herself. (*FZ*, 7)

Lane pilots his date to a fashionable French restaurant, and it is
only there that we see Franny as another of the Glass family suffering from "banana fever." She has begun to retreat into a world
of mysticism, but like Seymour, she realizes the importance of
an answer which will permit her to live in the real world. Her efforts at presenting a typical girl-on-a-football-weekend appearance
are part of a last stand in which she tries to face the public world.
Lane Coutell, the slick, falsely sophisticated representative of that
world, is reminiscent of Muriel Fedders and her mother, and of
Eloise's husband Lew. Franny is obviously on the verge of a nervous breakdown after a sudden depressing vision of the insignificance of the world around her that is emphasized by Lane's chatter
about an "A" paper on Flaubert that he has written for a professor
who lacks "'testicularity'." His chief interest in Franny rests in

being seen with "an unimpeachably right-looking girl—a girl who was not only extraordinarily pretty but, so much the better, not too categorically cashmere sweater and flannel skirt" (11).

In the beginning of the story Lane's own "phoniness" only encourages Franny to try more earnestly to fulfill the role he has outlined for her, but it gradually becomes clear that Franny suffers from an acute and oversensitive weariness with all that is phony in the world. Her mind wanders, and her lack of interest in Lane's distinctly "publishable" paper angers him. When he challenges her disinterestedness, she apologizes but adds that he is "'talking just like a section man'," and in her description of this Eastern college phenomenon, Franny begins to outline her disillusionment.

When Lane interrupts her frenzied dissection of the junior faculty member Franny confesses not only that she has felt "*destructive*" all week, but that she had to strain to write the "natural" letter to him. Listening to Lane's description of the events of the weekend, Franny becomes progressively depressed and begins to ridicule Wally Campbell, the person giving the inevitable cocktail party. But Wally is only a symbol of Franny's disgust with those individuals who resign themselves to the phoniness of the world: "'I don't mean there's anything horrible about him or anything like that. It's just that for four solid years I've kept seeing Wally Campbells wherever I go. . . . It's *everybody*, I mean. Everything everybody does is so—I don't know—not *wrong*, or even mean, or even stupid necessarily. But just so tiny and meaningless and—sad-making. And the worst part is, if you go bohemian or something crazy like that, you're conforming just as much as everybody else, only in a different way'" (25–26).

Franny's description of her illness—or at least of one of its major manifestations—is reminiscent of Celia's description of her "perplexing" illness in T. S. Eliot's "The Cocktail Party":

An awareness of solitude.
But that sounds so flat. I don't mean simply
That there's been a crash: though indeed there has been.
It isn't simply the end of an illusion
In the ordinary way, or being ditched.
Of course that's something that's always happening
To all sorts of people, and they get over it
More or less, or at least they carry on.
No. I mean that what has happened has made me aware
That I've always been alone. That one always is alone.
Not simply the ending of one relationship,
Not even simply finding that it never existed—

> But a revelation about my relationship
> With *everybody*. Do you know—
> It no longer seems worth while to *speak* to anyone. [2]

Indeed, one of the first details we learn about Franny in "Zooey" is that, following her weekend with Lane, she no longer wants to speak to anyone.

The only thing that Franny can think of worth concerning herself over is something which interests Lane only superficially—a small, pea-green book entitled *The Way of a Pilgrim*. The book has presumably been suggested to her by a professor, and she comes increasingly to see its message as her answer. When she almost loses control in the restaurant, she goes to the ladies' room and sits down with the book on her knees. "After a moment, she picked up the book, raised it chest-high, and pressed it to her—firmly, and quite briefly" (*FZ*, 22). The book seems momentarily to restore her control. The book which Franny clutches so zealously describes the search of a Russian peasant for the meaning of the Biblical commandment to "pray incessantly." The peasant learns the solution from a "starets"—"'some sort of terribly advanced religious person'" (33), who tells him to repeat the "Jesus Prayer" ("Lord Jesus Christ, have mercy on me") so often that the prayer becomes an automatic response of his heart. When the peasant has perfected his mystical prayer he walks all over Russia teaching people how to pray "'by this incredible method'" (34). "'He says',," Franny adds, "'that any name of God—any name at all—has this peculiar, self-active power of its own, and it starts working after you've sort of started it up'" (37). As Franny's excited description of the book continues, Lane's comments become as irrelevant ("'I hate to mention it, but I'm going to reek of garlic'" [34]) as the comments with which Franny had interrupted his discussion of Flaubert. Franny makes a final effort to adjust to Lane's idea of the "unimpeachably right-looking girl," but as she rises to leave, she faints, and when she awakens she is lying in a back room of the restaurant. The final satiric touch to Lane's insensitivity is given when he wonders if Franny does not simply need to go to bed with him.

"Zooey" begins on the Monday morning following Franny's weekend date with Lane; she has taken refuge on the couch in the Glass living room, where she clutches *The Way of the Pilgrim* and strokes the family cat, Bloomberg. Only two other members of the family are in the apartment, but the spirits of all the other brilliant Glass children crowd around Franny, "like so many Banquo's ghosts," threatening first to destroy her but suddenly offering her salvation. Just as Salinger warned us in "De Daumier-Smith's Blue Period" that he was not describing genuine mysticism, so he warns us in "Zooey" that what is to follow is not a mystical story but a love story which will take the form of a home movie (which in its close-ups, its attention to quotidian detail, and its casualness, it does). Pointing out that Nick Carraway in *The Great Gatsby* recognizes his cardinal virtue as honesty, the narrator says, "*Mine*, I think, is that I know the difference between a mystical story and a love story. I say that my current offering isn't a mystical story, or a religiously mystifying story, at all. *I* say it's a compound, or multiple, love story, pure and complicated" (49).

We are introduced to Zooey Glass at ten-thirty in the morning as he sits in "a very full bath" rereading a four-year-old letter from his brother Buddy. Among other things, the letter relates Buddy's arrival in Florida on the day following Seymour's suicide, but other than its value in filling in details in the ever-growing Glass legend, the letter from Buddy is important for the emphasis which it puts on the religious training which Franny and Zooey had received from their eldest brothers. Rather than urging the classics on the youngest children in the family, as they had urged them on the twins and Boo Boo, Buddy and Seymour decided to direct Franny and Zooey toward what is known in Zen as

no-knowledge. Dr. Suzuki says somewhere that to be in a state of pure consciousness—*satori*—is to be with God before he said, Let there be light. Seymour and I thought it might be a good thing to hold back this light from you and Franny (at least as far as we were able), and all the many lower, more fashionable lighting effects—the arts, sciences, classics, languages—till you were both able at least to conceive of a state of being where the mind knows the source of all light. We thought it would be wonderfully constructive to at least (that is, if our own "limitations" got in the way) tell you as much as we knew about the men—the saints, the arhats, the bodhisattvas, the jivanmuktas—who knew something or everything about this state of being. (65)

The description of this training for a state of pure consciousness is reinforced by a Taoist tale which Buddy (as narrator) repeats at the beginning of "Raise High the Roof Beam, Carpenters." The story had been read to Franny when she was an infant, but she always maintained that she could remember Seymour's reading it. In this brief Taoist allegory, Chiu-fang Kao has recently been retained by his Duke as a horse buyer, and he returns with the news that he has found a superlative horse—a dun-colored mare. When the animal turns out to be a coal-black stallion, the Duke is displeased, but his former horse-buyer exclaims with satisfaction,

"Has he really got as far as that? . . . Ah, then, he is worth ten thousand of me put together. There is no comparison between us. What Kao keeps in view is the spiritual mechanism. In making sure of the essential, he forgets the homely details; intent on the inward qualities, he loses sight of the external. He sees what he wants to see, and not what he does not want to see. He looks at the things he ought to look at, and neglects those that need not be looked at. So clever a judge of horses is Kao, that he has it in him to judge something better than horses." (*RHRB*, 5)

Chiu-fang Kao had achieved the state of pure consciousness which Buddy and Seymour envisioned for Franny and Zooey, and which Teddy McArdle possessed. Teddy's proposals represented Salinger's first consideration of Zen-oriented education. Teddy believed that the first thing to be done with children was to bring them together "'and show them how to meditate'." His primary interest was in teaching children "'who they *are*, not just what their names are and things like that . . . I'd get them to empty out everything their parents and everybody ever told them. I mean even if their parents just told them an elephant's big, I'd make them empty *that* out. An elephant's big only when it's next to something else—a dog or a lady, for example'." If the children wanted to learn other "stuff"—colors, names, categories—"'they could do it, if they felt like it, later on when they were older. But I'd want them to *begin* with all the real ways of looking at things . . .'" (*NS*, 142–143). Teddy's death prevents him from implementing his scheme of education, but Franny and Zooey are the products of controlled, intelligent experiments aimed at making them buyers who can always distinguish a "superlative horse." Franny's crisis, like Zooey's cynicism, is a result of this training, and her final victory is a throwing off of the banana fever of Buddhism, which for all its beauty and hope, is not a solution for modern Western man.

   Zooey's private reverie over Buddy's letter is broken by the entrance of his mother, and there follows a forty-seven–page dialogue in which we not only glimpse Zooey's cynicism (toward television, the theatre, writers, almost anyone who asks him to lunch), but also realize that beneath his cynical surface is a strong core of love. His bantering attitude toward Bessie is largely a "routine" which they have played so often that it is completely natural to them. Buddy does not understand this attitude, and in his letter had somewhat patronizingly requested, "Be kinder to Bessie, Zooey, when you can. I don't think I mean because she's our mother, but because she's weary" (57). At times Zooey's conversation with his mother seems no better integrated than Franny's conversation with Lane, but his preoccupied manner is largely the result of his own efforts to maintain an undistorted spiritual perspective. Bessie accuses Zooey of demonstrating a family failing, an inability to be "'any help when the chips are down'" (84). He scoffs at the idea of being asked to live Franny's life for her, and especially at the inevitable chicken broth Bessie offers as a cure-all. Bessie is right when she says "'You can't live in the world with such strong likes and dislikes'" (99), but she does not realize that Zooey is coming to a realization about love which will not only teach him that chicken broth is sacred, but will permit him to help Franny. Buddy (who, symbolically, can never be reached in a crisis) offers no help with his mysticism; Waker, the Catholic priest, is out of the question because, as Zooey urges, "'This thing with Franny is strictly non-sectarian'" (94); and Boo Boo is never considered.

Zooey makes the first important step toward relieving Franny's "fever" as well as his own when he realizes that *The Way of the Pilgrim* was not, as Franny told Lane, checked out of her school library, but was taken from the desk in Seymour and Buddy's old room. When he sees the pain which the mention of Seymour's name gives his mother, Zooey apologizes. "His apology had been genuine, and Mrs. Glass knew it, but evidently she couldn't resist taking advantage of it, perhaps because of its rarity" (102), to compare him unfavorably with Buddy. It is in his violent reaction to Bessie's reprimand that we first learn that Zooey is conscious of the sickness which he and Franny have inherited:

"Buddy, Buddy, *Buddy*," he said. "Seymour, Seymour, *Seymour*." He had turned toward his mother, whom the crash of the razor had startled and alarmed but not really frightened. "I'm so sick of their names I could cut my throat." His face was pale but very nearly expressionless. "This whole goddam house stinks of ghosts. I don't mind so much being haunted by a dead ghost, but I resent like *hell* being haunted by a half-dead one. I wish to *God* Buddy'd make up his mind. He does everything else Seymour ever did—or tries to. Why the hell doesn't he kill himself and be done with it?"

Mrs. Glass blinked her eyes, just once, and Zooey instantly looked away from her face. He bent over and fished his razor out of the wastebasket. "We're *freaks*, the two of us, Franny and I," he announced, standing up. "I'm a twenty-five-year-old freak and she's a twenty-year-old freak, and both those bastards are responsible. . . . The symptoms are a little more delayed in Franny's case than mine, but she's a freak, too, and don't you forget it. I swear to you, I could murder them both without even batting an eyelash. The great teachers. The great emancipators. My God. I can't even sit down to lunch with a man any more and hold up my end of a decent conversation. I either get so bored or so goddam preachy that if the son of a bitch had any sense, he'd break his chair over my head." (102–103)

When Zooey cites the fact that Franny's own symptoms are more "delayed" than his, we are able to see her revulsion and its crisis as a concentrated example of Zooey's own spiritual experience. Franny herself notes, after talking with Zooey from her couch-retreat, "'. . . we're not bothered by exactly the same things, but by the same kind of things, I think, and for the same reasons'" (143). In his efforts to bring Franny back into the world Zooey achieves final definition for his own struggle. Together they are able to scuttle out of the banana hole, achieving a victory important not only for its rejection of isolation but also for its emphasis on participation in the world.

In arguing against Franny's withdrawal, Zooey emphasizes her misuse of the Jesus Prayer, for instead of resisting a world whose emphasis is on piling up "'money, property, culture, knowledge, and so on and so on'" (147), she is attempting to pile up another kind of treasure, less material, but just as negotiable: "'. . . ninety per cent of all the world-hating saints in history,'" Zooey argues, "'were just as ac*quis*itive and unattractive, basically, as the rest of us are'" (147–148). Because he was brought up on the same perfectionist principles, Zooey understands Franny's mystical retreat from the world and her hope for some kind of miracle that will provide salvation. Her insistence on a mystical salvation, however, is only another example of the way in which they have been "'side-tracked. Always, always, always referring every goddam thing that happens right back to our lousy little egos'" (151). Zooey does not oppose the Jesus Prayer itself so much as "why and how and *where*" Franny is using it. Franny is not fulfilling any duty in life through the prayer but merely substituting it for her real duty. It is this fatal tendency to leave the realities of life behind which makes Franny and Zooey "freaks." "'You don't face any facts. This same damned attitude of not facing facts is what got you into this messy state of mind in the first place, and it can't possibly get you out of it'" (168). If Christ has a real function, it is not to take man up in his arms and relieve him of all his duties and make all his "nasty *Weltschmerzen*" go away.

In her dedication to the Jesus Prayer Franny has tried to make what Albert Camus regarded as the suicidal leap into faith. Franny's real crisis is not the result of the fact that she has reached an acute depth of despair, but that she is on the brink of becoming, like Seymour, a misfit who can never accept or be accepted by society. Franny is consequently in danger of joining the other Salinger heroes who refuse to come to terms with reality, confusing the life of isolation with the life of the spirit. Despite his disgust with stereotyped scripts and the "phonies" with whom he is so often cast, Zooey has fought to maintain a contact with reality. His realization of the danger of fleeing to the deceptive private world gives him an insight which the rest of the family lacks, and hence he is the only member to have forgiven Seymour his suicide because he is the only one who fully understands it. So anxious is Zooey to maintain his contact with reality—however painful it may be—that he is hesitant about the idea of going to Paris to make a movie. Any movement away from the specific world in which he has suffered seems distinctly suspect. To Franny the idea of making a movie in Paris is exciting, but Zooey counters her, "'It is *not* exciting. That's exactly the point. I'd enjoy doing it, yes. *God*, yes. But I'd hate like hell to leave New York. . . . I was *born* here. I went to *school* here. I've been *run over* here—*twice*, and on the same damn *street*. I have no business acting in Europe, for God's sake'" (136).

After trying unsuccessfully to convince Franny that the Jesus Prayer offers her no answer, Zooey enters Seymour and Buddy's old room. Picking up the phone still listed in Seymour's name, Zooey calls his sister and, disguising his voice, pretends to be Buddy. This is not the call from Seymour which Franny had said she wanted, but Buddy is so much the dead man's spiritual counterpart that there is little difference. Although Zooey's impersonation finally rings false, he has captured Franny's attention, and she is more prepared to listen than she was when he stretched out on the living room floor and lectured her. The absurd vision which Zooey is finally able to impart to Franny is that everything in the world, no matter how base or corrupt, is sacred. Salinger has continually reiterated the fact that "reality" has presented both young people impressions of deceit, pettiness, and insensitivity. The intention to see the world as sacred is, therefore, in total opposition to reality and a profound example of metaphysical absurdity. Until she adopts this vision, Zooey argues, she will never have the religious satisfaction she craves: "'You don't even have sense enough to *drink* when somebody brings you a cup of consecrated chicken soup—which is the only kind of chicken soup Bessie ever brings to anybody around this madhouse'" (194–195). Franny begins to be persuaded when Zooey argues that

"The only thing you can do now, the only religious thing you can do, is *act*. Act for God, if you want to—be *God's* actress, if you want to. . . . One other thing. And that's all. I promise you. But the thing is, you raved and you bitched . . . about the stupidity of audiences. The goddam 'unskilled laughter' coming from the fifth row. And that's right, that's right— God knows it's depressing. I'm not saying it isn't. But that's none of your business, really. That's none of your business, Franny. An artist's only concern is to shoot for some kind of perfection, and *on his own terms*, not anyone else's. You have no right to think about those things, I swear to you. Not in any real sense, anyway. You know what I mean?" (197–198)

Franny's realization—and now also Zooey's own—can come through dedication to her art. Camus saw art as the most complete and successful form of rebellion, since the artist reconstructs the world according to his own plan (his concern "to shoot for some kind of perfection"). "Art is the activity that exalts and denies simultaneously," and it therefore "should give us a final perspective on the content of rebellion." While Camus agrees with Nietzsche's dictum that "'No artist tolerates reality'," he also argues that "no artist can get along without reality."[3] A lack of toleration and an escape are two different things; "art disputes reality, but does not hide from it."[4] Nietzsche had argued that all forms of transcendence were slanders against this world and against life, but Camus envisions a nonsupernatural but "living transcendence, of which beauty carries the promise, which can make this mortal and limited world preferable to and more appealing than any other. Art thus leads us back to the origins of rebellion to the extent that it tries to give its form to an elusive value which the future perpetually promises, but of which the artist has a presentiment and wishes to snatch from the grasp of history."[5] Art is a paramount quixotic gesture by which man attempts to give order (at least an order in the same sense of making statements about individual experience or a state of being) to a disordered world. In support of his arguments, Camus cites Van Gogh's complaint as "the arrogant and desperate cry of all artists. 'I can very well, in life and in painting, too, do without God. But I cannot, suffering as I do, do without something that is greater than I am, that is my life—the power to create'."[6]

Zooey has shown his tormented sister the absurd gesture which she can make, and suggests that in making it she will not only

affirm her intention to find order and meaning in life but also realize the goal of "The Wise Child," whose obligation it is to both
know and be himself. Franny recognizes the validity of this gesture, but Zooey goes on to infuse her with the absurd belief that
will give the gesture its final meaning. He recalls that when as a
child he had rebelled against having to polish his shoes for the
"moronic" audience and sponsors of "It's a Wise Child," Seymour
had taken him aside and asked him to shine them for the Fat Lady.
"'He never did tell me who the Fat Lady was, but I shined
my shoes for the Fat Lady every time I ever went on the air again
. . .'" (FZ, 199). Zooey always pictured Seymour's Fat Lady sitting
on her porch listening to the radio, swatting flies, and dying of
cancer. He then learns that Seymour had once told Franny to be
funny for the Fat Lady, and the blaring radio and cancer were part
of the fantasy Franny had created just as they were part of Zooey's.
In the final moments of this "pure˙and complicated love story,"
Zooey explains the Fat Lady's identity:

"I don't care where an actor acts. It can be in summer stock, it can be
over a radio, it can be over *tele*vision, it can be in a goddam Broadway
theatre, complete with the most fashionable, most well-fed, most sun-
burned-looking audience you can imagine. But I'll tell you a terrible secret—Are you listening to me? *There isn't anyone out there who isn't
Seymour's Fat Lady.* That includes your Professor Tupper, buddy. And all
his goddam cousins by the dozens. There isn't anyone *any*where who isn't
Seymour's Fat Lady. Don't you know that? Don't you know that goddam
secret yet? And don't you know—*listen* to me now—*don't you know who
that Fat Lady really is?* . . . Ah, buddy. Ah, buddy. It's Christ Himself.
Christ Himself, buddy." (200)

For a moment all Franny can do—"for joy, apparently"—is cradle the phone in her hands, but at the conclusion of the story she
falls "into a deep, dreamless sleep" (201), like the sleep of Sergeant
X in "For Esmé—with Love and Squalor." While neither mysticism nor religion in its traditional sense "provides an answer to the
search of any of the members of the Glass family, a concern for
mystic and religious experience provides a path to Zooey's and
Franny's conception of perfect love . . . That conception includes,
embraces, and goes beyond the ordinary conceptions of religion
and morality (and in its humanness, stops short of mysticism) and
can properly be called by no other name than the simple and profound name of love."[7] To love the mercenaries, the butchers, the
deceivers, the phonies of the world with the idea that each of them
is Christ is to assume a preponderantly absurd stance. Zooey's
message is not to love man as Christ would have loved him, but to

love man *as* Christ. There is no appeal to a final supernatural authority, no desire for mystical transcendence, no hope that a better world awaits man as a reward for his struggle. Zooey is at last able to convince Franny that, as Sherwood Anderson's Dr. Parcival stated, "everyone in the world is Christ and they are all crucified."

To act with morality and love in a universe in which God is dead (or, at least, in which historical preconceptions of God frequently seem invalid) is perhaps the most acute problem of our age. Salinger's intense consideration of that problem in large part accounts for the fact that, while he is one of the least prolific authors writing today, he is the most popular. The progression from early stories in which the misfit hero can find genuine love only in children to the later stories in which mysticism is rejected in favor of an absurd love stance is a progression whose scope is perhaps not fully measured in the stories which Salinger has written, but more specifically in the personal struggle he has undergone in arriving at this philosophical position. There is no question that the author loves Seymour, and it is with an uneasy feeling that the reader is compelled to reject this Christ-like man. Salinger began the Glass saga with Seymour's suicide, and since that time has been writing his way around and back to that day in 1945 in order to show where Seymour failed. Seymour is at least partly exonerated for making "freaks" of Franny and Zooey when we note that it was his death (and its admission of failure) which saved the youngest Glass children; in a metaphorical sense in no way foreign to Salinger's intention, Seymour (who could, in fact, *see more* than his contemporaries) died that Franny and Zooey might live, and it is in this sense of his almost ritualistic death, rather than in the deluding mysticism of his life, that one seizes on the essence of this character's saintliness. Through Seymour's death, Zooey learns that the Fat Lady, the eternal vulgarian, must not be passed over for any mystical discipline. As Ihab Hassan has observed, "Zooey's message constitutes high praise of life. It is the sound of humility, calling us to *this* world. The vulgarian and the outsider are reconciled, not in the momentary flash of a quixotic gesture, nor even in the exclusive heart of a mystical revelation, but in the constancy of love."[8] And in this light it can, no doubt, be safely conjectured that "the sound of one hand clapping" is precisely, triumphantly, the commonplace sound of the Fat Lady swatting flies.

Epilogue

In articles, lectures, and interviews Saul Bellow has frequently attempted to assess and to defend the cultural relevance of the contemporary novel, which—like so many traditional aesthetic forms—seems repeatedly undermined by what he terms our "eschatological age," where the metaphysics of a mass society is common dinner-table talk and the fashions of alienation presuppose a world both shallow and centerless. When so many beliefs, attitudes, and attachments which once seemed impregnable now appear obsolete or merely irrelevant, it is only logical that the legitimacy of older art forms like the novel should also be questioned. The justification for yet "another" novel, Bellow concludes, is simply that someone has cared to turn his imagination to the world around him: ". . . this caring or believing or love alone matters. All the rest, obsolescence, historical views, manners, agreed views of the Universe, is simply nonsense and trash."[1] Bellow bases his plea for the modern novel on Simone Weil's statement that "To believe in the existence of human beings as such is love," and for Bellow the serious, significant novelist is always one whose aim is to express a belief in the existence of human beings *as such*, for this manifestation of concern and involvement can never be superfluous. The novelist's greatest challenge, however, comes in presenting this concern in such a manner that it establishes relevance without recourse to the distortions of romanticism or nihilism; for Bellow as (more tentatively) for Camus, the anti-novel embodies a fundamental aesthetic contradiction.

In light of the absurd hero as he has been seen in this study, Bellow's emphasis on the manifestation of love is of particular significance, for that hero's great concern has been either with learning how to love or with finding an environment in which love can be constructively expressed. Rabbit Angstrom, Cass Kinsolving, Augie March, Henderson, and Franny and Zooey Glass all embark on love quests. Like the saint, Rabbit desires to love one thing absolutely. Cass Kinsolving learns through his fall the significance of other human beings, and through a new humility and love for mankind he becomes a social reformer. In suddenly realizing his own inadequacies in ministering to his diseased friend Michele, Cass concluded that "Hell is not giving"; that conclusion is a close parallel, if not simply a paraphrase, of Sergeant X's hasty scrawl on the flyleaf of Goebbels' *Die Zeit Ohne Beispiel*: "'Fathers and teachers, I ponder, "What is hell?" I maintain that it is the suffering of being unable to love'." When Bellow's Henderson turns his attention to an implementation of the absurd vision, he decides first of all to "set love on a true course"; and Herzog's ultimate spiritual ease owes a major debt to Ramona's frank and uncomplicated love. The most intense statement of the humanizing love theme comes, of course, in Zooey's final, lyrical message to Franny.

These heroes all begin their quests with a vision of the apparent lack of meaning in the world, of the mendacity and failure of ideals, but they conclude with gestures of affirmation derived explicitly from their realization of the significance of love. Albert Maquet has argued that, placed in the context of the absurd world as Camus envisioned it, man is in a position "to edify, without God, a humanism of high nobility."[2] The love stance edifies because it reaffirms a belief in human beings *as such*, and it is this belief which promises to generate values to replace those which are lost as the traditional sacred society disappears. Such belief goes beyond the absurd, but it is important to remember that Camus considered the myth of the absurd as descriptive, not conclusive or programmatic, a provisional statement which was not intended to exclude a value system which might eventually transcend the absurd sensitivity.

Salinger's Teddy McArdle lamented the fact that "it's very hard to meditate and live a spiritual life in America," and the efforts of absurd heroes to achieve any recognizable degree of spiritual fulfillment are frequently painful and chaotic. As the absurd man's desire for unity and meaning increases, so too does his consciousness of the walls which enclose and trap him, but his struggle sheds light on what Camus called "the step taken by the mind when, starting from a philosophy of the world's lack of meaning, it ends by finding a meaning and depth in it."[3] The four writers discussed here share with Camus the paradoxical belief that, while the role of the individual undergoes ruthless diminishment in the modern world, only individual will and responsibility, only the sincere private gesture, can redeem the general existence and make it tenable.

Updike, Styron, Bellow, and Salinger suggest a patterning of attitudes and tensions fundamental to any discussion of the nature of the contemporary hero. Their initial response is to distrust conventional values and orthodox systems, and this profound skepticism in large part accounts for the irony which so frequently characterizes their work. That this irony is not a reflection of nihilism is indicated by the fact that each author has envisioned his most compelling hero as a sympathetic "knight" in search of order and value. Camus's absurd man, too, is involved in a quest, although he is a knight without God. In beginning with such a *tabula rasa*, Camus's knight sets a course which his counterparts in the American novel do not, of course, follow with exact precision. In the work of Salinger, for example, the spiritual quest takes a more familiar form, one which at least acknowledges the possibility of Christ as a representative of absolute values. To attempt to reconcile this tendency in Salinger's writing by reference to Camus's statement that "It is possible to be Christian and absurd,"[4] is merely to take advantage of the frequently ubiquitous treatment of absurdity in Camus's work; for it is impossible to be both absurd and Christian in any conventional sense. The failure of recourse to spiritual absolutes is strongly emphasized in Salinger's work, but their failure as values is not total. Similarly, Henderson's appeal to the "Something because of whom there is not Nothing" is one of Bellow's most memorable passages.

Such distinctions and divergences must be kept in mind if the reader is to avoid that *lèse majesté* by which critical formulation becomes academic dogma. While the myth of the absurd may serve as a useful critical tool in the study of many contemporary novels, it is as unwise to demand rigidity from such criticism as it is to demand of Camus's meditations the logic and consistency of a finalized philosophical system. Camus's investigation of the absurd is itself impressionistic and often lyrical, and as his own diverse fiction amply illustrates, even less finality can be demanded of the work of imagination which explores the dimensions of the absurd experience. Like the absurd hero himself, absurd fiction must have sufficient substance to stand apart from the myths and metaphysics which help to give it definition. The absurd sensitivity does not account for the artistic accomplishments of the authors considered here; but hopefully it does help to clarify their vision, to isolate the attitudes which ultimately shape their view of the life-enhancing alternatives which man may adopt when confronted by the dark, fragmented, absurd night of despair which colors so much of the modern imagination.

NOTES

THE MYTH OF THE ABSURD

1. Albert Camus, *The Myth of Sisyphus*, trans. Justin O'Brien, p. 5.
2. Ibid., p. 22.
3. Charles A. Glicksberg, "Camus's Quest for God," *Southwest Review* 44 (Summer 1959): 250.
4. R. W. B. Lewis, *The Picaresque Saint*, p. 60.
5. Ibid., p. 61.
6. John Cruickshank, *Albert Camus and the Literature of Revolt*, p. 146.
7. Ibid., p. 149.
8. Camus, *The Myth of Sisyphus*, p. 3.
9. Ibid., p. 10.
10. Ibid., p. 11.
11. Ibid., p. 22.
12. Cruickshank, *Albert Camus*, p. 57.
13. Ibid., p. 61.
14. Camus, *The Myth of Sisyphus*, p. 17.
15. Germaine Brée, *Albert Camus*, p. 188.
16. Cruickshank, *Albert Camus*, p. 88.
17. Camus, *The Myth of Sisyphus*, p. 90.
18. Ibid., p. 91.
19. Ibid., p. 89.
20. Ibid., p. 30.
21. Brée, *Albert Camus*, p. 204.
22. Quoted in ibid., pp. 44–45.
23. Jean-Paul Sartre, "Réponse à Albert Camus," *Les Temps Modernes* (August 1952), p. 345. Translated by David Galloway.
24. Albert Camus, *Actuelles, chroniques 1944–1948*, p. 111. Translated by David Galloway.
25. Camus, *The Myth of Sisyphus*, p. 45.
26. Leslie Fiedler, "No! In Thunder," *Esquire* 44 (September 1960): 79.
27. Brée, *Albert Camus*, p. 199.
28. Albert Maquet, *Albert Camus: The Invincible Summer*, trans. Herma Briffault, p. 108.

29. Northrop Frye, *Anatomy of Criticism*, p. 215.
30. Albert Camus, *The Rebel*, trans. Anthony Bower, p. 274.

THE ABSURD MAN AS SAINT

1. John Updike, "The Sea's Green Sameness," *New World Writing* 17 (1960): 59.
2. Whitney Balliett, "Books," *New Yorker*, November 5, 1960, p. 222.
3. Camus, *The Myth of Sisyphus*, p. 11.
4. John Updike, "Reflection," *New Yorker*, November 30, 1957, p. 216.
5. F. T. H. Fletcher, *Pascal and the Mystical Tradition*, p. 47.
6. Blaise Pascal, *Pensées*, III, 129–130.
7. Lewis, *The Picaresque Saint*, pp. 159–160.
8. Glicksberg, "Camus's Quest for God," p. 244.
9. Charles T. Samuels, "The Art of Fiction: John Updike," interview originally published in *Paris Review* (Winter 1968); reprinted in *Writers at Work: The Paris Review Interviews*, ed. George Plimpton. References here are to the collected edition.
10. Ibid., pp. 439–440.
11. See, for example, Larry E. Taylor, *Pastoral and Anti-Pastoral Patterns in John Updike's Fiction*, pp. 102–111.
12. John Updike, "Foreword," *Olinger Stories*, p. viii.
13. Ibid., p. v.
14. Taylor, *Pastoral and Anti-Pastoral Patterns in John Updike's Fiction*, pp. 102–103.
15. See Karl Barth, "Freedom in Fellowship," in *Dogmatics in Outline*, vol. 3, part 4, p. 54.
16. Samuels, "The Art of Fiction: John Updike," p. 451.
17. Camus, *The Myth of Sisyphus*, p. 11.
18. The first Maples story, "Snowing in Greenwich Village," was collected in *The Same Door*; the second, "Wife-Wooing," in *Pigeon Feathers*. The Maples stories in *The Music School* are "Giving Blood" and "Twin Beds in Rome."
19. Robert Detweiler, *John Updike*, p. 29.
20. Samuels, "The Art of Fiction: John Updike," p. 441.
21. Paul Tillich, "The Effects of Space Exploration on Man's Condition," in *The Future of Religions*, ed. Jerald C. Brauer, p. 50. The epigraph plays a more intricate role in the novel's thematic structure than it is possible to discuss in these pages. However, the reader should note Tillich's stress on "a mood favorable for the resurgence of religion but unfavorable for the preservation of a living democracy." Allusions to national and international politics form an important leitmotif in the novel, and the couples are generally disgruntled with the effectiveness of the annual town meeting in Tarbox. Tillich also stresses, in this chapter of *The Future of Religions*, that a society overly concerned with horizontal

exploration must inevitably lay such a stress on science and technology that an elite will be created of specialists who cannot share their knowledge with others. Note that the couples are repeatedly confused about what the scientists Ken Whitman and Ben Salz actually "do," and that the brilliant mathematician John Ong speaks a garbled Korean-English that only his wife can translate.

22. Glicksberg, "Camus's Quest for God," p. 250.

23. Samuels, "The Art of Fiction: John Updike," p. 443.

24. See, for example, Angela's remark on Michelangelo's drawings of male genitalia: "'Michelangelo's, the ones on Adam, are terribly darling and limp, with long foreskins . . .'" (389).

25. See "Foxy was Snow White" (288) and "You have woken me from my seven years' sleep" (265).

26. Robert Detweiler, "Updike's Couples: Eros Demythologized," Twentieth Century Literature 17 (October 1971): 242.

27. The italics are my own.

28. Quoted in John Updike, "Walt Whitman: Ego and Art," New York Review of Books, February 9, 1978, p. 36.

29. Ibid.

30. Frye, Anatomy of Criticism, p. 215.

31. Camus, The Myth of Sisyphus, p. 191.

32. Detweiler, John Updike, p. 152.

33. Ibid., pp. 155–159.

34. Norman Mailer, Of a Fire on the Moon, p. 40.

35. Ibid., p. 122.

36. Eugene Lyons, "John Updike: The Beginning and the End," Critique: Studies in Modern Fiction 14 (Spring–Summer 1972): 55.

37. Samuels, "The Art of Fiction: John Updike," p. 441.

38. John Updike, "Midpoint," in Midpoint and Other Poems, p. 42.

39. Ibid., p. 44.

40. David Daiches, George Eliot: Middlemarch, p. 66.

41. Ibid., p. 69.

42. John Updike, "Problems," in Problems and Other Stories, p. 152.

43. Quoted in John Updike, Buchanan Dying, p. vi.

44. Ibid., p. 10.

45. John Updike, "Transaction," in Problems and Other Stories, p. 93.

46. Samuels, "The Art of Fiction: John Updike," p. 454.

THE ABSURD MAN AS TRAGIC HERO

1. Peter Matthiessen and George Plimpton, "William Styron," in Writers at Work, p. 280. This interview was originally published in Paris Review 5 (Spring 1954): 42–57.

2. Ibid., p. 281.

3. Maxwell Geismar, "The Postwar Generation in American Arts and Letters," Saturday Review, March 15, 1953, p. 60.

4. Matthiessen and Plimpton, "William Styron," p. 275.
5. Ibid., p. 275.
6. Camus, *The Myth of Sisyphus*, p. 10.
7. Ibid., p. 11.
8. Ibid., p. 21.
9. Camus, *The Rebel*, pp. 13–14.
10. Maxwell Geismar, *American Moderns: From Rebellion to Conformity*, p. 250.
11. William Styron, "Prevalence of Wonders," *Nation*, May 2, 1953, p. 370.
12. Camus, *The Myth of Sisyphus*, p. 11.
13. Ibid., pp. 31–32.
14. Camus, *The Rebel*, p. 105.
15. Camus, *The Myth of Sisyphus*, p. 30.
16. Ibid., pp. 90–91.
17. Ibid., p. 90.
18. Quoted in Pierre Brodin, *Présences contemporaines: Ecrivains américains d'aujourd'hui*, pp. 210–211.
19. George Plimpton, "A Shared Ordeal: Interview with William Styron," in *William Styron's "Confessions of Nat Turner": A Critical Handbook*, ed. Melvin J. Friedman and Irving Malin, pp. 36–37. Plimpton's interview originally appeared in *New York Times*, October 8, 1967.
20. William Styron, "This Quiet Dust," *Harper's* 230 (April 1965): 146.
21. Cruickshank, *Albert Camus*, pp. 96–97.
22. Camus, *The Rebel*, p. 351.
23. Ibid., p. 32.
24. Mike Thelwell, "Mr. Styron and The Reverend Turner," *Massachusetts Review* 9 (Winter 1968): 29. Thelwell's review article was later collected in *William Styron's Nat Turner: Ten Black Writers Respond*, ed. John Henrik Clarke.
25. My own reflections on the form are contained in two essays: "Why the Chickens Came Home to Roost in Holcomb, Kansas," in *Truman Capote's "In Cold Blood": A Critical Handbook*, ed. Irving Malin, pp. 154–163; and "Der zeitgenössische non-fiction Roman," in *Die amerikanische Literatur der Gegenwart*, ed. Hans Bungert, pp. 187–204.
26. The most authoritative rebuttals to the attack on Styron's novel are found in Martin Duberman, "Historical Fictions," *New York Times Book Review*, August 11, 1968, pp. 1, 16–17; and Eugene Genovese, "Nat Turner's Black Critics," *New York Review of Books*, September 12, 1968, pp. 34–37.
27. Frederick J. Hoffman, "The Sense of Place," in *South*, ed. Louis D. Rubin, Jr., and Robert D. Jacobs, p. 61.
28. Camus, *The Myth of Sisyphus*, p. 3.
29. Styron, "This Quiet Dust," p. 140.

30. T. R. Gray, *The Confession, Trial and Execution of Nat Turner, the Negro Insurgent,* p. 11.
31. Albert Camus, *Caligula,* act 4, scene xii.
32. Quoted in Cruickshank, *Albert Camus,* p. 97.
33. Marc L. Ratner, *William Styron,* p. 138.
34. Wright Morris, "The Territory Ahead," in *The Living Novel,* ed. Granville Hicks, p. 146.
35. See William Styron, "Writers under Twenty-five," in *Under Twenty-five: Duke Narrative and Verse, 1945–1962,* ed. William M. Blackburn, p. 16.
36. Dante Alighieri, *The Inferno,* canto V, line 106.
37. John Gardner, "A Novel of Evil," *New York Times Book Review,* May 27, 1979, pp. 16–17.
38. Cruickshank, *Albert Camus,* p. 144.
39. Ibid., p. 145.
40. Quoted in *Newsweek,* October 16, 1967, p. 69.
41. Camus, *The Rebel,* p. 147.

THE ABSURD MAN AS PICARO

1. Paul Levine, "Saul Bellow: The Affirmation of the Philosophical Fool," *Perspective* 10 (Winter 1959): 165.
2. Camus, *The Myth of Sisyphus,* p. 49.
3. Cruickshank, *Albert Camus,* p. 159.
4. See Robert Penn Warren, "Man with No Commitments," *New Republic,* November 2, 1953, pp. 22–23.
5. Ihab Hassan, "Saul Bellow: Five Faces of a Hero," *Critique* 3 (September 1960): 30.
6. Richard Lehan, "Existentialism in Recent American Fiction: The Demonic Quest," *Texas Studies in Literature and Language* 1 (Summer 1959): 181–202.
7. See Saul Bellow, "Deep Readers of the World Beware!" *New York Times Book Review,* February 15, 1959, pp. 1, 34. Bellow's statements on symbolism recall Nathaniel Hawthorne's desire to write a novel "that should evolve some deep lesson and should possess physical substance enough to stand alone" (Nathaniel Hawthorne, *Mosses from an Old Manse* [Boston: Houghton Mifflin, 1882], p. 18). Bellow's article reflects one aspect of his prejudice against the novel "of literary derivation"; it is also a modern corollary to Twain's ironic notice at the beginning of *The Adventures of Huckleberry Finn.*
8. Richard Chase, "The Adventures of Saul Bellow: Progress of a Novelist," *Commentary* 27 (April 1959): 323.
9. Daniel Hughes, "Reality and the Hero: *Lolita* and *Henderson the Rain King,*" *Modern Fiction Studies* 6 (Winter 1960–1961): 357–358.
10. Hassan, "Saul Bellow," p. 35.

11. Camus, *The Myth of Sisyphus*, pp. 90–91.

12. Fiedler, "No! In Thunder," p. 79.

13. David Boroff, "Saul Bellow," *Saturday Review*, September 19, 1964, pp. 38–39.

14. James Dean Young, "Bellow's View of the Heart," *Critique* 7 (Spring 1965): 12.

15. Quoted in Tony Tanner, "Saul Bellow: The Flight from Monologue," *Encounter* 24 (February 1965): 65.

16. James Joyce, *Ulysses*, p. 277.

17. William York Tindall, *A Reader's Guide to James Joyce*, p. 130.

18. Ibid.

19. Joyce, *Ulysses*, p. 317.

20. Saul Bellow, "Scenes from Humanities—A Farce," *Partisan Review* 29 (Summer 1962): 345. Excerpts are from an earlier draft of *The Last Analysis*.

21. Ibid., p. 349.

22. Gordon L. Harper, "The Art of Fiction: Saul Bellow," *Paris Review* 9 (1966): 62.

23. Edward Lewis Wallant, *The Human Season*, p. 17.

24. Quoted in Richard Poirier, *The Performing Self*, pp. x–xii.

25. Leslie Fiedler, *Love and Death in the American Novel*, p. xxi.

26. Ibid.

27. See Norman Mailer, "The White Negro," in *Advertisements for Myself*, pp. 337–358.

28. Joseph Epstein, "Saul Bellow of Chicago," *New York Times Book Review*, May 9, 1971, p. 6.

29. Ibid., p. 5.

30. John W. Aldridge, *Time to Murder and Create*, pp. 233–234.

31. M. Gilbert Porter, *Whence the Power? The Artistry and Humanity of Saul Bellow*, pp. 178–179.

32. "Literature and Culture: An Interview with Saul Bellow," *Salmagundi* (1975), p. 5. The interview was conducted by Robert Boyers, Robert Orrill, Ralph Ciancio, and Edwin Moseley.

33. Other parallels are discussed above, in my analysis of *Rabbit Redux*.

34. Mailer, *Of a Fire on the Moon*, pp. 23–24.

35. "Literature and Culture: An Interview with Saul Bellow," p. 15.

36. Roger Shattuck, "A Higher Selfishness?" *New York Review of Books*, September 18, 1975, p. 22.

37. See pp. 223 and 264–265.

38. Camus, *The Myth of Sisyphus*, p. 10.

39. Joseph Epstein, "A Talk with Saul Bellow," *New York Times Book Review*, December 5, 1976, p. 92.

40. Nina Steers, "Successor to Faulkner?" *Show* 4 (September 1964): 38.

41. Saul Bellow, "'Off the Couch by Christmas,' Saul Bellow on His New Novel," *Listener*, November 20, 1975, p. 676.
42. Saul Bellow, "A Silver Dish," *New Yorker*, September 25, 1978, p. 40.
43. Ibid., p. 44
44. Cruickshank, *Albert Camus*, p. 88.
45. William Faulkner, "Nobel Prize Address," *Saturday Review*, July 28, 1962, p. 20. A reprint of the acceptance speech delivered in Stockholm on December 10, 1950.
46. Shattuck, "A Higher Selfishness?" p. 25.
47. Quoted in Brée, *Albert Camus*, p. 45.

THE LOVE ETHIC

1. Dan Wakefield, "Salinger and the Search for Love," *New World Writing* 14 (1958): 79–80.
2. T. S. Eliot, "The Cocktail Party," in *The Complete Poems and Plays of T. S. Eliot*, pp. 359–360.
3. Camus, *The Rebel*, p. 253.
4. Ibid., p. 258.
5. Ibid.
6. Ibid., p. 257.
7. Wakefield, "Salinger and the Search for Love," p. 82.
8. Ihab Hassan, *Radical Innocence: Studies in the Contemporary American Novel*, p. 283.

EPILOGUE

1. Saul Bellow, "Distractions of a Fiction Writer," in *The Living Novel*, ed. Granville Hicks, p. 20.
2. Maquet, *Albert Camus*, p. 109.
3. Camus, *The Myth of Sisyphus*, p. 31.
4. Ibid., p. 83.

BIBLIOGRAPHY

The following bibliography is divided into two parts. The first lists all works cited in the text and includes abbreviations used for quotations from primary sources. The second part includes book-length studies of Updike, Styron, Bellow, and Salinger, as well as significant references in general works and special issues of critical periodicals. The latter section replaces the extensive checklists contained in the first two editions of *The Absurd Hero*. In the last decade, studies of the writings of these four authors have become so numerous that it is no longer practicable to list them all here. Furthermore, each writer is now the subject of an annotated bibliography; these guides are also cited below under works recommended for further reading.

WORKS CITED

Aldridge, John W. *Time to Murder and Create*. New York: McKay, 1966.
Balliett, Whitney. "Books." *New Yorker*, November 5, 1960, pp. 222–224.
Barth, Karl. *Dogmatics in Outline*. Vol. 3. New York: Harper, 1959.
Bellow, Saul. *The Adventures of Augie March*. New York: Viking Press, 1953. *AAM*
———. *Dangling Man*. New York: Vanguard Press, 1944. *DM*
———. "Deep Readers of the World Beware!" *New York Times Book Review*, February 15, 1959, pp. 1, 34.
———. "Distractions of a Fiction Writer." In *The Living Novel*, ed. Granville Hicks, pp. 1–20. New York: Macmillan Company, 1957.
———. *Henderson the Rain King*. New York: Viking Press, 1959. *HRK*
———. *Herzog*. New York: Viking Press, 1964. *H*
———. *Humboldt's Gift*. New York: Viking Press, 1975. *HG*
———. "Literature and Culture: An Interview with Saul Bellow." *Salmagundi* (1975), pp. 6–23. [Interview conducted by Robert Boyers, Robert Orrill, Ralph Ciancio, and Edwin Moseley.]
———. *Mosby's Memoirs*. New York: Viking Press, 1968. *MM*
———. *Mr. Sammler's Planet*. New York: Viking Press, 1970. *MSP*
———. "'Off the Couch by Christmas,' Saul Bellow on His New Novel." *Listener*, November 20, 1975, p. 676.

————. "Scenes from Humanities—A Farce." *Partisan Review* 29 (Summer 1962): 327–349. [Excerpts from an earlier draft of *The Last Analysis* (1965).]
————. *Seize the Day.* New York: Viking Press, 1956. *SD*
————. "A Silver Dish." *New Yorker*, September 25, 1978, pp. 40–62.
————. *The Victim.* New York: Viking Press, 1956. *V*
Blackburn, William M., ed. *Under Twenty-five: Duke Narrative and Verse, 1945–1962.* Durham, N.C.: Duke University Press, 1963.
Boroff, David. "Saul Bellow." *Saturday Review*, September 19, 1964, pp. 38–39.
Brée, Germaine. *Camus.* New Brunswick, N.J.: Rutgers University Press, 1958.
Brodin, Pierre. *Présences contemporaines: Ecrivains américains d'aujourd'hui.* Paris: Les Nouvelles Editions Debresse, 1964.
Bungert, Hans, ed. *Die amerikanische Literatur der Gegenwart: Aspekte und Tendenzen.* Stuttgart: Reclam, 1977.
Camus, Albert. *Actuelles, chroniques 1944–1948.* Paris: Gallimard, 1950.
————. *Caligula.* Paris: Gallimard, 1944.
————. *The Myth of Sisyphus.* Trans. Justin O'Brien. New York: Vintage Books, 1959.
————. *The Rebel.* Trans. Anthony Bower. New York: Vintage Books, 1960.
Chase, Richard. "The Adventures of Saul Bellow: Progress of a Novelist." *Commentary* 27 (April 1959): 323–330.
Clarke, John Henrik, ed. *William Styron's Nat Turner: Ten Black Writers Respond.* Boston: Beacon Press, 1968.
Cruickshank, John. *Albert Camus and the Literature of Revolt.* New York: Galaxy Books, 1960.
Daiches, David. *George Eliot: Middlemarch.* London: Edward Arnold, 1963.
Detweiler, Robert. *John Updike.* New York: Twayne Publishers, 1972.
————. "Updike's *Couples*: Eros Demythologized." *Twentieth Century Literature* 17 (October 1971): 235–246.
Duberman, Martin. "Historical Fictions." *New York Times Book Review*, August 11, 1968, pp. 1, 16–17.
Eliot, T. S. "The Cocktail Party." In *The Complete Poems and Plays of T. S. Eliot*, pp. 295–387. New York: Harcourt, Brace, 1950.
Epstein, Joseph. "Saul Bellow of Chicago." *New York Times Book Review*, May 9, 1971, pp. 4, 12, 14, 16.
————. "A Talk with Saul Bellow." *New York Times Book Review*, December 5, 1976, pp. 3, 92–93.
Faulkner, William. "Nobel Prize Address." *Saturday Review*, July 28, 1962, p. 20.
Fiedler, Leslie. *Love and Death in the American Novel.* New York: Criterion Books, 1960.

————. "No! In Thunder." *Esquire* 44 (September 1960): 79–82.

Fletcher, F. T. H. *Pascal and the Mystical Tradition*. Oxford: Basil Blackwell, 1954.

Friedman, Melvin J., and Irving Malin, eds. *William Styron's "Confessions of Nat Turner": A Critical Handbook*. Belmont, Calif.: Wadsworth, 1970.

Frye, Northrop. *Anatomy of Criticism*. Princeton: Princeton University Press, 1957.

Galloway, David D. "Absurd Men, Absurd Art, Absurd Heroes." In *The Literature of the Western World*, vol. 6, ed. David Daiches and A. J. Thorlby. London: Aldus Books, 1970.

Gardner, John. "A Novel of Evil." *New York Times Book Review*, May 27, 1979, pp. 16–17.

Geismar, Maxwell. *American Moderns: From Rebellion to Conformity*. New York: Hill and Wang, 1958.

————. "The Postwar Generation in American Arts and Letters." *Saturday Review*, March 15, 1953, pp. 11–12, 60.

Genovese, Eugene. "Nat Turner's Black Critics." *New York Review of Books*, September 12, 1968, pp. 34–37.

Glicksberg, Charles A. "Camus's Quest for God." *Southwest Review* 44 (Summer 1959): 240–252.

Gray, T. R. *The Confession, Trial and Execution of Nat Turner, the Negro Insurgent*. Petersburg, Va.: John B. Edge, 1881. Reprinted by A.M.S. Press, 1975.

Harper, Gordon L. "The Art of Fiction: Saul Bellow." *Paris Review* 9 (1966): 49–73.

Hassan, Ihab. *Radical Innocence: Studies in the Contemporary American Novel*. Princeton: Princeton University Press, 1961.

————. "Saul Bellow: Five Faces of a Hero." *Critique* 3 (September 1960): 28–36.

Hoffman, Frederick J. "The Sense of Place." In *South*, ed. Louis D. Rubin, Jr., and Robert D. Jacobs, pp. 60–75. Garden City, N.Y.: Doubleday, 1961.

Hughes, Daniel. "Reality and the Hero: *Lolita* and *Henderson the Rain King*." *Modern Fiction Studies* 6 (Winter 1960–1961): 345–364.

Joyce, James. *Ulysses*. London: The Bodley Head, 1937.

Lehan, Richard. "Existentialism in Recent American Fiction: The Demonic Quest." *Texas Studies in Literature and Language* 1 (Summer 1959): 181–202.

Levine, Paul. "Saul Bellow: The Affirmation of the Philosophical Fool." *Perspective* 10 (Winter 1959): 163–176.

Lewis, R. W. B. *The Picaresque Saint*. Philadelphia: J. P. Lippincott, 1959.

Lyons, Eugene. "John Updike: The Beginning and the End." *Critique: Studies in Modern Fiction* 14 (Spring–Summer 1972): 44–59.

Mailer, Norman. *Advertisements for Myself*. New York: G. P. Putnam, 1959.

————. *Of a Fire on the Moon.* Boston: Little, Brown, 1970.

Malin, Irving, ed. *Truman Capote's "In Cold Blood": A Critical Handbook.* Belmont, Calif.: Wadsworth, 1968.

Maquet, Albert. *Albert Camus: The Invincible Summer.* Trans. Herma Briffault. New York: George Braziller, 1958.

Matthiessen, Peter, and George Plimpton. "William Styron." In *Writers at Work: The Paris Review Interviews,* ed. and with an introduction by Malcolm Cowley, pp. 268–282. New York: Viking Press, 1958.

Morris, Wright. "The Territory Ahead." In *The Living Novel,* ed. Granville Hicks. New York: Macmillan, 1957.

Pascal, Blaise. *Pensées,* III. In *Oeuvres de Blaise Pascal.* Vol. XIV. Paris: Librairie Hachette et Cie, 1904.

Poirier, Richard. *The Performing Self.* New York: Oxford University Press, 1971.

Porter, M. Gilbert. *Whence the Power? The Artistry and Humanity of Saul Bellow.* Columbia: University of Missouri Press, 1974.

Ratner, Marc L. *William Styron.* New York: Twayne, 1972.

Salinger, J. D. *The Catcher in the Rye.* New York: Modern Library, 1951. CR

————. *Franny and Zooey.* Boston: Little, Brown, 1961. FZ

————. *Nine Stories.* New York: New American Library, 1954. NS

————. *"Raise High the Roof Beam, Carpenters," and "Seymour: An Introduction."* Boston: Little, Brown, 1963. RHRB

Samuels, Charles T. "The Art of Fiction: John Updike." In *Writers at Work: The Paris Review Interviews,* ed. George Plimpton, pp. 427–454. New York: Viking Press, 1976.

Sartre, Jean-Paul. "Réponse à Albert Camus." *Les Temps Modernes* (August 1952), p. 345.

Shattuck, Roger. "A Higher Selfishness?" *New York Review of Books,* September 18, 1975, pp. 21–25.

Steers, Nina. "Successor to Faulkner?" *Show* 4 (September 1964): 36–38.

Styron, William. *The Confessions of Nat Turner.* New York: Random House, 1967. NT

————. *Lie Down in Darkness.* Indianapolis: Bobbs-Merrill, 1951. LDD

————. "The Long March." In *Best Short Stories of World War II,* ed. Charles A. Fenton. New York: Viking Press, 1957. LM

————. "Prevalence of Wonders." *Nation,* May 2, 1953, pp. 370–371.

————. *Set This House on Fire.* New York: Random House, 1959. STHF

————. *Sophie's Choice.* New York: Random House, 1979. SC

————. "This Quiet Dust." *Harper's* 230 (April 1965): 135–146.

Tanner, Tony. "Saul Bellow: The Flight from Monologue." *Encounter* 24 (February 1965): 58–70.

Taylor, Larry E. *Pastoral and Anti-Pastoral Patterns in John Updike's Fiction.* Carbondale: Southern Illinois University Press, 1971.

Tillich, Paul. *The Future of Religions.* Ed. Jerald C. Brauer. New York: Harper and Row, 1966.

Tindall, William York. *A Reader's Guide to James Joyce.* London: Thames and Hudson, 1959.

Updike, John. *Assorted Prose.* New York: Alfred A. Knopf, 1965. *AP*

———. *Bech: A Book.* Alfred A. Knopf, 1970. *B*

———. *Buchanan Dying.* New York: Alfred A. Knopf, 1974.

———. *The Carpentered Hen and Other Tame Creatures.* New York: Harper, 1954. *CH*

———. *The Centaur.* New York: Alfred A. Knopf, 1963. *C*

———. *The Coup.* New York: Alfred A. Knopf, 1978.

———. *Couples.* New York: Alfred A. Knopf, 1968. *Cs*

———. *Marry Me.* New York: Alfred A. Knopf, 1976. *MM*

———. *Midpoint and Other Poems.* New York: Alfred A. Knopf, 1969.

———. *A Month of Sundays.* New York: Alfred A. Knopf, 1975. *MS*

———. *The Music School.* New York: Fawcett Publications, 1967. *M*

———. *Of the Farm.* New York: Alfred A. Knopf, 1966. *OF*

———. *Olinger Stories.* New York: Vintage Books, 1964.

———. *Pigeon Feathers.* New York: Alfred A. Knopf, 1962. *PFe*

———. *The Poorhouse Fair.* New York: Alfred A. Knopf, 1959. *PFa*

———. *Problems and Other Stories.* New York: Alfred A. Knopf, 1979.

———. *Rabbit Redux.* New York: Alfred A. Knopf, 1971. *RRx*

———. *Rabbit, Run.* New York: Alfred A. Knopf, 1960. *RR*

———. "Reflection." *New Yorker,* November 30, 1957, p. 216.

———. "The Sea's Green Sameness." *New World Writing* 17 (1960): 54–59.

———. "Walt Whitman: Ego and Art." *New York Review of Books,* February 9, 1978, pp. 33–36.

Wakefield, Dan. "Salinger and the Search for Love." *New World Writing* 14 (December 1958): 68–85.

Wallant, Edward Lewis. *The Human Season.* New York: Harcourt, Brace, 1960.

Warren, Robert Penn. "Man with No Commitments." *New Republic,* November 2, 1953, pp. 22–23.

Young, James Dean. "Bellow's View of the Heart." *Critique* 7 (Spring 1965): 5–17.

FOR FURTHER READING

John Updike

Aldridge, John W. "John Updike and the Higher Theology." In *The Devil in the Fire: Retrospective Essays on American Literature and Culture, 1951–1971,* pp. 195–201. New York: Harper's Magazine Press, 1972.

———. "The Private Voice of John Updike." In *Time to Murder and Create: The Contemporary Novel in Crisis,* pp. 164–170. New York: McKay, 1966.

Allen, Mary. "John Updike's Love of 'Dull Bovine Beauty.'" In *The Necessary Blankness: Women in Major American Fiction of the Sixties*, pp. 97–132. Urbana: University of Illinois Press, 1976.

Alter, Robert. "Updike, Malamud, and the Fire This Time." In *Defenses of the Imagination: Jewish Writers and Modern Historical Crisis*, pp. 233–248. Philadelphia: Jewish Publication Society of America, 1978.

Bryant, Jerry H. "Novels of Ambiguity and Affirmation." In *The Open Decision: The Contemporary American Novel and Its Intellectual Background*, pp. 236–282. New York: Free Press, 1970.

Burchard, Rachael C. *John Updike: Yea Sayings*. Carbondale: Southern Illinois University Press, 1971.

Curtler, Betsy S. "Science, the Saving Grace of John Updike: *The Centaur* and *Couples*." In *A Festschrift for Professor Marguerite Roberts, on the Occasion of her Retirement from Westhampton College, University of Richmond, Virginia*, ed. Frieda Elaine Penninger, pp. 209–218. Richmond: University of Richmond, 1976.

Detweiler, Robert. *John Updike*. Twayne's United States Authors Series, no. 214. Ed. Sylvia E. Bowman. New York: Twayne Publishers, 1972.

———. "John Updike and the Indictment of Culture-Protestantism." In *Spiritual Crises in Mid-Century American Fiction*, pp. 14–24. Gainesville: University of Florida Press, 1964.

Enright, D. J. "Updike's Ups and Downs." *Holiday* 38 (November 1965): 162–164, 165. Reprinted in *Conspirators and Poets*, pp. 134–140. Chester Springs, Pa.: Dufour, 1966.

Finkelstein, Sidney. "Acceptance of Alienation: John Updike and James Purdy." In *Existentialism and Alienation in American Literature*, pp. 242–252. New York: International Publishers, 1965.

Gass, W. H. "Cock-a-doodle-doo." In *Fiction and the Figures of Life*, pp. 206–211. New York: Vintage, 1972.

Gearhart, Elizabeth A. *John Updike: A Comprehensive Bibliography with Selected Annotations*. Norwood, Pa.: Norwood Editions, 1978.

Gilman, Richard. "Fiction: John Updike." In *The Confusion of Realism*, pp. 62–68. New York: Random House, 1970.

Haas, Rudolf. "Griechischer Mythos im Modernen Roman: John Updikes *The Centaur*." In *Lebende Antike: Symposion für Rudolf Sühnel*, ed. Horst Meller and Hans-Joachim Zimmerman, pp. 513–527. Berlin: Erich Schmidt, 1967.

———. "John Updike: *The Centaur*." In *Der amerikanische Roman im 19. und 20. Jahrhundert*, ed. Edgar Lohner, pp. 337–352. Berlin: Erich Schmidt, 1974.

Hamilton, Kenneth. *John Updike: A Critical Essay*. Grand Rapids, Mich.: Wm. B. Eerdmans, 1967.

Hamilton, Kenneth, and Alice. *John Updike: A Critical Essay*. Grand Rapids, Mich.: Wm. B. Eerdmans, 1967.

———. *Novel Perspective: The Elements of John Updike*. Grand Rapids, Mich.: Wm. B. Eerdmans, 1970.

Harper, Howard M., Jr. "John Updike—the Intrinsic Problem of Human Existence." In *Desperate Faith: A Study of Bellow, Salinger, Mailer, Baldwin and Updike*, pp. 162–190. Chapel Hill: University of North Carolina Press, 1967.

Hassan, Ihab. "John Updike." In *Contemporary American Literature, 1945–1972: An Introduction*, pp. 60–63. New York: Ungar, 1973.

Herget, Winfried. "John Updike, 'Tomorrow and Tomorrow and so Forth' (1955)." In *Die amerikanische Short Story der Gegenwart: Interpretationen*, ed. Peter Freese, pp. 160–167. Berlin: Erich Schmidt, 1976.

Hicks, Granville. "Generations of the Fifties: Malamud, Gold, and Updike." In *The Creative Present*, ed. Norma Balakian and Charles Simmons, pp. 213–238. New York: Doubleday, 1963.

Hicks, Granville, with Jack Alan Robbins. "The Poorhouse Fair." *Literary Horizons: A Quarter Century of American Fiction*, pp. 107–133. New York: New York University Press, 1970.

Hyman, Stanley Edgar. "Chiron at Olinger High." In *Standards: A Chronicle of Books for Our Time*, pp. 128–132. New York: Horizon, 1966.

―――. "Couplings." In *The Critic's Credentials: Essays and Reviews*, ed. Phoebe Pettingell, pp. 107–111. New York: Atheneum, 1978.

Kazin, Alfred. "O'Hara, Cheever and Updike." *New York Review of Books*, April 19, 1973, pp. 14–19. Reprinted in "Professional Observers: Cozzens to Updike." In *Bright Book of Life: American Novelists and Storytellers from Hemingway to Mailer*, pp. 97–124. New York: Little, Brown, 1973.

Kort, Wesley A. "*The Centaur* and the Problem of Vocation." In *Shriven Selves: Religious Problems in Recent American Fiction*, pp. 64–89. Philadelphia: Fortress Press, 1972.

Kunkel, Francis L. "John Updike: Between Heaven and Earth." In *Passion and the Passion: Sex and Religion in Modern Literature*, pp. 75–98. Philadelphia: Westminster Press, 1975.

Landor, Mikhail. "Centaur-Novels: Landor on Bellow, Updike, Styron and Trilling." In *Soviet Criticism of American Literature in the Sixties—An Anthology*, ed. Carl R. Proffer, pp. 28–61. Ann Arbor, Mich.: Ardis, 1972.

LePellec, Yves. "Rabbit Underground." In *Les américanistes: New French Criticism on Modern American Fiction*, ed. Ira D. Johnson and Christian Johnson, pp. 94–109. Port Washington, N.Y.: Kennikat, 1978.

Lodge, David. "Post-Pill Paradise Lost: John Updike's *Couples*." *New Blackfriars* 51 (November 1970): 511–518. Reprinted in *The Novelist at the Crossroads, and Other Essays on Fiction and Criticism*, pp. 237–244. Ithaca, N.Y.: Cornell University Press, 1972.

Markle, Joyce B. *Fighters and Lovers: Themes in the Novels of John Updike*. New York: New York University Press, 1973.

―――. "On John Updike and 'The Music School.'" In *The American*

Short Story, ed. Calvin Skaggs, pp. 389–394; screenplay by John Korty, pp. 352–388. New York: Dell, 1977.

Meyer, Arlin G., with some additions by Michael A. Olivas. "Criticism of John Updike: A Selected Checklist." *Modern Fiction Studies* 20 (Spring 1974): 121–133.

Mizener, Arthur. "The American Hero as High-School Boy." In *The Sense of Life in the Modern Novel,* pp. 247–266. New York: Houghton Mifflin, 1964.

O'Connor, William Van. "John Updike and William Styron: The Burden of Talent." In *Contemporary American Novelists,* ed. Harry T. Moore, pp. 205–221. Carbondale: Southern Illinois University Press, 1964.

Olivas, Michael A. *An Annotated Bibliography of John Updike Criticism 1967–1973 and a Checklist of His Works.* New York: Garland Publishing Co., 1975.

Podhoretz, Norman. "A Dissent on Updike." In *Doings and Undoings,* pp. 251–257. New York: Farrar, Straus, 1964.

Rupp, Richard H. "John Updike: Style in Search of a Center." *Sewanee Review* 75 (Autumn 1967): 693–709. Reprinted in *Celebration in Postwar American Fiction, 1945–1967,* pp. 41–57. Coral Gables, Fla.: University of Miami Press, 1970.

Samuels, Charles Thomas. "The Art of Fiction XLIII: John Updike." *Paris Review* 45 (Winter 1968): 84–117. Reprinted in *Picked-Up Pieces* and *Writers at Work: The Paris Review Interviews,* ed. George Plimpton. 4th ser. New York: Viking, 1976.

———. *John Updike.* University of Minnesota Pamphlets on American Writers, no. 79. Minneapolis: University of Minnesota Press, 1969.

Sokoloff, B. A., and David E. Arnason. *John Updike: A Comprehensive Bibliography.* Bibliographies in Contemporary American Fiction. 1970. Reprinted, Folcroft, Pa.: Folcroft Press, 1971.

Tanner, Tony. "A Compromised Environment." In *City of Words: American Fiction 1950–1970,* pp. 273–294. New York: Harper and Row, 1971.

Taylor, C. Clarke. *John Updike: A Bibliography.* The Serif Series, gen. ed. Dean H. Keller. Kent, Ohio: Kent State University Press, 1968.

Thorburn, David, and Howard Eiland, eds. *Updike.* Twentieth Century Views. Englewood Cliffs, N.J.: Prentice-Hall, 1979.

Wahl, William B. "Updike's World and *Couples.*" In *Essays in Honor of Professor Tyrus Hillway,* ed. Erwin A. Stürzl, pp. 256–295. Salzburg: Institute für englische Sprache und Literatur, Universität Salzburg, 1977.

Walcutt, Charles Child. "The Centripetal Action: John Updike's *The Centaur* and *Rabbit, Run* and Wright Morris's *One Day.*" In *Man's Changing Mask: Modes and Methods of Characterization in Fiction,* pp. 326–332. Minneapolis: University of Minnesota Press, 1966.

Vargo, Edward P. *Rainstorms and Fire: Ritual in the Novels of John Updike.* Port Washington, N.Y.: Kennikat Press, 1973.

William Styron
Aldridge, John W. "The Society of Three Novels." In *In Search of Heresy*, pp. 126–148. New York: McGraw-Hill, 1956.
———. "William Styron and Derivative Imagination." In *Time to Murder and Create: The Contemporary Novel in Crisis*, pp. 30–51. New York: David McKay, 1966. Also in *The Devil in the Fire: Retrospective Essays on American Literature and Culture 1951–1971*, pp. 202–216. New York: Harper's Magazine Press, 1972.
Baumbach, Jonathan. "Paradise Lost: *Lie Down in Darkness* by William Styron." In *The Landscape of Nightmare: Studies in the Contemporary Novel*, pp. 123–137. New York: New York University Press, 1965.
Bradbury, John M. *Renaissance in the South: A Critical History of the Literature, 1920–1960*. Chapel Hill: University of North Carolina Press, 1963.
Bryant, Jerry H. *The Open Decision: The Contemporary American Novel and Its Intellectual Background*. New York: Free Press, 1970. [Pp. 264–268.]
Bryer, Jackson. *William Styron: A Reference Guide*, ed. Ronald Gottesman. A Reference Publication in Literature. Boston: G. K. Hall, 1978.
Core, George, ed. *Southern Fiction Today: Renascence and Beyond*. Athens: University of Georgia Press, 1969.
Davis, Robert Gorham. "The American Individualist Tradition: Bellow and Styron." In *The Creative Present: Notes on Contemporary Fiction*, ed. Nona Balakian and Charles Simmons, pp. 111–141. Garden City: Doubleday, 1963.
Detweiler, Robert. "William Styron and the Courage to Be." In *Four Spiritual Crises in Mid-Century American Fiction*, pp. 6–13. Gainesville: University of Florida Press, 1964.
Duff, John B., and Peter M. Mitchell, eds. *The Nat Turner Rebellion: The Historical Event and the Modern Controversy*. New York: Harper and Row, 1971.
Finkelstein, Sidney. "Cold War, Religious Revival, and Family Alienation: William Styron, J. D. Salinger and Edward Albee." In *Existentialism and Alienation in American Literature*, pp. 211–242. New York: International Publishers, 1965.
Fossum, Robert H. *William Styron: A Critical Essay*. Contemporary Writers in Christian Perspective. Grand Rapids, Mich.: Wm. B. Eerdmans, 1968.
Friedman, Melvin J. *William Styron*. Popular Writers Series, no. 3. Bowling Green, Ohio: Bowling Green University Press, 1974.
———, and A. J. Nigro, eds. *Configuration critique de William Styron*. Paris: Minard-Lettres Modernes, 1967.
Geismar, Maxwell. "The Shifting Illusion: Dream and Fact." In *American Dreams, American Nightmares*, ed. David Madden, pp. 45–57. Carbondale: Southern Illinois University Press, 1970.
———. "William Styron: The End of Innocence." In *American Moderns:*

From Rebellion to Conformity, pp. 239–250. New York: Hill and Wang, 1958.

Gossett, Louise Y. "The Cost of Freedom: William Styron." In *Violence in Recent Southern Fiction*, pp. 117–131. Durham, N.C.: Duke University Press, 1965.

Gray, Richard. *The Literature of Memory: Modern Writers of the American South*. Baltimore: Johns Hopkins University Press, 1977. [Pp. 284–305.]

Hassan, Ihab. "Encounter with Necessity: Three Novels by Styron, Swados and Mailer." In *Radical Innocence: Studies in the Contemporary American Novel*, pp. 124–152. Princeton: Princeton University Press, 1961.

————. "William Styron." In *Contemporary American Literature 1945–1972: An Introduction*, pp. 54–56. New York: Ungar, 1973.

Henderson, Harry B., III. "*The Fixer* and *The Confessions of Nat Turner*: The Individual Conscience in Crisis." In *Versions of the Past: The Historical Imagination in American Fiction*, pp. 273–277. New York: Oxford University Press, 1974.

Hoffman, Frederick J. "William Styron: The Metaphysical Hurt." In *The Art of Southern Fiction: A Study of Some Modern Novelists*, pp. 144–161. Carbondale: Southern Illinois University Press, 1967.

Kaufmann, Walter. "Tragedy Versus History: *The Confessions of Nat Turner*." In *Tragedy and Philosophy*, pp. 347–355. Garden City: Doubleday, 1968.

Kazin, Alfred. "The Alone Generation." In *Contemporaries*, pp. 214–216. Boston: Little, Brown, 1962.

Kort, Wesley A. "*The Confessions of Nat Turner* and the Dynamic of Revolution." In *Shriven Selves: Religious Problems in Recent American Fiction*, pp. 116–140. Philadelphia: Fortress Press, 1972.

Landor, Mikhail. "Centaur—Novels: Landor on Bellow, Updike, Styron and Trilling." In *Soviet Criticism of American Literature in the Sixties—An Anthology*, ed. Carl R. Proffer, pp. 28–61. Ann Arbor, Mich.: Ardis, 1972.

Leon, Philip W. *William Styron: An Annotated Bibliography of Criticism*. Westport, Conn.: Greenwood Press, 1978.

Ludwig, Jack. *Recent American Novelists*. University of Minnesota Pamphlets on American Writers, no. 22. Minneapolis: University of Minnesota Press, 1962. [Pp. 31–34.]

Mackin, Cooper R. *William Styron*. Southern Writers Series, no. 7. Austin, Tex.: Steck-Vaughn, 1969.

Meeker, Richard K. "The Youngest Generation of Southern Fiction Writers." In *Southern Writers: Appraisals in our Time*, ed. R. G. Simonini, Jr., pp. 162–191. Charlottesville: University of Virginia Press, 1961.

Morris, Robert K., and Irving Malin, eds. *The Achievement of William Styron*. Athens: University of Georgia Press, 1975.

O'Connor, William Van. "John Updike and William Styron: The Burden of Talent." In *Contemporary American Novelists*, ed. Harry T. Moore, pp. 205–221. Carbondale: Southern Illinois University Press, 1964.

Pearce, Richard. *William Styron*. University of Minnesota Pamphlets on American Writers, no. 98. Minneapolis: University of Minnesota Press, 1971.

Ratner, Marc L. *William Styron*. Twayne's United States Authors Series, no. 196. New York: Twayne Publishers, 1972.

Robb, Kenneth A. "William Styron's Don Juan." In *Kierkegaard's Presence in Contemporary American Life: Essays from Various Sources*, ed. Lewis A. Lawson, pp. 177–190. Metuchen, N.J.: Scarecrow Press, 1970.

Rubin, Louis D., Jr., and Robert D. Jacobs, eds. *South: Modern Southern Literature in its Cultural Setting*. Garden City: Doubleday, 1961.

Stevenson, David L. "William Styron and the Fiction of the Fifties." In *Recent American Fiction: Some Critical Views*, ed. Joseph L. Waldmeir, pp. 265–274. Boston: Houghton Mifflin, 1964.

Urang, Gunnar. "The Voices of Tragedy in the Novels of William Styron." In *Adversity and Grace: Studies in Recent American Literature*, ed. Nathan A. Scott, Jr., pp. 183–209. Chicago: University of Chicago Press, 1968.

Walcutt, Charles Child. "Idea Marching on One Leg." In *Man's Changing Mask: Modes and Methods of Characterization in Fiction*, pp. 251–257. Minneapolis: University of Minnesota Press, 1966.

Watkins, Floyd C. "*The Confessions of Nat Turner*: History and Imagination." In *Time and Place: Some Origins of American Fiction*, pp. 51–70. Athens: University of Georgia Press, 1977.

West, James L. W., III. *William Styron: A Descriptive Bibliography*. Boston: G. K. Hall, 1977.

Saul Bellow

Aldridge, John W. "The Society of Three Novels." In *In Search of Heresy*, pp. 125–148. New York: McGraw-Hill Book Co., 1956.

Alter, Robert. "Heirs of the Tradition." In *Rogue's Progress*, pp. 106–132. Cambridge, Mass.: Harvard University Press, 1964.

———. "Jewish Humor and the Domestication of Myth." In *Defenses of the Imagination: Jewish Writers and Modern Historical Crisis*, pp. 155–167. Philadelphia: Jewish Publication Society of America, 1978.

Baim, Joseph, and David P. Demarest, Jr. "*Henderson the Rain King*: A Major Theme and a Technical Problem." In *A Modern Miscellany*, ed. Joseph Baim and David P. Demarest, Jr., pp. 53–63. Pittsburgh: Carnegie-Mellon University, 1970.

Baumbach, Jonathan. "The Double Vision: *The Victim* by Saul Bellow." In *The Landscape of Nightmare*, pp. 35–54. New York: New York University Press, 1965.

Bellow, Saul. *Herzog: Text and Criticism*. Ed. Irving Howe. New York: Viking Press, 1976.

Bischoff, Peter. *Saul Bellows Romane: Entfremdung und Suche.* Bonn: Bouvier, 1975.

Boyers, Robert. "Nature and Social Reality in Bellow's 'Sammler.'" In *Excursions: Selected Literary Essays*, pp. 25–46. National University Publications, Literary Criticism Series. Port Washington, N.Y.: Kennikat, 1977.

Bryant, Jerry H. *The Open Decision: The Contemporary Novel and Its Intellectual Background.* New York: Free Press, 1970. [Pp. 341–369.]

Bus, Heiner. "Saul Bellow: 'Mr. Sammler's Planet.'" In *Amerikanische Erzählliteratur: 1950–1970*, ed. Frieder Busch and Renate Schmidt-v. Bardeleben, pp. 170–177. Kritische Informationen, 28. Munich: Fink, 1975.

Ciancio, Ralph. "The Achievement of Saul Bellow's *Seize the Day.*" In *Literature and Theology*, ed. Thomas F. Stanley and Lester F. Zimmermann, pp. 49–80. Tulsa, Okla.: University of Tulsa Press, 1969.

Clayton, John. *Saul Bellow: In Defense of Man.* Bloomington: Indiana University Press, 1968.

Cowley, Malcolm. "Naturalism: No Teacup Tragedies." In *The Literary Situation*, pp. 74–95. New York: Viking Press, 1954.

Davis, Robert Gorham. "The American Individualist Tradition: Bellow and Styron." In *The Creative Present*, ed. Norma Balakian and Charles Simmons, pp. 111–141. New York: Doubleday, 1963.

Detweiler, Robert. *Saul Bellow: A Critical Essay.* Grand Rapids, Mich.: Wm. B. Eerdmans, 1967.

Dommergues, Pierre. *L'aliénation dans le roman américain contemporain.* Paris: Union Générale d'Editions, 1976. [Pp. 220–227, 355–424.]

————. *Les U.S.A. à la recherche de leur identité; rencontre avec 40 écrivains americains.* Paris: Grasset, 1967. [Pp. 28–32, 55–57, 243–255.]

————, ed. *Saul Bellow.* Paris: Grasset, 1967.

Dutton, Robert R. *Saul Bellow.* Twayne United States Authors Series, no. 181. New York: Twayne Publishers, 1971.

Fiedler, Leslie. "Saul Bellow." *Prairie Schooner* 31 (Summer 1957): 103–110. Reprinted in *The Modern Critical Spectrum*, ed. Gerald J. and Nancy M. Goldberg, pp. 155–161. New York: Prentice-Hall, 1962. Also reprinted in *On Contemporary Literature*, ed. Richard Kostelanetz, pp. 286–295. New York: Avon, 1965.

————. *Waiting for the End.* New York: Stein and Day, 1965. [Pp. 61–64, 98–100.]

Finkelstein, Sidney. "Lost Convictions and Existentialism: Arthur Miller and Saul Bellow." In *Existentialism and Alienation in American Literature*, pp. 252–269. New York: International Publishers, 1965.

Gallo, Louis. *Like You're Nobody: Letters to Saul Bellow, 1961–62.* New York: Dimensions Press, 1966.

Galloway, David. "Saul Bellow, 'The Gonzaga Manuscripts' (1956)." In *Die amerikanische Short Story der Gegenwart: Interpretationen*, ed. Peter Freese, pp. 168–174. Berlin: E. Schmidt Verlag, 1976.

Gardner, John. *On Moral Fiction*. New York: Basic Books, 1978.

Garvin, Harry R., ed. *Makers of the Twentieth Century Novel*. Lewisburg, Pa.: Bucknell University Press, 1977.

Geismar, Maxwell. "Saul Bellow: Novelist of the Intellectuals." In *American Moderns: From Rebellion to Conformity*, pp. 210–224. New York: Hill and Wang, 1958.

Gindin, James. "Saul Bellow." In *Harvest of a Quiet Eye: The Novel of Compassion*, pp. 305–336. Bloomington: Indiana University Press, 1971.

Graff, Gerald. "Babbitt at the Abyss." In *Literature against Itself: Literary Ideas in Modern Society*, pp. 207–239. Chicago: University of Chicago Press, 1979.

Gross, Theodore L. "The Victim and the Hero." In *The Heroic Ideal in American Literature*, pp. 243–261. New York: Free Press, 1971.

Guttmann, Allen. "Mr. Bellow's America." In *The Jewish Writer in America: Assimilation and the Crisis of Identity*, pp. 178–221. New York: Oxford University Press, 1971.

Harper, Howard M., Jr. "Saul Bellow—The Heart's Ultimate Need." In *Desperate Faith: A Study of Bellow, Salinger, Mailer, Baldwin and Updike*, pp. 7–64. Chapel Hill: University of North Carolina Press, 1967.

Hassan, Ihab. "Major Novelists: Saul Bellow." In *Contemporary American Literature 1945–1972: An Introduction*, pp. 27–31. New York: Ungar, 1973.

Hendin, Josephine. *Vulnerable People: A View of American Fiction Since 1945*. New York: Oxford University Press, 1978. [Pp. 99–110.]

Hoffman, Frederick J. "The Fool of Experience: Saul Bellow's Fiction." In *Contemporary American Novelists*, ed. Harry T. Moore, pp. 80–94. Carbondale: Southern Illinois University Press, 1964.

Josipovici, Gabriel. "Herzog: Freedom and Wit." In *The World and the Book: A Study of Modern Fiction*, pp. 221–235. Stanford: Stanford University Press, 1971.

———. "Saul Bellow." In *The Lessons of Modernism and Other Essays*, pp. 64–84. London: Macmillan, 1977.

Kazin, Alfred. "The Earthly City of the Jews: Bellow to Singer." In *Bright Book of Life: American Novelists and Storytellers from Hemingway to Mailer*, pp. 125–162. Boston: Little, Brown, 1973. Reprinted in *Saul Bellow: Herzog*, ed. Irving Howe, pp. 481–488. New York: Viking, 1976.

Kegan, Robert. *The Sweeter Welcome: Voices for a Vision of Affirmation: Bellow, Malamud and Martin Buber*. Needham Heights, Mass.: Humanities, 1976.

Klein, Marcus. "A Discipline of Nobility: Saul Bellow's Fiction." *Kenyon*

Review 24 (Spring 1962): 203–226. Reprinted in *Recent American Fiction: Some Critical Views*, ed. Joseph J. Waldmeir, pp. 121–138. Also reprinted in *After Alienation*, pp. 33–70. Cleveland: World Publishing Co., 1964.

Knopp, Josephine Z. "Jewish America: Saul Bellow." In *The Trial of Judaism in Contemporary Jewish Writing*, pp. 126–156. Urbana: University of Illinois Press, 1975.

Kulshrestha, Chirantan. *Saul Bellow: The Problem of Affirmation*. New Delhi: Arnold Heinemann, 1978.

Landor, Mikhail. "Centaur—Novels: Landor on Bellow, Updike, Styron and Trilling." In *Soviet Criticism of American Literature in the Sixties—An Anthology*, ed. Carl R. Proffer, pp. 28–61. Ann Arbor, Mich.: Ardis, 1972.

Lebowitz, Naomi. *Humanism and the Absurd in the Modern Novel*. Evanston, Ill.: Northwestern University Press, 1971. [Pp. 117–122, 130–133.]

Lehan, Richard. "Into the Ruins: Saul Bellow and Walker Percy." In *A Dangerous Crossing: French Literary Existentialism and the Modern American Novel*, pp. 107–145. Carbondale: Southern Illinois University Press, 1973.

Lercangée, Francine. *Saul Bellow: A Bibliography of Secondary Sources*. Brussels: Center for American Studies, 1977.

Ludwig, Jack. *Recent American Novelists*. University of Minnesota Pamphlets on American Writers, no. 22. Minneapolis: University of Minnesota Press, 1962. [Pp. 7–18.] Reprinted in *On Contemporary Literature*, ed. Richard Kostelanetz, pp. 296–299. New York: Avon Books, 1964.

Lutwack, Leonard. "Bellow's Odysseys." In *Heroic Fiction: The Epic Tradition and American Novels of the Twentieth Century*, pp. 88–121. Carbondale: Southern Illinois University Press, 1971.

McConnell, Frank D. *Four Postwar American Novelists: Bellow, Mailer, Barth, and Pynchon*. Chicago & London: University of Chicago Press, 1977.

Majdiak, D. "The Romantic Self and *Henderson the Rain King*." In *Makers of the Twentieth Century Novel*, ed. Harry Raphael Garvin, pp. 276–289. Lewisburg, Pa.: Bucknell University Press, 1977.

Malin, Irving. *Jews and Americans*. Carbondale: Southern Illinois University Press, 1965. [Pp. 7–8, 23–29, 47–51, 73–75, 95–99, 116–119, 132–134, 149–152, 168–169.]

———. *Saul Bellow and the Critics*. New York: New York University Press, 1967.

May, Keith M. *Out of the Maelstrom: Psychology and the Novel in the Twentieth Century*. New York: St. Martin's Press, 1977.

Modern Fiction Studies 25, no. 1 (Spring 1979). [Saul Bellow Issue.]

Mudrick, Marvin. "Malamud, Bellow, Roth." In *On Culture and Literature*, pp. 200–233. New York: Horizon Press, 1970.

Nault, Marianne. *Saul Bellow: His World and His Critics: An Annotated International Bibliography*. Garland Reference Library of the Humanities, 59. New York: Garland, 1977.

Noreen, Robert G. *Saul Bellow: A Reference Guide*. Boston: G. K. Hall, 1978.

Opdahl, Keith M. *The Novels of Saul Bellow: An Introduction*. University Park: Pennsylvania State University Press, 1967.

Pearce, Richard. "Harlequin: The Character of the Clown in Saul Bellow's *Henderson the Rain King* and John Hawkes' *Second Skin*." In *Stages of the Clown: Perspectives on Modern Fiction from Dostoyevsky to Beckett*, pp. 102–116. Carbondale: Southern Illinois University Press, 1970.

Pinsker, Sanford. "The Psychological Schlemiels of Saul Bellow." In *The Schlemiel as Metaphor: Studies in the Yiddish and American Jewish Novel*, pp. 125–157. Carbondale: Southern Illinois University Press, 1971.

Podhoretz, Norman. "The Adventures of Saul Bellow." In *Doings and Undoings*, pp. 205–227. New York: Farrar, Straus, 1964.

Porter, M. Gilbert. *Whence the Power? The Artistry and Humanity of Saul Bellow*. Columbia: University of Missouri Press, 1974.

Rahv, Philip. "Saul Bellow's Progress." In *Myth and the Powerhouse*, pp. 218–224. New York: Farrar, Straus, 1965. Reprinted in *Literature and the Sixth Sense*, pp. 392–397. Boston: Houghton Mifflin, 1969. Also reprinted in *Essays on Literature and Politics, 1932–1972*, ed. Arabel J. Porter and Andrew J. Dvosin; with a Memoir by Mary McCarthy, pp. 62–66. Boston: Houghton Mifflin, 1978.

Richter, David H. *Fable's End: Completeness and Closure in Rhetorical Fiction*. Chicago: University of Chicago Press, 1974. [Pp. 5–6, 185–192, 201–202.]

Roth, Philip. "Imagining Jews." In *Reading Myself and Others*, pp. 215–246. New York: Farrar, Straus, 1975.

Rothermel, Wolfgang P. "Saul Bellow." In *Amerikanische Literatur der Gegenwart in Einzeldarstellungen*, ed. Martin Christadler, pp. 69–104. Stuttgart: Kröner, 1973.

Rovit, Earl. *Saul Bellow*. University of Minnesota Pamphlets on American Writers, no. 65. Minneapolis: University of Minnesota Press, 1967.

———, ed. *Saul Bellow: A Collection of Critical Essays*. Twentieth Century Views: Englewood Cliffs: Prentice-Hall, 1975.

Rupp, Richard H. "Saul Bellow: Belonging to the World in General." In *Celebration in Postwar American Fiction, 1945–1967*, pp. 189–208. Coral Gables, Fla.: University of Miami Press, 1970.

Salmagundi 30 (Summer 1975). [Saul Bellow Issue.]

Scheer-Schäzler, Brigitte. *Konstruktion als Gestaltung: Interpretationen zum zeitgenössischen amerikanischen Roman*. Salzburger Studien zur Anglistik und Amerikanistik. Vienna and Stuttgart: Braumüller, 1975.

———. *A Taste for Metaphors: Die Bildersprache als Interpretations-*

grundlage des modernen Romans dargestellt an Saul Bellows 'Herzog'.
Moderne Sprachen, Schriftenreihe 2. Vienna: Verband der Öster-
reichischen Neuphilologen, 1968.
Schraepen, Edmond, ed. *Saul Bellow and His Work: Proceedings of a
Symposium on Saul Bellow, Held at the Free University of Brussels on
December 10–11, 1977.* Brussels: Centrum voor Taal-en Literatuur-
wetenschap, Vrije Universiteit, 1978. [Contains essays by Edmond
Schraepen, Malcolm Bradbury, John Clayton, David Galloway, Keith
Opdahl, M. Gilbert Porter, Brigitte Scheer-Schäzler, and Tony
Tanner.]
Schulz, Max F. "Saul Bellow and the Burden of Selfhood." In *Radical
Sophistication: Studies in Contemporary Jewish American Novelists,*
pp. 110–153. Athens: Ohio University Press, 1970.
Scott, Nathan A., Jr. *Three American Moralists: Mailer, Bellow, Trilling.*
Notre Dame: University of Notre Dame Press, 1973. [Pp. 101–149,
221–225.]
Sherman, Bernard. "The Adventures of Augie March." In *The Invention
of the Jew: Jewish-American Education Novels 1916–1964,* pp. 132–
145. New York: Barnes and Noble, 1969.
Sokoloff, B. A., and Mark E. Posner. *Saul Bellow: A Comprehensive Bib-
liography.* Folcroft, Pa.: Folcroft Press, 1971.
Tanner, Tony. *City of Words: American Fiction, 1950–1970.* New York:
Harper and Row, 1971. [Pp. 64–72, 295–310.]
————. *Saul Bellow.* Edinburgh: Oliver and Boyd, 1965. Reprinted,
New York: Chips Book Shop, 1978.
Vernier, J. "Mr. Sammler's Lesson." In *Les américanistes: New French
Criticism on Modern American Fiction,* ed. Ira D. Johnson and Chris-
tian Johnson, pp. 16–36. National University Publications, Literary
Criticism Series. Port Washington, N.Y.: Kennikat, 1978.
Waldmeir, Joseph J., ed. *Recent American Fiction: Some Critical Views.*
Boston: Houghton Mifflin, 1963.
Weinberg, Helen. "The Heroes of Saul Bellow's Novels." In *The New
Novel in America: The Kafkan Mode in Contemporary Fiction,* Ithaca:
Cornell University Press, 1970. [Pp. 15–17, 29–54, 55–107, 165–168,
180–182.]

J. D. Salinger
Barr, Donald. "Ah, Buddy: Salinger." In *The Creative Present,* ed. Norma
Balakian and Charles Simmons, pp. 27–62. New York: Doubleday,
1963.
Baumbach, Jonathan. "The Saint as a Young Man: A Reappraisal of *The
Catcher in the Rye.*" *Modern Language Quarterly* 25 (December
1964): 461–472. Collected in *The Landscape of Nightmare,* pp. 55–67.
New York: New York University Press, 1965.
Belcher, William F., and James W. Lee, eds. *J. D. Salinger and the Crit-
ics.* Belmont, Calif.: Wadsworth, 1962.

Bode, Carl. "Mr. Salinger's *Franny and Zooey.*" In *The Half-World of American Culture: A Miscellany*, pp. 212–220. Carbondale: Southern Illinois University Press, 1965.

Booth, Wayne C. "Distance and Point of View: An Essay in Classification." *Essays in Criticism* 11 (January 1961): 60–79. Partially reprinted in Wayne C. Booth. *The Rhetoric of Fiction*, pp. 66, 155, 171, 213, 287. Chicago: University of Chicago Press, 1962.

Buchloh, Paul, ed. *Amerikanische Erzählungen von Hawthorne bis Salinger: Interpretationen.* Kieler Beiträge zur Anglistik und Amerikanistik, Bd. 6. Neumünster: Karl Wachholtz, 1968.

Burrows, David J.; Lewis M. Dabney; Milne Holton; and Grosvenor E. Powell. *Private Dealings: Modern American Writers in Search of Integrity.* Maryland: New Perspectives, 1974.

Detweiler, Robert. "J. D. Salinger and the Quest for Sainthood." In *Four Spiritual Crises in Mid-Century American Fiction*, pp. 36–43. Gainesville: University of Florida Press, 1964.

Faulkner, William. "A Word to Young Writers." In *Faulkner in the University: Class Conferences at the University of Virginia, 1957–1958*, ed. Frederick L. Gwynn and Joseph L. Blotner, pp. 241–245. Charlottesville: University of Virginia Press, 1959.

Fiedler, Leslie. "Boys Will Be Boys!" *New Leader* 41 (April 1958): 23–26. Collected (abridged) in Leslie Fiedler. *Love and Death in the American Novel*, p. 271. New York: Criterion Books, 1960; and in Leslie Fiedler. *No! In Thunder*, pp. 266–274. Boston: Beacon Press, 1960. Reprinted in Grunwald, *Salinger: A Portrait*, pp. 228–233.

Finkelstein, Sidney. "Cold War, Religious Revival, and Family Alienation: William Styron, J. D. Salinger and Edward Albee." In *Existentialism and Alienation in American Literature*, pp. 211–242. New York: International Publishers, 1965.

Freese, Peter. *Die amerikanische Kurzgeschichte nach 1945. Salinger, Malamud, Baldwin, Purdy, Barth.* Schwerpunkte Anglistik, 8. Frankfurt: Athenäum, 1974.

———. *Die Initiationsreise: Studien zum jugenlichen Helden im modernen amerikanischen Roman mit einer exemplarischen Analyse von J. D. Salinger's 'Catcher in the Rye'.* Neumünster: Wachholtz, 1971.

———. "Jerome David Salinger." In *Amerikanische Literatur der Gegenwart in Einzeldarstellungen*, ed. Martin Christadler, pp. 43–68. Stuttgart: Kröner, 1973.

———. "Jerome David Salinger: *The Catcher in the Rye.*" In *Der amerikanische Roman im 19. und 20. Jahrhundert: Interpretationen*, ed. E. Lohner, pp. 320–336. Berlin: E. Schmidt Verlag, 1974.

French, Warren. "The Age of Salinger." In *The Fifties: Fiction, Poetry, Drama*, pp. 1–39. De Land, Fla.: Everett/Edwards, 1972.

———. *J. D. Salinger.* New York: Twayne Publishers, 1963. Rev. ed. *J. D. Salinger.* Twayne's United States Authors Series, 40. Boston: Twayne Publishers, 1976.

————. "Steinbeck and J. D. Salinger: Messiah-Moulders for a Sick Society." In *Steinbeck's Literary Dimension: A Guide to Comparative
Studies*, ed. Tetsumaro Hayashi, pp. 105–115. Metuchen, N.J.: Scarecrow, 1973.

Gardner, John. *On Moral Fiction*. New York: Basic Books, 1978.

Geraths, Armin. "Salinger: 'The Laughing Man.'" In *Die amerikanische
Kurzgeschichte*, ed. Karl Heinz Göller and Gerhard Hoffman, pp.
326–336. Düsseldorf: Bagel, 1972.

Groene, Horst. "Jerome David Salinger, 'Uncle Wiggily in Connecticut'
(1948)." In *Die amerikanische Short Story der Gegenwart: Interpretationen*, ed. Peter Freese, pp. 110–118. Berlin: E. Schmidt Verlag,
1976.

Gross, Theodore L. "J. D. Salinger: Suicide and Survival in the Modern
World." In *The Heroic Ideal in American Literature*, pp. 262–271.
New York: Free Press, 1971.

Grunwald, Harvey A., ed. *Salinger: A Critical and Personal Portrait*.
New York: Harper, 1962.

Gwynn, Frederick L., and Joseph L. Blotner. *The Fiction of J. D. Salinger*. Pittsburgh: University of Pittsburgh Press, 1958. Sections reprinted in Grunwald, *Salinger: A Portrait*, pp. 102–114, 259–266; in
(abridged) Belcher and Lee, *J. D. Salinger and the Critics*, pp.
141–145; in (abridged) Marsden, *If You Really Want to Know*, pp.
45–47; in (abridged) Simonson and Hager, *Salinger's Catcher in the
Rye*, pp. 93–94; and in Laser and Fruman, *Studies in J. D. Salinger*,
pp. 85–87, 251–254.

Hamilton, Kenneth. *J. D. Salinger: A Critical Essay*. Grand Rapids,
Mich.: Wm. B. Eerdmans, 1967.

Harper, Howard M., Jr. "J. D. Salinger—Through the Glasses Darkly."
In *Desperate Faith: A Study of Bellow, Salinger, Mailer, Baldwin and
Updike*, pp. 65–95. Chapel Hill: University of North Carolina Press,
1967.

Hassan, Ihab. *Contemporary American Literature 1945–1972: An Introduction*. New York: Ungar, 1973. [Pp. 42–44, 64, 71, 88.]

————. "J. D. Salinger: The Quixotic Gesture." In *Radical Innocence:
Studies in the Contemporary American Novel*, pp. 259–289. Princeton: Princeton University Press, 1961.

Hipkiss, Robert A. *Jack Kerouac, Prophet of the New Romanticism: A
Critical Study of the Published Works of Kerouac and a Comparison of
Them to Those of J. D. Salinger, James Purdy, John Knowles, and Ken
Kesey*. Lawrence, Kan.: Regents Press, 1976.

Howe, Irving. "The Salinger Cult." In *Celebrations and Attacks: Thirty
Years of Literary and Cultural Commentary*, pp. 93–96. New York:
Horizon Press, 1978.

Kaplan, Robert B. *Catcher in the Rye Notes*. Lincoln, Neb.: Cliffs, 1976.

Kazin, Alfred. "The Alone Generation: A Comment on the Fiction of the
'Fifties.'" *Harper's* 209 (October 1959): 127–131. Reprinted in *Writing*

in America, ed. John Fischer and Robert B. Silvers, pp. 14–26. New Brunswick, N.J.: Rutgers University Press, 1960. Collected in Alfred Kazin. *Contemporaries*, pp. 207–217. Boston: Little, Brown, 1962.

———. *Bright Book of Life: American Novelists and Storytellers from Hemingway to Mailer*. Boston: Little, Brown, 1973.

———. "J. D. Salinger: Everybody's Favorite." *Atlantic* 158 (August 1961): 27–31. Collected in Alfred Kazin. *Contemporaries*, pp. 230–240. Boston: Little, Brown, 1962. Reprinted in Grunwald, *Salinger: A Portrait*, pp. 43–52; in Belcher and Lee, *J. D. Salinger and the Critics*, pp. 158–166; and in Laser and Fruman, *Studies in J. D. Salinger*, pp. 216–226.

Kermode, Frank. "Salinger." In *Modern Essays*, pp. 226–237. London: Collins, 1971.

Landor, Mikhail. "Centaur—Novels: Landor on Bellow, Updike, Styron and Trilling." In *Soviet Criticism of American Literature in the Sixties—An Anthology*, ed. Carl R. Proffer, pp. 28–61. Ann Arbor, Mich.: Ardis, 1972.

Laser, Marvin, and Norman Fruman, eds. *Studies in J. D. Salinger: Reviews, Essays and Critiques of "The Catcher in the Rye" and Other Fiction*. New York: Odyssey, 1963.

Lerner, Laurence. "City Troubles: Pastoral and Satire." In *The Uses of Nostalgia: Studies in Pastoral Poetry*, pp. 130–148. London: Chatto & Windus, 1972.

Lettis, Richard. *"Catcher in the Rye" by J. D. Salinger*. Woodbury, N.Y.: Barron, 1964.

Lundquist, James. *J. D. Salinger*. Modern Literature Monographs. New York: Ungar, 1978.

McCarthy, Mary Therese. "Characters in Fiction." *Partisan Review* 28 (March–April 1961): 171–191. Reprinted in *On the Contrary: Articles of Belief*, pp. 271–292. New York: Farrar, Straus, Cudahy, 1961.

———. "J. D. Salinger's Closed Circuit." *The Writing on the Wall, and Other Literary Essays*, pp. 35–41. New York: Harcourt, 1970.

Malin, Irving. *New American Gothic*, Carbondale: Southern Illinois University Press, 1962. [Pp. 26–35, 59–64, 117–120, 139–143.]

Marsden, Malcolm M., ed. *If You Really Want to Know: A Catcher Casebook*. Chicago: Scott, Foresman, 1963.

Miller, James Edwin. *J. D. Salinger*. University of Minnesota Pamphlets on American Writers, no. 51. Minneapolis: University of Minnesota Press, 1965.

Mizener, Arthur. "The American Hero as Poet: Seymour Glass." In *The Sense of Life in the Modern Novel*, pp. 227–246. Boston: Houghton Mifflin, 1964.

Ortseifen, Karl. "J. D. Salinger: *De Daumier-Smith's Blue Period*." In *Amerikanische Erzählliteratur: 1950–1970*, ed. Frieder Busch und Renate Schmidt v. Bardeleben, pp. 186–196. Kritische Informationen, 28. Munich: Fink, 1975.

Panichas, George Andrew. "J. D. Salinger and the Russian Pilgrim." In *The Reverent Discipline: Essays in Literary Criticism and Culture*, with a foreword by G. Wilson Knight, pp. 293–305. Knoxville: University of Tennessee Press, 1974.

Peden, William. *The American Short Story: Continuity and Change 1940–1975*. Boston: Houghton Mifflin, 1975.

Rees, Richard. "The Salinger Situation." In *Contemporary American Novelists*, ed. Harry T. Moore, pp. 95–105. Carbondale: Southern Illinois University Press, 1964.

Rosen, Gerald. *Zen in the Art of J. D. Salinger*. Modern Authors Monograph Series, 3. Berkeley: Creative Arts Book, 1977.

Rupp, Richard H. "J. D. Salinger: A Solitary Liturgy." In *Celebration in Postwar American Fiction, 1945–1967*, pp. 113–131. Coral Gables, Fla.: University of Miami Press, 1970.

Schulz, Max F. "J. D. Salinger and the Crisis of Consciousness." In *Radical Sophistication: Studies in Contemporary Jewish/American Novelists*, pp. 198–217. Athens: Ohio University Press, 1969.

Simonson, Harold P., and E. P. Hager, eds. *Salinger's "Catcher in the Rye": Clamor vs. Criticism*. New York: D. C. Heath, 1963.

Starosciak, Kenneth. *J. D. Salinger: A Thirty Year Bibliography, 1938–1968*. Wayzata, Minn.: Ross & Haines, 1971.

Stepf, Renate. *Die Entwicklung von J. D. Salingers short stories und Novelettes*. Europäische Hochschulschriften, Reihe XIV, 23. Bern and Frankfurt: Lang, 1975.

Tanner, Tony. *The Reign of Wonder: Naivety and Reality in American Literature*. New York: Cambridge University Press, 1965. [Pp. 339–349.]

Voss, Arthur. "The Short Story since 1940." In *The American Short Story: A Critical Survey*, pp. 302–343. Norman: University of Oklahoma Press, 1973.

Walcutt, Charles Child. "Anatomy of Alienation." In *Man's Changing Mask: Modes and Methods of Characterization in Fiction*, pp. 317–326. Minneapolis: University of Minnesota Press, 1966.

Weinberg, Helen. *The New Novel in America: The Kafkan Mode in Contemporary Fiction*. Ithaca, N.Y.: Cornell University Press, 1970. [Pp. 141–165, 174.]

Wiegand, William. "J. D. Salinger: Seventy-Eight Bananas." *Chicago Review* 11 (Winter 1958): 3–19. Reprinted in *Recent American Fiction: Some Critical Views*, ed. Joseph J. Waldmeir, pp. 252–264. New York: Houghton Mifflin, 1963. Also reprinted in Grunwald, *Salinger: A Portrait*, pp. 123–136; and (abridged) in Marsden, *If You Really Want to Know*, pp. 48–52.

INDEX

Absalom! Absalom!: 123
absurd hero: compared to traditional
  forms of heroism, ix; defined, 10,
  14–15; and types of fiction, 15–16,
  98–99. *See also* Camus, Albert
"Ace in the Hole": 23
Actuelles, Chroniques: 12
"Adam and Eve Sleeping": 56
Adams, Henry: 82
Adventures of Augie March, The: 43,
  138–147, 162, 174
Adventures of Huckleberry Finn, The:
  138–139, 166, 235 n. 7
Aldridge, John W.: 185–186
alienation: in contemporary literature,
  x, 14, 167, 169, 172, 228
American Dream, An: 108, 187, 188
Anatomy of Criticism: 15–16, 62
Anderson, Sherwood: *Winesburg,
  Ohio* of, 61, 227
anti-hero ("non-hero"): ix
anti-novel: 6, 228
anti-Semitism: in Bellow's work,
  135–138 passim, 175, 178,
  180–181; in Salinger's work,
  215–216
Arendt, Hannah: 117
Armies of the Night, The: 71
artist figure: 41–42, 88, 123, 127,
  194–195, 199–200
"Aspern Papers, The": 190
Assorted Prose: 58
As You Like It: 40
Auden, W. H.: 100

Balliett, Whitney: 22
Barth, John: xi
Barth, Karl: *Church Dogmatics* of, 37,
  44

Barthelme, Donald: xi
Beat Generation, the: xi
Bech: A Book: 61–65, 71, 79
"Bech Enters Heaven": 65
"Bech Takes Pot Luck": 63
Beckett, Samuel: ix, x, xiv
Bellow, Saul: and development of hero
  as picaro, 129–203; *Dangling Man*
  of, and Camus's *The Stranger*,
  129–130, 132, 133; and use of quest
  theme, 134, 138–139, 142, 145,
  149–153, 156, 161–163, 164,
  173–176, 229–230; and treatment
  of anti-Semitism, 135–138, 175,
  178, 180–181; *The Adventures of
  Augie March* of, and Twain's *The
  Adventures of Huckleberry Finn*,
  138–139, 140; narrative technique
  of, 138, 147, 153, 162–163,
  166–167, 174–175, 183–187,
  189–190, 192, 201; on childhood,
  141, 173; on materialism, 141, 173,
  192, 194, 195; on death, 149, 154,
  156, 178, 192–193, 195, 201, 202;
  Joyce's *Ulysses* as source for *Herzog*
  of, 165–166; on alienation,
  166–168, 172, 228–229; and Jewish
  hero, 172–173, 175–176, 193; cannibalism in work of, 192, 193–194,
  196; on sleep, 192, 197–199; and
  artist figure, 194–195, 199–200;
  mentioned, ix, xii, xiii, xiv, xv, 14,
  43, 61, 78, 205, 230
——, works of: *The Adventures of Augie
  March*, 43, 138–147, 162, 174;
  Dangling Man, xv, 129–134, 135,
  137, 138, 147, 173, 174, 186; "Deep
  Readers of the World, Beware!"
  235 n. 7; "Distractions of a Fiction

Writer," 228; "The Gonzaga Manu-
scripts," 190; *Henderson the Rain
King*, xv, 61, 78, 142, 146,
151–161, 182, 192, 198; *Herzog*,
146, 152, 161–174, 185, 186, 203;
Humboldt's Gift, 174, 190–201,
202; *Last Analysis*, 168; "Leaving
the Yellow House," 177; "Mosby's
Memoirs," 177; *Mr. Sammler's
Planet*, 71, 118, 174–190, 203; "The
Old System," 177; *Seize the Day*,
xv, 147–151, 183; "A Silver Dish,"
202; *The Victim*, 129, 134–138,
147, 183, 184
"Benito Cereno": 108, 181
Berger, Thomas: xi
Berlin Stories: 124
Berryman, John: 194, 199
Beyond the Pleasure Principle: 52
"Birthmark, The": 195
black humorists: xi
Blake, William: "Adam and Eve
Sleeping" of, 56
Blok, Alexander: "The Scythians" of,
59
Boroff, David: 162–163
Brée, Germaine: 10–11, 11–12, 13
Brodin, Pierre: 106
Brontë, Emily: *Wuthering Heights* of,
123
Browne, Sir Thomas: "Urn Burial" of,
82–83, 92
Buchanan Dying: 66, 79
Buechner, Frederich: *A Long Day's
Dying* of, 32
"Bulgarian Poetess, The": 61
Burr: 77
Burroughs, William: x
Butch Cassidy and the Sundance Kid:
69
Butor, Michel: 189

Caligula: 114–115, 117
Camus, Albert: ix, x, xiii, xiv, 25, 29,
36, 47, 55, 62, 67, 84, 106–112 passim, 114–115, 116–117, 125–126,
127, 144–145, 159, 198, 202, 203,
205, 208, 223, 228–230
—, works of: *Actuelles, Chroniques*,
12; *Caligula*, 114–115, 117; *Lettres*

à un ami allemand, 12, 13; *The
Myth of Sisyphus*, xi, 5–16 passim,
23, 62, 84, 86, 96, 97, 102, 103,
104, 110, 131, 132, 133, 161, 229;
The Plague, 16, 106, 160; *The Rebel*, 13, 14, 16, 90, 98, 109, 110, 225;
The Stranger, 8, 107, 129, 133
Capote, Truman: *In Cold Blood* of,
108, 112
Catch-22: 28
Catcher in the Rye, The: xiii, xv,
204–208
Centaur, The: 32–39, 41, 42, 44, 58, 60
Champagne, Comtesse de: 77
Chaplin, Charlie: 62
Chase, Richard: 153
childhood: and the child hero, 32; as
source of values, 87, 173, 204,
207–209 passim; as commentary on
adult world, 141, 204
Christianity: failure of, as contempo-
rary value system, 5; and meta-
physics of revolt, 14–15; in work of
Updike, 21, 26–32 passim, 44, 54,
55–56, 59, 64, 73–74; in work of
Styron, 114–115; in work of Sal-
inger, 205–206, 219, 223–224, 227,
230; and Camus's *The Myth of Sisy-
phus*, 230
Church Dogmatics: 37, 44
Clap Shack, The: 116
"Clean, Well-Lighted Place, A": 48
Cocktail Party, The: 218
*Confession, Trial and Execution of Nat
Turner, The*: 114
Confessions of Nat Turner, The: 105,
106, 107–115, 123, 127, 128, 181
Conrad, Joseph: 162
Cooper, James Fenimore: 39
Coup, The: 48, 66, 78–79
Couples: xv, 39, 44, 47, 48, 50–61,
62, 63, 64, 76, 77
Crane, Hart: 194
Cruickshank, John: 7, 9, 11, 110, 127,
133, 202

Daiches, David: 76
Dangling Man: xv, 129–134, 135,
137, 138, 147, 173, 174, 186
Dante: *Divine Comedy* of, 54, 122; *In-*

ferno of, 120, 121; mentioned, 116
"Dark, The": 48
Day of the Locust, The: 95, 138, 139, 171
death: Updike on, 50–53, 55, 57, 59, 61, 67, 72–73, 74, 78, 80; Styron on, 116, 125; Bellow on, 149, 154, 156, 178, 192–193, 195, 201, 202
"De Daumier-Smith's Blue Period": 209–211, 220
"Deep Readers of the World, Beware!": 235 n. 7
Defoe, Daniel: *Robinson Crusoe* of, 106
de Rougemont, Denis: *Love in the Western World* of, 48, 57, 58
Detweiler, Robert: 48, 59, 65, 66
DeVries, Peter: 50
Dickens, Charles: 189
"Distractions of a Fiction Writer": 228
Divine Comedy: 54, 122
Donleavy, J. P.: xi
Donne, John: "To the Earle of Carlile, and his Company, at Sion" of, 92
Dos Passos, John: 190
Dostoevski, Fyodor: influence of, on Camus, 7; and modern novel, 82; and Salinger's "For Esmé—With Love and Squalor," 214; mentioned, 80
"Down at the Dinghy": 215–216
Dreiser, Theodore: 199
"Dr. Heidegger's Experiment": 195
Driving Force of Spiritual Powers in World History, The: 197
"Effects of Space Exploration on Man's Condition, The": 53
1876: 77
Eliot, George: *Middlemarch* of, 76
Eliot, T. S.: *Waste Land* of, 57; *The Four Quartets* of, and Styron's *Set This House On Fire*, 92; and themes in Bellow's *Henderson the Rain King*, 152; "The Love Song of J. Alfred Prufrock" of, and Salinger's *The Catcher in the Rye*, 204; *The Cocktail Party* of, and Salinger's *Franny and Zooey*, 218; mentioned, 9
"Ethan Brand": 195

Euripides: 116
existentialism: xi
"Family Meadow, The": 48
Faulkner, William: *The Sound and the Fury* of, 83, 107, 121, 178; *Light in August* of, 108, 185; *Absalom! Absalom!* of, 123; mentioned, 9
Ferlinghetti, Lawrence: *Her* of, x
Fiedler, Leslie: 13, 161, 181
Fitzgerald, F. Scott: *The Great Gatsby* of, 93, 171, 220
Fletcher, F. T. H.: 27
"For Esmé—With Love and Squalor": 214–215, 226
Four Quartets, The: 92
"Four Sides of One Story": 48, 58
"Franny": xv, 214, 215, 217–219
Franny and Zooey: 215–227 passim. See also "Franny"; "Zooey"
Freud, Sigmund: *Beyond the Pleasure Principle* of, 52
Friedman, Bruce Jay: xi
Frost, Robert: pastoralism of, 39, 60, 178
Frye, Northrop: *Anatomy of Criticism* of, 15–16, 62
Future of Religions, The: 54
Gaddis, William: *The Recognitions* of, x
Geismar, Maxwell: 82, 83, 91
Genet, Jean: xiv
Glicksberg, Charles: 6, 29
Gluck, Christoph: *Orfeo* of, 122
"Gonzaga Manuscripts, The": 190
Goodman, Paul: 38
Gray, T. R.: 114
Great Gatsby, The: 93, 171, 220
Green, Henry: 46
"Hang of It, The": 204
"Hapworth 16, 1924": xii
Hassan, Ihab: 149, 161, 227
Hawkes, John: *Second Skin* of, 154; mentioned, xv
Hawthorne, Nathaniel: *The Scarlet Letter* of, xv, 77; *The House of the Seven Gables* of, 119, 195; compared to Bellow, 136; "The Birthmark," "Dr. Heidegger's Experiment," "Ethan Brand," and "Rappaccini's

Daughter" of, 195; *Mosses from an Old Manse* of, 235 n. 7
Heller, Joseph: *Catch-22* of, 28
Hemingway, Ernest: "A Clean, Well-Lighted Place" of, 48; mentioned, 9, 39, 162
Henderson the Rain King: xv, 61, 78, 142, 146, 151–161, 182, 192, 198
Her: x
"Hermit, The": 48
Herzog: 146, 152, 161–174, 185, 186, 203
Herzog, Maurice: 164, 166
Hoffman, Frederick J.: 112
Hogarth, William: 174, 189
Homer: *The Odyssey* of, 215
House of the Seven Gables, The: 119, 195
Hughes, Daniel: 161
Human Season, The: 176
Humboldt's Gift: 174, 190–201, 202
Husserl, Edmund: 7

In Cold Blood: 108, 112
Inferno: 120, 121
"In Football Season": 47
In the Clap Shack: 105–106
"Intimations of Immortality from Recollections of Early Childhood": 200
Ionesco, Eugene: ix, x
Isherwood, Christopher: *Berlin Stories* of, 124
"I Wandered Lonely as a Cloud": 65

James, Henry: 171, 190
Jarrell, Randall: 194
Joyce, James: compared to Camus, 9; and narrative technique in Styron's *Lie Down in Darkness*, 83; *Ulysses* of, and Updike's *Bech: A Book*, 63, 65; *Ulysses* of, as source for Bellow's *Herzog*, 165–167; *Ulysses* of, and Bellow's *Mr. Sammler's Planet*, 189
Jung, Carl: 32–33, 84

Kesey, Ken: xi, 39
Kierkegaard, Søren Aabye: 79, 112

Lardner, Ring: 24–25
Last Analysis: 168
"Last Day of the Furlough, The": 216

Lawrence, D. H.: 176
"Leaving the Yellow House": 177
Lehan, Richard: 152
Lettres à un ami allemand: 12, 13
Levine, Paul: 129
Lewis, R. W. B.: *The Picaresque Saint* of, 6, 28
Lie Down in Darkness: 82–89, 91–93, 105, 121, 141
"Lifeguard": 26
Light in August: 108, 185
Long Day's Dying, A: 32
Long March, The: xii, xv, 89–91, 105, 119
Loss of the Self, The: x
Love Declared: 57
Love in the Western World: 48, 57, 58
"Love Song of J. Alfred Prufrock, The": 204

McCarthy, Mary: 50
Mailer, Norman: *The Armies of the Night* of, 71; *Why Are We in Vietnam?* of, 71, 188; *Of a Fire on the Moon* of, 71–72, 80, 187–189; *An American Dream* of, 108, 187, 188; "The White Negro" of, 71, 181–182
Malamud, Bernard: *The Natural* of, 32, 61
Mann, Thomas: 112
Maquet, Albert: 14, 229
Marry Me: 48, 76, 78
Melville, Herman: *Moby Dick* of, 108; "Benito Cereno" of, 108, 181
Metalious, Grace: 50, 76
Middlemarch: 76
"Midpoint": 66, 75
Miller, Henry: xi, 50
Miller, Warren: xi
Moby Dick: 108
Modern Times: 62
Month of Sundays, A: 67, 76, 77
Morris, Wright: 9, 116
Morte d'Urban: 32
"Mosby's Memoirs": 177
Mosses from an Old Manse: 235 n. 7
Mozart, Wolfgang: 122
Mr. Sammler's Planet: 71, 118, 174–190, 203
Museums and Women: 48, 78
"Music School, The": 48

Music School, The: 47, 49
"My Blessed Man of Boston, My
    Grandmother's Thimble, and Fan-
    ning Island": 30–31
Myra Breckenridge: 77
Myron: 77
Myth of Sisyphus, The: xi, 5–16 pas-
    sim, 23, 62, 84, 86, 96, 97, 102, 103,
    104, 110, 131, 132, 133, 161, 229

Native Son: 108
Natural, The: 32, 61
Nietzsche, Friedrich: 7, 180, 225
Nine Stories: 209–215

Odyssey, The: 215
Oedipus Rex: 99–100 passim, 103,
    104
Of a Fire on the Moon: 71–72, 80,
    187–189
Of the Farm: xv, 39–47, 58, 60, 62,
    76, 79
O'Hara, John: 50
"Old System, The": 177
Olinger Stories: 39, 40
Orfeo: 122

"Packed Dirt, Churchgoing, A Dying
    Cat, A Traded Car": 30
Pascal, Blaise: as existential philoso-
    pher, xi; *Pensées* of, and Updike's
    Rabbit, Run, 27–28, 31; as inspira-
    tion for Updike's "Fanning Island,"
    30–31
Pawnbroker, The: 176
Pensées: 27–28, 31
"Perfect Day for Bananafish, A":
    211–212, 215
Picaresque Saint, The: 6, 28
Picasso, Pablo: 180
"Pigeon Feathers": 30, 39
Plague, The: 16, 106, 160
Poe, Edgar Allan: 194
Poorhouse Fair: 17–22, 70, 75, 82
Porter, Gilbert: 186
Potter, Beatrix: 66
Powers, J. F.: *Morte d'Urban* of, 32
"Prevalence of Wonders": 91
Problems and Other Stories: 48
Purdy, James: xi
Pynchon, Thomas: *V* of, xi, xiv, xv

quest theme, the: 5–6, 15–16, 23, 24,
    25, 27, 31, 61, 62, 66, 69–70, 134,
    139, 142, 149, 150–151, 152–153,
    156, 161–163, 173–174, 215,
    229–230

Rabbit, Run: 22–32, 39, 47, 48, 50,
    66, 67, 70, 96, 100
Rabbit Redux: 48, 54, 61, 62, 66–67,
    77, 187
"Raise High the Roof Beam, Carpen-
    ters": 213, 215, 216, 220–221
"Rappaccini's Daughter": 195
Ratner, Marc: 115
Rebel, The: 13, 14, 16, 90, 98, 109,
    110, 225
Recognitions, The: x
"Reflection": 23
Riis, Jacob: 189
Robbe-Grillet, Alain: xiv, 189
Robinson Crusoe: 106
Roth, Philip: *When She Was Good* of,
    61
Rubinstein, Richard L.: 117

"saint," the, in contemporary fiction:
    25–29 passim, 31, 32, 36, 153, 227
Salinger, J. D.: and use of love ethic
    with absurd hero, 204–227; and
    child hero, 204, 207–209 passim,
    227; and mystical experience,
    208–213 passim, 217–227 passim;
    on anti-Semitism, 215–216; men-
    tioned, ix, xii, xiii, xiv, xv, 14, 229,
    230
—, works of: *The Catcher in the Rye*,
    xiii, xv, 204–208; "De Daumier-
    Smith's Blue Period," 209–211, 220;
    "Down at the Dinghy," 215–216;
    "For Esmé—With Love and Squa-
    lor," 214–215, 226; "Franny," xv,
    214, 215, 217–219; "The Hang of
    It," 204; "Hapworth 16, 1924," xii;
    "The Last Day of the Furlough,"
    216; *Nine Stories*, 209–215; "A Per-
    fect Day for Bananafish," 211–212,
    215; "Raise High the Roof Beam,
    Carpenters," 213, 215, 216,
    220–221; "Seymour: An Introduc-
    tion," 215; "Soft-Boiled Sergeant,"
    204; "The Stranger," 204; "Teddy,"

209, 211, 221, 229; "This Sandwich Has No Mayonnaise," 204; "Uncle Wiggily in Connecticut," 216; "The Varioni Brothers," 204; "Zooey," xv, 215, 216, 219–227

Sartre, Jean-Paul: on Camus, 12; and work of Updike, 43, 44, 60; and work of Styron, 112; mentioned, 7

Sarraute, Nathalie: 189

Scarlet Letter, The; xv, 77

Schwartz, Delmore: 199

"Scythians, The": 59

"Sea's Green Sameness, The": 19

Second Skin: 154

Segal, Erich: 76

Seize the Day: xv, 147–151, 183

Set This House on Fire: 89, 91–105, 109, 112, 113

"Seymour: An Introduction": 215

Shakespeare, William: and work of Updike, 40, 53; and work of Styron, 116

Shattuck, Roger: 190, 203

Silone, Ignazio: 28

"Silver Dish, A": 202

Sinclair, Upton: 190

Skinner, B. F.: *Walden II* of, 17

"Soft-Boiled Sergeant": 204

Sophie's Choice: xv, 106, 112, 117–128, 176

Sophocles: *Oedipus Rex* of, 99–101 passim, 103, 104

Sound and the Fury, The: 83, 107, 121, 178

Southern, Terry: xi

Specimen Days: 49–50

Steiner, George: 121

Steiner, Rudolf: 196

Stern, Richard G.: xi

Stranger, The (Camus): 8, 107, 129, 133

"Stranger, The" (Salinger): 204

Styron, William: and development of tragic absurd hero, 81–128; on problems of contemporary novelist, 81–82; narrative technique of, xii, 82–83, 89, 91–92, 122–123, 124–125, 127–128; on childhood, 87; and artist figure, 88, 123, 127; on militarism and war, 89–91, 105–106, 116–117, 118, 119–120;

influence of classical tragedy on, 100–104 passim; Camus's influence on, 106–112; and Christ figure, 114–115; on death, 116, 125; mentioned, ix, xii, xiii, xv, 14, 205, 229

—, works of: *The Confessions of Nat Turner*, 105, 106, 107–115, 123, 127, 128, 181; *In the Clap Shack*, 105–106; *Lie Down in Darkness*, 82–89, 91–93, 105, 121, 141; *The Long March*, xii, xv, 89–91, 105, 119; "Prevalence of Wonders," 91; *Set This House on Fire*, 89, 91–105, 109, 112, 113; *Sophie's Choice*, xv, 106, 112, 117–128, 176; "This Quiet Dust," 109

"Superman": 24

Susann, Jacqueline: 50

Swift, Jonathan: 20

Sypher, Wylie: *The Loss of the Self* of, x

Tanner, Tony: 164

"Teddy": 209, 211, 221, 229

Tenants of Moonbloom, The: 56

theatre of the absurd: ix

"This Quiet Dust": 109

"This Sandwich Has No Mayonnaise": 204

Thoreau, Henry David: *Walden* of, 49; mentioned, 39

Tillich, Paul: "The Effects of Space Exploration on Man's Condition" of, 53; *The Future of Religions* of, 54; mentioned, xi

Tindall, William York: 165

Too Far to Go: 48

"To the Earle of Carlile, and his Company, at Sion": 92

"Toward Evening": 23–24

"Transaction": 79

True Grit: 69

Twain, Mark: and work of Updike, 36, 39; compared to Styron, 81–82; *The Adventures of Huckleberry Finn* of, 138–139, 166, 235 n. 7

2001: A Space Odyssey: 69

Ulysses: 63, 65, 165–167, 189

"Uncle Wiggily in Connecticut": 216

Updike, John: narrative technique of,

xii, 38, 46, 54, 61, 76, 79–80; and development of saintly hero, 17–80; and utopian novel, 17–22 passim; attitude of, toward Christianity, 21, 26–32 passim, 35, 36, 44, 54, 55–56, 59, 64, 73–74; and hero as athlete, 23–25, 38; and use of quest theme, 23, 24, 25, 27, 31–32, 61, 62, 66, 69–70, 229; and contemporary "saint," 25–29 passim, 31–32, 36, 47, 153; and child hero, 32; and use of mythology, 33–38 passim, 46, 50, 58, 60, 65; pastoralism of, 39, 40, 41, 42, 43, 45–46, 49, 57, 64, 65, 79; and artist figure, 41–42; and use of Tristan and Iseult myth, 48–49, 54, 57–58, 59, 77; on marriage, 48, 58, 78; on death, 50–53, 55, 57, 59, 61, 67, 72–73, 74, 78, 80; Shakespeare's technique and, 53; sexuality in work of, 57, 58; comic mode of, 62, 64, 65; history used by, 66; mentioned, ix, xii, xiii, xiv, xv, 14, 94, 95, 153, 187, 188, 205, 229
—, works of: "Ace in the Hole," 23; *Assorted Prose*, 58; *Bech: A Book*, 61–65, 71, 79; "Bech Enters Heaven," 65; "Bech Takes Pot Luck," 63; *Buchanan Dying*, 66, 79; "The Bulgarian Poetess," 61; *The Centaur*, 32–39, 41, 42, 44, 58, 60; *The Coup*, 48, 66, 78–79; *Couples*, xv, 39, 44, 47, 48, 50–61, 62, 63, 64, 76, 77; "The Dark," 48; "The Family Meadow," 48; "Four Sides of One Story," 48, 58; "The Hermit," 48; "In Football Season," 47; "Lifeguard," 26; *Marry Me*, 48, 76, 78; "Midpoint," 66, 75; *A Month of Sundays*, 67, 76, 77; *Museums and Women*, 48, 78; "The Music School," 48; *The Music School*, 47, 49; "My Blessed Man of Boston, My Grandmother's Thimble, and Fanning Island," 30–31; *Of the Farm*, xv, 39–47, 58, 60, 62, 76, 79; *Olinger Stories*, 39, 40; "Packed Dirt, Churchgoing, A Dying Cat, A Traded Car," 30; "Pigeon Feathers,"

30, 39; *Poorhouse Fair*, 17–22, 70, 75, 82; *Problems and Other Stories*, 48; *Rabbit, Run*, 22–32, 39, 47, 48, 50, 66, 67, 70, 96, 100; *Rabbit Redux*, 48, 54, 61, 62, 66–76, 77, 187; "Reflection," 23; "The Sea's Green Sameness," 19; "Superman," 24; *Too Far to Go*, 48; "Toward Evening," 23–24; "Transaction," 79
"Urn Burial": 82–83, 92

V: xi
Valéry, Paul: 9
"Varioni Brothers, The": 204
Victim, The: 129, 134–138, 147, 183, 184
Vidal, Gore: *Burr, 1876, Myra Breckenridge*, and *Myron* of, 76–77

Wakefield, Dan: 213, 226
Walden: 49
Walden II: 17
Wallant, Edward Lewis: novels of, xii, xiv; *The Tenants of Moonbloom* of, 56; *The Human Season* and *The Pawnbroker* of, 176
Warren, Robert Penn: 145
Waste Land: 57
Weil, Simone: 228
West, Nathanael: *The Day of the Locust* of, 95, 138, 139, 171
When She Was Good: 61
"White Negro, The": 71, 181–182
Whitman, Walt: Updike compared to, 35, 49, 60; *Specimen Days* of, 49–50
Why Are We in Vietnam?: 71, 188
Winesburg, Ohio: 61
Wordsworth, William: "I Wandered Lonely as a Cloud" of, 65; "Intimations of Immortality from Recollections of Early Childhood" of, 200
Wright, Richard: *Native Son* of, 108
Wuthering Heights: 123
Wyeth, Andrew: 60

Young, James Dean: 163

Zola, Emile: 189
"Zooey": xv, 215, 216, 219–227